WELCOME TO TORONTO

Cultured and cosmopolitan, Toronto nevertheless manages to remain relaxed, livable, and fun all at the same time. Canada's center of the arts and media has plenty of pleasant tree-lined streets in Yorkville for window-shopping and wandering; a host of independent galleries in West Queen West with edgy works; big-name music festivals year-round; and an adventurous, constantly evolving food scene. Toronto's impressive sights may be what pull you in, but its vibrant neighborhoods, artistic happenings, and friendly locals will make you want to return.

TOP REASONS TO GO

★ **CN Tower:** Rising 1,815 feet in the air, this icon has stupendous panoramic views.

★ **Foodie Paradise:** Sophisticated restaurants, excellent ethnic spots, markets.

★ **Nonstop Shopping:** High-end designer flagships and a plethora of vintage shops.

★ **Festival City:** A star-studded film festival, the Nuit Blanche all-nighter, and more.

★ **Hip and Happening:** Urbanites flock to West Queen West, Old Town, and beyond.

★ **The Waterfront:** The Beach's boardwalk and car-free Toronto Islands help you unwind.

Fodor's TORONTO

Publisher: Amanda D'Acierno, *Senior Vice President*

Editorial: Arabella Bowen, *Editor in Chief*; Linda Cabasin, *Editorial Director*

Design: Fabrizio La Rocca, *Vice President*, *Creative Director*; Tina Malaney, *Associate Art Director*; Chie Ushio, *Senior Designer*; Ann McBride, *Production Designer*

Photography: Melanie Marin, *Associate Director of Photography*; Jessica Parkhill and Jennifer Romains, *Researchers*

Maps: Rebecca Baer, *Senior Map Editor*; David Lindroth, Ed Jacobus, *Cartographers*

Production: Linda Schmidt, *Managing Editor*; Evangelos Vasilakis, *Associate Managing Editor*; Angela L. McLean, *Senior Production Manager*

Sales: Jacqueline Lebow, *Sales Director*

Marketing & Publicity: Heather Dalton, *Marketing Director*; Katherine Fleming, *Senior Publicist*

Business & Operations: Susan Livingston, *Vice President*, *Strategic Business Planning*; Sue Daulton, *Vice President*, *Operations*

Fodors.com: Megan Bell, *Executive Director*, *Revenue & Business Development*; Yasmin Marinaro, *Senior Director*, *Marketing & Partnerships*

Writers: Andrew Dobson, Kathryn Lane, Sarah Richards, and Yvonne Tsui

Editors: Alexis Crisman Kelly, Maria Teresa Hart, Kristan Schiller, Caroline Trefler

Production Editor: Evangelos Vasilakis

24th Edition

ISBN 978-0-8041-4193-2

ISSN 1044-6133

SPECIAL SALES

This book is available at special discounts for bulk purchases for sales promotions or premiums. For more information, e-mail specialmarkets@randomhouse.com

PRINTED IN CHINA

10 9 8 7 6 5 4 3

CONTENTS

CONTENTS

MAPS

ABOUT THIS GUIDE

Fodor's Recommendations

Everything in this guide is worth doing—we don't cover what isn't—but exceptional sights, hotels, and restaurants are recognized with additional accolades. **Fodor's**Choice★ indicates our top recommendations; and **Best Bets** call attention to notable hotels and restaurants in various categories. Care to nominate a new place? Visit Fodors.com/contact-us.

Trip Costs

We list prices wherever possible to help you budget well. Hotel and restaurant price categories from **$** to **$$$$** are noted alongside each recommendation. For hotels, we include the lowest cost of a standard double room in high season. For restaurants, we cite the average price of a main course at dinner or, if dinner isn't served, at lunch. For attractions, we always list adult admission fees; discounts are usually available for children, students, and senior citizens.

Hotels

Our local writers vet every hotel to recommend the best overnights in each price category, from budget to expensive. Unless otherwise specified, you can expect private bath, phone, and TV in your room. For expanded hotel reviews, facilities, and deals visit Fodors.com.

Restaurants

Unless we state otherwise, restaurants are open for lunch and dinner daily. We mention dress code only when there's a specific requirement and reservations only when they're essential or not accepted. To make restaurant reservations, visit Fodors.com.

Credit Cards

The hotels and restaurants in this guide typically accept credit cards. If not, we'll say so.

Top Picks

★ **Fodor's**Choice

Listings

- Address
- Branch address
- Telephone
- Fax
- Website
- E-mail
- Admission fee
- Open/closed times
- Subway
- Directions or Map coordinates

Hotels & Restaurants

- Hotel
- Number of rooms
- Meal plans
- Restaurant
- Reservations
- Dress code
- No credit cards
- Price

Other

- See also
- Take note
- Golf facilities

EXPERIENCE TORONTO

TORONTO TODAY

Torontonians have a hard time defining their city. It's culturally diverse, to be sure, but this, the city's most touted trait, is the polar opposite of a unifying characteristic. So what exactly is Toronto all about? It's a bit confused. Americans call Torontonians friendly and the city clean, while other Canadians say its locals are rude and egocentric. Toronto is often touted as "livable," a commendable if dull virtue. Admittedly, Toronto is not as exciting as New York, as quaint as Montréal, as glitzy as Los Angeles, as outdoorsy as Vancouver, or as historic as London. Instead, it's a patchwork of *all* these qualities. Toronto is the complete package. And comparatively (despite what Canadian compatriots believe) Toronto *is* clean, safe, and just all-around nice. Torontonians say "sorry" when they jostle you. They recycle and compost. They obey traffic laws. Toronto is like the boy next door you eventually marry after fooling around with New York or Los Angeles. Why not cut the charade and start the love affair now?

Diverse City

Toronto is one of the most immigrant-friendly cities on the planet, and the city's official motto, "Diversity Our Strength," reflects this hodgepodge of ethnicities. More than half its population is foreign-born, and half of all Torontonians are native speakers of a foreign language. (The "other" national language of French, however, is not one of the most commonly spoken languages here, trailing Chinese, Portuguese, Punjabi, and Tagalog.) In a few hours in Toronto you can travel the globe, from Little India to Little Italy, Koreatown to Greektown, or at least eat your way around it, from Polish pierogi to Chinese dim sum to Portuguese salt-cod fritters.

A City of Neighborhoods

Every city has neighborhoods, but Toronto's are particularly diverse, distinctive, and walkable. Some were once their own villages, and many, such as the Danforth (Greektown), Little Portugal, and Chinatown, are products of the ethnic groups who first settled them. For the most part, boundaries aren't fixed and are constantly evolving: on a five-minute walk down Bloor Street West you can pass a Portuguese butcher, an Ethiopian restaurant, a hip espresso bar, and a Maltese travel agency. In the '70s and '80s, areas such as Yorkville and Queen West were transformed by struggling-artist types and

WHAT'S HOT IN TORONTO NOW?

After years of continuous condo construction and a recent building boom that included a bevy of luxury hotels, Toronto's distinctive skyline is becoming a blur of glossy high-rise buildings. The CN Tower still stretches above it all, making the loftiest architecture appear pretty insignificant.

In preparation for the 2015 Pan American Games, an Athlete's Village is springing up on the vacant Don Lands, where the Don River meets the lake, which will give Torontonians access to another swath of previously off-bounds shoreline. Just before the games begin, the UPExpress train will start running between Pearson International Airport and

have since grown into downright affluent, retail powerhouses. In the last decade once run-down neighborhoods including West Queen West and Leslieville, have blossomed into funky, boho areas with enviable shopping and eating options with housing prices to match. Barring a change in fortune, gentrification is set to continue to more areas.

Canada's Culture Center

The Toronto International Film Festival, the Art Gallery of Ontario, Canada's center for magazine and book publishing, national ballet and opera companies, the Toronto Symphony Orchestra—these are just a handful of the many reasons Toronto attracts millions of arts and culture lovers each year to live, work, and play. On any given day or night, you'll find events to feed the brain and the spirit: art gallery openings, poetry readings, theatrical releases, film revues, dance performances, and festivals showcasing the arts, from the focused Toronto Jazz Festival and the North by Northeast indie rock extravaganza to events marrying visual and performing arts, like Nuit Blanche and Luminato.

On the Waterfront

Lake Ontario forms Toronto's very obvious southern border, but residents who live out of its view often forget it's there until they attend an event at the Ex or the Harbourfront Centre. It's one of the city's best features, especially in the summer, providing opportunities for boating, ferrying to the Toronto Islands, or strolling, biking, or jogging beside the water. The lakeshore is more of an attraction than ever, with ongoing initiatives to revitalize the waterfront and create more parks, beaches, and walkways.

Gastronomical

There's no shortage of amazing restaurants in this city, and local and fresh produce is all the rage. Celebrity chefs like Lynn Crawford, Mark McEwan, and Jamie Kennedy give locavores street cred. Toronto's cornucopia of cultures means you can sample almost any cuisine, from Abyssinian to Yemeni. Nowhere is Torontonians' love of food more apparent, perhaps, than at St. Lawrence Market, where you can pick up nonessentials like fiddlehead ferns, elk burgers, truffle oil, and mozzarella *di bufala*. In warm weather, farmers' markets bring the province's plenty to the city.

Union Station—a much needed direct link from downtown to the city's main airport.

And speaking of airports and shoreline, the controversial Toronto Island Airport, squeezed between the edge of Toronto Island and Harbourfront, is pushing to add more flights and bigger planes. That would provide local jet setters even greater convenience, but annoy the lakeshore's residents to no end.

The subway is being extended into the northern suburbs where so many Torontonians live, and a light rail line is under construction along Eglinton, through North Toronto's cosmopolitan hub.

WHAT'S WHERE

1 Harbourfront, the Entertainment District, and the Financial District. Between the waterfront and Queen Street, the city's main attractions are packed in: the CN Tower, the Harbourfront Centre, the Hockey Hall of Fame, and Ripley's Aquarium of Canada. Most of the lofty peaks in Toronto's skyline are in this epicenter of Canadian financial power, as well as the restaurants, theaters, and clubs of King St. West.

2 Old Town and the Distillery District. Stroll through the Old Town past Victorian buildings to the foodie paradise St. Lawrence Market. Farther east, the Distillery District offers great shopping and cafés.

3 Dundas Square Area. The square hosts frequent performances in summer, and the surrounding neighborhood has Broadway-style theaters and department stores.

4 Chinatown, Kensington Market, and Queen West. Busy and bustling, the sidewalks here are overflowing. Wander through the much-loved hippy-punk hangout of Kensington Market and scoff dumplings in Chinatown. Don't miss the Canadian and contemporary art at the Art Gallery of Ontario (AGO).

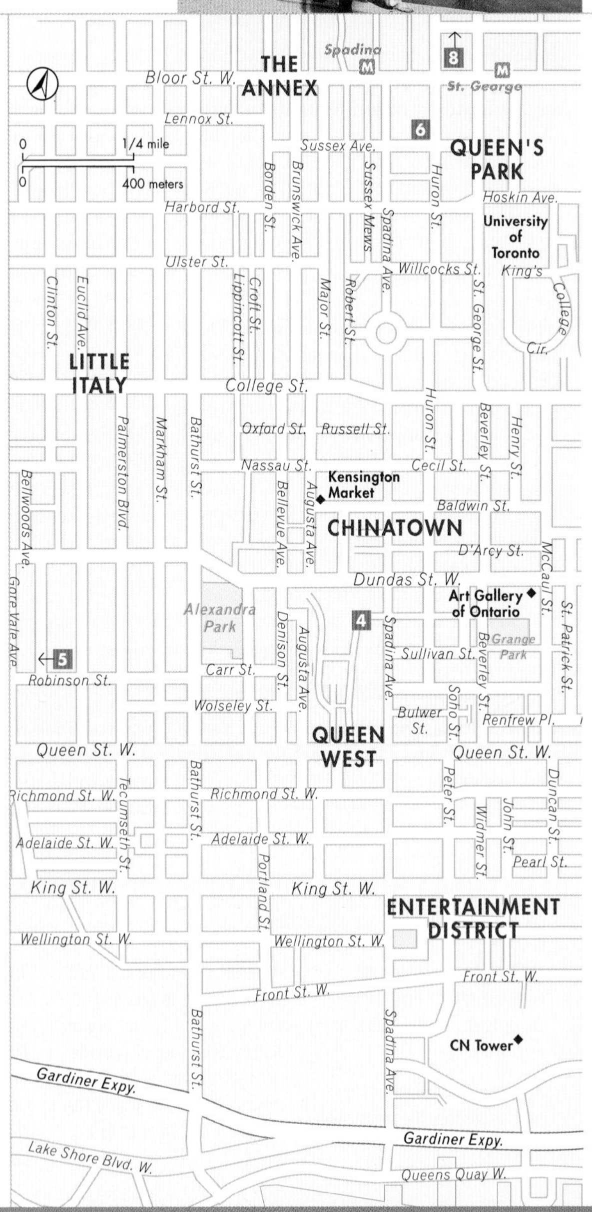

Royal Ontario Museum
YORKVILLE
Asquith Ave.
Bay
Bloor-Yonge
Bloor St. E.
Avenue Rd.
St. Thomas St.
Bay St.
Hayden St.
Charles St. E.
Museum
Queen's Park
Isabella St.
Yonge St.
Church St.
Gloucester St.
St. Joseph St.
Dundonald St.
Wellesley
Wellesley St. W.
Wellesley St. E.
Jarvis St.
Queen's Park Cir. W.
Queen's Park Cir. E.
Breadalbane St.
Maitland Ave.
Ontario Legislative Building
Grosvenor St.
Alexander St.
CHURCH-WELLESLEY
Grenville St.
Wood St.
College St.
College
Carlton St.
Queen's Park
Carlton St.
Allan Gardens
University Ave.
Elizabeth St.
Bay St.
Gerrard St. W.
Gerrard St. E.
George St.
Pembroke St.
Seaton St.
O'Keefe St.
Elm St.
Gould St.
St. Patrick
Chestnut St.
Edward St.
Dundas St. W.
Dundas
Dundas St. E.
Simcoe St.
DUNDAS SQUARE AREA
Victoria St.
Shuter St.
City Hall
Nathan Phillips Square
James St.
Queen
Mutual St.
Moss Gardens
Pullan Pl.
Osgoode
Queen St. E.
Nelson St.
York St.
Richmond St. E.
FINANCIAL DISTRICT
Adelaide St. E.
Toronto St.
OLD TOWN
Sherbourne St.
King St. E.
Colborne St.
Front St. E.
Wellington St. W.
Wellington St. E.
Hockey Hall of Fame
St. Lawrence Market
The Esplanade
Union
The Esplanade
Gardiner Expy.
Brenner Blvd.
Lake Shore Blvd. E.
DISTILLERY DISTRICT
Harbour St.
Queens Quay E.
HARBOURFRONT
Lake Ontario

5 East and West of the City Center. Many of the city's most alluring spots are here. The leafy residential streets and boardwalk of The Beach beckon, while funkified Leslieville offers boho shopping and great brunch spots. The Danforth is super lively in the evening with packed patios. And West Queen West steps up the city's hip quotient.

6 Queen's Park, the Annex, and Little Italy. Stately Queen's Park is home to the Ontario legislature and the ivy-covered buildings of the U of T campus. Farther west lies Little Italy, packed with cool cafés. North of the campus you'll hit the Annex, the city's academic and artsy haunt.

7 Yorkville, Church-Wellesley, and Rosedale. Yorkville itself is refined and classy, the narrow streets lined with chic cafés and high-end boutiques. North of here is the moneyed residential neighborhood of Rosedale, which lies east of Yonge. A nudge east and south is Toronto's "queer and queer-positive"Church-Wellesley neighborhood.

8 Greater Toronto. Top attractions such as Canada's Wonderland theme park, the Ontario Science Centre, and the Toronto Zoo lure visitors from downtown.

TORONTO PLANNER

Getting Here

Most flights arrive and depart from Pearson International Airport (YYZ), about a 30-minute drive northwest of downtown. Cabs are a C$50–C$65 flat rate (varies by destination) for most downtown locations. The Toronto Transit Commission (TTC) operates the 192 Airport Rocket, a shuttle bus to the Kipling subway station; the TTC fare of C$3 applies. The Airport Express bus costs C$30 and runs every half hour to five central hotels. The UPExpress train to Union Station downtown is due to start running in spring 2015. It will also connect with the Bloor-Danforth subway line near Dundas West station. The Billy Bishop Toronto City Airport (YTZ), better known as the Toronto Island Airport, right downtown, is served only by Porter Airlines, which flies to Chicago, Newark (New Jersey), Boston, Washington, D.C., and several cities in northern Ontario and in eastern Canada, including Montréal. Amtrak and VIA Rail trains pull into Union Station, at the intersection of Bay and Front streets.

Visitor Information

Tourism Toronto ☎ *800/499-2514, 416/203-2500* 🌐 *www.seetorontonow.com.*

When to Go

Toronto is most pleasant from late spring through early fall, when there are outdoor concerts, frequent festivals, and open-air dining. On the other hand, some hotels drop their prices up to 50% in the off-season. Fall through spring is prime viewing time for dance, opera, theater, and classical music. The temperature frequently falls below freezing from late November into March, when snowstorms can wreak havoc on travel plans, although Toronto's climate is mild by Canadian standards, thanks to the regulating properties of Lake Ontario. Still, snow is substantial enough to lure skiing enthusiasts to the resorts north of the city. A few underground shopping concourses, such as the PATH in the Financial District downtown, allow you to avoid the cold in the winter months.

Getting Around

Traffic is dense and parking expensive within the city core. If you have a car, leave it at your hotel. **TIP→ In the city, take taxis or use the excellent TTC subway, streetcar, and bus system.**

Car Travel. A car is helpful to access some further-flung destinations, but it isn't necessary and can be a hassle. Street parking is sometimes difficult; garages and lots usually charge C$3–C$5 per hour or C$10–C$20 per day.

Taxi Travel. Taxis here are easy to hail, or you can call ☎ *416/829–4222* for pickup. The meter starts at C$4 and you are charged C25¢ for each additional 0.155 km (roughly 1/10 mile) after the first 0.155 km.

TTC Travel. The Toronto Transit Commission operates the subway, streetcars, and buses that easily take you to most downtown attractions. The subway is clean and efficient, with trains arriving every few minutes; streetcars and buses are a bit slower. A single transferable fare is C$3; day (C$10.75) and week (C$38.50) passes are available. A day pass covers up to two adults and four children on weekend days and holidays. Most systems operate from about 6 am to 1 am Monday through Saturday and 9 am to 1 am Sunday.

Getting Oriented

The boundaries of what Torontonians consider downtown, where most of the city sights are located, are subject to debate, but everyone agrees on the southern cutoff—Lake Ontario and the Toronto Islands. The other coordinates of the rectangle that compose the city core are roughly High Park to the west, the DVP (Don Valley Parkway) to the east, and Eglinton Avenue to the north. A few sights beyond these borders make excellent half- or full-day excursions. An ideal way to get a sense of the city's layout is from one of the observation decks at the CN Tower on a clear day; the view is especially lovely at sunset.

Most city streets are organized on a grid system: with some exceptions, street numbers start at zero at the lake and increase as you go north. On the east–west axis, Yonge (pronounced "young") Street, Toronto's main north–south thoroughfare, is the dividing line: you can expect higher numbers the farther away you get from Yonge.

Making the Most of Your Time

Planning is the key to maximizing your experience. First, book a hotel near the activities that most interest you. If you're here to see a Broadway-style show, get the view from the CN Tower, stroll the lakefront, stomp your feet at a Raptors game, or soak up some culture at the ballet, opera, or symphony, go for a room in or near Harbourfront. If food, shopping, or museums are your passion, affluent Yorkville might be better suited (bonus: it's at the axis of both major subway lines). To live like a local, wandering neighborhood streets and patronizing funky cafés and shops, consider the Queen West boutique hotels.

In a short trip you can do a lot but not everything. Decide on your priorities, and don't overbook. Allow time for wandering. Schedule coffee (or Ontario microbrew) breaks. Be realistic about your sightseeing style. If you tend to scour every inch of a museum, you could spend an entire afternoon at the ROM (Royal Ontario Museum); if you're selective, you can breeze through in an hour.

Plan your days geographically. Kensington and Chinatown make an excellent combo; High Park and The Beach, not so much.

Ditch the car and get a TTC day pass for unlimited travel on the subways and streetcars.

Savings Tips

- Toronto CityPASS (🌐 *www.citypass.com*) saves money and time as it lets you bypass ticket lines. Admission fees to the CN Tower, Casa Loma, the Royal Ontario Museum, the Ontario Science Centre, and the Toronto Zoo are included for a one-time fee of C$61.50 plus tax—a savings of more than C$50, valid for nine days.
- Buying a day or weekly pass on the TTC can save you money and make getting around the city easier.
- Many events listed on the city's website (🌐 *www.toronto.ca/events*) are free. The Harbourfront Centre (🌐 *www.harbourfrontcentre.com*) hosts numerous free cultural programs and festivals year-round.
- Some museums and art collections have free (or pay-what-you-can) admission all the time, including the Gallery of Inuit Art in the TD Centre, the Museum of Contemporary Canadian Art, and the Harbourfront Centre's Power Plant gallery. But even the major museums, including the Royal Ontario Museum, the Bata Shoe Museum, Gardiner Museum of Ceramic Art, Textile Museum of Canada, and Art Gallery of Ontario, have one or two free, pay-what-you-can, and/or half-price evening(s) per week, usually Wednesday, Thursday, or Friday, and usually beginning after 4 pm.

TORONTO TOP ATTRACTIONS

CN Tower

(A) Since it opened as a communications tower in 1976, the CN Tower has defined Toronto's skyline and is the city's most iconic structure. Everyone has to step onto the glass floor, hovering more than 1,000 feet above the ground, at least once. You can sometimes see Niagara Falls from the Sky Pod. At nearly 1,500 feet it was the highest observation deck in the world for more than 30 years, until the Guangzhou TV & Sightseeing Tower in China crushed its record in 2009.

Historic Distillery District

(B) The 1832 Gooderham and Worts distillery was restored and revitalized in 2003 to create a pedestrian-only mini-village of cobblestone streets and brick buildings housing restaurants, shops, galleries, and theaters. The design perfectly incorporates the original Victorian industrial architecture, and the Distillery District is a great place to while away an afternoon or evening. Concerts and other events take place outdoors in summer.

Hockey Sites

(C) To truly experience Canadian culture you should school yourself at the Hockey Hall of Fame. Its prized possession is the original 1892 Stanley Cup. The Maple Leafs are Toronto's National Hockey League team, and though they haven't won the Stanley Cup since 1967, fans are loyal and tickets are notoriously tough to get. **TIP→ If you can't nab a Leafs ticket, head to the Ricoh Coliseum to catch the Marlies, Toronto's AHL team.**

Great Markets

(D) St. Lawrence Market is as much a destination for its brick 1844 exterior as for its city block of meats, cheeses, produce, and prepared foods inside. It's the quintessential place to grab one of the city's famed peameal bacon sandwiches (we said "famed," not "gourmet").

1

G

E

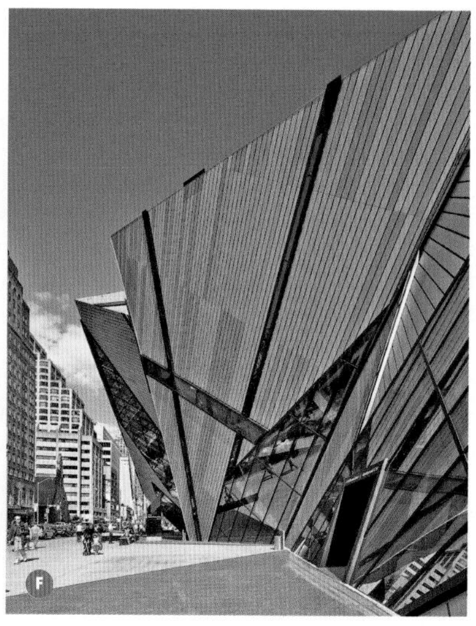

F

Kensington Market is an entirely different beast: several blocks square of used-clothing stores, head shops, cheap ethnic and vegetarian eats, and shops selling spices, fish, and baked goods. Streets teem with browsers, buskers, and bicycles. The best—albeit busiest—time to go is when cars are prohibited, the last Sunday of every month between May and October.

Toronto Islands

(E) A short ferry ride from Harbourfront, the car-free islands are a relaxing respite from the concrete jungle. Take a picnic, lie on the beach, or ride a bicycle on the boardwalk. The kiddie amusement park on Centre Island attracts families. Don't forget your camera: the view of Toronto's skyline from here is unparalleled.

Top Museums

(F) Your first stop should be the Art Gallery of Ontario (AGO), with its collection of nearly 80,000 works spanning almost 2,000 years of art. Then hit the Royal Ontario Museum (ROM) with a world-class Age of Dinosaurs gallery. And don't miss the changing exhibitions at the Design Exchange and the Bata Shoe Museum's staggering collection of footwear. And opening in 2014, the Aga Khan Museum and Ismaili Centre, a groundbreaking, expansive cultural center dedicated to the Muslim world.

Queen West

(G) Many a visitor falls in love with Toronto after a foray to historically bohemian Queen Street West. Though the entire strip has spirit, the ragtag artist-forged businesses keep moving west. Begin with the spiffy chain stores near Spadina and see how the record shops, boutiques, cafés, bookstores, bars, and galleries change as you head west.

TOP EXPERIENCES

Wining and Dining

Those in search of haute cuisine are pampered in Toronto, where some of the world's finest chefs vie for the attention of the city's sizable foodie population. Toronto's range of exceptional eateries, from creative Asian fusion to more daring molecular gastronomy, offers wining and dining potential for every possible palate. Aromas of finely crafted sauces and delicately grilled meats emanate from eateries in Yorkville, where valet service and designer handbags are de rigueur, and the strip of bistros in the Entertainment District gets lively with theatergoing crowds. Weekdays at lunch, the Financial District's Bay Street is a sea of Armani suits, crisply pressed shirts, and clicking heels heading to power lunches to make deals over steak frites. To conduct your own taste tests, check out some of the following places:

Bistro 990. Staff here are sure to be attentive—they're used to serving celebrities and power-wielding bigwigs who fill the tables on weekday afternoons.

Bymark. An ultramodern and ultracool spot primed for the Financial District set; chef-owner Mark McEwan aims for perfection with classy contemporary fare.

Canoe. Toronto's most famous "splurge" place. Sit back, enjoy the view, and let the waiter pair your dish with a recommended local Ontario wine.

Colborne Lane. Star chef Claudio Aprile's venture is *the* place to sample cutting-edge creations that blur the boundary between dinner and science project.

Fressen. Dimly lit, ultra-trendy vegan nouvelle cuisine with a wine list to rival any steak house.

Hot Hoods

Toronto's coolness doesn't emanate from a downtown core or even a series of town centers. The action is everywhere in the city. Dozens of neighborhoods, each with its own scene and way of life, coexist within the vast metropolitan area. Here are a few worth investigating:

West Queen West. As Queen Street West (to Bathurst Street or so) becomes more commercial and rents increase, more local artists and designers have moved farther west; it's also home to a burgeoning night scene and experimental restaurants.

Kensington Market. This well-established bastion of bohemia for hippies of all ages is a grungy and multicultural several-block radius of produce, cheese, by-the-gram spices, fresh empanadas, used clothing, head shops, and funky restaurants and cafés.

The Annex. The pockets of wealth nestled in side streets add diversity to this scruffy strip of Bloor, the favorite haunt of the intellectual set, whether starving student or world-renowned novelist.

The Beach. This bourgeois-bohemian neighborhood (also called The Beaches) is the habitat of young professionals who frequent the yoga studios and sushi restaurants along Queen Street East and walk their pooches daily along Lake Ontario's boardwalk.

Performing Arts

Refurbished iconic theaters such as the Royal Alexandra and Ed Mirvish theaters host a number of big-ticket shows in elegant surroundings. More modern venues such as the Princess of Wales highlight local and Broadway performances. The Four Seasons Centre is home to both the National Ballet of Canada and the Canadian Opera Company, which shares the

music scene with the Toronto Symphony Orchestra and mainstream concerts at the Sony Centre and Massey Hall. Indie artists are attracted to the bars and grimy music venues on Queen Street West. (True theater buffs will also want to leave Toronto to hit the festivals of Stratford and Niagara-on-the-Lake.) A few of the many venues worth visiting are:

Massey Hall. Since 1894, this has been one of Toronto's premier concert halls. British royals have been entertained here and legendary musicians have performed: Charlie Parker, Dizzy Gillespie, George Gershwin, Bob Dylan, and Luciano Pavarotti, to name a few. Orchestras, musicals, dance troupes, and comedians also perform at this palpably historic venue.

Rivoli. In this multifaceted venue, you can dine while admiring local art, catch a musical act, or watch stand-up. Before they were megastars, Beck, the Indigo Girls, Iggy Pop, Janeane Garofalo, and Tori Amos all made appearances here.

Elgin and Winter Garden Theatres. These two 1913 Edwardian theaters, one stacked on top of the other, provide sumptuous settings for classical music performances, musicals, opera, and Toronto International Film Festival screenings.

The Second City. The comedic troupe here always puts on a great performance. Photo collages on the wall display the club's alumni, including Mike Myers, Dan Aykroyd, and Catherine O'Hara.

Architecture

At one point, Toronto's only celebrated icon was the CN Tower, but architects have been working hard to rejuvenate the cityscape in the new millennium—at a dizzying pace. Since 2006, the city has unveiled the transparent-glass-fronted Four Seasons Centre for the Performing Arts (Jack Diamond), the Royal Ontario Museum's deconstructed-crystal extension (Daniel Libeskind), the wood-and-glass Art Gallery of Ontario (Frank Gehry), and a redesign of the Sony Centre for the Performing Arts with attached residential 58-story, all-glass, swooping L Tower (Libeskind). A series of high-rises topping 50 stories—not the least of which is the 60-story, glass-spired Trump Tower—is changing the skyline of the city forever.

Fine examples include:

Philosopher's Walk. This scenic path winds through the University of Toronto, from the entrance between the Royal Ontario Museum and the Victorian Royal Conservatory of Music, past Trinity College's Gothic chapel and towering spires. Also look for University College, an 1856 ivy-covered Romanesque Revival building, set back from the road across Hoskin Avenue.

ROMwalks. From May through October, free themed walks organized by the Royal Ontario Museum tour some of the city's landmark buildings, such as the Church of the Redeemer, the St. Lawrence Market, and the Royal York Hotel.

Art Gallery of Ontario. A C$250-million renovation added thousands of square feet of gallery space in the AGO's Frank Gehry–designed building in 2008. The wooden facades, glass roofs, and four-story blue titanium wing are spectacular to admire from the outside or within.

Sharp Centre for Design. Locals are split by Will Alsop's salt-and-pepper rectangle held aloft by giant colored-pencil-like stilts standing above the Ontario College of Art and Design.

TORONTO WITH KIDS

Toronto is one of the most livable cities in the world, with many families residing downtown and plenty of activities to keep them busy. *Throughout this guide, places that are especially appealing to families are indicated by FAMILY in the margin.*

Always check what's on at the **Harbourfront Centre,** a cultural complex with shows and workshops for ages 1 to 100. On any given day you could find a circus, clown school, musicians, juggling, storytelling, or acrobat shows. Even fearless kids' (and adults') eyes bulge at the 1,465-foot glass-elevator ride up the side of the **CN Tower,** and once they stand on the glass floor, their minds are officially blown.

Kids won't realize they're getting schooled at the **ROM,** with its Bat Cave and dinosaur skeletons, and the **Ontario Science Centre,** with interactive exhibits exploring the brain, technology, and outer space; documentaries are shown in the massive OMNIMAX dome. Out at the eastern end of the suburb of Scarborough, the well-designed **Toronto Zoo** is home to giraffes, polar bears, and gorillas. Less exotic animals hang at **Riverdale Farm,** in the more central Cabbagetown: get nose-to-nose with sheep, cows, and pigs.

Spending a few hours on the **Toronto Islands** is a good way to decompress. The Centreville Amusement Park and petting zoo is geared to the under-seven set, with tame rides, such as the log flume and antique carousel. Alternatively, pile the whole family into a surrey to pedal along the carless roads, or lounge at the beach at Hanlan's Point (warning: clothing-optional) or Ward's Island (clothes generally worn). The **Canadian National Exhibition (CNE),** aka "the Ex," is a huge three-week fair held in late August with carnival rides, games, food, puppet shows, a daily parade, and horse, dog, and cat shows. Kids can also pet and feed horses at the horse barn or tend to chickens and milk a cow on the "farm." But the mother of all amusement parks is a half-hour drive north of the city at **Canada's Wonderland,** home of Canada's biggest and fastest roller coaster. In winter, **ice-skating** at the Harbourfront Centre is the quintessential family activity.

Young sports fans might appreciate seeing a **Blue Jays** (baseball), **Maple Leafs** (hockey), **Raptors** (basketball), or Toronto **FC** (soccer) game. To take on Wayne Gretzky in a virtual game and see the original Stanley Cup, head to the **Hockey Hall of Fame.**

Intelligent productions at the **Young People's Theatre** don't condescend to kids and teens, and many are just as entertaining for adults. The **TIFF Kids International Film Festival** takes place in April, with films for ages 2 to 13. Teens and tweens who aren't tuckered out after dark might get a kick out of a retro double feature at the **Polson Pier Drive-In,** right downtown.

For the latest on upcoming shows and events, plus an overwhelming directory of stores and services, go to the website Toronto4Kids (🌐 *www.toronto4kids.com*).

TORONTO LIKE A LOCAL

To get a sense of Toronto's culture, start by familiarizing yourself with the rituals of daily life. These are a few highlights.

Leafs Nation

What do the Leafs and the *Titanic* have in common? They both look great until they hit the ice. Cue rim shot. Leafs fans—or "Leafs Nation" as they are known collectively—are accustomed to jokes, rooting as they do for a team that hasn't won the Stanley Cup since 1967. Despite heartbreak after heartbreak, they stand by every year praying for a slot in the playoffs. If the opportunity arises to attend a game (don't bank on it—nearly everyone has been sold out for six decades), count yourself luckier than most Torontonians. If not, try for a Marlies AHL game at the Ricoh Coliseum. For hockey fans or an intro to the sport, the Hockey Hall of Fame is a must. Seeing a hockey game at a sports bar is a true Canadian pastime: grab a brewski and join locals in heckling the refs on bad calls. When the Leafs score, the mirth is contagious.

International Outlook

With around half the urban population born outside Canada, and even more with foreign roots, Toronto redefines "cosmopolitan." Ethnic enclaves—Little Portugal, Greektown, Corso Italia (the "other Little Italy," on St. Clair West), and Koreatown—color downtown. It's fun to explore the architecture and shopping in each neighborhood, and dining out can be as exotic as you choose. Toronto's multiculturalism is evident in many of its annual festivals: the glittering Scotiabank Caribbean Carnival along the waterfront; the Pilaros Taste of the Danforth, featuring Greek musicians, dances, and plenty of souvlaki; the raucous celebration of Mexican Independence Day in Nathan Phillips Square; and the India Bazaar's annual festival with dancing, *chaat* (savory snacks), and henna tattooing.

Coffee, Coffee Everywhere

Morning rush hour is the best time to observe, but not participate in (lines are out the door), the ritual of caffeine and sugar intake at Tim Horton's, a coffee chain with a distinctly Canadian image and affordable prices. Go for a "double-double" (two cream, two sugar) and a box of Timbits (donut holes). But plenty of Torontonians eschew "Tim's" for more quality brews, and the city has no shortage of independently owned cafés with stellar espresso, exquisitely steamed milk, and often a fair-trade and organic option, especially along Queen Street (east of Broadview or west of Spadina) and in the Annex and Little Italy. Some of the best are Crema (Danforth, the Junction), Sam James (the Annex), Dark Horse (Chinatown, Riverside, and Queen West), and Manic (Little Italy).

Lake Escapes

You don't need a car to escape Toronto's bustle and summer heat to indulge in a calm, cool day by the lake. A rite of passage for every Torontonian is a warm-weather trip to the islands—a 15-minute ferry trip from downtown—for a barbecue, picnic, bike rides, or the Centreville amusement park. Or head to the east side of the city for strolls along the boardwalk in The Beach neighborhood. Those with wheels spend weekends on the Niagara Peninsula dallying in antiques shops in charming towns and sampling wines or head north to relax in the Muskoka Lakes cottage country or hike and camp in Algonquin Provincial Park.

TORONTO'S BEST FESTIVALS

Festivals keep Toronto lively even when cold winds blow in off Lake Ontario in winter. Themes range from art to food, Caribbean culture to gay pride. Most national championship sports events take place in and around Toronto.

Tourism Toronto. Tourism Toronto maintains an online calendar of nearly every event in the city. ☎ *416/203–2500, 800/499–2514* 🌐 *www.seetorontonow.com.*

January–February

Winterlicious. A winter culinary event offering discount prix-fixe menus at top restaurants as well as themed tastings and food-prep workshops. ☎ *416/395–0490* 🌐 *www.toronto.ca/winterlicious.*

April

TIFF Kids International Film Festival. Taking place in April, this children's film festival holds screenings for kids and teens aged (roughly) 2–13. ☎ *416/599–8433, 888/599–8433* 🌐 *tiff.net.*

April–November

Shaw Festival. Held from late spring until fall in quaint Niagara-on-the-Lake, this festival presents plays by George Bernard Shaw and his contemporaries. Niagara-on-the-Lake is a two-hour drive south of Toronto. ☎ *905/468–2172, 800/511–7429* 🌐 *www.shawfest.com.*

Stratford Festival. One of the best known Shakespeare festivals in the world, this event was created in the 1950s to revive a little town two hours west of Toronto that happened to be called Stratford (and its river called the Avon). The festival includes at least five Shakespeare plays as well as other classical and contemporary productions. Respected actors from around the world participate. ☎ *519/273–1600, 800/567–1600* 🌐 *www.stratfordfestival.ca.*

April–May

Hot Docs. North America's largest documentary film fest, Hot Docs takes over independent cinemas for two weeks. ☎ *416/203–2155* 🌐 *www.hotdocs.ca.*

Scotiabank Contact Photography Festival. More than 200 galleries and other venues mount photo exhibits by 1,000 different artists for this photography festival, throughout the entire month of May. ☎ *416/539–9595* 🌐 *www.scotiabankcontactphoto.com.*

June

Luminato. For 10 days, this citywide arts festival combines visual arts, music, theater, dance, literature, and more in hundreds of events, many of them free. ☎ *416/368–3100* 🌐 *luminatofestival.com.*

North by Northeast (*NXNE*). Modeled after South by Southwest in Austin, Texas, this is a seven-day music and film festival. ☎ *416/863–6963* 🌐 *nxne.com.*

Pride Week. Rainbow flags fly high during Pride Week, the city's premier gay and lesbian event. It includes 10 days of cultural and political programs, concerts, a street festival, and a parade, and is centered around the Church-Wellesley corridor. ☎ *416/927–7433* 🌐 *www.pridetoronto.com.*

Toronto Jazz Festival. For 10 days this festival brings big-name jazz artists to city jazz clubs and other indoor and outdoor venues. ☎ *416/928–2033* 🌐 *torontojazz.com.*

July

Beaches International Jazz Festival. In the east-end Beach (aka Beaches) neighborhood, this event is a free, 10-day jazz, blues, and Latin music event and street festival ☎ *416/698–2152* 🌐 *www.beachesjazz.com.*

Honda Indy. At this summer fixture, cars speed around an 11-turn, 1.77-mile track that goes through the Canadian National Exhibition grounds and along Lakeshore Boulevard. ☎ *416/588–7223* 🌐 *www.hondaindytoronto.com.*

Summerlicious. Almost 200 restaurants in Toronto create prix-fixe menus—some at bargain prices—for this two-week culinary event. ☎ *416/395–0490* 🌐 *www.toronto.ca/summerlicious.*

Toronto Fringe Festival. This 10-day event is the city's largest theater festival. It features new and developing plays by emerging artists. ☎ *416/966–1062* 🌐 *www.fringetoronto.com.*

July–August

Scotiabank Caribbean Carnival Toronto. One of the largest festivals in North America, Caribana is a three-week celebration of Carribean culture, with calypso, steel pan, soca, and reggae music; fiery cuisine; and plenty of revelry. The celebrations culminate in a massive parade on the first Saturday of August. ☎ *416/391–5608* 🌐 *www.torontocaribbeancarnival.com.*

August

Canadian National Exhibition. With carnival rides, concerts, an air show, a dog show, a garden show, and a "Mardi Gras" parade, this 2½-week-long fair is the biggest in Canada. It's been held at the eponymous fairgrounds on the Lake Ontario waterfront since 1879. ☎ *416/393–6300* 🌐 *www.theex.com.*

Rogers Cup. Founded in 1881, this is an ATP Masters 1000 event for men and a Premier event for women. It's held on the York University campus, with the men's and women's events alternating between Toronto and Montréal each year. ☎ *416/665–9777* 🌐 *www.rogerscup.com.*

Scotiabank BuskerFest. This is no ordinary street festival: aerialists, fire-eaters, dancers, contortionists, musicians, and more perform along Yonge Street between Queen and College for four days in August. 🌐 *www.torontobuskerfest.com.*

SummerWorks Performance Festival. Plays, concerts, and performances are mounted at local theaters during this 11-day theater festival. ☎ *416/628–8216* 🌐 *www.summerworks.ca.*

September

The Toronto International Film Festival. Renowned worldwide, this festival is considered more accessible to the public than Cannes, Sundance, or other major film festivals. A number of films make their world or North American premieres at this 11-day festival each year, some at red-carpet events attended by Hollywood stars. ☎ *416/968–3456, 877/968–3456* 🌐 *tiff.net.*

October

Nuit Blanche. Concentrated in Toronto's downtown core, this all-night street festival has interactive contemporary art installations and performances. 🌐 *www.scotiabanknuitblanche.ca.*

November

Royal Agricultural Winter Fair. Held since 1922 at the Ex, this 10-day fair is a highlight of Canada's equestrian season each November, with jumping, dressage, and harness-racing competitions. ☎ *416/263–3400* 🌐 *www.royalfair.org.*

SPORTS AND OUTDOORS

Toronto has a love–hate relationship with its professional sports teams, and fans can sometimes be accused of being fair-weather, except when it comes to hockey, which has always attracted rabid, sell-out crowds whether the Maple Leafs win, lose, or draw. In other words, don't count on getting Leafs tickets but take heart that sports bars will be filled with fired-up fans. It can be a cinch, however, to score tickets to Blue Jays (baseball), Raptors (basketball), Argos (football), and Toronto FC (soccer) games—depending on who they play.

StubHub. Ticket reseller StubHub is a good resource for sold-out games. ☎ *866/788–2482* 🌐 *www.stubhub.com.*

If you prefer to work up a sweat yourself, consider golf at one of the GTA's courses, ice-skating at a city rink in winter, or exploring the many parks and beaches *(see the Exploring chapter).*

Baseball

Toronto Blue Jays. Toronto's professional baseball team plays April through September. Interest in the team has gradually fallen since they won consecutive World Series championships in 1992 and 1993. Recent seasons have seen many young players trying to make their mark. The spectacular Rogers Centre (formerly the SkyDome) has a fully retractable roof; some consider it one of the world's premier entertainment centers. ✉ *Rogers Centre, 1 Blue Jays Way, Harbourfront* ☎ *416/341–1234 ticket line, 888/OK–GO–JAY toll free ticket line* 🌐 *www.bluejays.com* Ⓜ *Union.*

Basketball

Toronto Raptors. The city's NBA franchise, this team played its first season in 1995–96. For several years they struggled mightily to win both games and fans in this hockey-mad city, but the Raptors have finally come into their own, and games often sell out. Single-game tickets are available beginning in September; the season is from October through April. ✉ *Air Canada Centre, 40 Bay St., at the Gardiner Expwy., Harbourfront* ☎ *855/985–5000 Ticketmaster* 🌐 *www.nba.com/raptors* Ⓜ *Union.*

Football

Toronto Argonauts. The Toronto Argonauts Canadian Football League (CFL) team has a healthy following. American football fans who attend a CFL game discover a faster, more unpredictable and exciting contest than the American version. The longer, wider field means quarterbacks have to scramble more. Tickets for games (June–November) are usually a cinch to get. ✉ *Rogers Centre, 1 Blue Jays Way, Harbourfront* ☎ *855/985–5000 Ticketmaster* 🌐 *www.argonauts.ca* Ⓜ *Union.*

Hockey

Toronto Maple Leafs. Hockey is as popular as you've heard here, and Maple Leafs fans are particularly ardent. Even though the Leafs haven't won a Stanley Cup since 1967, they continue to inspire fierce devotion in Torontonians. If you want a chance to cheer them on, you'll have to get on the puck. **TIP→ Buy tickets at least a few months in advance or risk the game's being sold out.** No matter the stats, Leafs tickets are notoriously the toughest to score in the National Hockey League. The regular hockey season is October–mid-April. ✉ *Air Canada Centre, 40 Bay St., at Gardiner Expwy., Harbourfront* ☎ *855/465–3237 Ticketmaster* 🌐 *www.mapleleafs.com* Ⓜ *Union.*

Toronto Marlies. If you're keen to see some hockey while you're in town, go to a Toronto Marlies game at Ricoh Coliseum. The level of play is very high, and

tickets are cheaper and easier to come by than those of the Marlies' NHL affiliate, the Toronto Maple Leafs. ✉ *Ricoh Coliseum, 100 Princes Blvd., Harbourfront* ☎ *416/263–3900* 🌐 *www.marlies.ca/* Ⓜ *Union, then 509 Harbourfront streetcar west; or Bathurst, then 511 streetcar.*

Soccer

Toronto's British roots combined with a huge immigrant population have helped make the Toronto Football Club (TFC), the newest addition to the city's pro-sports tapestry, a success. And during events like the FIFA World Cup, UEFA European Championship, and Copa América (America Cup), sports bars and cafés with TVs are teeming.

Toronto FC. Canada's first Major League Soccer team and Toronto's first professional soccer team in years, Toronto FC has a 20,000-seat stadium. Fans get seriously pumped up for these games, singing fight songs, waving flags, and throwing streamers. Games sometimes sell out; single-game tickets go on sale a few days before the match. The season is March–October. ✉ *BMO Field, 170 Princes' Blvd., Exhibition Place* ☎ *1-855/985–5000 Ticketmaster* 🌐 *www.torontofc.ca* Ⓜ *Union, then 509 Harbourfront streetcar west; 511 Bathurst streetcar south.*

Golf

The golf season lasts only from April to late October. Discounted rates are usually available until mid-May and after Canadian Thanksgiving (early October). All courses are best reached by car.

Angus Glen Golf Club. Deemed Canada's best new course by *Golf Digest* when it opened in 1995, this club has remained one of the country's best places to play, hosting the Canadian Open in 2002 and 2007 on its par-72 South and North courses, respectively. It's a 45-minute drive north of downtown. ✉ *10080 Kennedy Rd., Markham* ☎ *905/887–0090, 905/887–5157 reservations* 🌐 *www.angusglen.com.*

Don Valley Golf Course. About a 20-minute drive north of downtown this is a par-71, 18-hole municipal course. Despite being right in the city, it's a lovely, hilly course with water hazards and tree-lined fairways. ✉ *4200 Yonge St., North York* ☎ *416/392–2465* 🌐 *www.toronto.ca/parks/golf.*

Glen Abbey Golf Club. This Jack Nicklaus–designed 18-hole, par-73 club is considered to be Canada's top course. The Canadian Open was held here for the 26th time in 2013. It's in the affluent suburb of Oakville, about 45 minutes east of the city. ✉ *1333 Dorval Dr., just north of QEW, Oakville* ☎ *905/844–1800* 🌐 *www.clublink.ca.*

Ice-Skating

Harbourfront Centre. This spacious, outdoor rink is often voted the best in the city due to its lakeside location and DJ'd skate nights. Skate rentals are C$8. ✉ *235 Queens Quay W, at Lower Simcoe St., Harbourfront* ☎ *416/973–4866* 🌐 *www.harbourfrontcentre.com/skating* Ⓜ *Union.*

Toronto Parks, Forestry & Recreation Rink Hotline. The favorite city-operated, outdoor rinks are the forested, west-side **High Park** and the tiny **Nathan Phillips Square,** surrounded by towering skyscrapers in the heart of the Financial District. City rinks are free, and most don't have rental facilities, although the Nathan Phillips Square Rink does. ☎ *311 Toronto Parks, Forestry & Recreation rink hotline* 🌐 *www.toronto.ca/parks/skating.*

AROUND THE WORLD WALKING TOUR

How fast can you circumnavigate the globe? Forget 80 days—in Toronto you can do it in a mere 80 minutes (give or take). These neighborhoods are food-centric, so start out hungry.

Chinatown

Start on Chinatown's periphery with a photo op. Three of the city's most recognizable buildings are visible here: the whimsically modernist **Sharp Centre for Design**, the **CN Tower** in the distance, and the Frank Gehry–designed **Art Gallery of Ontario.** Move west to the **Chinese Bakery** and fuel up with sticky rice cakes and salty pork cookies. **Ten Ren Tea** is a favorite for bubble tea, milk tea, and traditional green tea. The intersection of Dundas and Spadina is one of the busiest in the city. The **Royal Bank of Canada building** here has a colorful history. Opened as a Yiddish theater in 1921, it became a burlesque theater and then a Chinese-language cinema before closing in the 1990s. All along Spadina, sidewalks spill over with bins of exotic fruit and dried fish, stacks of rattan baskets, and racks of inexpensive clothing. Slip into Tap Phong Tranding Co. Inc. where you'll find aisles of rice bowls and bamboo steamers; it supplies dining ware to many of the area's restaurants. Chinese restaurants are plentiful, but Thailand, Japan, Korea, and Vietnam are also represented. For a full meal of noodles, try **Swatow,** and for inexpensive dim sum at any time of day (or night), drop into **Rol San.**

Kensington Soup

Cross Spadina to the global marketplace of **Kensington Market,** via St. Andrew Street. In the early 20th century this was an overwhelmingly Jewish neighborhood; one of the few remnants is the 1930 **Minsk Synagogue.** Over half the shops on Kensington Avenue are vintage—take your pick, but the mother of them all is the 38-year-old **Courage My Love.** Then plunk yourself down on **Fika's** perfect patio for a coffee. Deeper into the market you'll find the choice of eatables overwhelming—how about a roast beef dinner between two slices of bread from **Sanagan's Meat Locker** or a "double" (chickpea sandwich) from Caribbean **Patty King**? An empanada from **Jumbo Empenada** will let you on to their patio, which is a great place to watch the carnival go round on the market's busiest block. Up the street there are unique gifts at **Good Egg** and the **Blue Banana;** wood-fired bagels at **Nu Bügel;** and fresh-squeezed juice at **Urban Herbivore.**

On the Continent

Along College Street, the freneticism peters out. Pop into **She Said Boom** to browse the collection of second-hand fiction, philosophy and vinyl, then head to the deliberately disheveled **Manic Coffee** to review your finds. Head farther west past Bathurst along College and you'll hit Little Italy. At Clinton, you'll find **Café Diplomatico**, a Little Italy institution since 1968: its sidewalk patio is a great place to chill with a Peroni or granita. Sadly, espresso isn't its forte. The Italian bakeries, restaurants, and gelato shops multiply closer to the heart of Little Italy, around College and Grace streets. End your cultural tour with a taste of Portugal: a traditional *pastel de nata* (custard pastry) at **Nova Era.**

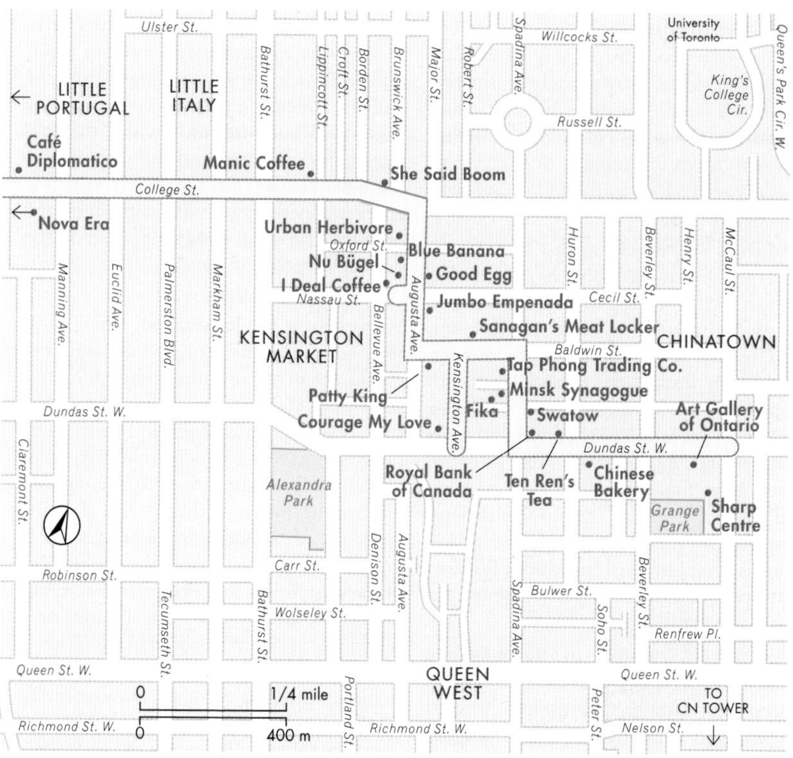

Where to Start:	At the Art Gallery of Ontario (AGO).
Time/Length:	Two hours at a leisurely pace; longer if you're tempted by one of the many coffee shops or restaurants along the way. About 1½ miles.
Where to Stop:	Almost anywhere in Kensington or Little Italy is suited to whiling away minutes or hours; favorites are Fika and Café Diplomatico.
Best Time to Go:	Any sunny day will do, though some shops and restaurants are closed Monday. Ending up in Little Italy at teatime (or pre-dinner drinks time) is a plan.
Worst Time to Go:	In this case the early bird doesn't catch the worm: start before 10 am and you'll be faced with shuttered storefronts. After 5 pm Kensington Market starts to wind down.
Highlights:	Art Gallery of Ontario, Sharp Centre for Design, Chinatown, Kensington Market, Little Italy.

GREAT ITINERARIES

Five Days in Toronto

To really see Toronto, a stay of at least one week is ideal. However, these itineraries are designed to inspire thematic tours of some of the city's best sights, whether you're in town for one day or five. We've also included a two-to-three-day escape to the Niagara region.

One Day: Architecture and Museums

Start at Queen and Bay by pondering Finnish architect Viljo Revell's eye-shaped **City Hall** and then its regal predecessor, **Old City Hall,** across the street. From here, head south through the **Financial District** to admire the skyscrapers before swinging west on Front Street to the spectacular **CN Tower.** It's not hard to find—just look up. If you have more time, walk up to King and catch a streetcar east to Parliament, then walk south to the restored Victorian industrial buildings of the **Historic Distillery District**; choose any of the amazing restaurants here for lunch.

Begin the afternoon at the **Royal Ontario Museum.** If the steep entrance fee makes you wince, admire the modern Crystal gallery from outside before moving on to the **Gardiner Museum of Ceramic Art,** across the street, or the quirky **Bata Shoe Museum** at St. George Street.

One Day: Shopping Around the World

Before the crowds descend at lunchtime, head for the aesthetically chaotic Spadina Avenue–Dundas Street intersection, the core of **Chinatown,** to browse the stalls overflowing with exotic fruits and vegetables, fragrant herbal tonics, and flashy Chinese baubles. Either pause here for a steaming plate of fried noodles, or try one of the juice bars, vegan restaurants, or empanada stands in nearby **Kensington Market** (head west on Dundas to Augusta and turn right). After lunch, browse the South American and Caribbean shops and groceries, modern cafés, and funky clothing boutiques. Take the College streetcar east to Coxwell Avenue (about a 30-minute ride), where the dazzling bejeweled saris and shiny bangles of the **India Bazaar** beckon. A fiery madras curry washed down with a mango *lassi* (yogurt drink) or Kingfisher beer is the perfect way to end the day.

One Day: With Kids

Start early at the **Toronto Zoo,** where 700-plus acres of dense forests and winding creeks are home to more than 5,000 animals and 460 species. (Allow for extra time if you are reaching the zoo by public transportation, which could take over an hour.) Or venture out to the equally enthralling indoor exhibits and demonstrations of the **Ontario Science Centre.** If your kids are sports fans, the **Hockey Hall of Fame,** at Yonge and Front streets, might be just the ticket. If it's the summer or a weekend, head to Harbourfront. There's always kid-friendly activities and performances; watching the glass blowers in the open workshops is fascinating. In winter, rent some skates and get on the ice. Combine Harbourfront with a ride up the **CN Tower** to test your nerves on the glass floor that "floats" over a 1,122-foot drop and take in a view that extends far enough to let you see the mist from Niagara Falls. Head east down Queen's Quay just past Jarvis to **Against the Grain** where you can toast a fun-filled day with a Shirley Temple right next to the water's edge.

One Day: Island Life

Pick up picnic supplies from **St. Lawrence Market** (closed Sunday and Monday), whose stalls offer a cornucopia of imported delicacies and delicious prepared foods. From here, walk to

the **docks** at the foot of Bay Street and Queen's Quay to catch one of the ferries to the **Toronto Islands;** the view of the city skyline is an added bonus. In summer, kids have the run of **Centre Island. Hanlan's Point** is infamous for its nude bathing, and **Ward's Island** has a great sandy beach and a restaurant, the Rectory Café, with a shady patio. One of the allures of Island life is the slow pace, so spend the afternoon rambling. If you'd like to cover more ground, rent a bicycle at the pier on Centre Island. Winter is not without charms—namely, cross-country skiing, snowshoeing, and skating on the frozen streams. When you're back downtown in the evening, keep the outdoorsy theme going with an alfresco dinner in the **Danforth, Little Italy,** or the **Historic Distillery District**—Toronto's only pedestrian-friendly entertainment village.

One Day: Neighborhood Watching

Begin the day window-shopping along the rows of restored Victorian residences on **Yorkville Avenue,** or reading at a sidewalk café along **Cumberland Street.** In the 1960s, before the country's most exclusive shops settled here, Yorkville was a hippie haven, attracting emerging Canadian musical artists like Joni Mitchell and Gordon Lightfoot. The shops spill onto **Bloor Street West,** and the strip between Yonge Street and Avenue Road is sometimes referred to as Toronto's Fifth Avenue. The **Royal Ontario Museum** is worth a peek, even if just from the street, to admire the shiny crystal-inspired modern structure. In stark contrast to Yorkvillian sophistication, the grungy shops along Bloor, west of Spadina, are housed in less lovingly restored turn-of-the-20th-century storefronts. Rest your legs in either **Future Bakery & Café,** a student-friendly outpost for comfort food, or the more upscale, Mediterranean spot **Splendido.** In the evening, take in a play, a concert, or a comedy show downtown at the **Second City.**

A Few Days: Niagara Getaway

If you have a few days to spare, start by succumbing to the force and brilliance of **Niagara Falls.** A ride on the **Maid of the Mist** is highly recommended, and in the afternoon—especially if you have kids—you may want to experience **Clifton Hill** in all its tacky, amusement-filled glory. Alternatively, head along the scenic Niagara Parkway to visit the **Botanical Gardens** or **White Water Walk,** more peaceful and natural attractions. Get dressed up for dinner at the Skylon Tower or another restaurant overlooking the falls and tuck in for a night at the slots. Admire the **fireworks** at 10 pm (Friday and Sunday in summer) from either your falls-view hotel room or the **Table Rock Centre.** The next day, a good breakfast is essential, perhaps at one of the many options in the Fallsview Casino Resort, to prepare for a day of wine tasting and strolling in bucolic **Niagara-on-the-Lake.** You'll need a car to follow the beautiful Niagara Parkway north to Niagara-on-the-Lake's **Queen Street** for shopping. Nibble and tipple the day away along the **Wine Route,** which follows Highway 81 as far west as Grimsby. Dinner at one of the wineries or the excellent restaurants, such as **Peller Estates Winery Restaurant**, then a night in one of the region's boutique hotels or luxurious B&Bs is an indulgent end to a great weekend. If you're here during the **Shaw Festival** (April–October), book a ticket for a play by George Bernard Shaw or one of his contemporaries.

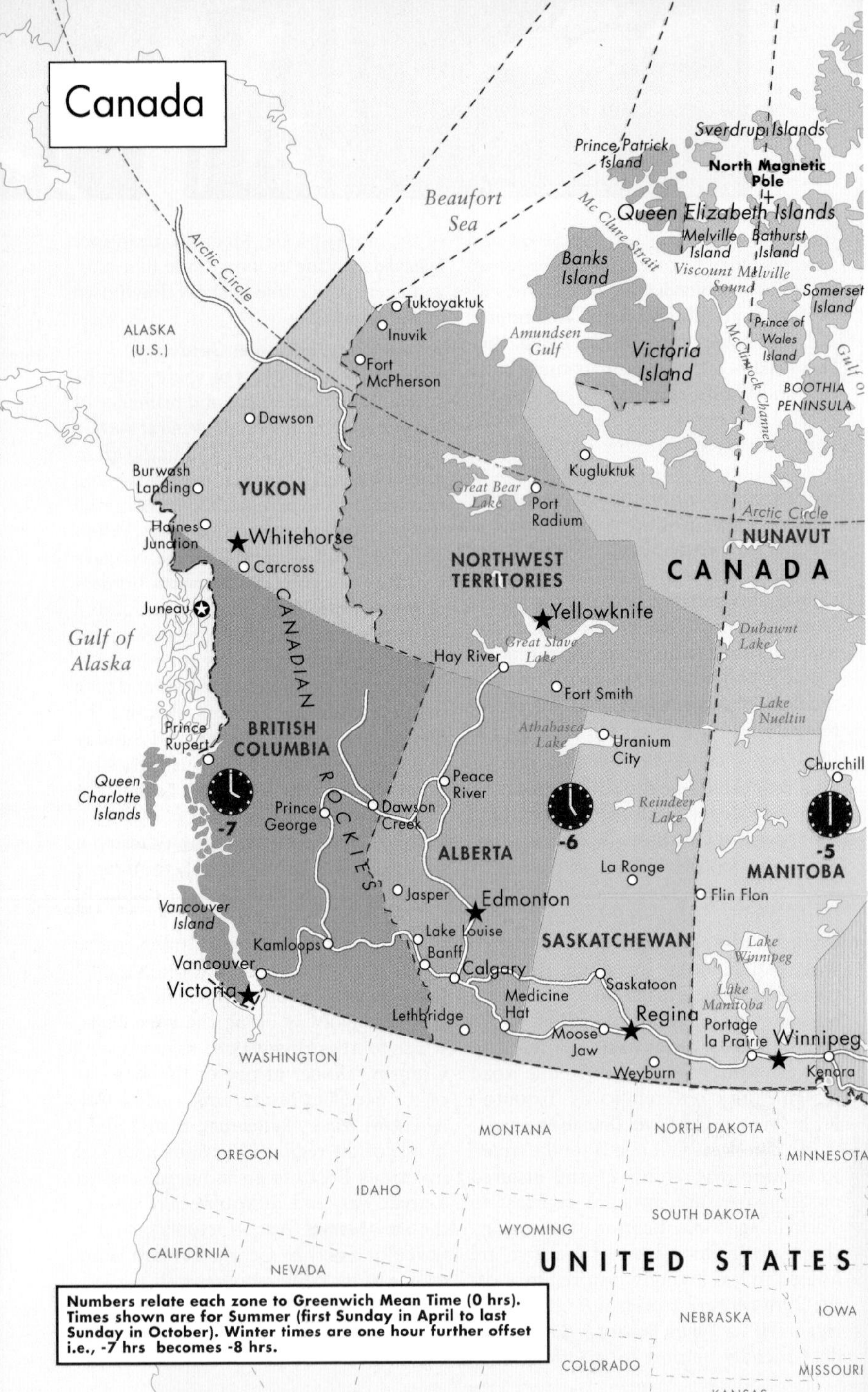
Canada
Beaufort Sea
Arctic Circle
ALASKA (U.S.)
Sverdrup Islands
Prince Patrick Island
North Magnetic Pole
Queen Elizabeth Islands
Mc Clure Strait
Melville Island
Bathurst Island
Banks Island
Viscount Melville Sound
Somerset Island
Tuktoyaktuk
Inuvik
Amundsen Gulf
Prince of Wales Island
Fort McPherson
Victoria Island
McClintock Channel
BOOTHIA PENINSULA
Gulf of
Dawson
Kugluktuk
Burwash Landing
YUKON
Great Bear Lake
Port Radium
Arctic Circle
Haines Junction
Whitehorse
NUNAVUT
Carcross
NORTHWEST TERRITORIES
CANADA
CANADIAN ROCKIES
Juneau
Yellowknife
Gulf of Alaska
Dubawnt Lake
Great Slave Lake
Hay River
Fort Smith
Lake Nueltin
Prince Rupert
BRITISH COLUMBIA
Athabasca Lake
Uranium City
Churchill
Peace River
Queen Charlotte Islands
Prince George
Dawson Creek
Reindeer Lake
-7
-6
-5
ALBERTA
La Ronge
MANITOBA
Jasper
Edmonton
Flin Flon
Vancouver Island
Lake Louise
SASKATCHEWAN
Lake Winnipeg
Kamloops
Banff
Vancouver
Calgary
Saskatoon
Victoria
Medicine Hat
Lake Manitoba
Regina
Lethbridge
Moose Jaw
Portage la Prairie
Winnipeg
WASHINGTON
Weyburn
Kenora
MONTANA
NORTH DAKOTA
OREGON
MINNESOTA
IDAHO
SOUTH DAKOTA
WYOMING
CALIFORNIA
UNITED STATES
NEVADA
NEBRASKA
IOWA
COLORADO
MISSOURI
KANSAS
Numbers relate each zone to Greenwich Mean Time (0 hrs).
Times shown are for Summer (first Sunday in April to last
Sunday in October). Winter times are one hour further offset
i.e., -7 hrs becomes -8 hrs.

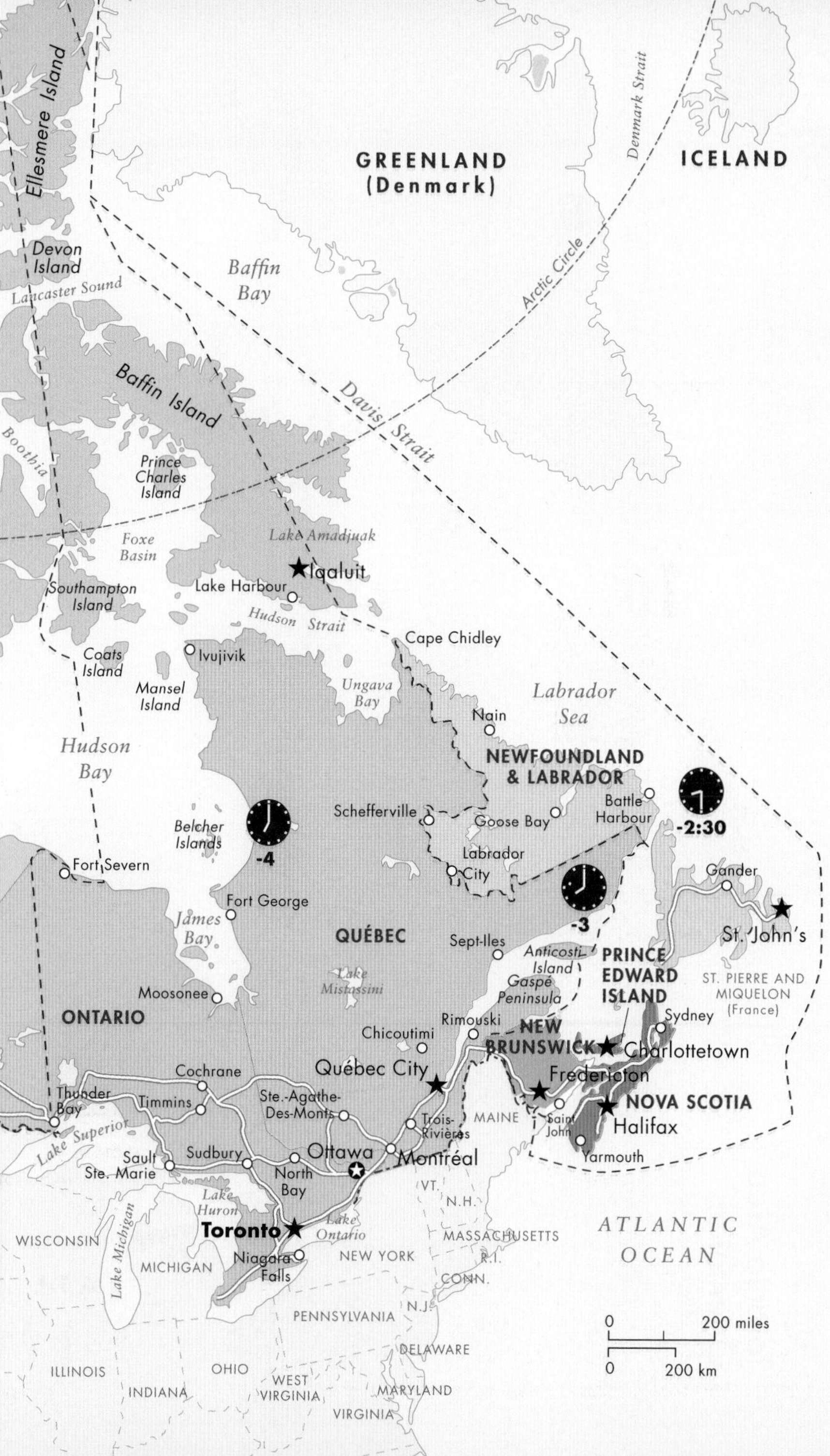

GREENLAND
(Denmark)
ICELAND
Denmark Strait
Ellesmere Island
Devon Island
Lancaster Sound
Baffin Bay
Arctic Circle
Baffin Island
Davis Strait
Boothia
Prince Charles Island
Foxe Basin
Lake Amadjuak
Iqaluit
Southampton Island
Lake Harbour
Hudson Strait
Cape Chidley
Coats Island
Ivujivik
Ungava Bay
Labrador Sea
Mansel Island
Nain
Hudson Bay
NEWFOUNDLAND & LABRADOR
Battle Harbour
-2:30
Schefferville
Goose Bay
Belcher Islands
-4
Labrador City
Fort Severn
Gander
-3
Fort George
St. John's
James Bay
QUÉBEC
Sept-Iles
Anticosti Island
PRINCE EDWARD ISLAND
Gaspé Peninsula
Lake Mistassini
ST. PIERRE AND MIQUELON (France)
Moosonee
ONTARIO
Rimouski
NEW BRUNSWICK
Sydney
Chicoutimi
Charlottetown
Cochrane
Québec City
Fredericton
Thunder Bay
Timmins
Ste.-Agathe-Des-Monts
NOVA SCOTIA
MAINE
Trois-Rivières
Saint John
Halifax
Lake Superior
Sault Ste. Marie
Sudbury
Ottawa
Montréal
Yarmouth
North Bay
VT.
Lake Huron
N.H.
Lake Michigan
Toronto
Lake Ontario
ATLANTIC OCEAN
WISCONSIN
MASSACHUSETTS
Niagara Falls
MICHIGAN
NEW YORK
R.I.
CONN.
N.J.
PENNSYLVANIA
0
200 miles
DELAWARE
0
200 km
ILLINOIS
OHIO
WEST VIRGINIA
INDIANA
MARYLAND
VIRGINIA

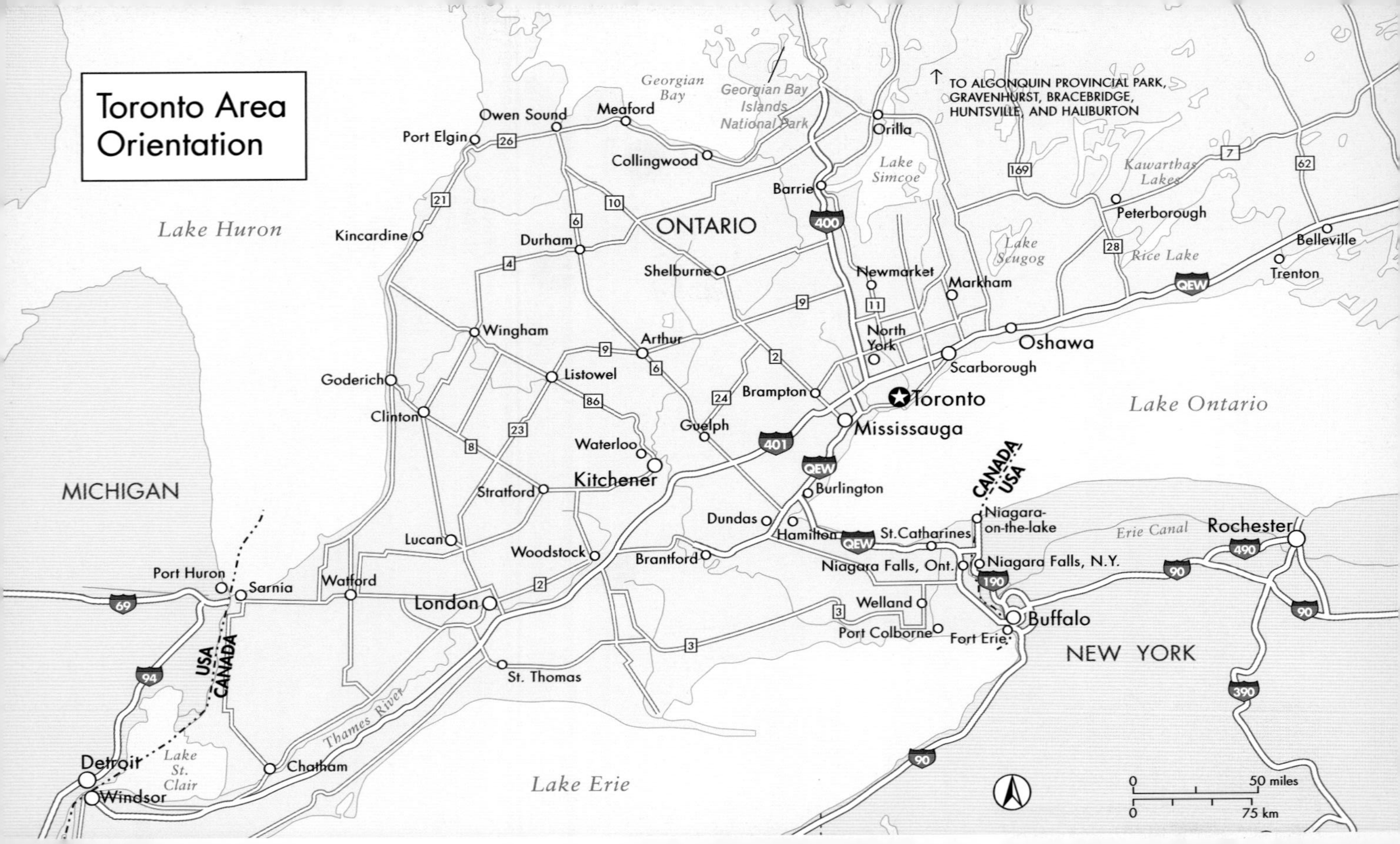

Toronto Area Orientation
TO ALGONQUIN PROVINCIAL PARK, GRAVENHURST, BRACEBRIDGE, HUNTSVILLE, AND HALIBURTON
Georgian Bay
Georgian Bay Islands National Park
Lake Huron
Lake Simcoe
Kawarthas Lakes
Lake Scugog
Rice Lake
Lake Ontario
Lake Erie
Lake St. Clair
Thames River
Erie Canal
ONTARIO
MICHIGAN
NEW YORK
CANADA
USA
Owen Sound
Meaford
Port Elgin
Collingwood
Orilla
Barrie
Kincardine
Durham
Shelburne
Newmarket
Markham
Peterborough
Belleville
Trenton
Wingham
Arthur
North York
Oshawa
Scarborough
Goderich
Listowel
Brampton
Toronto
Clinton
Guelph
Mississauga
Waterloo
Kitchener
Stratford
Burlington
Dundas
Hamilton
St.Catharines
Niagara-on-the-lake
Rochester
Lucan
Woodstock
Brantford
Niagara Falls, Ont.
Niagara Falls, N.Y.
Port Huron
Sarnia
Watford
London
Welland
Port Colborne
Fort Erie
Buffalo
St. Thomas
Detroit
Windsor
Chatham
26
21
10
6
4
9
11
2
24
86
23
8
3
7
169
62
28
400
401
QEW
190
490
90
390
69
94
0
50 miles
75 km

2

EXPLORING TORONTO

Visit Fodors.com for advice, updates, and bookings

Updated by Sarah Richards

"Toronto is like New York, as run by the Swiss," the actor Peter Ustinov is rumored to have said. Indeed, this is a big, beautiful, and efficient city, one that has emerged from relative obscurity over the past half-century to become the center of culture, commerce, and communications in Canada. With its colorful ethnic mix, rich history, and breathtaking architecture, Toronto is nonstop adventure, from the top of the CN Tower to as far as the eye can see.

More than half the 2.79 million residents who now live in Toronto were born and raised somewhere else, often very far away. Nearly 500,000 Italians give Greater Toronto one of the largest communities outside Italy; while South Asians, the biggest visible minority group inside Toronto, account for 12% of the population (nearly 300,000 people). It's also the home of the largest Chinese community in Canada and the largest Portuguese community in North America. The city hosts close to 200,000 Jewish people, nearly as many Muslims, and tens of thousands of Germans, joined by Greeks, Hungarians, East Indians, West Indians, Vietnamese, Maltese, South Americans, and Ukrainians—more than 80 ethnic groups in all, speaking more than 140 different languages and dialects. Toronto is also the home of Canada's largest gay and lesbian community.

Although the assimilation of these various cultures into the overall fabric of the city is ongoing, several ethnic neighborhoods have become attractions for locals and visitors. These include Kensington Market (west of Spadina Avenue between College and Dundas), Chinatown (around the Spadina Avenue and Dundas Street intersection), Greektown (Danforth Avenue between Chester and Jones), Little Italy (College Street between Euclid and Shaw), Little Poland (Roncesvalles Avenue between Queen and Dundas), Portugal Village (Dundas Street West, west of Bathurst), Little India (Gerrard Street between Coxwell and Greenwood), and Koreatown (Bloor Street West between Bathurst and Christie).

A BRIEF HISTORY OF TORONTO

The city officially became Toronto on March 6, 1834, but its roots are much older. In the early 1600s a Frenchman named Etienne Brûlé was sent into the not-yet-Canadian wilderness by the famous explorer Samuel de Champlain to see what he could discover. He found the river and portage routes from the St. Lawrence to Lake Huron, possibly Lakes Superior and Michigan, and eventually Lake Ontario. The native Huron peoples had known this area between the Humber and Don rivers for centuries—and had long called it "Toronto," believed to mean "meeting place."

A bustling village called Teiaiagon grew up here, which became the site of a French trading post. After the British won the Seven Years' War, the trading post was renamed York in 1793. More than 40 years later the city again took the name Toronto. Following an unsuccessful American invasion in 1812, several devastating fires, and a rebellion in 1837, there was a slow but steady increase in the population of white Anglo-Saxon Protestants leading into the 20th century. Since World War II, Toronto has attracted residents from all over the world. Unlike the American "melting pot," Toronto is more of a "tossed salad" of diverse ethnic groups.

What this immigration has meant to Toronto is the rather rapid creation of a vibrant mix of cultures that echoes turn-of-the-20th-century New York City—but without the slums, crowding, and tensions. Torontonians embrace and take pride in their multicultural character, their tradition of keeping a relatively clean and safe city, and their shared belief in the value of everyone getting along and enjoying the basic rights of good health care, education, and a high standard of living.

Toronto is also filled with boutiques, restaurants, and cafés, and there are plenty of shops, both aboveground and on the PATH, Toronto's underground city—an 29-km-long (18-mile-long) subterranean walkway lined with eateries, shops, banks, and medical offices.

And then there are the oft-overlooked gems of Toronto, such as the beach-fringed Toronto Islands. These eight tree-lined islands—and more than a dozen smaller islets—that sit in Lake Ontario just off the city's downtown have been attracting visitors since 1833, especially during summer, when their more than 550 acres of parkland are most irresistible. From any of the islands you have spectacular views of Toronto's skyline, especially as the setting sun turns the skyscrapers to gold, silver, and bronze.

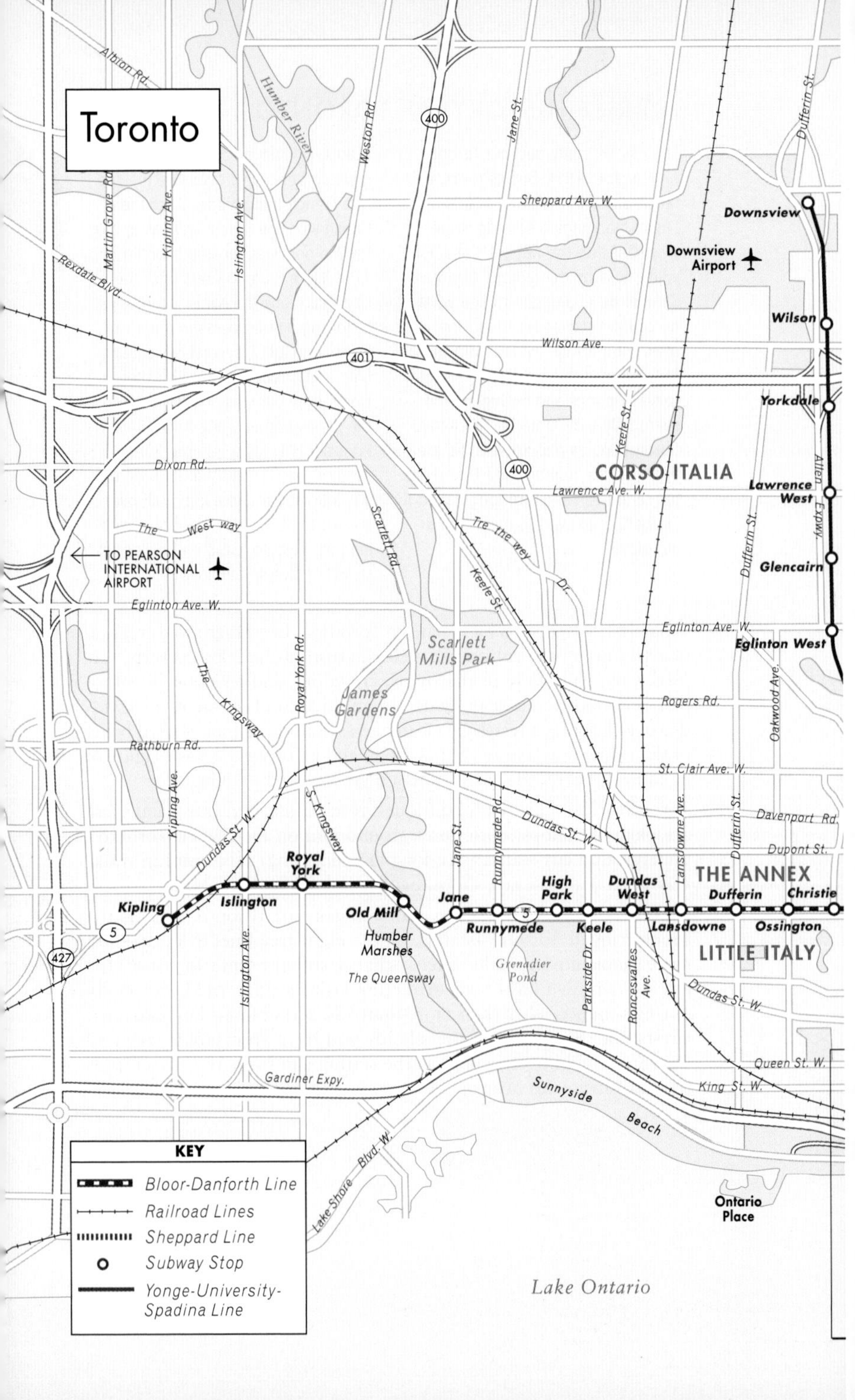

Toronto
KEY
Bloor-Danforth Line
Railroad Lines
Sheppard Line
Subway Stop
Yonge-University-Spadina Line
Downsview
Downsview Airport
Wilson
Yorkdale
Lawrence West
Glencairn
Eglinton West
CORSO ITALIA
THE ANNEX
LITTLE ITALY
Kipling
Islington
Royal York
Old Mill
Jane
Runnymede
High Park
Keele
Dundas West
Lansdowne
Dufferin
Ossington
Christie
TO PEARSON INTERNATIONAL AIRPORT
Scarlett Mills Park
James Gardens
Humber Marshes
Grenadier Pond
Sunnyside Beach
Ontario Place
Lake Ontario
Humber River
Albion Rd.
Martin Grove Rd.
Kipling Ave.
Islington Ave.
Rexdale Blvd.
Weston Rd.
Jane St.
Sheppard Ave. W.
Wilson Ave.
Dufferin St.
Keele St.
Allen Expwy.
Dixon Rd.
The West way
Lawrence Ave. W.
Scarlett Rd.
Tre the wey Dr.
Eglinton Ave. W.
Royal York Rd.
The Kingsway
Rathburn Rd.
Rogers Rd.
Oakwood Ave.
St. Clair Ave. W.
Davenport Rd.
Dupont St.
Dundas St. W.
S. Kingsway
Runnymede Rd.
Lansdowne Ave.
The Queensway
Parkside Dr.
Roncesvalles Ave.
Queen St. W.
King St. W.
Gardiner Expy.
Lake Shore Blvd. W.
400
401
427
5

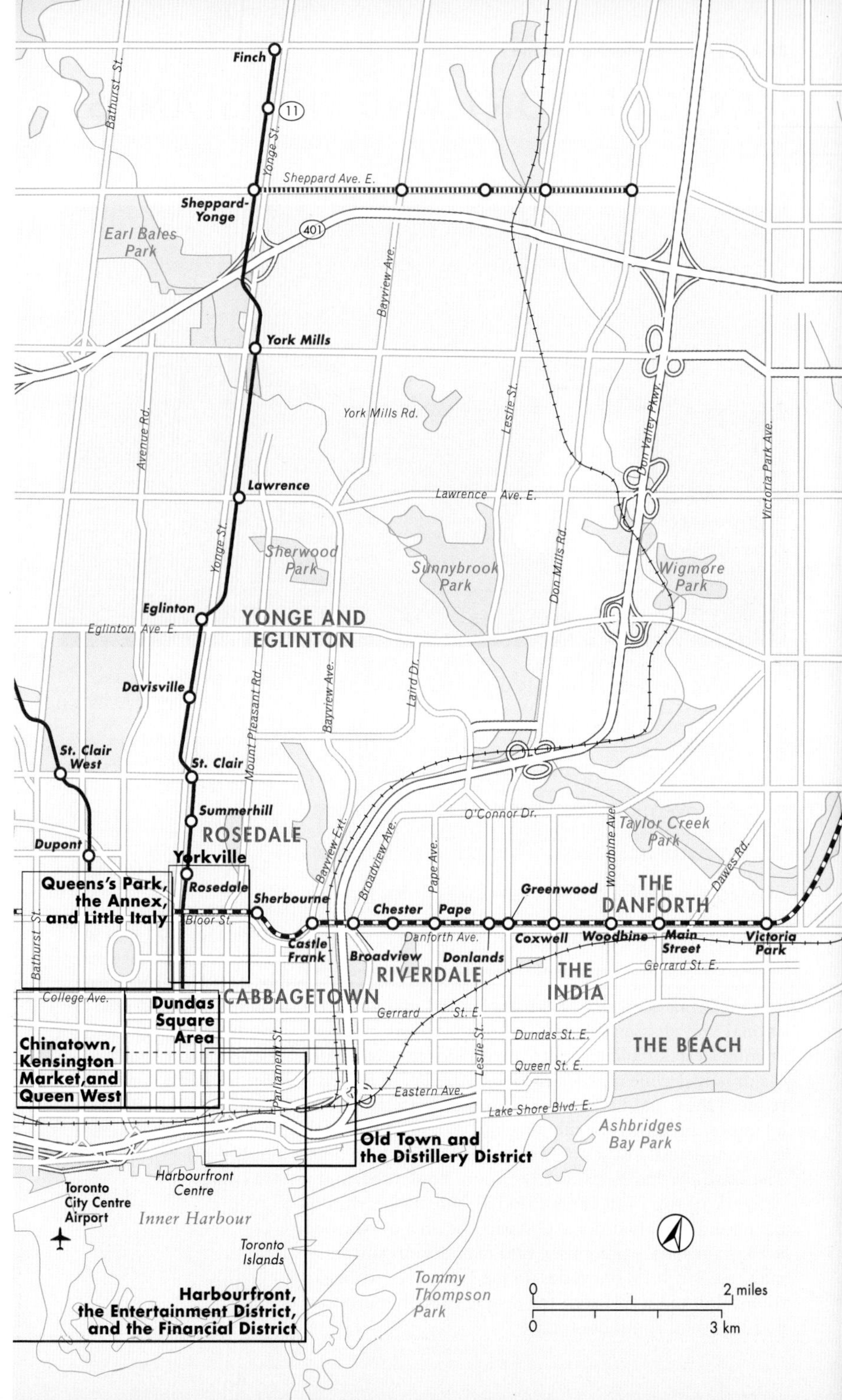

Finch
11
Bathurst St.
Yonge St.
Sheppard Ave. E.
Sheppard-Yonge
401
Earl Bales Park
Bayview Ave.
York Mills
Avenue Rd.
York Mills Rd.
Leslie St.
Don Valley Pkwy.
Victoria Park Ave.
Lawrence
Lawrence Ave. E.
Don Mills Rd.
Sherwood Park
Sunnybrook Park
Wigmore Park
Eglinton
Eglinton Ave. E.
YONGE AND EGLINTON
Davisville
Mount Pleasant Rd.
Bayview Ave.
Laird Dr.
St. Clair West
St. Clair
Summerhill
ROSEDALE
O'Connor Dr.
Woodbine Ave.
Taylor Creek Park
Dupont
Yorkville
Bayview Ext.
Broadview Ave.
Pape Ave.
Dawes Rd.
Queens's Park, the Annex, and Little Italy
Rosedale
Sherbourne
Greenwood
THE DANFORTH
Chester
Pape
Bloor St.
Danforth Ave.
Coxwell
Woodbine
Main Street
Victoria Park
Castle Frank
Broadview
Donlands
Gerrard St. E.
RIVERDALE
THE INDIA
College Ave.
Dundas Square Area
CABBAGETOWN
Gerrard
St. E.
Parliament St.
Leslie St.
Dundas St. E.
THE BEACH
Chinatown, Kensington Market, and Queen West
Queen St. E.
Eastern Ave.
Lake Shore Blvd. E.
Ashbridges Bay Park
Old Town and the Distillery District
Toronto City Centre Airport
Harbourfront Centre
Inner Harbour
Toronto Islands
Tommy Thompson Park
Harbourfront, the Entertainment District, and the Financial District
0
2 miles
0
3 km

HARBOURFRONT AND THE ISLANDS

The new century has brought renewed interest to Toronto's Harbourfront. Cranes dot the skyline as condominium buildings seemingly appear overnight. Pedestrian traffic increases as temperatures rise in spring and summer. Everyone wants to be overlooking, facing, or playing in Lake Ontario.

(above) Enjoying the skyline from one of Toronto's ferries
(top right) A performance of the Luminato Cirque du Soleil
(bottom right) One of the Toronto ferries

The lakefront is appealing for strolls, and myriad recreational and amusement options make it ideal for those craving fresh air and exercise or with kids in tow. Before the drastic decline of trucking due to the 1970s oil crisis reduced the Great Lakes trade, Toronto's waterfront was an important center for shipping and warehousing. It fell into commercial disuse and was neglected for a long time. The Gardiner Expressway, Lake Shore Boulevard, and a network of rusty rail yards stood as hideous barriers to the natural beauty of Lake Ontario; the area overflowed with grain silos, warehouses, and malodorous towers of malt, used by local breweries. In the 1980s the city began to develop the waterfront for people-friendly purposes, and the trend continues today.

BEST TIME TO GO

If it's sun and sand you're looking for, you'll want to aim for a visit in June, July, or August. The cool breeze coming off Lake Ontario can be the perfect antidote to one of Toronto's hot and humid summer days, but in the off-season it can make things a little chilly if you aren't packing an extra layer.

WAYS TO EXPLORE

BOAT

The best way to enjoy the waterfront is to get right onto Lake Ontario. There are many different boat tours—take your pick from the vendors lining the Harbourfront's lakeside boardwalk—but most offer the same deal: a pleasant, hour-long jaunt around the harbor for about C$20. More extravagant packages include dinner and dancing at sunset.

To soak up the sun and skyline views, use the public ferry to head for the **Toronto Islands**. The best beaches are those on the southeast tip of Ward's Island, Centre Island Beach, and the west side of Hanlan's Point. The most secluded and natural beach on the islands is Hanlan's Beach, backed by a small dunes area, a portion of which is clothing-optional. Most families with kids head for Centre Island Beach.

BIKE AND STROLL

To get away from busy downtown and stretch your legs, the Toronto Islands are the perfect destination. This car-free open space has paved trails for biking, in-line skating, or strolling; miles and miles of green space to explore; and picture-perfect vistas of the surrounding lake and skyline.

Bicyclists, power-walkers, and Sunday strollers alike enjoy the **Martin Goodman Trail**, the Toronto portion of the 219-mile Lake Ontario Waterfront Trail. The string of beaches along the **eastern waterfront** (east of Coxwell Avenue) is connected by a continuous boardwalk that parallels the Martin Goodman Trail. At the western end of this walking and biking trail is **Sunnyside Park Beach**, once the site of a large amusement park, and now a favorite place for a swim in the "tank" (a huge heated pool) or a snack at the small restaurant inside the handsomely restored 1922 Sunnyside Bathing Pavilion. Between the eastern and western beaches is the downtown stretch of the trail that hugs the waterfront and passes by a sewage treatment plant (no, it's not all pretty), marinas, a waterfowl conservation area, a sugar refinery, the Harbourfront, and the Toronto Islands ferry terminal.

FESTIVALS AND EVENTS

The **Canadian National Exhibition** (CNE, or "the Ex") takes place the last two weeks of August and Labor Day weekend, attracting more than 3 million people each year. It began in 1879 primarily as an agricultural show and today is a collection of carnival workers pushing C$5 balloons, midway rides, bands, horticultural and technological exhibits, parades, dog swims, horse shows, and (sometimes) top-notch performances. Stick around for nightly fireworks at 10.

Throughout the year, the **Harbourfront Centre** hosts a dizzying array of festivals, covering cultural celebrations such as Kuumba (February) and the Mexican Day of the Dead (November), foodie-friendly fêtes like the Hot & Spicy Festival (August) and Vegetarian Food Fair (September), and literary events such as the International Festival of Authors (October).

HARBOURFRONT, ENTERTAINMENT DISTRICT, AND THE FINANCIAL DISTRICT

Packed into this area, which runs from Bay Street east to Parliament Street and from Queen Street south to Lake Ontario, you'll find the city's main attractions and historical roots and the financial hub of the nation. As many of its attractions are outdoors, this downtown core is especially appealing during warm weather, but should a sudden downpour catch you off guard, shelter can be found in the area's museums and underground shopping city.

GETTING HERE

To get to the Harbourfront, take the 509 Queens Quay streetcar from Union Station. The Entertainment District is around St. Andrew and Osgoode subway stations. The Financial District is at Queen, King, and Union stations.

TIMING

If you have kids in tow, plan on spending a whole day in the Harbourfront area. If you're going to the Toronto Islands, add 45 minutes total traveling time just to cross the bay and return on the same ferry. Depending on what you're planning at the Bell Lightbox, you could spend an hour browsing an exhibit or several hours taking in a few movies. Museum buffs will want to linger for at least an hour each in the Hockey Hall of Fame and the Design Exchange.

HARBOURFRONT

In fair weather, the Harbourfront area is appealing for strolls, and myriad recreational and amusement options make it ideal for those traveling with children. The nearby Toronto Islands provide a perfect escape from the sometimes-stifling summer heat of downtown.

2

TORONTO DAY TOURS

Tourism Toronto. Tourism Toronto can provide further tour information. ☎ *416/203–2500, 800/499–2514* 🌐 *www.seetorontonow.com.*

BOAT TOURS

If you want to get a glimpse of the skyline, try a boat tour. There are many boat-tour companies operating all along the boardwalk of Harbourfront.

Great Lakes Schooner Company. To further your appreciation for man-made beauty, the company lets you see Toronto's skyline from the open deck of the 165-foot three-mastered *Kajima.* Two-hour tours are available early June to the end of September and cost C$22. ☎ *416/203–2322* 🌐 *www.tallshipcruisestoronto.com.*

BUS TOURS

For a look at the city proper, take a bus tour around the city. If you want the freedom to get on and off the bus when the whim strikes, take a hop-on, hop-off tour.

Toronto City Tours. Two-hour guided tours are offered in 24-passenger buses for C$40. ☎ *416/868–0400* 🌐 *www.torontobusco.com.*

Gray Line Sightseeing Bus Tours. Gray Line has London-style double-decker buses and turn-of-the-20th-century trolleys. They also have tours of Niagara Falls. ✉ *610 Bay St., north of Dundas St., Dundas Square Area* ☎ *800/594–3310* 🌐 *www.grayline.ca.*

SPECIAL-INTEREST TOURS

Toronto Field Naturalists. About 150 guided tours are scheduled thoughout the year, each focusing on an aspect of nature, such as geology or wildflowers, and with starting points accessible by public transit. ☎ *416/593–2656* 🌐 *www.torontofieldnaturalists.org.*

Toronto Bruce Trail Club. This hiking club arranges day and overnight hikes around Toronto and its environs. ☎ *416/763–9061* 🌐 *www.torontobrucetrailclub.org.*

WALKING TOURS

Heritage Toronto. To get a feel for Toronto's outstanding cultural diversity, check out one of the 56 walking tours offered from April to early October. They last 1½ to 2 hours and cover one neighborhood or topic, such as the history of a wealthy, influential family. ☎ *416/338–3886* 🌐 *www.heritagetoronto.org.*

Royal Ontario Museum. The museum runs 1½- to 2-hour ROMwalk tours on such topics as Cabbagetown, a now-trendy, heritage neighborhood with many houses dating to the 1850s. Several free walks are given weekly. ☎ *416/586–8097* 🌐 *www.rom.on.ca/programs.*

A Taste of the World. Food-, literary-, and ghost-theme tours of various lengths are offered in several neighborhoods. Reservations are essential; prices range from C$25–50. ☎ *416/923–6813* 🌐 *www.torontowalksbikes.com.*

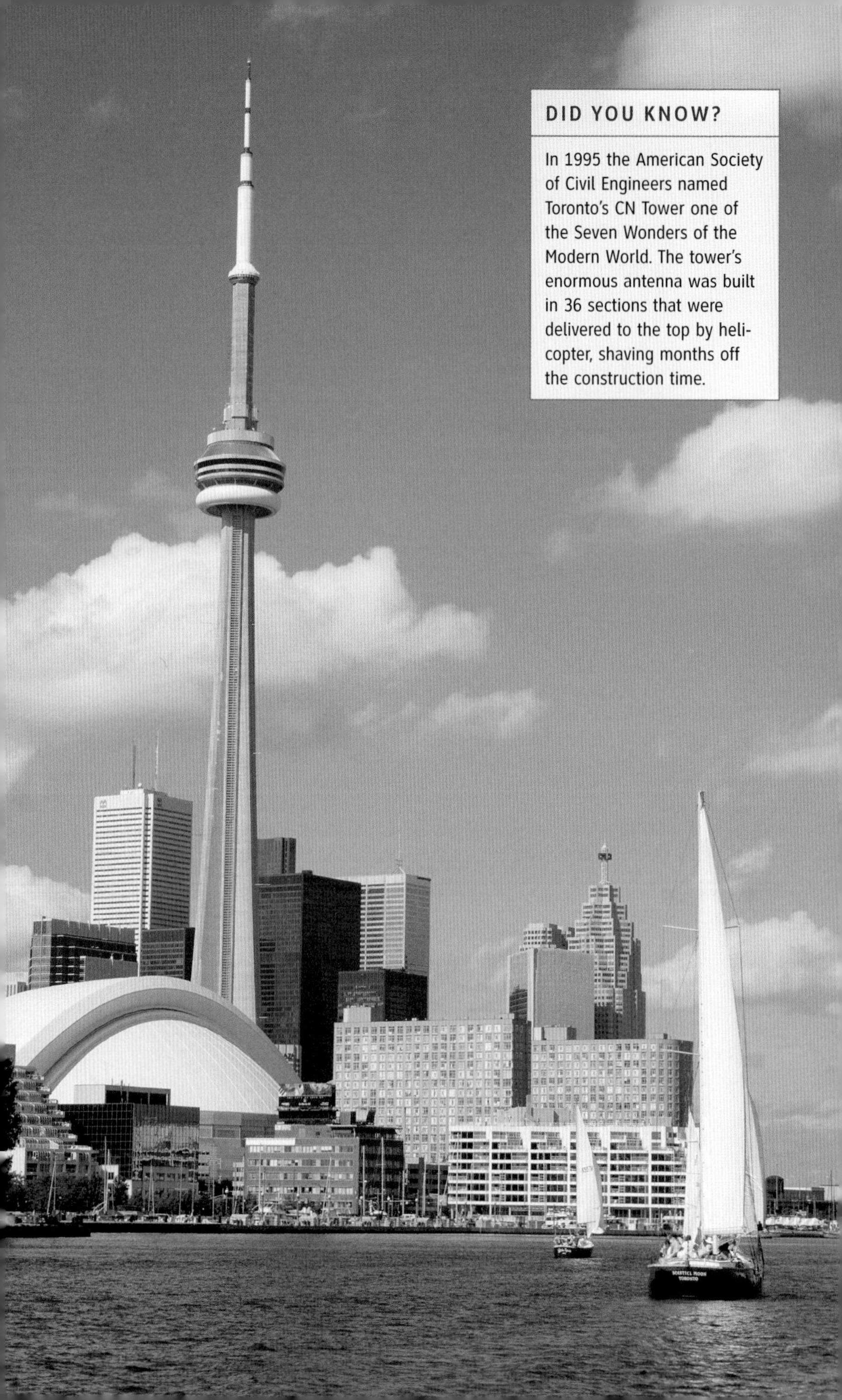

DID YOU KNOW?

In 1995 the American Society of Civil Engineers named Toronto's CN Tower one of the Seven Wonders of the Modern World. The tower's enormous antenna was built in 36 sections that were delivered to the top by helicopter, shaving months off the construction time.

TOP ATTRACTIONS

FAMILY Fodor's Choice ★ **CN Tower.** The tallest freestanding tower in the Western Hemisphere, this landmark stretches 1,815 feet and 5 inches high and marks Toronto with its distinctive silhouette. The CN Tower is tall for a reason: prior to the opening of this telecommunications tower in 1976, so many tall buildings had been built over the previous decades that lower radio and TV transmission towers had trouble broadcasting. The C$63 million building weighs 130,000 tons and contains enough concrete to build a curb along Highway 401 from Toronto to Kingston, some 262 km (162 miles) to the east. It's worth a visit if the weather is clear, despite the steep fee. Six glass-front elevators zoom up the outside of the tower at 20 feet per second, and the ride takes less than a minute—a rate of ascent similar to that of a jet taking off. Each elevator has one floor-to-ceiling glass wall—three opaque walls make the trip easier on anyone prone to vertigo—and all have glass floor panels for the dizzying thrill of watching the earth disappear before your eyes.

There are four observation decks. The **Glass Floor Level,** which is exactly what it sounds like, is about 1,122 feet above the ground. This may be the most photographed indoor location in the city—lie on the transparent floor and have your picture taken from above like countless visitors before you. Don't worry—the glass floor can support 85,000 pounds. Above is the **Look Out Level,** at 1,136 feet; one floor more, at 1,150 feet, is the excellent **360 Revolving Restaurant.** If you're here to dine, your elevator fee is waived. At an elevation of 1,465 feet, the **Sky Pod** is the world's highest public observation gallery. All the levels provide spectacular panoramic views of Toronto, Lake Ontario, and the Toronto Islands. On really clear days you may see Lake Simcoe to the north and the mist rising from Niagara Falls to the south. Adrenaline junkies can try the **EdgeWalk** attraction, which allows harnessed tower-goers to roam "hands free" around a 5-foot ledge outside the tower's main pod. Reservations are required.

On the ground level, the **Marketplace at the Tower** has 12,500 square feet of shopping space with quality Canadian travel items and souvenirs, along with a shop selling Inuit art. There's also the **Fresh Market Cafe,** with seating for 300; the **Maple Leaf Cinema,** which screens the 20-minute documentary *The Height of Excellence,* about the building of the Tower; and the **Themed Arcade,** with the latest in virtual-game experiences and the Himalamazon motion picture ride based loosely on the Himalayan and Amazon regions. **TIP→ Peak visiting hours are 11 to 4; you may wish to work around them, particularly on weekends.** Ticket packages get more expensive with more attractions included. ✉ *301 Front St. W, at Bremner Blvd., Harbourfront* ☎ *416/868–6937, 416/362–5411 restaurant, 416/601–3833 EdgeWalk* 🌐 *www.cntower.ca* 🎟 *First two observation levels and Sky Pod C$32; observation levels, Sky Pod, and Edgewalk C$175* ⏲ *Daily 9 am–11 pm* Ⓜ *Union.*

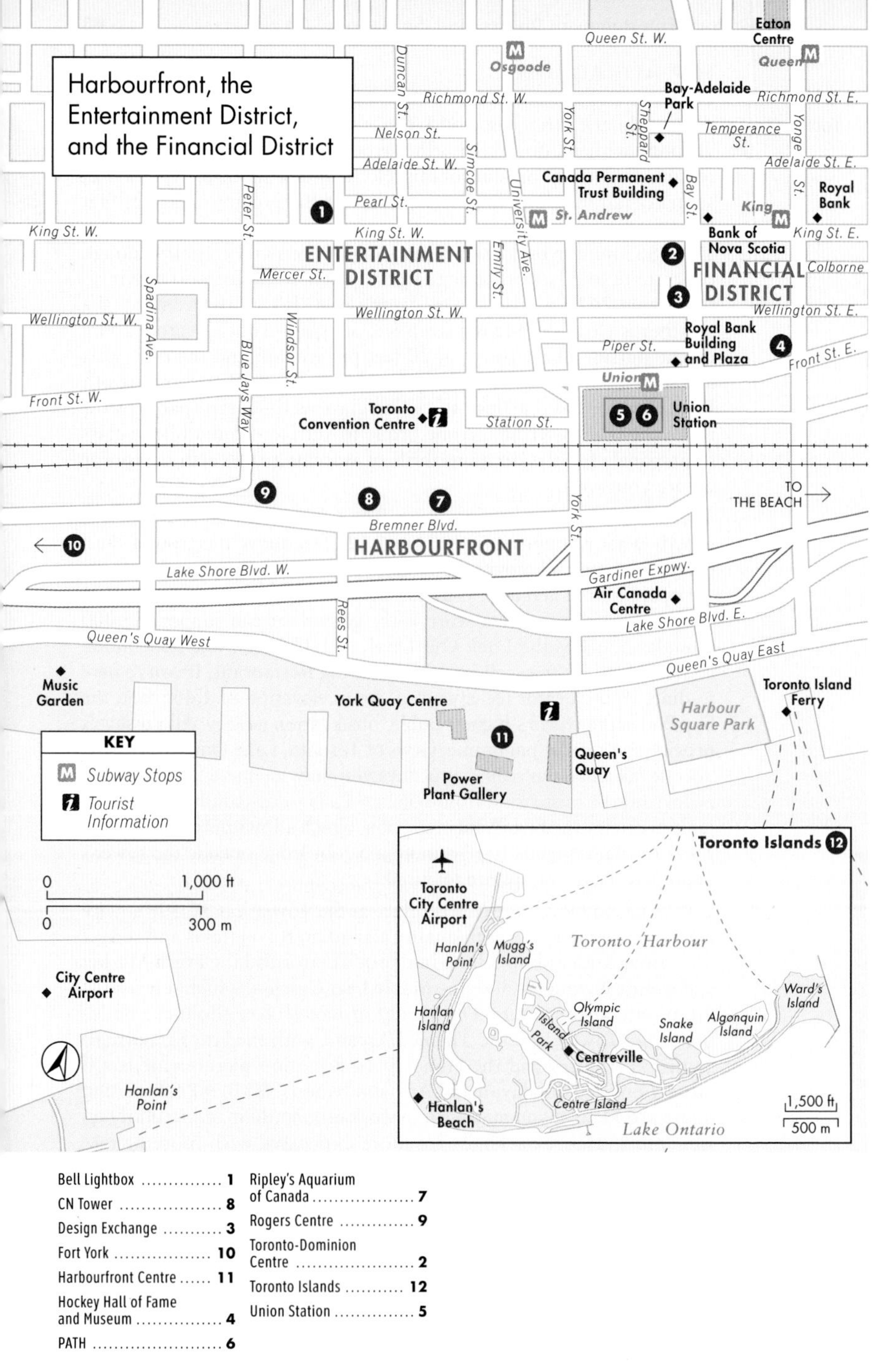

Bell Lightbox	1
CN Tower	8
Design Exchange	3
Fort York	10
Harbourfront Centre	11
Hockey Hall of Fame and Museum	4
PATH	6
Ripley's Aquarium of Canada	7
Rogers Centre	9
Toronto-Dominion Centre	2
Toronto Islands	12
Union Station	5

FAMILY **Toronto Islands.** These eight narrow, tree-lined islands, plus more than a dozen smaller islets, just off the city's downtown in Lake Ontario, provide a gorgeous green retreat with endless outdoor activities. The more than 550 acres of parkland are hard to resist, especially in the summer, when they're usually a few degrees cooler than the city.

WORD OF MOUTH

"I love the Toronto Islands. Great way to escape the sometimes soulless skyscrapers of downtown Toronto and get into an oasis of greenery; the views of Lake Ontario from the islands are just gorgeous."

—Daniel.Williams

Sandy beaches fringe the islands; the best are on the southeast tip of Ward's Island, the southernmost edge of Centre Island, and the west side of Hanlan's Island. In 1999 a portion of Hanlan's Beach was officially declared "clothing-optional" by Toronto's City Council. The declaration regarding Ontario's only legal nude beach passed without protest—perhaps a testament to the city's live-and-let-live attitude. The section frequented by gays and lesbians is at the east end; the straight section is more westerly. There are free changing rooms near each side. Lake Ontario's water is declared unfit for swimming a few days every summer, so call ☎ *416/392–7161* or check 🌐 *www.toronto.ca/beach* for water-quality reports. In the summer, Centre Island has bike and rowboat rentals and Centreville Amusement Park. Bring picnic fixings or something to grill in one of the park's barbecue pits, or grab a quick (and expensive) bite at one of the snack bars. Note that the consumption of alcohol in a public park is illegal in Toronto. There are supervised wading pools, baseball diamonds, volleyball nets, tennis courts, and even a disc-golf course. The winter can be bitterly cold on the islands, but snowshoeing and cross-country skiing with downtown Toronto over your shoulder are appealing activities.

All transportation is self-powered: no private cars are permitted. The boardwalk from Centre Island to Ward's Island is 2½ km (1½ miles) long. Centre Island gets so crowded that no bicycles are allowed on its ferry from the mainland during summer weekends. Consider renting a bike for an hour or so once you get there and working your way across the islands. Bike rentals can be found south of the Centre Island ferry docks on the Avenue of the Islands.

You may want to take one of the equally frequent ferries to Ward's or Hanlan's Island. Both islands have tennis courts and picnic and sunbathing spots. Late May through early September, the ferries run between the docks at the bottom of Bay Street and the Ward's Island dock between 6:35 am and 11:45 am; for Centre and Hanlan's islands, they begin at 8 am. Ward's Island Ferries run roughly at half-hour intervals most of the working day and at quarter-hour intervals during peak times such as summer evenings. On Canada Day (July 1) the lines are slow moving. In winter the ferries run only to Ward's Island on a limited schedule. ✉ *Ferries at foot of Bay St. and Queen's Quay, Harbourfront* ☎ *416/392–8186 for island information, 416/392–8193 for ferry information* 🌐 *www.toronto.ca/parks/island* 🎫 *Ferry C$7 round-trip* Ⓜ *Union, then streetcar 509 or 510.*

WORTH NOTING

Fort York. The most historic site in Toronto is a must for anyone interested in the city's origins. Toronto was founded in 1793 when the British built Fort York to protect the entrance to the harbor during Anglo-American strife. Twenty years later the fort was the scene of the bloody Battle of York, in which explorer and general Zebulon Pike led U.S. forces against the fort's outnumbered British, Canadian, and First Nations defenders. The Americans won this battle—their first major victory in the War of 1812—and burned down the provincial buildings during a six-day occupation. A year later British forces retaliated when they captured Washington, D.C., and torched its public buildings, including the Executive Mansion. Exhibits include restored barracks, kitchens, and gunpowder magazines, plus changing museum displays. There are guided tours, marching drills, and cannon firings daily during the summer months. ✉ *250 Fort York Blvd., between Bathurst St. and Strachan Ave., Harbourfront* ☎ *416/392–6907* 🌐 *www.fortyork.ca* 🎫 *C$9* 🕐 *Mid-May–Aug., daily 10–5; Sept.–mid-May, weekdays 10–4, weekends 10–5* Ⓜ *Bathurst, then streetcar 511 south.*

FAMILY **Harbourfront Centre.** Stretching from just west of York Street to Spadina Avenue, this culture-and-recreation center is a match for San Francisco's Pier 39 and Baltimore's Inner Harbor. The original Harbourfront opened in 1974, rejuvenating more than a mile of city. Today Harbourfront Centre, a streamlined version of the original concept, draws more than 3 million visitors to the 10-acre site each year. **Queen's Quay Terminal** (✉ *207 Queen's Quay W* ☎ *416/203–0510* 🌐 *www.qqterminal.com*) at Harbourfront Centre is a former Terminal Warehouse building, where goods shipped to Toronto were stored before being delivered to shops in the city. In 1983 it was transformed into a magnificent, eight-story building with specialty shops, eateries, the 450-seat Fleck Dance Theatre—and harbor views. Exhibits of contemporary painting, sculpture, architecture, video, photography, and design are mounted at the **Power Plant** (✉ *231 Queen's Quay W* ☎ *416/973–4949* 🌐 *www.thepowerplant.org* 🕐 *Sun, Tues., and Wed. 10–6, Thurs.–Sat. 10–8; tours Sun. at 2*). It can be spotted by its tall red smokestack. It was built in 1927 as a power station for the Terminal Warehouse's ice-making plant. Developed by renowned cellist Yo-Yo Ma and garden designer Julie Moir Messervy, the **Music Garden** on the south side of Queen's Quay was planned for Boston, but when that venue fell through, Toronto was the pair's next choice. The garden is Yo-Yo Ma's interpretation of Johann Sebastian Bach's Cello Suite No. 1 (which consists of six movements—Prelude, Allemande, Courante, Sarabande, Minuet, and Gigue). Each movement is reflected in the park's elaborate design: undulating riverscape, a forest grove of wandering trails, a swirling path through a wildflower meadow, a conifer grove, a formal flower parterre, and giant grass steps. **York Quay Centre** (✉ *235 Queen's Quay W* ☎ *416/973–4000; 416/973–4866 rink info; 416/973–4963 craft studio*) hosts concerts, theater, readings, and even skilled artisans. The Craft Studio, for example, has professional craftspeople working in ceramics, glass, metal, and textiles from February to December (Tuesday through Sunday), in full view of the public. A shallow pond outside is used for canoe lessons in warmer months and as the largest artificial ice-skating rink in North America in more wintry times. At the nearby Nautical Centre, many private firms rent boats and give lessons in sailing and canoeing. Among the seasonal events in Harbourfront Centre are the Ice Canoe Race in late January, Winterfest in February, a jazz festival in June, Canada Day celebrations and the Parade of Lights in July, the Authors' Festival and Harvest Festival in October, and the Swedish Christmas Fair in November. ✉ *410 Queen's Quay W, Harbourfront* ☎ *416/973–4000 event hotline, 416/973–4600 offices* 🌐 *www.harbourfrontcentre.com* Ⓜ *Union, then streetcar 509 or 510 west.*

2

Ripley's Aquarium of Canada. North America's largest aquarium is sleek, angular, watery blue, and shaped like a shark. It contains more than 450 species of marine life spread out between 45 exhibit spaces. Maintaining their philosophy to "foster environmental education, conservation, and research," Ripley's also lives up to its reputation for providing a wow-inducing entertainment venue. One exhibit simulates a Caribbean scuba diving experience complete with bountiful tropical fish, coral reefs, and a bright blue sky above. Although the focus is on Canadian marine wildlife, sharks are a dominant theme: you can wind your way through tunnels that take you right into the almost 80,000-gallon shark tank, which houses at least six varieties of sharks. The shark pattern on the roof is an unexpected treat for visitors peering down on the aquarium from the top of the CN Tower. ✉ *288 Bremner Blvd., Harbourfront* ☎ *647/351–3474* 🌐 *www.ripleyaquariums.com/canada* 🎟 *C$30.*

QUICK BITES

There are plenty of places inside Queen's Quay for a quick sandwich, freshly squeezed juice, or ice-cream concoction. You can also check out one of the food trucks outside selling french fries.

FAMILY **Rogers Centre.** One of Toronto's most famous landmarks, the Rogers Centre is home to baseball's Blue Jays and was the world's first stadium with a fully retractable roof. Rogers Communications, the owner of the Blue Jays, bought the stadium, formerly known as the SkyDome, in February 2005 for a mere C$25 million. A new playing surface and a state-of-the-art integrated scoring and display system were added, including two color screens that display the action on either side of the outfield wall. One way to see the 52,000-seat stadium is to buy tickets for a Blue Jays or Argos game or one of the many other events that take place here. You might watch a cricket match, Wrestlemania, a monster-truck race, a family ice show, or a rock concert—even the large-scale opera *Aïda* has been performed here. You can also take a one-hour guided walking tour. Depending on several factors, you may find yourself in the middle of the field, in a press box, in the dressing rooms, or, if a roof tour is available, 36 stories above home plate on a catwalk. ✉ *1 Blue Jays Way, tour entrance at Front and John Sts., between Gates 1 and 2, Harbourfront* ☎ *416/341–2770 for tours, 416/341–3663 for events and shows, 416/341–1234 for ticket information, 888/654–6529 for Blue Jays information* 🌐 *www.rogerscentre.com* 🎟 *Tour C$16* ⏲ *Tours 11–4 hourly (canceled during special events)* Ⓜ *Union.*

The Bell Lightbox is the focal point for the annual Toronto International Film Festival.

ENTERTAINMENT DISTRICT

The neighborhood originally got its name from the strip of nightclubs along Richmond Street West, but these days the neighborhood is so much more than that. The vibe is boisterous with pre-theater crowds and movie buffs hitting the TIFF Bell Lightbox; a string of new hotels and restaurants have opened to field the crowds.

TOP ATTRACTIONS

Escape to Shangri-La. In the Shangri-La's Lobby Lounge, where guests check in, a band performs, a fireplace soothes, and silk-clad waitresses seemingly float from sunken couch to sunken couch bringing light meals and cocktails to a mix of locals and hotel guests. You can take in the scene over Afternoon Tea, offered seven days a week. This experience starts at $45 per person for a three-tier spread that includes a pot of one of the expertly blended teas—there are two tea sommeliers on staff to explain the 72 varieties of tea. Expect delicate pastries, buttery scones with homemade jam, and clever twists on finger sandwiches, such as Brie, apple, and ham on marble rye on the menu. ✉ *Shangri-La Hotel, 188 University Ave., Entertainment District* ☎ *647/788–8888.*

TIFF Bell Lightbox. A five-story architectural masterpiece in the city's center, this glass-paneled building houses the year-round headquarters of the internationally acclaimed, wildly popular Toronto International Film Festival. Throughout the year—except in September when TIFF fever paralyzes the city—visitors can attend film-related lectures, watch screenings, and enjoy smaller film festivals, including TIFF.kids, a celebration of children's film that takes place each April. A stellar educational program includes summer camps, ongoing workshops—how to produce a stop-motion movie, for example—and gallery exhibitions that highlight big-shot filmmakers such as Tim Burton and Federico Fellini; faculty and university students get free admission to special "higher learning" TIFF offerings (a limited number of tickets become available one hour before each event; check online for the full calendar). The TIFF Cinematheque, open to the public, plays world cinema classics and contemporary art house films all year. Hit the concession stand for gourmet treats far beyond the standard popcorn fare, or head to one of the two restaurants in the complex for the traditional dinner-and-a-movie pairing. ✉ *Reitman Square, 350 King St. W, at John St., Entertainment District* ☎ *416/599–8433, 888/599–8433* 🌐 *tiff.net* ⏲ *Box office 8 am–midnight.*

FINANCIAL DISTRICT

Toronto's Financial District pleases many tourists with its unique and wonderful architectural variety of skyscrapers. Most of the towers have bank branches, restaurants, and retail outlets on their ground floors and are connected to the PATH, an underground city of shops and tunnels.

TOP ATTRACTIONS

Design Exchange. A delightful example of streamlined Moderne design (a later and more austere version of art deco), this building is clad in polished pink granite and smooth buff limestone, with stainless-steel doors. Between 1937 and 1983 the DX (as it's now known) was home to the Toronto Stock Exchange. Don't miss the witty stone frieze carved above the doors—a banker in top hat marching behind a laborer and sneaking his hand into the worker's pocket. Only in Canada, where socialism has always been a strong force, would you find such a political statement on the side of a stock exchange. In the early 1990s the building reopened as a nonprofit center devoted to promoting Canadian design. The permanent collection consists of more than 600 pieces that span six decades from 1945 to the present; it includes furniture, graphic design, housewares, lighting, and tableware. Check the website for information about rotating exhibits which make good use of the old trading floor. And stop into the Design Exchange shop to browse witty gifts like stackable "totem pole" mugs or kerchiefs with stenciled mustaches. ✉ *234 Bay St., at King St., Financial District* ☎ *416/363–6121* 🌐 *www.dx.org* 🎫 *C$22* ⏲ *Sun.–Wed. 10–6, Thurs.–Sat. 10–9* Ⓜ *King, St. Andrew.*

FAMILY **Hockey Hall of Fame and Museum.** Even if you're not a hockey fan, it's worth a trip here to see this shrine to Canada's favorite sport. Exhibits include the original 1893 Stanley Cup, as well as displays of goalie masks, skate and stick collections, great players' jerseys, video displays of big games, and a replica of the Montréal Canadiens' locker room. Grab a stick and test your speed and accuracy in the "shoot out" virtual experience, or strap on a goalie mask and field shots from big-name players like Wayne Gretzky and Mark Messier with the "shut out" computer simulation. It's also telling that this museum is housed in such a grand building, worthy of any fine art collection. A former Bank of Montréal branch designed by architects Darling & Curry

DID YOU KNOW?

The Caribbean Carnival Toronto festival was created in 1967 as a community heritage project to celebrate Canada's centennial and was such a success that it's been held every year since. This two-and-a-half-week summer celebration highlights the food, costumes, music, and art of Caribbean cultures, and attracts more than a million visitors each year.

in 1885, the building is covered with beautiful ornamental details. Note the richly carved Ohio stone and the Hermès figure supporting the chimney near the back. At the corner of Front and Yonge streets, the impressive statue—a seventeen-foot bronze entitled *Our Game*—is a busy photo op. **TIP→ Entrance is through Brookfield Place on the lower level of the east side.** ✉ *Brookfield Place, 30 Yonge St., at Front St., Financial District* ☎ *416/360–7765* 🌐 *www.hhof.com* 🎫 *C$17.50* ⏲ *Sept.–June, weekdays 10–5, Sat. 9:30–6, Sun. 10:30–5; July and Aug., Mon.–Sat. 9:30–6, Sun. 10–6* Ⓜ *Union.*

DOWN TOWN

According to the *Guinness Book of World Records,* the PATH is the biggest underground shopping complex in the world. Maps to guide you through this labyrinth are available in many downtown news and convenience stores.

2

Toronto-Dominion Centre. Ludwig Mies van der Rohe, a virtuoso of modern architecture, designed this five-building masterwork, though he died before its completion in 1985. As with his acclaimed Seagram Building in New York, Mies stripped the TD Centre's buildings to their skin and bones of bronze-color glass and black-metal I-beams. The tallest building, the Toronto Dominion Bank Tower, is 56 stories high. The only decoration consists of geometric repetition, and the only extravagance is the use of rich materials, such as marble counters and leather-covered furniture. In summer, the plazas and grass are full of office workers eating lunch and listening to one of many free outdoor concerts. Inside the low-rise, square banking pavilion at King and Bay streets is a virtually intact Mies interior.

Inside the TD Centre's Waterhouse Tower is the **Museum of Inuit Art** (✉ *79 Wellington St. W* ☎ *416/982–8473* 🎫 *Free* ⏲ *Weekdays 8–6, weekends 10–4* Ⓜ *St. Andrew*). It's one of just a few such galleries in North America. The collection, equal to that of the Smithsonian, focuses on the bank's renowned collection of Inuit art from the vast Arctic region in northern Canada. ✉ *55 King St. W, at Bay St., Financial District* Ⓜ *St. Andrew.*

WORTH NOTING

QUICK BITES

Brookfield Place. A modern office and retail complex cleverly designed to incorporate the facades of the Bank of Montréal and other older buildings under a vaulted glass roof, Brookfield Place is one of the most impressive architectural spaces in Toronto. The atrium under the glass canopy makes a lovely place to sit and enjoy a cup of coffee and pastry from Richtree Market, or a snack at the mozzarella bar, Obikà. ✉ ***181 Bay St., between Front St. W and Wellington St. W, Financial District*** Ⓜ ***Union.***

PATH. This subterranean universe emerged in the mid-1960s partly to replace the retail services in small buildings that were demolished to make way for the latest skyscrapers and partly to protect office workers from the harsh winter weather. As each major building went up, its developers agreed to build and connect their underground shopping areas with others and with the subway system. You can walk

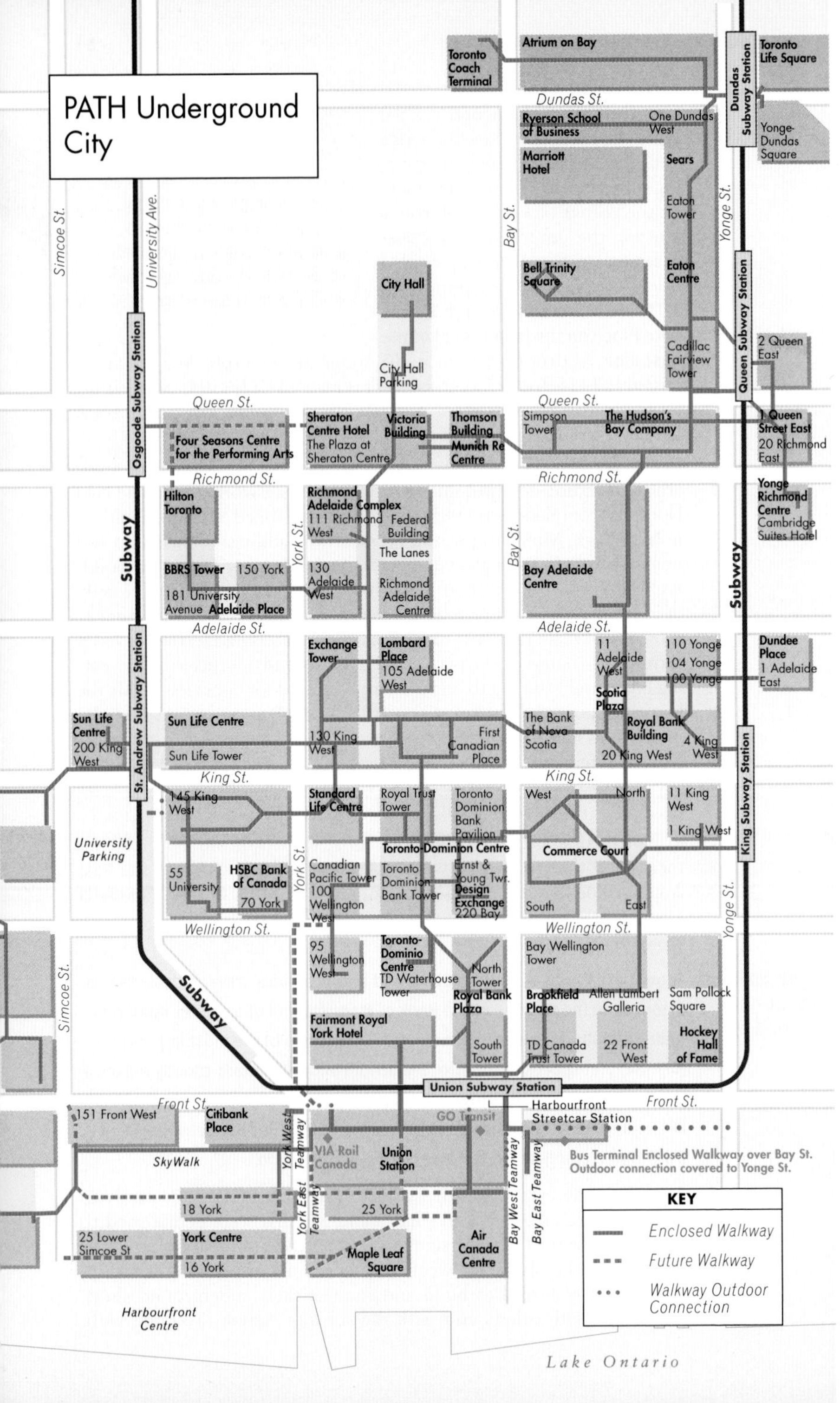

PATH Underground City
Toronto Coach Terminal
Atrium on Bay
Toronto Life Square
Dundas Subway Station
Dundas St.
Ryerson School of Business
One Dundas West
Yonge-Dundas Square
Marriott Hotel
Sears
Eaton Tower
Yonge St.
Bay St.
University Ave.
Simcoe St.
City Hall
Bell Trinity Square
Eaton Centre
Queen Subway Station
Osgoode Subway Station
Cadillac Fairview Tower
2 Queen East
City Hall Parking
Queen St.
Four Seasons Centre for the Performing Arts
Sheraton Centre Hotel
The Plaza at Sheraton Centre
Victoria Building
Thomson Building
Munich Re Centre
Simpson Tower
The Hudson's Bay Company
1 Queen Street East
20 Richmond East
Richmond St.
Hilton Toronto
Richmond Adelaide Complex
111 Richmond West
Federal Building
Yonge Richmond Centre
Cambridge Suites Hotel
Subway
York St.
The Lanes
BBRS Tower
150 York
130 Adelaide West
Richmond Adelaide Centre
Bay Adelaide Centre
181 University Avenue
Adelaide Place
Adelaide St.
St. Andrew Subway Station
Exchange Tower
Lombard Place
105 Adelaide West
11 Adelaide West
110 Yonge
104 Yonge
100 Yonge
Dundee Place
1 Adelaide East
Scotia Plaza
Sun Life Centre
200 King West
Sun Life Centre
Sun Life Tower
130 King West
First Canadian Place
The Bank of Nova Scotia
Royal Bank Building
20 King West
4 King West
King Subway Station
King St.
145 King West
Standard Life Centre
Royal Trust Tower
Toronto Dominion Bank Pavilion
West
North
11 King West
1 King West
University Parking
Toronto-Dominion Centre
Commerce Court
55 University
HSBC Bank of Canada
70 York
Canadian Pacific Tower
100 Wellington West
Toronto Dominion Bank Tower
Ernst & Young Twr.
Design Exchange
220 Bay
South
East
Wellington St.
95 Wellington West
Toronto-Dominio Centre
TD Waterhouse Tower
North Tower
Royal Bank Plaza
Bay Wellington Tower
Brookfield Place
Allen Lambert Galleria
Sam Pollock Square
Fairmont Royal York Hotel
South Tower
TD Canada Trust Tower
22 Front West
Hockey Hall of Fame
Union Subway Station
Front St.
151 Front West
Citibank Place
York West Teamway
GO Transit
Harbourfront Streetcar Station
VIA Rail Canada
Union Station
Bay West Teamway
Bay East Teamway
Bus Terminal Enclosed Walkway over Bay St.
Outdoor connection covered to Yonge St.
SkyWalk
18 York
York East Teamway
25 York
KEY
Enclosed Walkway
Future Walkway
Walkway Outdoor Connection
25 Lower Simcoe St
York Centre
16 York
Maple Leaf Square
Air Canada Centre
Harbourfront Centre
Lake Ontario

from beneath Union Station to the Fairmont Royal York hotel, the Toronto-Dominion Centre, First Canadian Place, the Sheraton Centre, the Bay, Eaton Centre, and City Hall without ever seeing the light of day, encountering everything from art exhibitions to buskers (the best are the winners of citywide auditions, who are licensed to perform throughout the subway system) and walkways, fountains, and trees. There are underground passageways in other parts of the city—one beneath Bloor Street and another under College Street (both run from Yonge to Bay Street)—but this is the city's most extended subterranean network. ✉ *Financial District.*

Union Station. Historian Pierre Berton wrote that the planning of Union Station recalled "the love lavished on medieval churches." Indeed, this train depot can be regarded as a cathedral built to serve the god of steam. Designed in 1907 and opened by the Prince of Wales in 1927, it has a 40-foot-high Italian-tile ceiling and 22 pillars weighing 70 tons apiece. The main hall, with its lengthy concourse and light flooding in from arched windows at each end, was designed to evoke the majesty of the country that spread out by rail from this spot. The names of the towns and cities across Canada that were served by the country's two railway lines, Grand Trunk (incorporated into today's Canadian National) and Canadian Pacific, are inscribed on a frieze along the inside of the hall. As train travel declined, the building came very near to being demolished in the 1970s, but public opposition eventually proved strong enough to save it, and Union Station is now a vital transport hub. Commuter, subway, and long-distance trains stop here. ✉ *65–75 Front St. W, between Bay and York Sts., Financial District* Ⓜ *Union.*

OLD TOWN AND THE DISTILLERY DISTRICT

Old Town is a mishmash of restored historic attractions and trendy new developments. Farther east, the historic Distillery District is one of Toronto's hottest entertainment destinations. It's filled with restored Victorian-era factories that house contemporary galleries, bustling pubs, and chic restaurants.

OLD TOWN

Old Town is where the city got its municipal start as the village of York in 1793. It now has a pleasing natural disorder with leafy streets that crisscross at odd angles, and a blend of old and new buildings that are home to residential and commercial space alike.

TOP ATTRACTIONS

Fodor's Choice ★ **St. Lawrence Market.** Both a lovely landmark and an excellent place to sample Canadian bacon, this market was originally built in 1844 as the first true Toronto city hall. The building now has an exhibition hall upstairs—the Market Gallery—where the council chambers once stood. The food market, which began growing up around the building's square in the early 1900s, is considered one of the world's best. Local and imported foods such as fresh shellfish, sausage varieties, and cheeses are renowned. Stop and snack on Canadian bacon, also known as "peameal bacon," at the Market's Carousel Bakery. The plain brick building across Front Street, on the north side, is open on Saturday mornings for the 200-year-old farmers' market; it's a cornucopia of fine produce and homemade jams, relishes, and sauces from farms just north of Toronto. On Sunday the wares of more than 80 antiques dealers are on display in the same building. ✉ *Front and Jarvis Sts., Old Town* ☎ *416/392-7219* 🌐 *www.stlawrencemarket.com* ⏲ *Tues.–Thurs. 8–6, Fri. 8–7, Sat. 5 am–5 pm; farmers' market Sat. 5 am–3 pm; antiques market Sun. 5 am–5 pm* Ⓜ *Union.*

The outstanding St. Lawrence food market, one of the finest in the world, sells a huge variety of local and imported specialties.

WORTH NOTING

Flatiron Building. One of several wedge-shape buildings scattered all over North America, Toronto's Flatiron occupies the triangular block between Wellington, Scott, and Front streets. It was erected in 1892 as the head office of the Gooderham and Worts distilling company. On the back of the building, a witty trompe l'oeil mural by Derek Besant is drawn around the windows, making it appear that part of the building has been tacked up on the wall and is peeling off. ✉ *49 Wellington St. E, between Church and Scott sts., Old Town* Ⓜ *King.*

St. James Cathedral. Even if bank towers dwarf it now, this Anglican church with noble Gothic spires has the tallest steeple in Canada. Its illuminated clock once guided ships into the harbor. This is the fourth St. James Cathedral on this site; the third burned down in the Great Fire of 1849. As part of the church's bicentennial in 1997, a new peal of bells was installed. Stand near the church most Sundays after the 9 am service ends (about 10:10 am) and be rewarded with a glorious concert of ringing bells. ✉ *65 Church St., at King St., Old Town* ☎ *416/364–7865* 🌐 *www.stjamescathedral.on.ca* Ⓜ *King.*

St. Lawrence Hall. Erected on the site of the area's first public meeting space, the St. Lawrence Hall, built in 1850–51, demonstrates Renaissance Revival architecture at its finest. Erected for musical performances and balls, it is here that famed opera soprano Jenny Lind sang, where antislavery demonstrations were held, and where P. T. Barnum first presented the midget Tom Thumb. Take time to admire the exterior of this architectural gem, now used for everything from concerts to wedding receptions and graduation parties. If there's no event

Flatiron Building 5
St. James Cathedral 2
St. Lawrence Hall 3
St. Lawrence Market 4
Toronto's First Post Office 1
Ontario Spring Water Sake Company 6

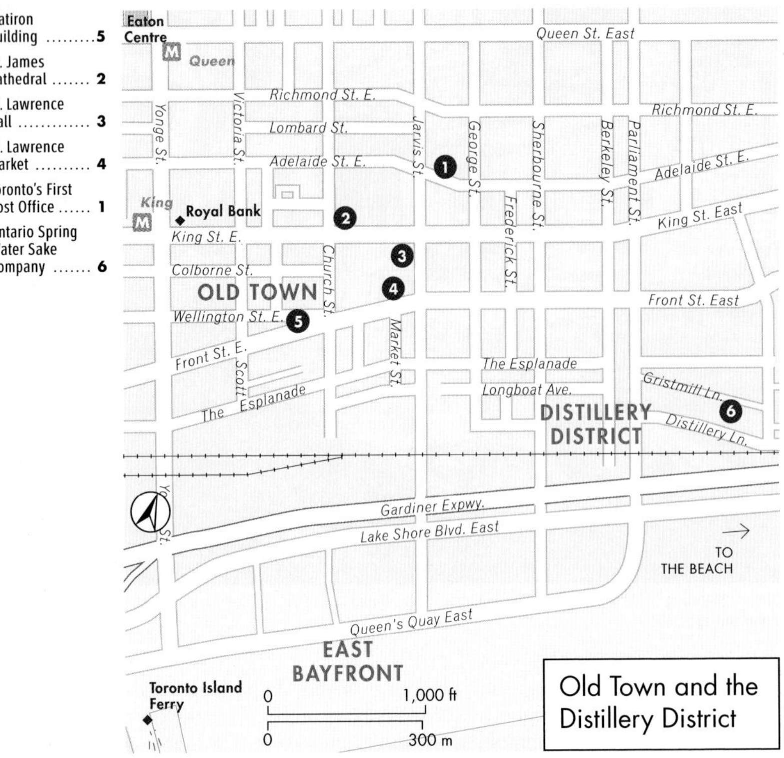

scheduled, you can take a peek at the photos in the East Room on the third floor; the various notable figures displayed once performed or lectured here. ✉ *157 King St. E, Old Town* ☎ *416/392–7809* 🌐 *www.stlawrencemarket.com* Ⓜ *Union.*

FAMILY **Toronto's First Post Office.** Dating from 1833, this small working post office continues to use quill pens, ink pots, and sealing wax—you can use the old-fashioned equipment to send a letter for C$2. Exhibits include reproductions of letters from the 1820s and 1830s. Distinctive cancellation stamps are used on all outgoing cards and letters. ✉ *260 Adelaide St. E, Old Town* ☎ *416/865–1833* 🌐 *www.townofyork.com* 🎫 *Free* ⏲ *Weekdays 9–5:30, Sat. 10–4, Sun. noon–4* Ⓜ *King.*

DISTILLERY DISTRICT

Utterly charming, this excellently restored collection of Victorian industrial buildings, complete with interlinking cobblestone lanes, has become a hub of independent eateries, boutiques, and galleries. The carefully preserved former Gooderham and Worts Distillery (founded in 1832) has been reborn as a cultural center. The 13-acre site includes 45 19th-century buildings and a pedestrian-only village that houses more than 100 tenants—including galleries, artist studios and workshops, boutiques, a few breweries, upscale restaurants, bars, and cafés.

The cobblestoned Historic Distillery District is now home to more than 100 upscale galleries, shops, and restaurants.

Other delicious detours include the Soma Chocolatemaker, Mill Street Brewpub, and Brick Street Bakery. Live music, outdoor exhibitions, fairs, and special events take place year-round, but summer months are the best time to visit. Hour-long walking tours take place seven days a week (C$19; 416/642–0051 to reserve); or you can join one of the 30-minute-long Segway lesson-tours (C$39; Tues.–Sun. 11–6) at Segway of Ontario (in Building 37). You can also combine a Segway lesson with a ghost tour for C$49 (Tue.–Sun. 5, 6, and 7 pm).

TOP ATTRACTIONS

Ontario Spring Water Sake Company. A member of the Brewing Society of Japan, Toronto's first sake distillery only uses water from the nearby town of Huntsville—it's highly regarded by the brewery's *toji* (brewmaster) for its soft quality and minimal chemicals—and special sake rice from Japan. You can take an hour-long guided tour (*Thursday at 5 pm, Saturday and Sunday at 1 and 5 pm*), where you observe traditional Japanese methods of producing sake, learn about the *junmei* ("pure-rice") brewing style, and sample four different kinds of sake. There's also a small store that offers products infused with the house sake such as soaps, salad dressings, and dipping sauces; ceramic ware from Japan and sake glasses; and T-shirts emblazoned with "IZUMI." If you can't make it to the Distillery District, pick up a bottle of their sake at any LCBO, or liquor store, and many of the more upscale restaurants in Toronto (look for its brand name, IZUMI). *55 Mill St., Bldg. 4, Distillery District* *416/365–7253* *ontariosake.com* *tours C$15* *Mon.–Sat. 11–7, Sun. noon–6.*

DUNDAS SQUARE AREA

Yonge Street is the central vein of Toronto, starting at Lake Ontario and slicing the city in half as it travels through Dundas Square and north to the suburbs. Tourists gather below the enormous billboards and flashy lights in Dundas Square, especially in the summer, when the large public area comes alive with outdoor festivals and entertainment. The few sights in this neighborhood, namely the Eaton Centre and Nathan Phillips Square, get a lot of attention from both locals and visitors.

Tourists always end up here, whether they want to or not. Usually it's the enticement of nonstop shopping in the Eaton Centre, Toronto's biggest downtown shopping mall, or the shops lining Yonge Street, nearby. Others see the allure of outdoor markets, ethnic food festivals, and street concerts in the bright and lively, larger-than-life Dundas Square.

To catch a glimpse of what locals are up to, grab lunch and dine alfresco at Nathan Phillips Square. Under the omnipresent gaze of City Hall—the two curving buildings were designed to resemble a watchful eye—nearby suits from the Financial District and spent shoppers populate the benches in all weather. During the winter, the water fountain at Nathan Phillips Square becomes an ice-skating rink that draws in gaggles of giggling teenage girls, young couples holding hands, and little ones testing out their skates for the first time.

There's also a selection of distinct museums. History buffs will enjoy the MacKenzie House, the former home of Toronto's first mayor; contemporary fashion and design are highlighted at the Museum for Textiles; and at the Toronto Police Museum, kids can hop aboard a 1914 paddy wagon or examine their own fingerprints.

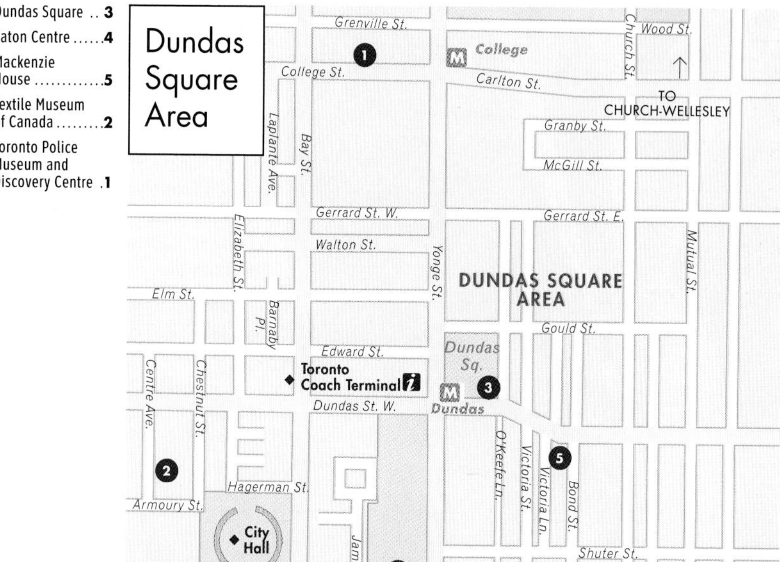

GETTING HERE

The subway stations Dundas and Queen, conveniently at either end of the Eaton Centre, are the main transportation hubs for this part of the city. There are also streetcar lines running along Dundas and Queen streets, linking this area to Chinatown and Kensington Market, and Queen West respectively.

TIMING

Depending on your patience and the contents of your wallet, you could spend anywhere from one to ten hours in the colossal Eaton Centre, literally shopping until you drop. The MacKenzie House, Museum for Textiles, and Toronto Police Museum merit an hour each; and you could easily while away an afternoon people-watching in Dundas Square or Nathan Phillips Square.

TOP ATTRACTIONS

Dundas Square. A public square surrounded by oversize billboards and explosive light displays, Toronto's answer to New York's Times Square is becoming one of the fastest-growing tourist destinations in the city. Visitors and locals converge on the tables and chairs that are scattered across the square when the weather is fine, and kids (and the young at heart) frolic in the 20 water fountains that shoot out of the cement floor like miniature geysers. From May to October, there's something

DID YOU KNOW?

Toronto kicks off the holiday season each year with the Cavalcade of Lights in Nathan Phillips Square. The festival includes fireworks, live music performances, and the lighting of the city's official Christmas tree.

happening every weekend—it could be an artisan market, an open-air film viewing, a summertime festival, or a live musical performance. ✉ *Yonge St., at Dundas St., Dundas Square Area* 🌐 *www.ydsquare.ca* Ⓜ *Dundas.*

WORD OF MOUTH

"I've never been but I hear the Textile Museum is supposed to be great. It's very central— around Dundas and University."

—goddesstogo

2

Eaton Centre. The 3-million-square-foot Eaton Centre shopping mall has been both praised and vilified since it was built in the 1970s, but it remains incredibly popular. From the graceful glass roof, arching 127 feet above the lowest of the mall levels, to artist Michael Snow's exquisite flock of fiberglass Canada geese floating poetically in open space, there's plenty to appreciate.

Such a wide selection of shops and eateries can be confusing, so here's a simple guide: Galleria Level 1 contains two food courts; popularly priced fashions; photo, electronics, and music stores; and much "convenience" merchandise. Level 2 is directed to the middle-income shopper; Level 3, suitably, has the highest fashion and prices. Named for the store (Eaton's) that once anchored it, its biggest tenants are now Sears and H&M. The southern end of Level 3 has a skywalk that connects the Centre to the seven floors of the Bay (formerly Simpsons) department store, across Queen Street.

Safe parking garages with spaces for some 1,800 cars are sprinkled around Eaton Centre. The building extends along the west side of Yonge Street all the way from Queen Street up to Dundas Street (with a subway stop at each end). ✉ *220 Yonge St., Dundas Square Area* ☎ *416/598–8560* 🌐 *www.torontoeatoncentre.com* ⏲ *Weekdays 10–9, Sat. 9:30–7, Sun. 11–6* Ⓜ *Dundas, Queen.*

Mackenzie House. Once home to journalist William Lyon Mackenzie, Toronto's first mayor (elected in 1834) and designer of the city's coat of arms, this Greek Revival row house is now a museum. Among the period furnishings and equipment preserved here is an 1845 printing press, which visitors may try. Mackenzie served only one year as mayor. In 1837, he gathered some 700 supporters and marched down Yonge Street to try to overthrow the government, but his minions were roundly defeated, and he fled to the United States with a price on his head. When Mackenzie was pardoned by Queen Victoria years later, he returned to Canada and was promptly elected once again to the legislative assembly. By this time, though, he was so down on his luck that a group of friends bought his family this house. Mackenzie enjoyed the place for only a few years before his death in 1861. His grandson, William Lyon Mackenzie King, became the longest-serving prime minister in Canadian history. ✉ *82 Bond St., at Dundas St. W, Dundas Square Area* ☎ *416/392–6915* 🎟 *C$7* ⏲ *Jan.–Apr., weekends noon–5; May–Sept., Tues.–Sun. noon–5; Sept.–Dec., Tues.–Fri. noon–4, weekends noon–5* Ⓜ *Dundas.*

QUICK BITES

Trinity Square Café. The Trinity Square Café at the Church of the Holy Trinity is a charming eatery serving sandwiches, soups, pastries, and tea. It's open for lunch weekdays 11:30 am to 2:30 pm. The church itself is fully operational and available for quiet contemplation in the midst of one of downtown Toronto's busiest sections. ✉ ***19 Trinity Sq., facing Bay St., Dundas Square Area*** ☎ ***416/598–2010*** 🌐 ***trinitysquarecafe.webs.com*** Ⓜ ***Dundas.***

WORTH NOTING

Textile Museum of Canada. Ten galleries showcase over 12,000 cultural artifacts—men's costumes from northern Nigeria and ceremonial masks from Papua New Guinea, for example—as well as the latest in contemporary design. Rugs, cloth, and tapestries from around the world are exhibited. Wednesday evenings (after 5) admission is pay what you can. ✉ *55 Centre Ave., at Dundas St. W, Dundas Square Area* ☎ *416/599–5321* 🌐 *www.textilemuseum.ca* 🎟 *C$15* ⏲ *Thurs.–Tues. 11–5, Wed. 11–8* Ⓜ *St. Patrick.*

FAMILY **Toronto Police Museum and Discovery Centre.** A replica of a 19th-century police station, a collection of firearms, and exhibits about infamous crimes are the highlights at this museum devoted exclusively to the Toronto police. Interactive displays include law-and-order quizzes and the opportunity to study your own fingerprints. Kids have fun with the 1914 paddy wagon, car-crash videos, and, especially, a Harley-Davidson they can jump on. They also enjoy climbing in and out of a car sliced in half and hearing a dispatcher squawk at them. **TIP→ Visits must be made ahead of time.** ✉ *40 College St., at Bay St., Dundas Square Area* ☎ *416/808–7020* ✉ *museum@torontopolice.on.ca* 🌐 *www.torontopolice.on.ca/museum* 🎟 *C$3* ⏲ *Weekdays 8–4* Ⓜ *College.*

CHINATOWN, KENSINGTON MARKET, AND QUEEN WEST

The areas along Dundas and Queen streets typify Toronto's ethnic makeup and vibrant youthfulness. To many locals, the Dundas and Spadina intersection means Chinatown and Kensington Market, while Queen West, which was the home of 1990s comedy troupe Kids in the Hall and pop-rockers Barenaked Ladies, has always been a haven for shoppers and trendsetters.

Chinatown and Kensington Market, often explored together, are popular destinations for tourists and locals alike. On a weekend morning, the sidewalks are jam-packed with pedestrians shopping for cheap produce and Chinese trinkets, lining up for a table at one of Chinatown's many restaurants, or heading to "the Market" for a little afternoon shopping. On the last Sunday of each month (May–October), Kensington Market goes car-free, and the streets explode with live entertainment, street performances, and vendors selling handicrafts and clothing.

Queen West is busy any time of the year, mostly with teenagers hanging out at the MuchMusic building and young fashionistas-in-training shopping up a storm.

GETTING HERE

The Osgoode subway station is ideal for getting to Queen West, as is the 501 streetcar. The 510 Spadina streetcar (which originates at the Spadina subway station) services Chinatown and Kensington Market.

TIMING

In Queen West, the Campbell House merits at least a half hour; the Art Gallery of Ontario an hour or more. Chinatown is at its busiest (and most fun) on Sunday, but be prepared for very crowded sidewalks and much jostling. Kensington is great any time, although it can feel a bit sketchy at night, and it gets mobbed on weekend afternoons. Just strolling around any of these neighborhoods can gobble up an entire afternoon.

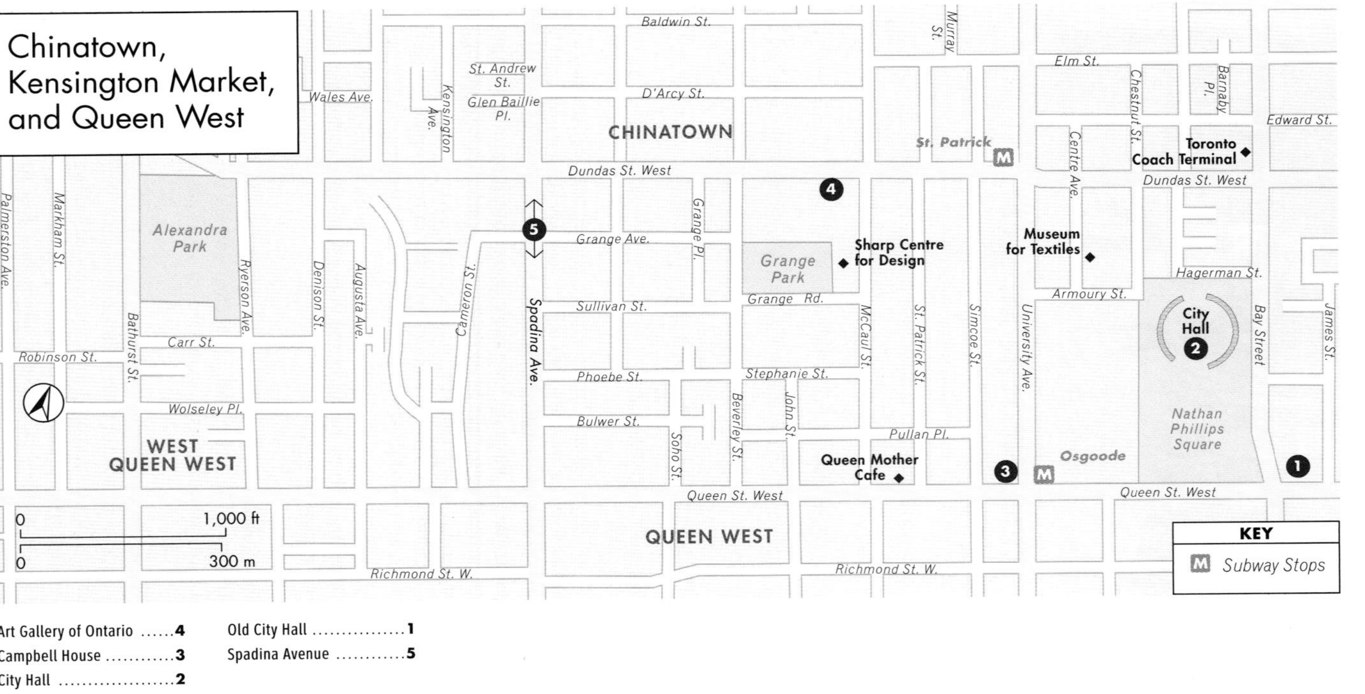
Chinatown, Kensington Market, and Queen West
Baldwin St.
Murray St.
Elm St.
Wales Ave.
Kensington Ave.
St. Andrew St.
Glen Baillie Pl.
D'Arcy St.
Chestnut St.
Barnaby Pl.
Edward St.
CHINATOWN
St. Patrick
Centre Ave.
Toronto Coach Terminal
Dundas St. West
Dundas St. West
Palmerston Ave.
Markham St.
Alexandra Park
Grange Pl.
Museum for Textiles
Grange Ave.
Sharp Centre for Design
Grange Park
Hagerman St.
Ryerson Ave.
Denison St.
Augusta Ave.
Cameron St.
Spadina Ave.
Sullivan St.
Grange Rd.
Armoury St.
Bathurst St.
Carr St.
McCaul St.
St. Patrick St.
Simcoe St.
University Ave.
City Hall
Bay Street
James St.
Robinson St.
Phoebe St.
Stephanie St.
Wolseley Pl.
Bulwer St.
Beverley St.
John St.
Pullan Pl.
Nathan Phillips Square
Soho St.
WEST QUEEN WEST
Queen Mother Cafe
Osgoode
Queen St. West
Queen St. West
0
1,000 ft
0
300 m
QUEEN WEST
Richmond St. W.
Richmond St. W.
KEY
Subway Stops
Art Gallery of Ontario 4
Campbell House 3
City Hall 2
Old City Hall 1
Spadina Avenue 5

CHINATOWN

Compact and condensed, Toronto's Chinatown—which is actually the main or original Chinatown in the city, as five other areas with large Chinese commercial districts have sprung up elsewhere—covers much of the area of Spadina Avenue from Queen Street to College Street, running along Dundas Street nearly as far east as Bay Street. The population is more than 100,000, which is especially impressive when you consider that just over a century ago there was only a single Chinese resident, Sam Ching, who ran a hand laundry on Adelaide Street.

Especially jumbled at its epicenter, the Spadina–Dundas intersection, Chinatown's rickety storefronts selling (real and fake) jade trees, lovely sake sets, Chinese herbs, and fresh fish are packed every day of the week. On Sunday, Chinese music blasts from storefronts, cash registers ring, and bakeries, markets, herbalists, and restaurants do their best business of the week.

TOP ATTRACTIONS

Fodor's Choice ★ **Art Gallery of Ontario.** The AGO is hard to miss: the monumental glass and titanium facade designed by Toronto native son Frank Gehry hovering over the main building is a stunning beauty. Near the entrance, you'll find visitors of all ages climbing in and around Henry Moore's large *Two Forms* sculpture, on the corner of Dundas and McCaul streets. Inside, the collection, which had an extremely modest beginning in 1900, is now in the big leagues, especially in terms of its exhibitions of landscape paintings from the 19th and 20th centuries. Be sure to take a pause in the light and airy Walker Court, to admire Gehry's spiraling Baroque Stair; climb the staircase and look straight up for the best view.

The Canadian Wing includes major works by such northern lights as Emily Carr, Cornelius Krieghoff, David Milne, and Homer Watson, plus the Thomson Collection with pieces by Paul Kane, Tom Thomson, and Lawren Harris. The AGO also has a growing collection of works by such world-famous artists as Rembrandt, Hals, Van Dyck, Hogarth, Reynolds, Chardin, Renoir, de Kooning, Rothko, Oldenburg, Picasso, Rodin, Degas, Matisse, and many others. A rediscovered early-17th-century piece by Flemish painter Peter Paul Rubens, *Massacre of the Innocents*, was unveiled in 2008. The brand-new Weston Family Learning Centre offers art courses, camps, lectures, and interactive exhibitions for adults and children alike. If you have time, take a peek at the open excavation of buried artifacts sealed in the foundations of the Grange, the original site of the Art Gallery of Toronto, which was built in 1817. Themed tours take in unusual sites, such as the Grange kitchen, or specific genres, like Canadian art; check the website for dates and times. Free AGO Highlights tours run daily at 1 pm; the meeting point is the Walker Court. ✉ *317 Dundas St. W, at McCaul St., Chinatown* ☎ *416/979–6648* 🌐 *www.ago.net* 🎟 *C$19.50; permanent collection free on Wed. after 6 pm* ⏲ *Tues. and Thurs.–Sun. 10–5:30, Wed. 10–8:30* Ⓜ *St. Patrick.*

WORTH NOTING

Spadina Avenue. Spadina (pronounced "Spa-*dye*-nah"), running from the lakeshore north to College Street, has never been chic. For decades it has housed a collection of inexpensive stores, factories that sell wholesale if you have connections, ethnic food stores, and eateries, including some first-class, if modest-looking, Chinese restaurants. Each new wave of immigrants—Jewish, Chinese, Portuguese, East and West Indian, South American—has added its own flavor to the mix, but Spadina–Kensington's basic bill of fare is still bargains galore. Here you can find discounts of up to half off the prices of Yorkville stores, yards of remnants piled high in bins, designer clothes minus the labels, and the occasional rock-and-roll nightspot and interesting greasy spoon. A streetcar line runs down the wide avenue to Front Street. ✉ *Chinatown.*

WORD OF MOUTH

"I was glad I went to the AGO (Art Gallery of Ontario) for the first time, as I especially enjoyed their collection of 19th- and early-20th-century Canadian art. In particular, Cornelius Krieghoff... with his panoramas of 19th-century life in Quebec. His paintings... give the viewer a sense of what life was like not so long ago."

—Daniel_Williams

KENSINGTON MARKET

This collection of colorful storefronts, crumbling brick houses, delightful green spaces, and funky street stalls titillates all the senses. On any given day you can find Russian rye breads, barrels of dill pickles, fresh fish, imported cheese, and ripe fruit. Kensington's collection of vintage-clothing stores is the best in the city.

The site sprang up in the early 1900s, when Russian, Polish, and Jewish inhabitants set up stalls in front of their houses. Since then the district, or "market"—named after the area's major street—has become a sort of United Nations of stores. Unlike the members of the UN, however, these vendors get along well with one another. Jewish and Eastern European shops sit side by side with Portuguese and Caribbean ones, as well as with a sprinkling of Vietnamese and Chinese establishments. **TIP→** Saturday or Sunday are the best days to visit, preferably by public transit; parking is difficult. Also note that the neighborhood is pedestrianized from dawn to dusk on the last Sunday of every month.

QUICK BITES

King's Café. In a neighborhood where the bohemian vegetarian lifestyle is the norm, King's Café has become a mainstay for diners seeking healthy grub with an Asian accent. Artists, students, and young professionals flock to this serene and airy interior with wide windows overlooking bustling Augusta Avenue. Specialties include enoki mushrooms in seaweed and spinach and King's Special Vegetable Soup, a hearty broth with homemade veggie nuggets, taro, and fried tofu. ✉ *192 Augusta Ave., Kensington Market* ☎ *416/591–1340* Ⓜ *St. Patrick, then streetcar 505 west.*

Toronto's network of streetcars provides an excellent method of transportation for getting around downtown.

QUEEN WEST

Along Queen Street West, from University Avenue to Bathurst Street is a shopper's dream. John Fluevog, HMV, American Apparel, Zara, Lululemon—they all have outposts here. The area also attracts tourists for its iconic landmarks: the Horseshoe Tavern at 370 Queen Street West has been here since the 1940s and was a springboard for such megastars as Bryan Adams and Stompin' Tom Connors; the open-air Nathan Phillips Square at City Hall, and the historic Campbell House.

TOP ATTRACTIONS

City Hall. Toronto's modern city hall resulted from a 1958 international competition to which some 520 architects from 42 countries submitted designs. The winning presentation by Finnish architect Viljo Revell was controversial—two curved towers of differing height—but logical: an aerial view of City Hall shows a circular council chamber sitting like an eye between the two tower "eyelids," which contain the offices of 44 municipal wards, with 44 city councillors. A remarkable mural within the main entrance, *Metropolis,* was constructed by sculptor David Partridge from 100,000 nails. Revell died before his masterwork was opened in 1965, but within months City Hall became a symbol of a thriving metropolis, with a silhouette as recognizable as the Eiffel Tower. Robert Fulford's book *Accidental City* details the positive influence the development of this building has had on Toronto's civic life.

Annual events at City Hall include the Spring Flower Show in late March; the Toronto Outdoor Art Exhibition in early July; and the yearly Cavalcade of Lights from late November through Christmas, when more than 100,000 sparkling lights are illuminated across both new and old city halls.

In front of City Hall, 9-acre **Nathan Phillips Square** (named after the mayor who initiated the City Hall project) has become a gathering place, whether for royal visits, protest rallies, picnic lunches, or concerts. The reflecting pool is a delight in summer, and even more so in winter, when office workers skate at lunch. The park also holds a Peace Garden for quiet meditation and Henry Moore's striking bronze sculpture *The Archer.* ✉ *100 Queen St. W, at Bay St., Queen West* ☎ *416/338–0338, 416/338–0889 TDD* 🌐 *www.toronto.ca* ⏲ *Weekdays 8:30–4:30* Ⓜ *Queen.*

WORD OF MOUTH

"I'd recommend Chinatown—Kensington Market is nearby…and has Wanda's Pie in the Sky. [Enjoy] people watching from their patio on a sunny corner and all sorts of REALLY GOOD pies."

—morningglory47

QUICK BITES

Queen Mother Café. Queen Street West is lined with cafés and restaurants, and one solid choice is the Queen Mother Café, a neighborhood institution popular with art students and broadcast-media types. Serving Lao-Thai and Italian cuisine, the "Queen Mum" is open until 1 am (Sunday until midnight) for wholesome meals and rich desserts at reasonable prices. ✉ ***208 Queen St. W, at St. Patrick St., Queen West*** ☎ ***416/598–4719*** Ⓜ ***Osgoode.***

WORTH NOTING

Campbell House. The Georgian mansion of Sir William Campbell, the sixth chief justice of Upper Canada, is now one of Toronto's best house museums. Built in 1822 in another part of town, the Campbell House was moved to this site in 1972. It has been restored with elegant early-19th-century furniture. Costumed guides detail the social life of the upper class. Note the model of the town of York as it was in the 1820s and the original kitchen. ✉ *160 Queen St. W, Queen West* ☎ *416/597–0227* 🌐 *www.campbellhousemuseum.ca* 🎫 *C$6* ⏲ *Oct.–May, Tues–Fri., 9:30–4:30; Jun.–Sept., Tues–Fri., 9:30–4:30, weekends noon–4:30* Ⓜ *Osgoode.*

Old City Hall. Opened in 1899, and used until 1965 when "new" City Hall was built across the street, the old municipal building is still the home of the provincial courts, county offices, and marriage bureau. This imposing building was designed by E.J. Lennox, who was also the architect for Casa Loma and the King Edward Hotel. Note the huge stained-glass window as you enter. The fabulous gargoyles above the front steps were apparently the architect's witty way of mocking certain turn-of-the-20th-century politicians; he also carved his name under the eaves on all four faces of the building. The building has appeared in countless domestic and international TV shows and feature films. ✉ *60 Queen St. W, Queen West* ⏲ *Weekdays 8:30–5* Ⓜ *Queen.*

DID YOU KNOW?

Henry Moore's *Two Large Forms* anchors the northeast corner of the Art Gallery of Ontario. The museum houses the world's largest public collection of the British artist's sculptures.

EAST AND WEST OF THE CITY CENTER

Toronto is sprawling, there's no doubt about it. However, the city's excellent public transportation system makes it a cinch to get outside the city center to explore the Toronto that locals know and cherish. And you should do just that: hit a trendy strip like Ossington to experience Toronto's burgeoning hipster culture; take in the vibe of a busy sidewalk café in Leslieville, teeming with young families; stroll the boardwalk and enjoy the lake breezes in The Beach; or satisfy a hungry belly with Greek food along the Danforth or a spicy curry in Little India.

WEST QUEEN WEST, PARKDALE, AND OSSINGTON

Grunge meets chic along Queen Street west of Bathurst, dubbed "West Queen West" by locals. While it's still possible to find a run-down hardware store shouldering a high-end hipster bar, more of the latter are moving in these days. Almost completely devoid of the familiar chains that plague older sister Queen West, this area is instead filling with vegan spa resorts, trendy ethnic restaurants, and European kitchenware shops; much farther west a bustling art scene is blossoming.

The neighborhood's landmarks, the **Drake Hotel** and the **Gladstone Hotel,** enjoy much success for their creative, eclectic decor and their happening nightlife. Businesses like these, which revolutionized the once-shabby district and gave it its current über-cool image, helped pave the way for a second wave of émigrés. An eclectic smattering of restaurants and more than 300 art galleries vie for real estate with fair-trade coffee shops and boutiques featuring Canada's hottest new designers. Trinity Bellwoods Park punctuates the neighborhood at the center and provides a beautiful setting for a picnic or a bench break.

West Queen is home to an increasing number of trendy boutiques and cutting-edge galleries.

Farther west, after the overpass next to the Gladstone Hotel, is Parkdale, a once crime-infested and still fairly run-down neighborhood that's become home to North America's largest Tibetan community. Apartment buildings streaked with prayer flags and shops offering everything from beef *momos* (dumplings) to singing bowls have been a welcome improvement over the once derelict storefronts.

The previously shady strip along Ossington Street, north of Queen West, is Toronto's newest *it* spot. Fashion designers, artists and musicians, and creative restaurateurs have flooded the street, and the area now attracts attention for its sudden and celebrated gentrification.

THE BEACH

Queen Street *West* represents the city's of-the-moment trends, but The Beach neighborhood, 15 minutes east of the Queen subway stop, is old-school bohemian. This pricey area is bounded by Neville Park Road to the east and Woodbine Avenue to the west. The main strip, Queen Street *East*, has a funky flair and a small-town feel, and it's easy to spend an afternoon strolling the delightful yet crowded (in summer) boardwalk along the shore of Lake Ontario. Musicians often perform at the parks fronting the boardwalk, where you're also likely to see artists selling their wares. You could also do some window-shopping on Queen Street East, which is lined with antiques stores and specialty boutiques and shops. An annual jazz festival in July attracts more than 400 musicians and thousands of listeners to this laid-back community.

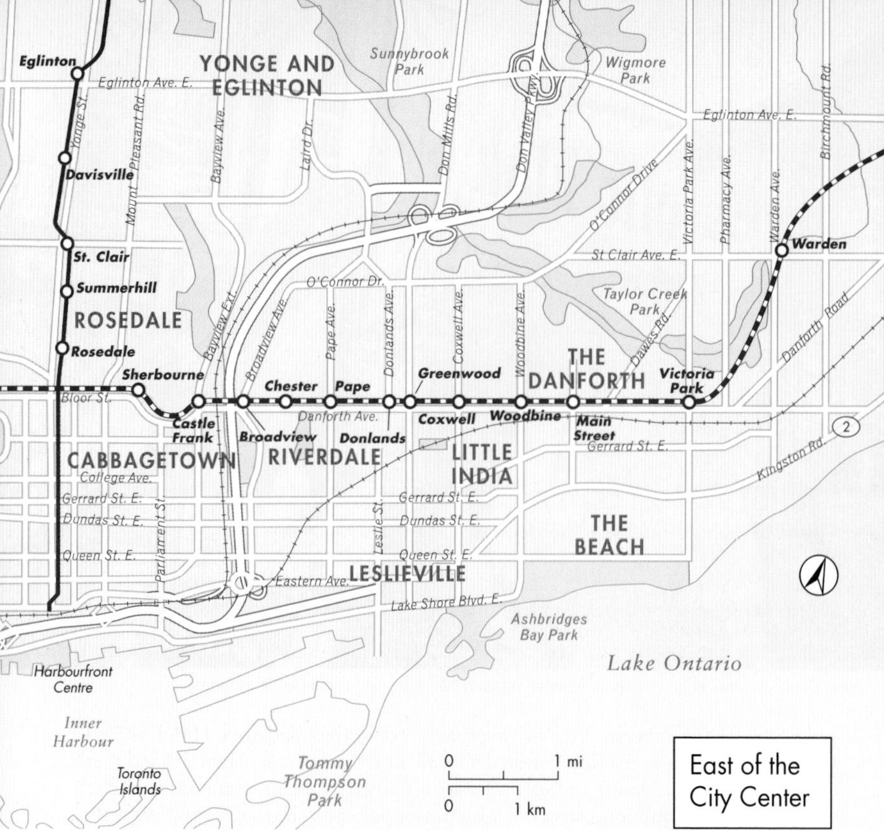

East of the City Center

This neighborhood's official name has been a source of controversy since the 1980s. It boils down to whether you view the four separate beaches—Woodbine, Balmy, Kew, and Scarboro—as one collective entity or plural. When the area decided to welcome tourists with fancy, emblematic street signs, the long-running debate surfaced. "The Beach" folks won, but not before the dispute was settled fairly with a democratic vote in spring 2006.

THE DANFORTH

Once English-settled, this area along Danforth Avenue named after Asa Danforth, an American contractor who cut a road into the area in 1799, has a dynamic ethnic mix, although it's primarily a Greek community. You'll now find bright organic-juice bars, boisterous patios overflowing with late-night revelers, and some of the best souvlaki this side of the Atlantic.

The western end, between Broadview and Chester subway stations, is a health nut's haven. Juice bars, vegetarian food emporia, yoga studios, and stores devoted to holistic healing, naturopathic medicine, and environmentally friendly clothing and cleaning products abound.

The Danforth neighborhood serves some of the best Greek food in North America.

East of Chester subway station is the area referred to as "Greektown." Late-night taverns, all-night fruit markets, and some of the best Greek food in North America keep this neighborhood busy at all hours. A number of bakeries offer mouthwatering baklava, *tyropita* (cheese pie), and *touloumbes* (fried cinnamon-flavored cakes soaked in honey) if you prefer to snack and stroll. **TIP→ Summer is the best season to visit, as most eateries have patios open and are busy until the wee hours of morning.**

Every August the Taste of the Danforth (☎ *416/469–5634* 🌐 *www.tasteofthedanforth.com*) pays tribute to the little nook of foodie paradise here. More than a million visitors come to sample the fare—mainly dolmades, souvlaki, and other Greek specialties—for C$1 to C$5 per taste. The festival motto—"Don't eat for a week before coming"—is helpful advice.

But it's not just about food. Between bites, you might want to check out the independent, original boutiques in the neighborhood that offer everything from fair-trade gifts to funky kitchenware. For those who like to live on the edge, there's even a shop that sells nothing but hot sauce, with samplers ranging from mild to "smack my ass."

LITTLE INDIA

"Little India" and "Indian Village" both refer to Gerrard India Bazaar, the largest collection of South Asian restaurants, sari stores, and Bollywood movie-rental shops in North America. Follow your nose through the sweets shops, food stalls, and curry restaurants, and allow your eyes to be dazzled by storefront displays of jewelry, Hindu deities, and swaths of sensuous fabrics ablaze with sequins.

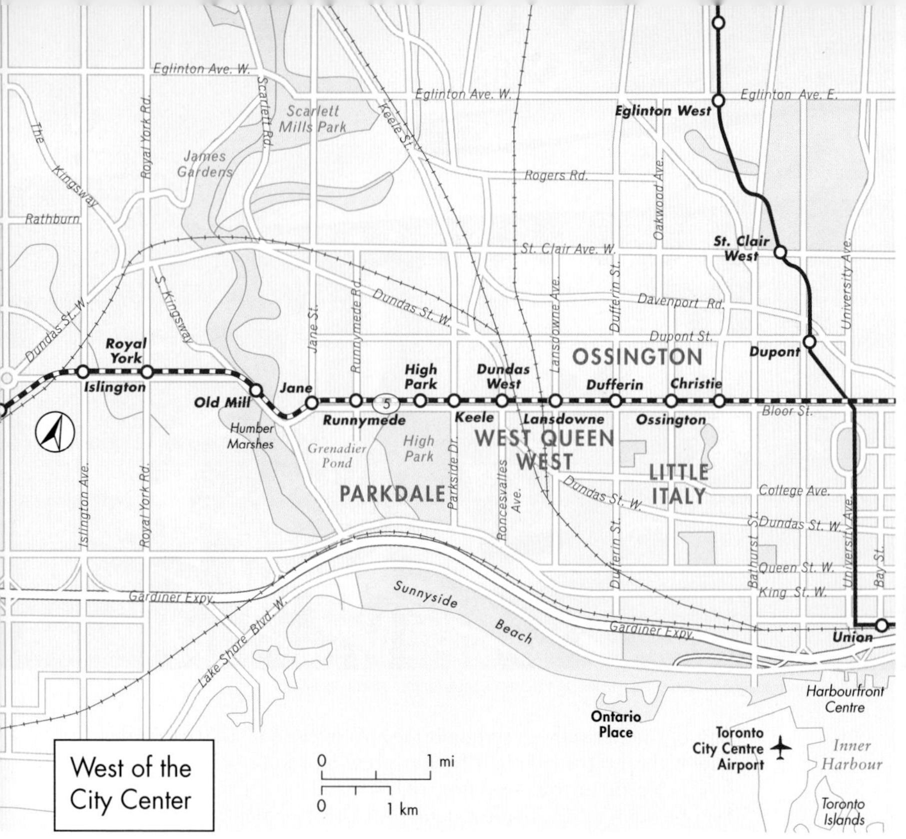

Mornings are generally quiet. Afternoons see a trickle of visitors, but the area really comes alive in the evening, when those with hungry bellies stroll in search of a fiery madras, creamy korma, or hearty masala curry. Many of the restaurants offer buffet lunches and dinners for around C$12 per person, which draw huge crowds on the weekends. Sunday afternoons set the familiar scene of Indian families crowding the sidewalks, enjoying corn on the cob and *paan* (a mild Indian stimulant of spices, fruits, and sometimes sugar wrapped in leaves of the betel pepper), and window-shopping their way up and down Gerrard Street.

As this area represents such a diverse group of people, there are many festivals throughout the year. During the biggest event, the three-day Festival of South Asia in August, stages are set for colorful music and dance performances, and the streets fill with the tantalizing scents of snack stalls and the calls of vendors peddling everything from henna tattoos to spicy corn on the cob. In late autumn, the Hindu Festival of Lights (Diwali) and the end of Ramadan (Eid) are celebrated together with another fun and fiery street fête. For more information on the festivals, contact ☎ *416/465–8513*.

LESLIEVILLE

Perhaps because of its location, far from much-hyped and highly publicized West Queen West and Ossington, Leslieville has been quietly gentrifying into a colorful and exciting strip of interior design shops, hip eateries, funky boutiques, and independent cafés that is often labeled by trend-spotters (much to the disdain of locals) as Toronto's Brooklyn. Interior design shops stand out, but the vibe has more of a community feel due to a tight-knit collection of shop owners with regular customers. And like the nearby Beach neighborhood, the sidewalks are often filled with baby strollers and dog walkers.

It's quaint at times, with dusty antiques shops, old-fashioned ice cream parlors, and the occasional old-school appliance shop thrown into the mix, but the offerings lean more toward local designer boutiques, cute bakeries, organic butcher shops, cheese emporia, homey diners, chic eateries, and, in keeping with the chilled-out vibe of the area, an unusually large selection of independent coffee shops.

GETTING HERE

To explore Leslieville, take the 501 Queen streetcar east from downtown to Coxwell Avenue and walk west along Queen Street East.

TOP ATTRACTIONS

Tommy Thompson Park. This park comprises a peninsula that juts 5 km (3 miles) into Lake Ontario. It was created from the sand dredged for a new port of entry and the landfill of a hundred skyscrapers (trucks still dump landfill here Monday to Friday). It has quickly become one of the best areas in the city for cycling, jogging, walking, sailing, photography, and, especially, bird-watching. The strange, artificial peninsula is home (or stopover) to the largest colony of ring-billed seagulls in the world and dozens of species of terns, ducks, geese, and snowy egrets. At the end of the spit, you'll find a red-and-white lighthouse, in addition to amazing views of downtown and an awesome sense of isolation in nature. Bird-watching is best from mid-May to mid-October. To get here, head east along Queen Street to Leslie Street, then south to the lake. No private vehicles are permitted in the park. ✉ *Entrance at the foot of Leslie St., south of Lakeshore Blvd. East, Leslieville* ☎ *416/661–6600* 🌐 *www.tommythompsonpark.ca* ⏲ *Weekends Apr.–Nov., daily 9–6; Dec.–Mar., daily 9–4:30* Ⓜ *Queen, then streetcar 501 east.*

QUEEN'S PARK, THE ANNEX, AND LITTLE ITALY

This vast area that encompasses a huge chunk of Toronto's downtown core holds several important attractions, but it couldn't feel further from a tourist trap if it tried, bringing together Toronto's upper crust, Ontario's provincial politicians, Canada's intellectual set, and a former Italian neighborhood turned entertainment district. Take a break in one of The Annex's many casual spots and you could be rubbing shoulders with a student cramming for an exam, a blocked author looking for inspiration, or a busy civil servant picking up a jolt of caffeine to go.

The large, oval Queen's Park circles the Ontario Provincial Legislature and is straddled by the sprawling, 160-acre downtown campus of the University of Toronto. Wandering this neighborhood will take you past century-old colleges, Gothic cathedrals, and plenty of quiet benches overlooking leafy courtyards and student-filled parks.

The University of Toronto's campus overflows west into The Annex, where students and scholarly types while away the hours after class. This frantic section of Bloor Street West abounds with ethnic restaurants and plenty of student-friendly cafés and bars, plus two of the city's must-see attractions: the Bata Shoe Museum and Casa Loma.

Similarly energetic is Little Italy, where music spills out of trendy eateries and patios are packed in the summertime. The myriad wine bars and boutique clubs in this neighborhood attract a young professional crowd.

GETTING HERE

Use the subway to reach the University of Toronto (St. George and Queen's Park stations), Casa Loma (Dupont station), The Annex (Spadina and Bathurst stations), and Queen's Park (Queen's Park station). Little Italy can be reached by streetcar 505 along College Street (east).

TIMING

The Queen's Park and Annex areas are nice places to take a stroll any time of year because many of the attractions bring you indoors. A visit to the legislature and one or two of the museums or libraries would make a nice half-day (or more) program. Give yourself at least a few hours for a full tour of Casa Loma and about an hour for the Bata Shoe Museum. Make an evening of dinner and drinks in the trendy Little Italy area.

WORD OF MOUTH

"I second the Bata Shoe Museum (not nearly as frivolous as I thought it would be, rather historically fascinating to tell the truth!)." —Daniel_Williams

QUEEN'S PARK

Many visitors consider this the intellectual hub of Toronto. Surrounding the large oval-shape patch of land are medical facilities to the south and the University of Toronto to the west and east. To most locals, Queen's Park is chiefly synonymous with politics, as the Ontario Legislative Building sits in its center.

TOP ATTRACTIONS

Hart House. A neo-Gothic student center built in 1911–19, Hart House represents the single largest gift to the University of Toronto. Vincent Massey, a student here at the turn of the 20th century, regretted the absence of a meeting place and gym for students and convinced his father to build one. It was named for Vincent's grandfather, Hart, the founder of Massey-Ferguson, once the world's leading supplier of farm equipment. Originally restricted to male students, Hart House has been open to women since 1972.

Keep your eyes peeled for artwork scattered throughout the building, including a revolving collection of works by famed Canadians like Emily Carr and evocative landscape paintings by the Group of Seven. Hart House founder Vincent Massey filled the walls of the house with artwork so that the students would "consciously or unconsciously... develop an interest in it." The project to build a permanent collection, which holds more than 600 important works by both emerging and established Canadian artists, began in 1922 with the purchase of the painting Georgian Bay, November, by Group of Seven member A. Y. Jackson. Two hundred works are on display throughout the building, most of which can be viewed by anyone willing to wander in and out of the rooms. Each year a new piece is added, carefully chosen by a committee made up of mainly students, and today the collection is reported to be worth close to C$17 million. The **Justina Barnicke Gallery** (☎ *416/978–8398* ⏲ *Mon.–Fri. noon–5, Sat. 1–5*) comprises two rooms of mixed-media art showcasing homegrown talent. The stained-glass windows and vaulted ceiling in the Great Hall are impressive, but so is chef Suzanne Baby's cuisine at the resident **Gallery Grill** (☎ *416/978–2445* ⏲ *Sept.–June, weekdays 11:30–2:30, Sun. 11–2*). Try one of the grilled fish dishes, a juicy steak, or a creative vegetarian torte while enjoying the elegant surroundings. ✉ *U of T, 7 Hart House Circle, Queen's Park* ☎ *416/978–2452* 🌐 *www.harthouse.utoronto.ca* Ⓜ *Museum.*

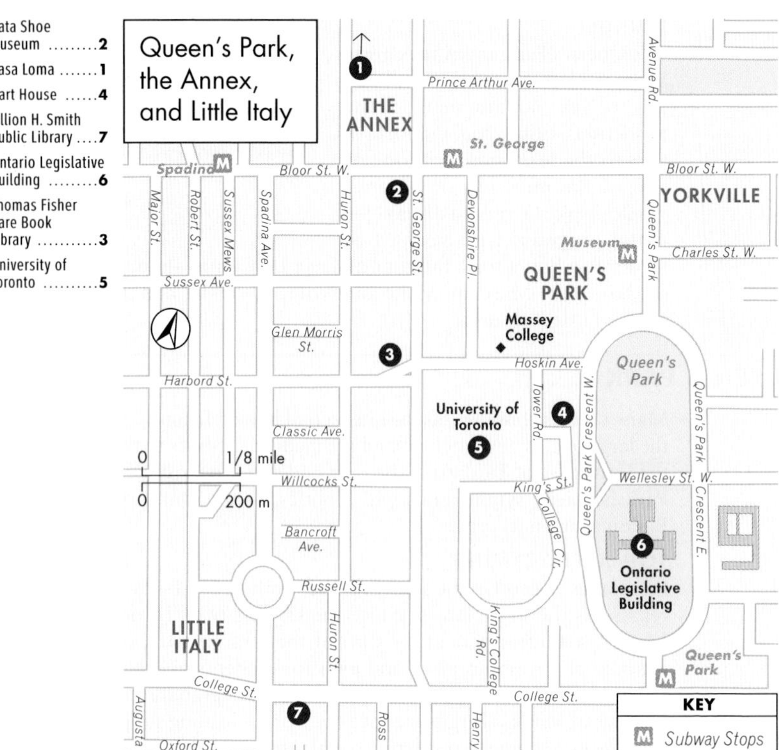

University of Toronto. Almost a city unto itself, U of T has a staff and student population of around 60,000. The institution dates to 1827, when King George IV signed a charter for a "King's College in the Town of York, Capital of Upper Canada." The Church of England had control then, but by 1850 the college was proclaimed nondenominational, renamed the University of Toronto, and put under the control of the province. Then, in a spirit of Christian competition, the Anglicans started Trinity College, the Methodists began Victoria, and the Roman Catholics began St. Michael's; by the time the Presbyterians founded Knox College, the whole thing was a bit out of hand. Now the 10 schools and faculties are united, and they welcome anyone who can meet the admission standards and afford the tuition, which, thanks to government funding, is still somewhat reasonable. The architecture is interesting, if uneven, as one might expect on a campus that's been built in bits and pieces over 150 years. ✉ *Visitors Centre, 25 King's College Circle, Queen's Park* ☎ *416/978–5000* 🌐 *www.utoronto.ca* Ⓜ *St. George, Queen's Park.*

WORTH NOTING

FAMILY **Lillian H. Smith Branch of the Toronto Public Library.** Honoring the memory of the city's first children's librarian, this branch maintains nearly 60,000 items in three children's collections, ranging from the 14th century to the present. In addition, the Merril Collection of Science Fiction, Speculation and Fantasy includes about 50,000 items, on everything from parapsychology to UFOs. The Electronic Resource Centre has 32 public terminals for online access. ✉ *239 College St., between Spadina Ave. and St. George St., Queen's Park* ☎ *416/393–7746* 🌐 *www.torontopubliclibrary.ca* *Free* ⏲ *Mon.–Fri. 9–8:30, Sat. 9–5* Ⓜ *Queen's Park.*

Ontario Legislative Building. Like City Hall, this home to the provincial parliament was the product of an international contest among architects, in this case won by a young Briton residing in Buffalo, New York. The 1893 Romanesque Revival building, made of pink Ontario sandstone, has a wealth of exterior detail; inside, the huge, lovely halls echo half a millennium of English architecture. The long hallways are hung with hundreds of oils by Canadian artists, most of which capture scenes of the province's natural beauty. Take one of the frequent, 30-minute-long tours from the lobby to see the chamber where the 130 MPPs (members of Provincial Parliament) meet. The two heritage rooms—one each for the parliamentary histories of Britain and Ontario—are filled with old newspapers, periodicals, and pictures. The many statues dotting the lawn in front of the building, facing College Street, include one of Queen Victoria and one of Canada's first prime ministers, Sir John A. Macdonald. The lawn is also the site of Canada Day celebrations and the occasional political protest. These buildings are often referred to simply as Queen's Park, after the park surrounding them. ✉ *1 Queen's Park, Queen's Park* ☎ *416/325–7500* 🌐 *educationportal.ontla.on.ca* *Free* ⏲ *Guided tours: mid-May–early Sept., weekdays 9:30–5:30, weekends 9–4; early Sept.–mid-May, weekdays 9–4* Ⓜ *Queen's Park.*

Thomas Fisher Rare Book Library. Early writing artifacts such as a Babylonian cuneiform tablet, a 2,000-year-old Egyptian papyrus, and books dating to the beginning of European printing in the 15th century are shown here in rotating exhibits, which change three times annually. Subjects of these shows might include William Shakespeare, Galileo Galilei, Italian opera, or contemporary typesetting. Registration is required upon entry, so bring some form of identification with you. ✉ *U of T, 120 St. George St., Queen's Park* ☎ *416/978–5285* 🌐 *fisher.library.utoronto.ca* *Free* ⏲ *Weekdays 9–5* Ⓜ *St. George.*

THE ANNEX

Born in 1887, when the burgeoning town of Toronto engulfed the area between Bathurst Street and Avenue Road north from Bloor Street to the Canadian Pacific Railway tracks at what is now Dupont Street, the countrified Annex soon became an enclave for the well-to-do; today it attracts an intellectual set. Timothy Eaton of department-store fame built a handsome structure at 182 Lowther Avenue (since demolished). The prominent Gooderham family, owners of a distillery, erected a lovely red castle at the corner of St. George Street and Bloor Street, now the home of the exclusive York Club.

As Queen Victoria gave way to King Edward, old money gave way to new money and ethnic groups came and went. Upon the arrival of developers many Edwardian mansions were demolished to make room for bland 1960s-era apartment buildings.

Still, The Annex, with its hundreds of attractive old homes, can be cited as a prime example of Toronto's success in preserving lovely, safe streets within the downtown area. Examples of late-19th-century architecture can be spotted on Admiral Road, Lowther Avenue, and Bloor Street, west of Spadina Avenue. Round turrets, pyramid-shape roofs, and conical spires are among the pleasures shared by some 20,000 Torontonians who live in this vibrant community, including professors, students, writers, lawyers, and other professional and artsy types. Bloor Street between Spadina and Palmerston keeps them fed and entertained with its bohemian collection of used-record stores, whole-foods shops, juice bars, and restaurants from elegant Italian to aromatic Indian.

TOP ATTRACTIONS

Bata Shoe Museum. Created by Sonja Bata, wife of the founder of the Bata Shoe Company, this shoe museum holds a permanent collection of 10,000 varieties of foot coverings and, through the changing fashions, highlights the craft and sociology of making shoes. Some items date back more than 4,000 years. Pressurized skydiving boots, iron-spiked shoes used for crushing chestnuts, and smugglers' clogs are among the items on display. Elton John's boots have proved wildly popular, but Marilyn Monroe's red leather pumps give them a run for their money. Ongoing exhibits feature the bear-fur shoes of samurai and Napoléon Bonaparte's black silk socks. Admission is free every Thursday from 5 to 8 pm. ✉ *327 Bloor St. W, at St. George St., The Annex* ☎ *416/979–7799* 🌐 *www.batashoemuseum.ca* 🎟 *C$14* ⏲ *Mon.–Wed., Fri., and Sat. 10–5, Thurs. 10–8, Sun. noon–5* Ⓜ *St. George.*

FAMILY **Casa Loma.** A European-style castle, Casa Loma was commissioned by Sir Henry Pellatt, a soldier and financier. This grand display of extravagance has 98 rooms, two towers, creepy passageways, and lots of secret panels. The home's architect, E. J. Lennox, also designed Toronto's Old City Hall and the King Edward Hotel. Pellatt spent more than C$3 million to construct his dream (that's in 1913 dollars), only to lose his house to the taxman just over a decade later. Some impressive details are the giant pipe organ; the reproduction of Windsor Castle's Peacock Alley; the majestic, 60-foot-high ceiling of the Great Hall; the mahogany-and-marble stable, reached by a long, underground passage; and the extensive, 5-acre estate gardens (open May–October). The rooms are copies of those in English, Spanish, Scottish, and Austrian castles. This has been the location for many a horror movie and period drama, an episode of the BBC's *Antiques Roadshow*, and several Hollywood blockbusters, including *Chicago* and *X-Men*. Included in the admission price are a self-guided audio tour (available in eight languages) and a docudrama about Pellatt's life. **TIP→ A tour of Casa Loma is a good 1½-km (1-mile) walk, so wear sensible shoes.** And if you're traveling with young children, note strollers must be left on the first floor. ✉ *1 Austin Terr., The Annex* ☎ *416/923–1171* 🌐 *www.casaloma.org* 🎟 *C$20.55* ⏲ *Daily 9:30–5, last admission at 4* Ⓜ *Dupont.*

LITTLE ITALY

Once a quiet strip of College Street with just a few unfrequented clothing shops and the odd, obstinate pizzeria, Little Italy has become one of the hippest haunts in Toronto. This is the southern edge of the city's Italian community, and though not much remains of this heritage—most Italians now live in the suburbs and throughout the city—the flavor lingers on many a table and in a few food markets.

Whether you're in the mood for old-school Italian trattorias (think checkered tablecloths) or polished martini bars, Little Italy won't disappoint. Pasta and pizza aren't the only things on the menus here—new ethnic restaurants open monthly, and every corner holds fashionable cafés and diners to match.

Surprisingly, this edge of downtown has a nightlife that rivals the clubs and bars of the Entertainment District (around Adelaide Street West). Bars and coffeehouses are busy into the night, and summer months bring out booming cruise-mobiles, patio revelers, and plenty of pedestrian animation.

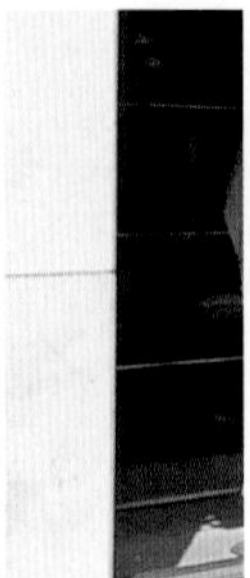

YORKVILLE, CHURCH-WELLESLEY, AND ROSEDALE

Yorkville and Church-Wellesley may be stacked together, but their personalities are quite different. Yorkville whispers a tony elegance, where as Church-Wellesley is a casual, out-and-proud LGBT community. Farther northeast, Rosedale is a place to window-shop for fantasy Victorian houses.

YORKVILLE

Toronto's equivalent to Fifth Avenue or Rodeo Drive, Yorkville, and Bloor Street in particular, is a dazzling spread of high-price stores stocked with designer clothes, furs, and jewels along with restaurants, galleries, and specialty boutiques. It's also where much of the excitement takes place in September during the annual Toronto International Film Festival, reportedly the world's largest and most people-friendly film festival, where the public actually gets to see premieres and hidden gems and attend industry seminars. Klieg lights shine over skyscrapers, bistros serve alcohol until 2 am, cafés teem with the well-heeled, and everyone practices air kisses. Yorkville is also home to a unique park on Cumberland Street, designed as a series of gardens along old property lines and reflecting both the history of the Village of Yorkville and the diversity of the Canadian landscape.

TOP ATTRACTIONS

FAMILY **Royal Ontario Museum.** Since its inception in 1912, the ROM, Canada's largest museum, has amassed more than 6 million items. What sets the ROM apart is that science, art, and archaeology exhibits are all appealingly presented in one gigantic complex. A C$200-million refurbishment project, envisioned by world-renowned architect Daniel Libeskind (the designer of the Jewish Museum in Berlin), added 40,000 square feet and the ultramodern **Michael Lee-Chin Crystal** gallery in 2009—a series of interlocking prismatic cubes spilling out onto Bloor Street.

George R. Gardiner Museum of Ceramic Art ...**2**

Royal Ontario Museum **1**

Toronto Reference Library **3**

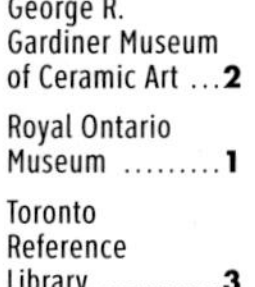

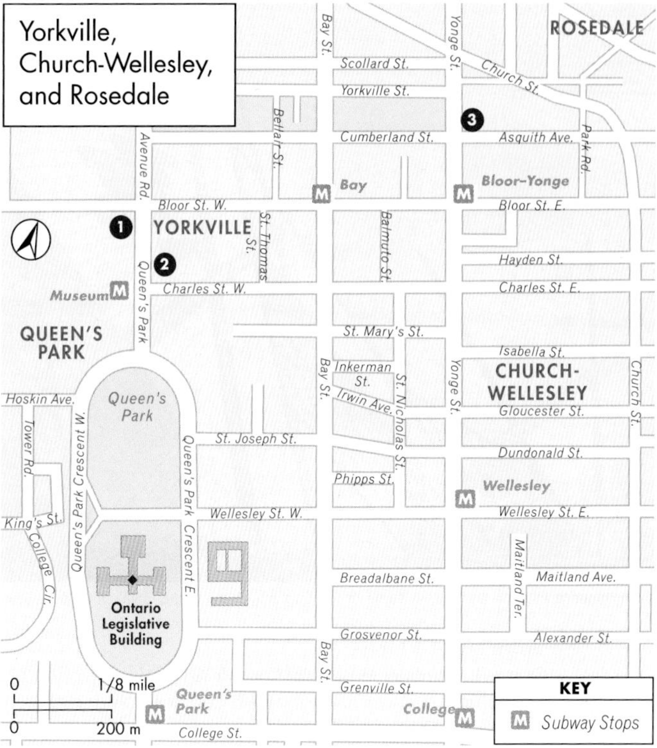

Highlights include the **Learning Centre**—a state-of-the-art educational facility for the 220,000 schoolchildren expected annually—and the **Crystal Court,** a four-story atrium slashed on all sides by sliver-thin windows through which light pours into the open space. A look through the windows reveals parts of the treasures inside, such as the frightful creatures from the **Age of Dinosaurs** exhibit standing guard. The **ROM Contemporary Culture** hangs 110 feet over Bloor Street from its fourth-floor perch. The **Crystal Five Bistro,** "C5" for short, on the fifth floor feels a bit like the lounge on Star Trek's Enterprise, and turns out a selection of perfectly presented tapas and the region's finest wines.

The **Daphne Cockwell Gallery of Canada** exhibits an impressive range of First Peoples historical objects and artifacts, from pre-colonial time to the present. The **Chinese Sculpture Gallery** in the Matthews Family Court displays 25 stone Buddhist sculptures dating from the 2nd through 16th centuries; and the **Gallery of Korea** is North America's largest permanent gallery devoted to Korean art and culture. The **Sir Christopher Ondaatje South Asian Gallery** houses the best objects of a 7,000-piece collection that spans 5,000 years, from Bangladesh, Bhutan, India, the Maldives, Nepal, Pakistan, Sri Lanka, and Tibet. ✉ *100 Queen's Park, Yorkville* ☎ *416/586–8000* 🌐 *www.rom.on.ca* 🎟 *C$16; C$10 Fri. 4:30–8:30* ⏲ *Mon.–Thurs. and weekends 10–5:30, Fri. 10–8:30* Ⓜ *Museum.*

A striking modern addition showcases some of the 6 million items in the Royal Ontario Museum's collection.

WORTH NOTING

George R. Gardiner Museum of Ceramic Art. This collection of rare ceramics includes 17th-century English delftware and 18th-century yellow European porcelain; its pre-Columbian collection dates to Olmec and Maya times. Other galleries feature Japanese Kakiemon-style pottery and Chinese white-and-blue porcelain. If your visit coincides with lunchtime, hit the Gardiner Bistro for light dishes like West Coast salmon with local greens. Free guided tours take place at 2 pm daily; or you can join a drop-in session in the clay studio (*Wed. and Fri. 6–8 pm; Sun. 1–3 pm* *C$15*). **TIP→ Admission is half-price on Friday after 4 (or free on the third Friday of every month after 4).** *111 Queen's Park Crescent, Yorkville* *416/586–8080, 416/362–1957 Restaurant reservations* *www.gardinermuseum.on.ca* *C$12* *Mon.–Thurs. 10–6, Fri. 10–9, weekends 10–5* *Museum.*

Toronto Reference Library. Designed by one of Canada's most admired architects, Raymond Moriyama, who also created the Ontario Science Centre, this five-story library is arranged around a large atrium, affording a wonderful sense of open space. There is a small waterfall in the foyer, and glass-enclosed elevators glide swiftly and silently up and down. One-third of the more than 4 million items—spread across 45 km (28 miles) of shelves—are open to the public. Audio carrels are available for listening to nearly 30,000 music and spoken-word recordings. The largest Performing Arts Centre in a public library in Canada is on the fifth floor; the **Arthur Conan Doyle Room** (*Tues., Thurs., and Sat. 2–4, and by appointment*), which is of special interest to Baker Street regulars, is on the fifth floor. It houses the world's finest public collection of Holmesiana, including records, films, photos, books, manuscripts, letters, and even cartoon books starring Sherlock Hemlock of *Sesame Street.* ✉ *789 Yonge St., Yorkville* ☎ *416/395–5577* 🌐 *www.torontopubliclibrary.ca* ⏲ *Mon.–Thurs. 9:30–8:30, Fri. and Sat. 9:30–5:30, Sun. 1:30–5 (Sept.–June only)* Ⓜ *Bloor-Yonge.*

CHURCH-WELLESLEY

Colorful rainbow flags fly high and proud in this vibrant neighborhood, a little east of downtown. The area is energetic and boisterous any time of year, but absolutely frenetic during the annual Pride festival and parade in June. Given its long history, the area has evolved into a tight-knit, well-established community, with pharmacies, grocery stores, and dry cleaners rubbing shoulders with a mix of new and decades-old gay- and lesbian-centric nightspots.

ROSEDALE

This posh residential neighborhood northeast of Yorkville has tree-lined curving roads (it's one of the few neighborhoods to have escaped the city's grid pattern), many small parks, and a jumble of oversized late-19th-century and early-20th-century houses in Edwardian, Victorian, Georgian, and Tudor styles. An intricate ravine system weaves through this picturesque corner of downtown, its woodsy contours lined with old-money and old-world majesty. The neighborhood is bounded by Yonge Street, Don Valley Parkway, St. Clair Avenue, and Rosedale Ravine.

DID YOU KNOW?

A statue of Sir John A. Macdonald, Canada's first prime minister, presides over the grounds of the Ontario Legislative Building. You can take tours of the pink sandstone building and observe the provincial parliament in session.

2

GREATER TORONTO

Toronto's wealth of diverse neighborhoods and fascinating attractions cater to most tastes, but explore beyond downtown to find the ethnic enclaves, parks, museums, and attractions that make the Greater Toronto Area even more intriguing. Most of these must-sees are accessible by public transportation, although a car would make the journey to some of the more far-flung destinations more convenient.

GETTING HERE

High Park is on the subway line. Buses run from various downtown subway stations to Edwards Gardens, the Ontario Science Centre, the Toronto Zoo, and Black Creek Pioneer Village. You'll need a car to visit the Kortright Centre for Conservation and the McMichael Canadian Art Collection. A special GO Transit bus serves Canada's Wonderland in summer.

TIMING

You can explore each Greater Toronto sight independently or combine a couple of sights in one trip. The Ontario Science Centre and Edwards Gardens are very close together, for example, and would make a manageable day trip; and, if you're driving from the city, you could visit Black Creek Pioneer Village and the Kortright Centre for Conservation on the way to the McMichael Canadian Art Collection.

BLOOR WEST VILLAGE

TOP ATTRACTIONS

FAMILY **High Park.** One of North America's loveliest parks, High Park (at one time the privately owned countryside "farm" of John George Howard, Toronto's first city architect) is especially worth visiting in summer, when the many special events include professionally staged Shakespeare productions. Hundreds of Torontonians and guests arrive

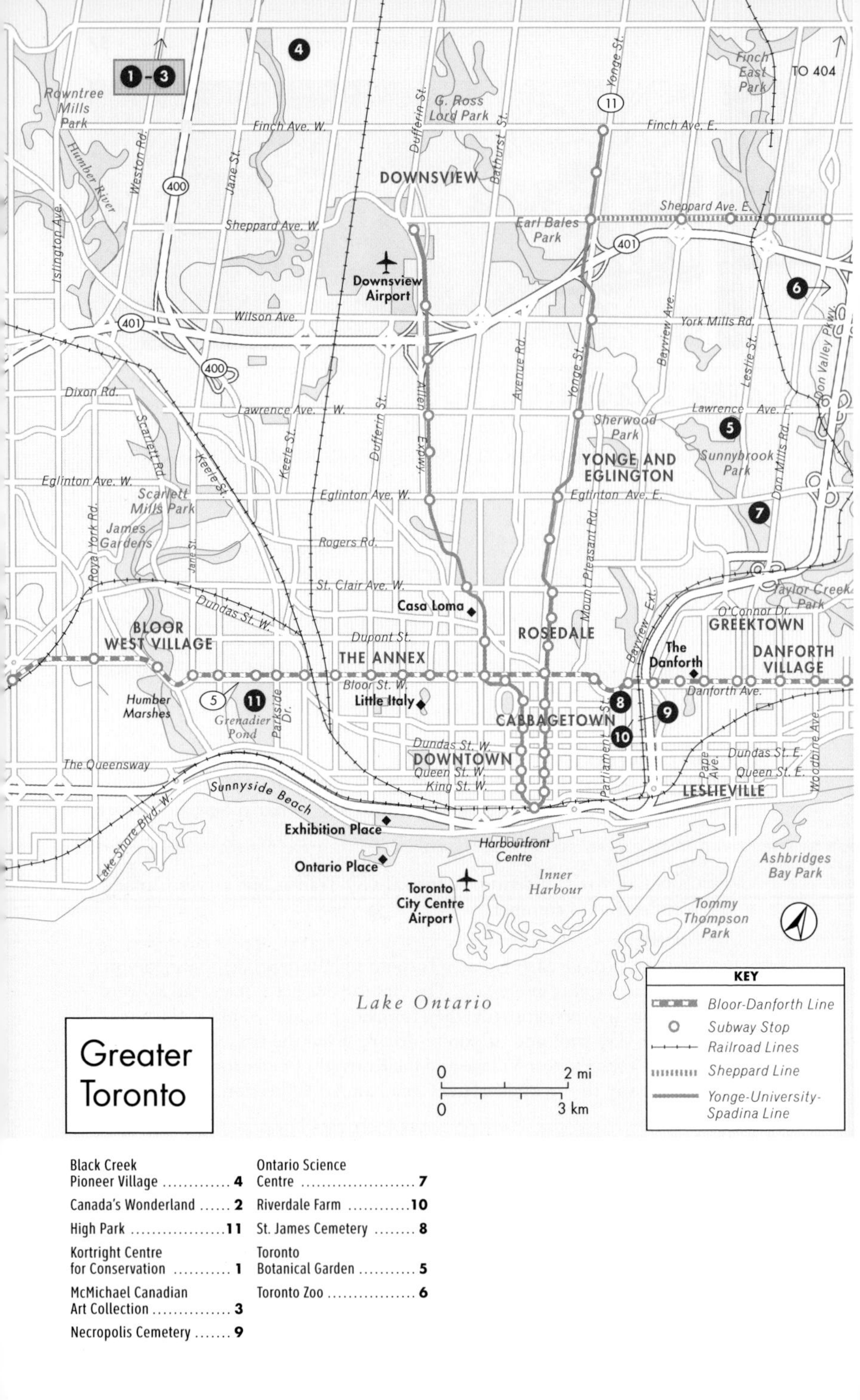

Black Creek Pioneer Village 4
Canada's Wonderland 2
High Park 11
Kortright Centre for Conservation 1
McMichael Canadian Art Collection 3
Necropolis Cemetery 9
Ontario Science Centre 7
Riverdale Farm 10
St. James Cemetery 8
Toronto Botanical Garden 5
Toronto Zoo 6

at dinnertime and picnic on blankets before the show. Admission is by donation. **Grenadier Pond** in the southwest corner of the park is named after the British soldiers who, it's said, crashed through the soft ice while rushing to defend the town against invading American forces in 1813. In summer there are concerts on Sunday afternoons, and there is skating in winter. At the south end of High Park, near Colborne Lodge, is the **High Park Zoo**, which is open daily from dawn to dusk. It's more modest than the Toronto Zoo but a lot closer to downtown and free. Even young children won't tire walking among the deer, Barbary sheep, emus, yaks, llamas, peacocks, and buffalo. **Colborne Lodge** (☎ *416/392–6916* *C$7* ⏲ *Jan.–Apr., Fri.–Sun. noon–4; May–Aug., Tues.–Sun. noon–5; Sept., weekends noon–5; Oct.–Dec., Tues.–Sun. noon–4*) was built more than 150 years ago by Howard on a hill overlooking Lake Ontario. This Regency-style "cottage" contains its original fireplace, bake oven, and kitchen, as well as many of Howard's drawings and paintings. Other highlights of the 398-acre park are a large swimming pool, tennis courts, fitness trails, and hillside gardens with roses and sculpted hedges. There's limited parking along Bloor Street north of the park, and along the side streets on the eastern side. **TIP→ June through August, on the first and third Sundays, free 1.5-hour walking tours depart across the street from Grenadier Restaurant.** ✉ *Bordered by Bloor St. W, Gardiner Expressway, Parkside Dr., and Ellis Park Rd. Main entrance off Bloor St. W at High Park Ave., Bloor West Village* ☎ *416/392–1748 walking tours* Ⓜ *High Park.*

CABBAGETOWN

TOP ATTRACTIONS

Riverdale Farm. This spot once hosted the city's main zoo, but it's now home to a rural community representative of a late-19th-century farm. Permanent residents include Clydesdale horses, cows, sheep, goats, pigs, donkeys, ducks, geese, chickens, and a small assortment of other domestic animals. While it's not a petting zoo per se, kids get a real kick out of watching farmers go about their daily chores which include feeding animals, cleaning the grounds, and bathing the animals. The playground adjacent to the farm has a wading pool. On Tuesdays (3–7 pm) from mid-May to late October, there's a great farmers' market on the grounds. ✉ *201 Winchester St., Cabbagetown* ☎ *416/392–6794* *Free* ⏲ *Daily 9–5.*

WORTH NOTING

Necropolis Cemetery. This nonsectarian burial ground, established in 1850, is the final resting place for many of Toronto's pioneers, including William Lyon Mackenzie, Toronto's first mayor. The cemetery's chapel, gate, and gatehouse date from 1872; the buildings constitute one of the most attractive groupings of small Victorian-era structures in Toronto. ✉ *200 Winchester St., Cabbagetown* ⏲ *Apr.–Sept. 8–8, Oct.–Mar. 8–5:30.*

St. James Cemetery. At the northeast corner of Parliament and Wellesley streets, this cemetery contains interesting burial monuments, including the small yellow-brick Gothic Chapel of St. James-the-Less with a handsome spire rising from the church nave. Built between 1859 and 1860, it's still considered one of the most beautiful church buildings in the country. ✉ *635 Parliament St., Cabbagetown* ⏲ *Apr.–Sept. 8–8, Oct.–Mar. 8–5:30.*

NORTH TORONTO

TOP ATTRACTIONS

FAMILY **Ontario Science Centre.** It has been called a museum of the 21st century, but it's much more than that. Where else can you stand at the edge of a black hole, work hand-in-clamp with a robot, or land on the moon? Even the building itself is extraordinary: three linked pavilions float gracefully down the side of a ravine and overflow with exhibits that make space, technology, and communications fascinating. The 25,000-square-foot Weston Family Innovation Centre, rife with hands-on activities, is all about experience and problem solving. Make a music soundtrack, take a lie-detector test, and measure fluctuations in your body chemistry as you flirt with a virtual celebrity.Younger visitors learn through play in KidSpark, a space specially designed for children eight and under to enjoy and explore. The CA Technologies Planetarium, Toronto's only public planetarium, uses state-of-the-art technology to take participants on a trip to the outer reaches of the universe. Demonstrations of glassblowing, papermaking, lasers, electricity, and more take place daily; check the schedule when you arrive. The museum has a cafeteria, a restaurant, and a gift store with a cornucopia of books and scientific doodads. ✉ *770 Don Mills Rd., at Eglinton Ave., North Toronto, North York* ☎ *416/696–1000* 🌐 *www.ontariosciencecentre.ca* 🎟 *C$22, parking C$10 (cash only)* ⏲ *Fri.–Wed. 10–5, Thurs. 10–8* Ⓜ *Eglinton, then No. 34 Eglinton East bus to Don Mills Rd. stop; then walk ½ block south.*

FAMILY **Toronto Botanical Garden and Edwards Gardens.** The beautiful 17 contemporary botanical garden areas and adjacent estate garden (once owned by industrialist Rupert Edwards) flow into one of the city's most visited ravines. Paths wind along colorful floral displays and exquisite rock gardens. Refreshments and picnic facilities are available, but no pets are allowed. There's also a signposted "teaching garden" for kids to touch and learn about nature. Free general tours between May and early September depart Tuesdays at 10 am or Thursday at 6 pm; additional guided tours (fee) can be arranged for small groups of seniors, children, ESL students, or adults with a special interest (history, econature, etc.). For a great ravine walk, start at the gardens' entrance and head south through Wilket Creek Park and the winding Don River valley. Pass beneath the Don Valley Parkway and continue along Massey Creek. After hours of walking (or biking or jogging) through almost uninterrupted park, you reach the southern tip of Taylor Creek Park on Victoria Park Avenue, just north of the Danforth. From here you can catch a subway back to your hotel. ✉ *777 Lawrence Ave. E, entrance at southwest corner of Leslie St. and Lawrence Ave. E,*

The futuristic Ontario Science Centre engages visitors of all ages with hands-on exhibits and workshops.

North Toronto, North York ☎ *416/397–1340, 416/397–1366 tours* 🌐 *www.torontobotanicalgarden.ca* ⏲ *Daily dawn–dusk* Ⓜ *Eglinton, then bus 54 or 54A.*

OUTLYING SUBURBS

TOP ATTRACTIONS

FAMILY **Canada's Wonderland.** Yogi Bear, Fred Flintstone, and Scooby Doo are part of Canada's first theme park, filled with more than 200 games, rides, restaurants, and shops. Favorite attractions include KidZville, home of the Nickelodeon cartoon characters, the Rugrats; the Sky-Rider stand-up looping inverted roller coaster; and Windseeker, which features thirty-two 301-foot swings. At Planet Snoopy, nine rides star *Peanuts* characters Charlie Brown, Snoopy, Lucy, and Linus. The Whitewater Bay wave pool, the Black Hole waterslide, and a children's interactive water-play area are all a part of Splash Works, the 20-acre on-site water park. Look for the strolling *Star Trek* characters and the Fun Shoppe, arcade, miniature golf, and batting cages. Other entertainment includes concerts, musicals, light shows, fireworks, and cliff divers. Check newspapers, chain stores, and hotels for discount coupons. **TIP→ The park is about 30 minutes north of downtown Toronto by car or via the "Wonderland Express" GO Bus from the Yorkdale and York Mills subway stations.** ✉ *9580 Jane St., Outlying Suburbs, Vaughan* ☎ *905/832–7000, 905/832–8131 Kingswood Theatre tickets* 🌐 *www.canadaswonderland.com* 🎟 *C$47* ⏲ *Late May–June, weekdays 10–6, Sat. 10–10, Sun. 10–8; late June–Aug., daily 10–10; Sept., weekends 10–8; Oct., weekends 10–5.*

McMichael Canadian Art Collection. On 100 acres of lovely woodland in Kleinburg, 30 km (19 miles) northwest of downtown, the McMichael is the only major gallery in the country with the mandate to collect Canadian art exclusively. The museum holds impressive works by Tom Thomson, Emily Carr, and the Group of Seven landscape painters, as well as their early-20th-century contemporaries. These artists were inspired by the wilderness and sought to capture it in bold, original styles. First Nations art and prints, drawings, and sculpture by Inuit artists are well represented. Strategically placed windows help you appreciate the scenery as you view art that took its inspiration from the vast outdoors. Inside, wood walls and a fireplace set a country mood. Free guided tours take place every Saturday and Sunday at 12:30 (museum) and 2 (special exhibits). ✉ *10365 Islington Ave., west of Hwy. 400 and north of Major Mackenzie Dr., Outlying Suburbs, Kleinburg* ☎ *888/213–1121, 905/893–1121* 🌐 *www.mcmichael.com* 🎟 *C$15, parking C$5* ⏲ *Daily 10–5.*

FAMILY **Toronto Zoo.** With its varied terrain, from river valley to dense forest, the Rouge Valley was an inspired choice of site for this 710-acre zoo in which mammals, birds, reptiles, and fish are grouped according to their natural habitats. Enclosed, climate-controlled pavilions have botanical exhibits, such as the Africa pavilion's giant baobab tree. Look over an Events Guide, distributed at the main entrance, to help plan your day; activities might include chats with animal keepers and animal and bird demonstrations. An "Around the World Tour" takes approximately three hours and includes the Africa, Americas, Australasia, Indo-Malayan, and "Canadian Domain" pavilions. From late April through early September, the Zoomobile can take you through the outdoor exhibit area.

From 2013 until 2018, Er Shun and Da Mao, a pair of Chinese pandas, will call the Toronto Zoo their home. Should there be any offspring during their stay, the zoo will adopt the babies until they're old enough to leave their birth home. In addition to viewing the couple up close, the brand-new Panda Interpretive Centre is also worth exploring.

The African Savanna is the country's finest walking safari, a dynamic reproduction that brings rare and beautiful animals and distinctive geological landscapes to the city's doorstep. You can also dine in the Savanna's Safari Lodge and camp overnight in the Serengeti Bush Camp (reservations required). The zoo is a 30-minute drive east from downtown. ✉ *Meadowvale Rd., Exit 389 off Hwy. 401, Outlying Suburbs, Scarborough* ☎ *416/392–5929, 416/392–5947 for camping reservations* 🌐 *www.torontozoo.com* 🎟 *C$28, parking C$10* ⏲ *May–Aug., daily 9–7; Sept. and Oct. daily 9–6; Nov.–Apr. daily 9:30–4:30* Ⓜ *Kennedy, then bus 86A or Don Mills, then bus 85.*

WORTH NOTING

FAMILY **Black Creek Pioneer Village.** Less than a half-hour drive from downtown is a rural, mid-19th-century living-history-museum village that makes you feel as though you've gone through a time warp. Black Creek Pioneer Village is a collection of 40 buildings from the 19th and early-20th centuries, including a town hall, a weaver's shop, a printing shop, a blacksmith's shop, and a school complete with a dunce cap. The mill dates from the 1840s and has a 4-ton wooden waterwheel that grinds up to a hundred barrels of flour a day (bags are available for purchase).

As men and women in period costumes go about the daily routine of mid-19th-century Ontario life, they explain what they're doing and answer questions. Visitors can see farm animals; take free wagon rides, Victorian dance classes, and 19th-century baseball lessons; and explore a hands-on discovery center. There's a great brewery-restaurant for lunch or afternoon tea (reservation required). In winter you can also skate, toboggan, or hop on a sleigh ride. ✉ *1000 Murray Ross Pkwy., near the intersection of Jane St. and Steeles Ave., Outlying Suburbs, North York* ☎ *416/736–1733* 🌐 *www.blackcreek.ca* 🎫 *C$15, parking C$7* ⏲ *May and June, weekdays 9:30–4, weekends 11–5; July and Aug., weekdays 10–5, weekends 11–5; Sept.–Dec., weekdays 9:30–4, weekends 11–4:30* Ⓜ *Finch, then bus 60 west or Jane, then bus 35.*

Kortright Centre for Conservation. Only 15 minutes north of the city, this delightful conservation center has three aquariums, more than 16 km (10 miles) of hiking trails through forest, meadow, river, and marshland, and a renewable-energy cottage that demonstrates what life would be like off the grid (interior tours first Saturday of every month at 11:30, 1:30, and 3 from February to October). In winter some of the trails are reserved for cross-country skiing (C$18 to use the trail; equipment rentals available). In the magnificent woods there have been sightings of foxes, coyotes, rabbits, deer, wild turkeys, pheasants, chickadees, finches, and blue jays. Seasonal events include a dogsled race, a spring maple-syrup festival, and a Christmas crafts fair. Nature day camps and day-long energy conservation workshops are offered throughout the year for an extra fee. To get here, drive 3 km (2 miles) north along Highway 400, exit west at Major Mackenzie Drive, and continue south 1 km (½ mile) on Pine Valley Drive to the gate. ✉ *9550 Pine Valley Dr., Outlying Suburbs, Woodbridge* ☎ *905/832–2289, 416/667–6295 for workshops and camps* 🌐 *www.kortright.org* 🎫 *C$6.50, special events C$10, parking C$4 (weekends only)* ⏲ *Daily 10–4:30.*

3

WHERE TO EAT

Updated by Yvonne Tsui

Toronto's calling card—its ethnic diversity—offers up a potent mix of cuisines. But with that base, the city's chefs are now pushing into new territory. Gone are the days of chefs gunning for white linen tablecloths; now pop-up vendors such as Fidel Gastro's Lisa Marie and Seven Lives Tacos Y Mariscos draw a cult following big enough to open up brick-and-mortar locations.

And it's not enough to have consistently good food: kitchens are pushed to be creative and embrace food trends. Spanish tapas and Korean fusion have replaced French and Thai as the newest crazes in the city and izakayas are out while ramen is in. Farm-to-table shows no sign of slowing down, with many menus citing the source of their meats and produce. While Toronto is still young as a foodie travel destination, it's drawing in the crowds, or at a minimum world-famous chefs such as Daniel Boulud and David Chang, who have landed in Toronto with Café Boulud and Momofuku. And as locals will tell you, first come the chefs, then come the savvy foodie travelers, always posting a tweet or photo to Instagram at the city's newest hot spots.

PLANNER

With new restaurants and shops opening up farther away from the downtown core, tourists have a lot more area to cover. We make it easy by sorting restaurants by price, cuisine, and neighborhood. Search our "Best Bets" chart for top recommendations. But good eats aren't limited to the city core. *For recommended restaurants in the Greater Toronto Area, refer to the Greater Toronto section near the end of the chapter.*

DISCOUNTS

For 2½ weeks between January and February, more than 100 of the city's best restaurants offer the **Winterlicious** Program, where a fixed-price, three-course lunch is C$15 to C$25, and dinner is C$25 to C$40, and the regular menu is still served. Similarly, **Summerlicious** runs for around two weeks in July. For more details, see 🌐 *www.toronto.ca/special_events*.

THE ANNEX
Cheap eats, great ethnic food
YORKVILLE
Discerning tastes for heavy wallets
DANFORTH
Traditional Greek fare
LITTLE ITALY
From red-sauce joints to sleek and modern
CHINATOWN AND KENSINGTON MARKET
Noodle shops and hippie havens
DUNDAS SQUARE AREA
Flashy chains and sporty bars
QUEEN WEST
Funky and bohemian eateries with an ethnic edge
OSSINGTON
Up-and-coming casual spots
ENTERTAINMENT DISTRICT
Trendy and hip, bustling at night
FINANCIAL DISTRICT AND HARBOURFRONT
High end business dining: steak houses to take-out sushi
QUEEN'S PARK
University of Toronto
Ontario Legislative Building
Toronto Coach Terminal
City Hall
Nathan Phillips Square
Grange Park
Queen's Park
King's College Cir.
St. George
Museum
Bay
Bloor-Yonge
Wellesley
College
Queen's Park
St. Patrick
Dundas
Queen
Osgoode
Union
Bloor St. W.
Cumberland St.
Charles St. E.
Madison Ave.
Sussex Ave.
Avenue Rd.
Hoskin Ave.
St. Joseph St.
Wellesley St. W.
Maitland Ave.
Willcocks St.
Grosvenor St.
Alexander St.
Grenville St.
College St.
Carlton St.
Gerrard St. W.
Cecil St.
Baldwin St.
D'Arcy St.
Elm St.
Gould St.
Edward St.
Dundas St. W.
Dundas St. E.
Sullivan St.
Shuter St.
Renfrew Pl.
Pullan Pl.
Queen St. W.
Queen St. E.
Nelson St.
Richmond St. E.
Adelaide St. E.
Pearl St.
King St. W.
King St. E.
Wellington St. W.
Front St. W.
Gardiner Expy.
Bremner Blvd.
Lake Shore Blvd. E.
Harbour St.
Queens Quay W.
Queens Quay E.
Borden St.
Brunswick Ave.
Major St.
Huron St.
St. George St.
Queen's Park Cir. W.
Queen's Park Cir. E.
Bay St.
Yonge St.
Church St.
Jarvis St.
Bellevue Ave.
Spadina Ave.
Beverley St.
Henry St.
University Ave.
Elizabeth St.
McCaul St.
Chestnut St.
St. Patrick St.
Simcoe St.
Augusta Ave.
Soho St.
Victoria St.
Mutual St.
Peter St.
Widmer St.
John St.
Duncan St.
York St.
0
1/4 mile
0
400 meters

DRESS

With the exception of high-end restaurants, the dining atmosphere in Toronto is generally cool and relaxed, with patrons donning trendy and polished attire. In the more elegant and upscale restaurants, or around the Financial District, men are likely to feel more comfortable wearing a jacket. Conversely, in the Kensington Market area, casual comfort is the style of choice. In the aggressively air-conditioned summer months, women are advised to bring a light sweater or jacket when heading out, especially in the evening. We mention dress only when men are required to wear a jacket or a jacket and tie.

FOODIE FESTIVALS

Because of long winters, weekends in the summer are celebrated to their fullest. What better way than food festivals to showcase Canadian culture?

The annual **Taste of the Danforth Festival** celebrates the mouthwatering diversity of the city as it welcomes millions to the Danforth strip each August. 🌐 *www.tasteofthedanforth.com.*

Taste of Little Italy. A smaller event when compared to the Danforth Festival, Taste of Little Italy takes place in June on College Street, where Italian-centric cuisine and live music are celebrated. 🌐 *www.tasteoflittleitaly.ca.*

MEALTIMES

Lunch typically starts at 11:30 or noon, and dinner service begins around 5:30 or 6. Many restaurants close between lunch and dinner (roughly 2:30 to 5:30). On weekdays, kitchens usually close around 10:30 pm. Chinatown, Yorkville, and Danforth have some late-night spots. There are few all-night restaurants in the city. Unless otherwise noted, the restaurants listed in this guide are open daily for lunch and dinner. *In the Exploring chapter, look for "Quick Bites" places—perfect for a snack while sightseeing.*

ORIENTATION

Throughout the chapter, you'll see mapping symbols and coordinates (✣ 1:F2) after property names or reviews. To locate the property on a map, turn to the Toronto Dining maps within this chapter. The first number after the ✣ symbol indicates the map number. Following that are the property's coordinates on the map grid.

RESERVATIONS

Reservations are always a good idea; we mention them only when they're essential or not accepted. Book as far ahead as you can. (Large parties should always call to check the reservations policy.) Many restaurants have lounges and sections for walk-ins only.

SMOKING

Toronto restaurants prohibit smoking, including areas outdoors under an awning or overhang. Some let diners get away with smoking in open-air outdoor dining areas.

TIPPING AND TAXES

There is no hard and fast rule when it comes to tipping; it is optional but customary, and some restaurants include gratuities on the bill for parties of six or more. It's common to leave 15%–20% for standard or good service and 20% or more for exceptional service. If you have brought your own wine or cake for a special occasion, it's proper etiquette to tip more for the extra service. The percentage of tips is generally calculated on the subtotal. Goods and Services Tax and Provincial Sales Tax were combined into the Harmonized Sales Tax of 13%, meaning the tax on alcohol was lowered, and food and alcohol are no longer taxed separately.

WHAT IT COSTS

Credit cards are widely accepted in Toronto restaurants though some may accept only MasterCard and Visa. Cafés and burger joints may accept debit cards as well.

Prices in the reviews are the average cost of a main course at dinner or, if dinner is not served, at lunch.

RESTAURANT REVIEWS

Listed alphabetically within neighborhoods.

HARBOURFRONT, ENTERTAINMENT DISTRICT, THE FINANCIAL DISTRICT

It skirts a serene Lake Ontario, yet is the engine that drives the city. The area is one of historic marvels like St. Lawrence Market, tourist hot spots ranging from the Hockey Hall of Fame to the Princess of Wales Theater, and a lovely waterfront for biking or a stroll. It's also home to a jumble of glassy 50-story skyscrapers and the business types that fill them. Little wonder, then, that from steak houses to take-out sushi, you'll find it here.

HARBOURFRONT

The vibe here is decidedly beachy: Take a stroll along the lake stopping by for a lunch on breezy patios. If you brought your bathing suit, head to Sugar Beach—an urban oasis where locals sunbathe. Or work off that lunch by renting one of the city's Bixi bikes and pedal around, until you're ready for dinner.

$$$ CANADIAN

Against the Grain Urban Tavern. With one of the city's best patios, Against the Grain overlooks the water and is steps away from Cherry Beach, a sandy oasis where locals go to sunbathe without leaving downtown's core. The menu capitalizes on this relaxed, beachy vibe by focusing on shared plates, which makes for groups of friends. Dishes such as chicken wings and lobster tacos offer comforting classics while the pan-seared Cornish hen with corn, grape tomato, and edamame succotash veers off toward the adventurous. **TIP→ Validate your parking if you park underground.** $ *Average main: C$21* ✉ *Corus Building, 25 Dockside Dr., Corus Building, Harbourfront* ☎ *647/344-1562* 🌐 *corusquay.atgurbantavern.ca* *Reservations essential* M *Union* ⊕ *2:C6.*

BEST BETS FOR TORONTO DINING

Where can I find the best food the city has to offer? Fodor's writers and editors have selected their favorite restaurants by price, cuisine, and experience *in the lists below*. In the first column, the Fodor's Choice properties represent the "best of the best" across price categories. You can also search by area—just peruse our complete reviews on the following pages.

Fodor's Choice ★

By Price

$

$$

$$$

$$$$

By Cuisine

CHINESE

FRENCH

ITALIAN

MODERN CANADIAN

By Experience

CELEB-SPOTTING

CHILD-FRIENDLY

MOST ROMANTIC

$$$ AMERICAN **E11even.** A New York–style restaurant of wooden tables and booths, E11even serves well-executed dishes from its predominantly American menu. The doubled-cut bacon with maple sherry glaze is an excellent example of sweet and savory, and the dry-aged rib eye is a model piece of steak that's both tender and flavorful. Wine choices are presented on an iPad, where a full description of the characteristics of each option is given. *Average main: C$30 15 York St., Harbourfront 416/815–1111 www.e11even.ca Closed Sun. 1:F6.*

$$$$ STEAKHOUSE **Harbour Sixty Steakhouse.** Bucking the trend toward relaxed fine dining, Harbour Sixty goes for sheer opulence, the drama of which is apparent from the get-go as you walk up stone steps to the grand entrance of the restored Harbour Commission building. A baroque-inspired foyer leads to a sleek marble bar. On the lower level is the wall-to-wall wine storage, which houses bottles from their 36-page wine list. But never fear, the kitchen's skills rise to the occasion with starters like the zesty shrimp cocktail. Bone-in rib steak is a specialty, and the fluffy and luscious coconut cream pie is a must-eat for dessert. The comfortable high-backed armchairs and spacious, curved booths are particularly hard to abandon after the tab is settled. *Average main: C$40 60 Harbour St., Harbourfront 416/777–2111 www.harboursixty.com No lunch Sat. or Sun. Union 1:F6.*

$$ AMERICAN **Real Sports Bar & Grill.** The larger-than-life giant screen at the Real Sports Bar is the next best thing to stadium seats. With several screens playing tennis, football, hockey, and baseball—there's sure to be a game for every sports fan. Of course, part of the thrill of being at a sports event is the food. And the saucy ribs and refreshing salads don't disappoint. If you're having trouble deciding on a burger, get the slider trio, featuring one of everything in bite-sized versions. And don't make it to the first commercial break without sampling the beer blends. *Average main: C$19 15 York St., Harbourfront 416/815-7325 www.realsports.ca Reservations essential Union 1:F6.*

ENTERTAINMENT DISTRICT

This neighborhood seems quiet, but comes to life at night and on weekends when women put on their little black dresses and men don their best button-ups. A row of nightclubs and bars beckon post-dinner. Or, for a more refined evening, catch a show at the theater or head over to the TIFF Bell Lightbox to see what's playing.

$$ INTERNATIONAL Fodor's Choice ★ **Beast.** Carnivores will revel in the full-on meat menu at Beast Restaurant where chef Scott Vivian serves up dishes such as succulent pork hocks with kimchi and candied peanuts or buttery marrow with parsley, horseradish, and house-made bread. The dining room's centaur paintings are a little odd, but the decor is secondary to what's on the plate: all sourced locally and made in-house. Brunch-goers can kick off their meal appropriately with maple-bacon donuts. And every Friday at noon "the Beastwich" take-out lunch special is served with a side and dessert for $10 cash. Get there on time; it sells out within the hour. *Average main: C$13 96 Tecumseth St., King West 647/352-6000 www.thebeastrestaurant.com Closed Mon. and Tues. No lunch Wed.–Fri. St. Andrew 1:C6.*

$$$ ITALIAN
Buca. Amidst an abundance of extremes in this neighborhood—stodgy pasta drowned in marinara or authentic dishes in superformal dining rooms—Buca is a refreshing alternative of rustic-yet-stylish Italian classics. Tucked into an alleyway just off King Street, the repurposed boiler room has exposed brick walls, metal columns, and wooden tables that reflect the natural philosophy behind the food by Chef Rob Gentile. Start with the selection of cured meats including *soppresata*, beef tongue and *n'duja* or *nodini*, warm bread knots seasoned with rosemary and sea salt. For a simple pasta, order the *lorghittas*, with olives, capers, anchovies, golden plums, tomato sauce, and *cacio di fossa* cheese. End your meal with an insanely luscious dessert, such as *panna cotta* made from buffalo mozzarella topped with candied pistachio and strawberry gellée. Wines are meticulously procured from Italy by the sommelier to complement the dishes. *Average main: C$23 ✉ 604 King St. W, Entertainment District ☎ 416/865–1600 ⊕ www.buca.ca ⊗ No lunch on weekends Ⓜ Osgoode ✢ 1:C6.*

$ MEXICAN Fodor's Choice ★
Burrito Boyz. One of the best places to stuff yourself silly, Burrito Boyz answers the call for rice-filled tortillas stuffed with succulent halibut or hearty steak at all hours. And vegetarians also have options, like soy or sweet potato. Pick your base and pile it on with some of the seventeen toppings. The casual eatery is always busy, but it's the most alive in the wee hours of the morning with the post-clubbing crowd looking to refuel and sleep soundly on a full stomach. It's not a bad approach: the burritos are so supersized, the second half can double as a late lunch. *Average main: C$7 ✉ 218 Adelaide St. W, Entertainment District ☎ 647/439-4065 ⊕ www.burritoboyz.ca Ⓜ St. Andrew ✢ 1:E6.*

$ CANADIAN
Cheesewerks. A tribute to all things fromage-focused, Cheesewerks is a comfort-food bonanza. Choose your carb (nachos, bread, macaroni, or quesadilla) and then top it with your favorite gooey combination. Those wanting something a little more upscale can indulge in a savory pot of fondue with artisan bread, roasted seasonal vegetables, and apples. And dessert doesn't stray from the theme with a decadent sweet grilled cheese: buttery bread stuffed with mascarpone and your choice of chocolate bar, topped with mixed fruit, and finally served up with maple syrup. This is a great place to hole up on a cold, wet day with one of the venue's board games. *Average main: C$10 ✉ 56 Bathurst St., King West ☎ 416/243-3327 ⊕ www.cheesewerks.com Reservations essential ⊗ Closed Mon. Ⓜ Union ✢ 1:C6.*

$$ EUROPEAN Fodor's Choice ★
Edulis. European-bistro-meets-local-forager, that's the theme at Edulis, a restaurant devoted to classic rustic dishes. Bentwood chairs, rough-hewn wood walls, and burlap breadbaskets evoke a farmhouse-like feel, and the soft lighting adds to the intimacy. Given the restaurant's name, a reference to edible mushrooms, you'll find all manner of fungi on the menu, from porcini to truffles. Savor intricate dishes such as truffle-poached lobster or roast duck breast in a wild cranberry mostarda. Gourmands can preorder entire lobes of foie gras, milk-fed piglet with perfectly crispy crackling, or succulent Chantecler chicken in hay. *Average main: C$18 ✉ 169 Niagara St., King West ☎ 416/703-4222 ⊕ www.edulisrestaurant.com Reservations essential ⊗ Closed Mon. and Tues. No lunch. Ⓜ St. Andrew ✢ 1:B6.*

$$$ FRENCH **The Fifth Grill.** Enter through the Easy Social Club, a main-floor dance club, and take a freight elevator to this semiprivate dining club and loft space with the right balance of formality and flirtation. The mood is industrial-strength romance. In winter, sit on a sofa in front of a huge fireplace; in summer, dine on the gazebo terrace. Entrées include a wide variety of steaks, butter-poached lobster, and rack of lamb with duck fat and garlic. Vegetarian offerings include the risotto of the day and roasted garlic gnocchi. *Average main: C$30 225 Richmond St. W, Entertainment District 416/979–3005 www.thefifthgrill.com Reservations essential Closed Sun.–Wed. No lunch M Osgoode 1:E5.*

$$ THAI Fodor's Choice ★ **Khao San Road.** Named for a street in Bangkok bursting with nightlife and excellent street eats, Khao San Road lives up to its moniker. Start with a refreshing Thai iced tea—a blend of Thai spices, black tea, and condensed milk could double as dessert. The garlic tofu might just be the vegetarian equivalent of chicken nuggets with a sweet-and-sour tamarind dip. For heartier dishes, opt for the *khao soi,* a dish of egg noodles in a rich coconut milk sauce; or try the warming *gaeng massaman,* a tamarind-infused curry with peanuts, potatoes, and deep-fried shallots. Ingredients are sourced directly from Thailand wherever possible—you couldn't get any closer to Khao San Road without heading to Pearson International Airport. *Average main: C$14 326 Adelaide St. W, Entertainment District 647/352-5773 www.khaosanroad.ca Reservations not accepted Closed Sun. M St. Andrew 1:E6.*

$$$ MODERN CANADIAN Fodor's Choice ★ **Luma.** Duck out of a double feature at the TIFF Bell Lightbox to grab a meal at Luma. Echoing the Lightbox's artistic nature, this restaurant plays with global flavors and mostly Canadian ingredients. Within the bustling glass-paneled film festival and film education venue, the restaurant is a mini oasis on the second floor complete with a patio overlooking the lively Entertainment District and the CN Tower. But the star attraction is Jason Bangerter's delectable dishes, and his commitment to sustainable seafood. Try the crispy calamari coated in rice puffs with candied lemon peel or roasted Vidalia onion salad with blue cheese and pine nuts, and finish on a sweet note with a cheesecake parfait of goat's cheese, lavender-infused filo pastry, and macerated strawberries. *Average main: C$28 330 King St. W, Entertainment District 647/288–4715 No lunch Sat. Closed Sun. 1:E6.*

$$ SEAFOOD **Rodney's Oyster House.** A den of oceanic delicacies, this playful basement raw bar is frequented by solo diners and showbiz types. Among the options are soft-shell steamer clams, a variety of smoked fish, and "Oyster Slapjack Chowder," plus Merigomish oysters from Novia Scotia or perfect Malpeques from owner Rodney Clark's own oyster beds on Prince Edward Island. A zap of Rodney's in-house line of condiments or a splash of vodka and freshly grated horseradish are eye-openers. **TIP→ Shared meals and half orders are okay. Be sure to ask about the daily "Grace's soup" and "white-plate" specials.** *Average main: C$20 469 King St. W, Entertainment District 416/363–8105 www.rodneysoysterhouse.com Closed Sun. M St. Andrew 1:D6.*

$$$$ MODERN CANADIAN

✕ **Toca.** The swanky Ritz Carlton dining experience comes to Toronto in the form of Toca. Here diners partake in dishes like smoked eggplant, salmon en papillote, and halibut fish croquettes with squid ink tempura, or homemade cavatelli pasta and well-aged steaks for the traditionalists. The dining room, a blend of tasteful beige and brown, has a curvaceous wood-beamed ceiling and a glass cheese cave. High rollers can sit at the chef's table, inside a private dining nook in the kitchen. **TIP→ Skip your hotel breakfast and come Sundays for the Market Brunch; a cold seafood station of oysters, shrimp, and lobster await, or sample a made-to-order omelet. Another enticement: it's all-you-can-drink mimosas and Bellinis.** $ *Average main: C$40* ✉ *181 Wellington St. W, Entertainment District* ☎ *416/585-2500* 🌐 *www.tocarestaurant.ca* ⏲ *No lunch Sat.* ✥ *1:F6.*

TORONTO'S POUTINE

A Québécois classic traditionally made from french fries, cheese curds, and gravy is getting dressed up and refined. Modern takes might include pulled pork and other meats, as well as different sauces and ethnic spices. Poutini (🌐 *www.poutini.com*) and Smoke's Poutinerie (🌐 *www.smokespoutinerie.com*) are restaurants dedicated to it. Caplansky's (🌐 *www.caplanskys.com*) makes the gravy with their famous smoked meat.

$$$ MODERN CANADIAN Fodor's Choice ★

Victor. Just off King Street in the boutique Hôtel Le Germain, Victor exudes an easy cool, with plate-glass walls, wood plank floors, and just the right amount of black leather. The kitchen also contributes to the hip factor, with former Top Chef Canada contestant David Chrystian at the helm. His Toronto Tasting menu is inspired by the city's various ethnic neighborhoods; order à la carte or indulge in the full seven-course tasting menu. Regular dishes do playful twists on international standards, like the sushi pizza with sashimi, lobster salad, and avocado. But if you just want to take in the buzzy atmosphere, swing by to enjoy a drink in the swanky lounge. $ *Average main: C$30* ✉ *Hôtel Le Germain Toronto, 30 Mercer St., Entertainment District* ☎ *416/883–3431* 🌐 *www.victorrestaurant.com* ⏲ *No lunch* ✥ *1:E6.*

$ GERMAN

✕ **WVRST.** You don't need to wait around until Oktoberfest to drink great German beer and indulge in delicious bratwurst; just walk into WVRST, a beer hall in King West. Choose from a selection of sausages, from the traditional pork to vegetarian, or get a little wild with selections such as pheasant, duck, or bison. And since you're already indulging, be sure to order a side of duck fat fries; they're double fried and delicious. Just leave the lederhosen at home. $ *Average main: C$7* ✉ *609 King St. W, King West* ☎ *416-703-7775* 🌐 *www.wvrst.com* Ⓜ *St. Andrew* ✥ *1:C6.*

$ THAI

✕ **Young Thailand.** Chef Wandee Young impressed Toronto's taste buds when she launched Canada's first Thai restaurant in 1980. Her gently spiced authentic staples are just as delicious now. Within the open dining room with white walls and black accents and small Thai decorations, you can order from a traditional menu of chicken satay with peanut sauce, Thai-spiced calamari with sweet chili, and refreshing salad rolls are a nice start. Move on to zingy lemon chicken soup and shared mains like green mango salad, red-curry beef, spicy basil chicken, and Thai-style eggplant. It's pretty hard to order wrong here. $ *Average main: C$12* ✉ *936 King St. W, King West* ☎ *416/366–8424* 🌐 *www.youngthailand.com* ⏲ *No lunch Sun.* Ⓜ *Dundas* ✣ *1:A6.*

THE FINANCIAL DISTRICT

As one of the city's major employment hubs and the center for business, The Financial District has no shortage of places to eat. Venues cater to all the worker bees, from the assistant out on an espresso run to the executives with large expense accounts. Luckily, these restaurants are also good bets for visitors, too.

$$ EUROPEAN

✕ **Beer Bistro.** A culinary tribute to beer, the creative menu here incorporates its star ingredient in every dish, but in subtle and clever ways without causing a malted-flavor overload. Start the hoppy journey with a Taster flight of three draft beers, chosen from almost 20 options, arranged from mild to bold. Follow that with a beer-bread pizza made with oatmeal stout; a mussel bowl, available in five different broths; pulled pork *Primanti* (sandwich); house-smoked pork, or Dragon Stout and Skor ice cream. The warm, modern interior includes a huge angled mirror on the wall above the kitchen, which allows a peek into the heart of the restaurant. The patio is a joy in summer. $ *Average main: C$19* ✉ *18 King St. E, Financial District* ☎ *416/861–9872* 🌐 *www.beerbistro.com* Ⓜ *King* ✣ *1:G6.*

$$$$ MODERN CANADIAN

✕ **Bymark.** Wood, glass, and water create drama in a space anchored by a 5,000-bottle wine "cellar" inside a two-story glass column. *Top Chef Canada* judge Mark McEwan has created a refined modern menu showcasing sophisticated seafood dishes, like brioche-crusted halibut, and simply prepared meats, like the signature 8-ounce burger with molten Brie de Meaux and grilled Porcini mushrooms. The glass-encased bar upstairs oozes extreme comfort and has a good view of architect Ludwig Mies van der Rohe's Toronto Dominion Centre Plaza. Bar dishes are as luxurious as they are casual, as exhibited by the shrimp tacos with citrus-spiked aioli. $ *Average main: C$40* ✉ *66 Wellington St. W, Concourse Level, Financial District* ☎ *416/777–1144* 🌐 *www.bymark.ca* ⏲ *Closed Sun.* Ⓜ *St. Andrew* ✣ *1:G6.*

$$$$ MODERN CANADIAN Fodor's Choice ★

✕ **Canoe.** Huge dining-room windows frame breathtaking views of the Toronto Islands and the lake at this restaurant, thanks to a location on the 54th floor of the Toronto Dominion Bank Tower. But once your food arrives, your focus will return to the plate. Begin with dishes like the Wellington County beef tartare with applewood-smoked bacon and pretzel toast. Entrées like smoked duck with mushrooms and foie gras nod to both tradition and trend. Classic Canadian desserts such as sticky toffee pudding and raisin butter tart round out the exceptional meal. **TIP→ Book a table at the chef's rail for a close-range perspective on the kitchen's artistry.** $ *Average main: C$44* ✉ *Toronto-Dominion Centre, 66 Wellington St. W, 54th fl., Financial District* ☎ *416/364–0054* 🌐 *www.oliverbonacini.com/ourrestaurants/canoe* ✍ *Reservations essential* ⏲ *Closed weekends* Ⓜ *King* ✣ *1:G6.*

CLOSE UP

Local Chains Worth a Taste

For those times when all you want is a quick bite, consider these local chains where you're assured of fresh, tasty food and good value.

Freshii: A healthier choice (formerly Lettuce Eatery) where baseball-capped salad artists get through the lunch rush like a championship team. The interior is all steely white and blond wood, and designer greens and custom-made sandwiches clearly appeal to the masses. The Cobb is a standout. 🌐 *www.freshii.com.*

Harvey's: Harvey's says it makes a hamburger a beautiful thing, and we agree—whether it's a beef, salmon, or veggie burger. Made-to-order toppings will please even the most discerning kids. The fries are a hit, too. 🌐 *www.harveys.ca.*

Lick's: Great Homeburgers and turkey burgers, plus the best veggie burger you'll ever taste. Onion rings, fresh fries, extra-thick milk shakes, and frozen yogurt will keep you coming back for more. 🌐 *www.lickshomeburgers.com.*

Milestones: Duck into the cool comfort of this very happening spot for Cajun popcorn shrimp or stone-oven pizza. Spit-roasted half chicken with curly fries and gloriously spicy corn-bread muffins may be the kitchen's best. 🌐 *www.milestonesrestaurants.com.*

Second Cup: You'll find coffees plain and fancy, as well as flavored hot chocolates, a variety of teas, Italian soft drinks, and nibbles that include muffins, bagels, and raspberry–white chocolate scones. 🌐 *www.secondcup.com.*

Spring Rolls: For Asian favorites on the fly: appealing soups and spiced salads, savory noodle dishes, and spring rolls all satiate lunchtime hunger pangs. 🌐 *www.springrolls.ca.*

Swiss Chalet Rotisserie and Grill: Children are welcome at this Canadian institution known for its rotisserie chicken and barbecued ribs, in portions that suit every family member. **TIP→ Ask for extra sauce for your french fries.** 🌐 *www.swisschalet.ca.*

Tim Horton's: It never closes, and coffee is made fresh every 20 minutes. Check out the variety of fresh donuts, muffins, bagels, and soup-and-sandwich combos. The Canadian Maple donut is an obvious front-runner. 🌐 *www.timhortons.com.*

$$$ SEAFOOD

The Chase. Located on the fifth floor of the historic Dineen Building and overlooking the Financial District, The Chase offers an excellent fine-dining balance of casual and refined. In good weather you can choose to sit on the rooftop patio, but those seated in the elegant Park Avenue–style dining room won't miss out; the marvelous Chambord-style lighting fixtures and the floor-to-ceiling windows provide an equally glamorous setting. The menu, composed of dishes meant for sharing, has a selection of fish flown in fresh daily. The crab *gnudi* is soft and delicate; the beef tartare is smooth and satisfying; and the lime meringue cake with coconut cream is a perfect ending paired with a bold espresso. **TIP→ For a relaxed take on The Chase, head downstairs to The Chase Fish & Oyster Bar and grab a drink and the daily shuck.** *Average main: C$21* ✉ *10 Temperance St., 5th fl, Financial District*

647/348-7000 www.thechasetoronto.com Reservations essential No lunch Sat. Closed Sun. King 1:G5.

$$$ INTERNATIONAL **Far Niente.** Classic fine dining gets a face-lift at this opulent, yet comfortable, New York–inspired restaurant. A mainstay since the '90s, Far Niente remains modern with oversized pendant lamp shades, soft lighting, circular banquettes, and a palate of black and camel. Chef Jordan St. Amand takes simple ingredients and creates luxurious inventions, like maple duck salad and seafood tagliatelle. The impressive global wine selection, with more than 4,400 bottles, ensures there's a glass for taste. *Average main: C$30 187 Bay St., Financial District 416/214–9922 www.farnienterestaurant.com Reservations essential Closed Sun. No lunch Sat. King 1:F6.*

3

$$ BRITISH **The Gabardine.** Cozy and unpretentious, this gastro-pub stands out from the other restaurants in the area that cater mostly to those with a corporate AmEx. An airy room of white walls, ceilings, and counters is the backdrop for pub classics like chicken liver pâté or salt cod fritters, but updated with gourmet touches like aioli and piri piri for the latter. Moist and juicy roasted brined pork with black-eyed pea ragout is comforting, as is the house-ground sirloin bacon cheeseburger with aioli. *Average main: C$20 372 Bay St., Financial District 647/352–3211 www.thegabardine.com Closed weekends 1:G5.*

$$$ AMERICAN **Reds Wine Tavern.** Repurposed wine bottles and glasses assembled as giant chandeliers hover above the tables at Reds Wine Tavern and offer a nod to chef Michael Hunter's modern tavern fare. The bustling ground-floor restaurant is the place to sample international picks from the broad wine list, and the charcuterie tasting plate. The menu specializes in shareable plates and fresh seafood. Indulge in a beef tartare (mixed tableside to your preferred level of spice); bite into a juicy cheeseburger with a duo of Morbier and fontina cheeses; and finish with decadent flourless chocolate cake. *Average main: C$28 77 Adelaide St. W, Financial District 416/862–7337 www.redswinetavern.com Closed Sun. No lunch Sat. King 1:F6.*

$$$ SEAFOOD Fodor's Choice ★ **Starfish.** Patrick McMurray—a walking encyclopedia of shellfish lore and winner of the 48th World Oyster Opening Championship in Galway, Ireland (won by shucking 30 oysters in under three minutes)—has curated the most unusual tastes from the sea here in the most diverse oyster bar in North America. Oysters from Ireland, England, Scotland, and North America are all available in this casual bistro with simple wooden tables and chairs and a maritime-themed bar. Ingredients used are local and sustainable, and the menu changes daily subject to whatever Mother Nature washes ashore. From the kitchen, a whole Atlantic lobster, European sea bream, crisp salads, and homemade desserts will make you fall for Starfish hook, line, and sinker. *Average main: C$25 100 Adelaide St. E, Financial District 416/366–7827 www.starfishoysterbed.com King 1:H6.*

$$ ITALIAN FAMILY **Terroni.** Open shelving lined with Italian provisions decorates this cool pizza joint, but it's the thin-crust pies, bubbled and blistered to perfection and the generous panini, that keep diners coming. The menu suits all pizza lovers—from the simple Margherita to the bombastic Polentona of tomato, mozzarella, fontina, speck (smoked prosciutto),

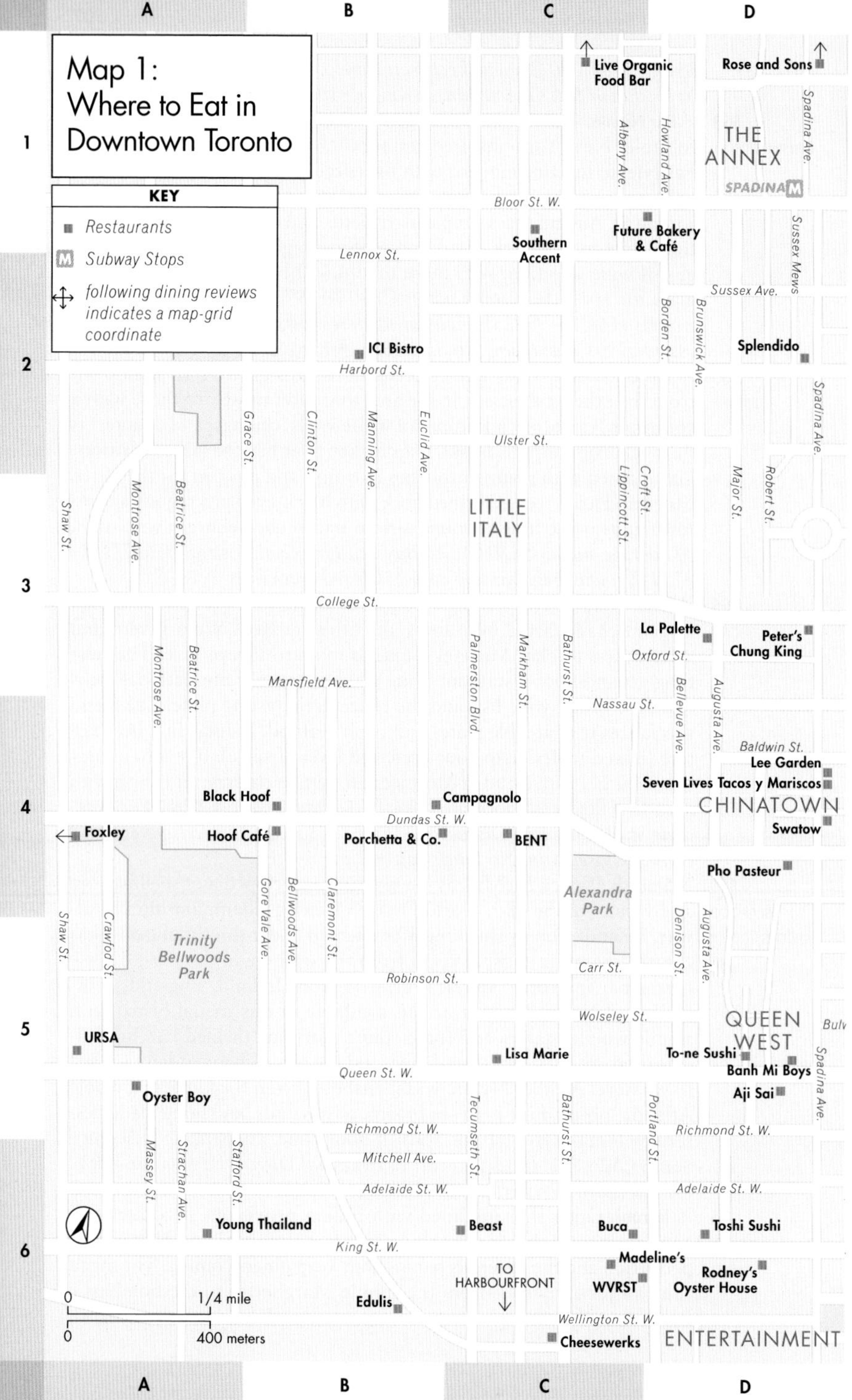

Map 1:
Where to Eat in
Downtown Toronto
KEY
Restaurants
Subway Stops
following dining reviews indicates a map-grid coordinate
A
B
C
D
1
2
3
4
5
6
Live Organic Food Bar
Rose and Sons
THE ANNEX
SPADINA
Albany Ave.
Howland Ave.
Spadina Ave.
Bloor St. W.
Southern Accent
Future Bakery & Café
Lennox St.
Sussex Ave.
Sussex Mews
Borden St.
Brunswick Ave.
ICI Bistro
Harbord St.
Splendido
Grace St.
Clinton St.
Manning Ave.
Euclid Ave.
Ulster St.
Lippincott St.
Croft St.
Major St.
Robert St.
Shaw St.
Montrose Ave.
Beatrice St.
LITTLE ITALY
College St.
La Palette
Peter's Chung King
Oxford St.
Mansfield Ave.
Palmerston Blvd.
Markham St.
Bathurst St.
Nassau St.
Bellevue Ave.
Augusta Ave.
Baldwin St.
Lee Garden
Seven Lives Tacos y Mariscos
CHINATOWN
Black Hoof
Campagnolo
Dundas St. W.
Swatow
Foxley
Hoof Café
Porchetta & Co.
BENT
Pho Pasteur
Gore Vale Ave.
Bellwoods Ave.
Claremont St.
Alexandra Park
Crawfod St.
Trinity Bellwoods Park
Denison St.
Carr St.
Robinson St.
Wolseley St.
QUEEN WEST
URSA
Lisa Marie
To-ne Sushi
Banh Mi Boys
Queen St. W.
Oyster Boy
Aji Sai
Tecumseth St.
Portland St.
Richmond St. W.
Mitchell Ave.
Massey St.
Strachan Ave.
Stafford St.
Adelaide St. W.
Young Thailand
Beast
Buca
Toshi Sushi
King St. W.
Madeline's
TO HARBOURFRONT
WVRST
Rodney's Oyster House
0
1/4 mile
400 meters
Edulis
Wellington St. W.
Cheesewerks
ENTERTAINMENT

E
F
G
H
1
2
3
4
5
6
YORKVILLE
Dyne
Sotto Sotto
One
Asuka
Crêpes à GoGo
Café Boulud
The Host
Truffles
Ciao Wine Bar
Morton's
7 West Cafe
QUEEN'S PARK
Queen's Park
UNIVERSITY OF TORONTO
King's College Cir.
ONTARIO LEGISLATIVE BUILDING
CHURCH-WELLESLEY
Guu Izakaya
DUNDAS SQUARE AREA
Wah Sing Seafood Restaurant
Matahari Grill
Barberian's
TORONTO COACH TERMINAL
Lai Wah Heen (Metropolitan Hotel)
Spadina Garden
Grange Park
CITY HALL
Nathan Phillips Square
Nota Bene
The Gabardine
The Chase
The Fifth Grill
OLD TOWN
Khao San Road
Burrito Boyz
Terroni
Reds Wine Tavern
FINANCIAL DISTRICT
Starfish
Beer Bistro
Origin
Vertical
Luma
Bymark
Canoe
Kultura
Romagna Mia Osteria Pizzeria
Victor
E11even
Far Niente
PJ O'Brien
Toca
Real Sports Bar & Grill
Harbour Sixty Steakhouse
Irish Embassy Pub & Grill
Takesushi
Future Bakery & Café
DISTRICT
TO TORONTO CONVENTION CENTER
ST. GEORGE
BLOOR-YONGE
BAY
MUSEUM
WELLESLEY
COLLEGE
QUEEN'S PARK
ST. PATRICK
DUNDAS
OSGOODE
QUEEN
ST. ANDREW
KING
Hazelton Ave.
Lowther Ave.
Scollard St.
Yorkville Ave.
Cumberland St.
Park Rd.
Rosedale Valley Rd.
Asquith Ave.
Madison Ave.
Avenue Rd.
St. Thomas St.
Bloor St. E.
Hayden St.
Charles St. E.
Huron St.
St. George St.
Bay St.
Yonge St.
Church St.
Hoskin Ave.
St. Joseph St.
Dundonald St.
Queen's Park Cir. W.
Queen's Park Cir. E.
Willcocks St.
Wellesley St. W.
Wellesley St. E.
Breadalbane St.
Maitland Ave.
Russell St.
Grosvenor St.
Alexander St.
Jarvis St.
Grenville St.
Wood St.
College St.
Carlton St.
Beverley St.
Henry St.
Elizabeth St.
University Ave.
Cecil St.
Gerrard St. W.
Gerrard St. E.
O'Keefe St.
Elm St.
Gould St.
D'Arcy St.
Chestnut St.
Edward St.
Dundas St. W.
Dundas St. E.
Victoria St.
Sullivan St.
McCaul St.
St. Patrick St.
Simcoe St.
Shuter St.
James St.
Mutual St.
Soho St.
Renfrew Pl.
Pullan Pl.
Queen St. W.
Queen St. E.
Peter St.
York St.
Richmond St. E.
Nelson St.
Adelaide St. E.
Widmer St.
John St.
Duncan St.
Pearl St.
Toronto St.
King St. W.
Colborne St.
Mercer St.
Wellington St. W.
Wellington St. E.

and pine nuts. Daily specials are hit and miss, but desserts—like a flourless wedge of Nutella chocolate cake—are universally delicious. Try the other location at 720 Queen Street West if you are in the Queen Street West area. Ⓢ *Average main: C$15* ✉ *57 Adelaide St. E, Financial District* ☎ *416/504–1992* 🌐 *www.terroni.ca* ⏲ *Closed Sun.* Ⓜ *Queen* ✣ *1:H6.*

$$$ JAPANESE ✕ **Takesushi.** Dramatic black and deep-blue decor with a central grove of bamboo sets the stage for a food experience that focuses on presentation, with both a sushi bar and table service. Master chefs thrill customers with an array of spectacular items: black cod with miso paste and king crab salad roll—just to start. Progress to fresh and beautifully made sushi and sashimi for the main. You can pair those with a vast selection of sake and sake cocktails. Ⓢ *Average main: C$22* ✉ *22 Front St. W, Financial District* ☎ *416/862–1891* 🌐 *www.takesushi.ca* ✍ *Reservations essential* ⏲ *Closed Sun. No lunch Sat.* Ⓜ *King* ✣ *1:H6.*

$$$ ITALIAN ✕ **Vertical.** Tucked away off First Canadian Place's food court, this slick, crimson-lit substantial and symmetrical dining room demands your attention. A starter of seared scallops with squid ink and corn introduces you to Vertical's rich signature flavors. Other highlights on the Italian menu include house-made pastas like pappardelle with slow-braised boar ragu, whole fish on the grill, and other sustainable seafood selections. The patio, cloistered within the building, is a secret hideaway for those in the area. Ⓢ *Average main: C$27* ✉ *First Canadian Place, 100 King St. W, main mezzanine, Financial District* ☎ *416/214–2252* 🌐 *www.verticalrestaurant.ca* ⏲ *Closed weekends* Ⓜ *King* ✣ *1:F6.*

OLD TOWN AND THE DISTILLERY DISTRICT

OLD TOWN

One of the most historic neighborhoods in Toronto, Old Town is home to major landmarks such as the St. James Cathedral and the St. Lawrence Market Building; formerly the home of the province's food terminal where restaurateurs would awaken at the wee hours of the morning to get their hands on the best produce. Today, it is still one of the go-to places to find the season's freshest ingredients.

$$ IRISH ✕ **Irish Embassy Pub & Grill.** Popular both with the après-work crowd and late-night carousers, this handsome pub is the place for hearty homemade food and a proper pint. The soaring ceilings and columns and mahogany wood make an authentic backdrop for the approachable lineup of imported beers, such as Guinness, Smithwick's, Harp, and Kilkenny. As for the pub food, the chicken curry and the *poutine*, with bacon lardons, garlic, mayo, and cheddar cheese, satisfy traditional and nontraditional palates alike. Ⓢ *Average main: C$18* ✉ *49 Yonge St., Old Town* ☎ *416/866–8282* 🌐 *www.irishembassypub.com* Ⓜ *King* ✣ *1:G6.*

$$ ASIAN FUSION Fodor's Choice ★ ✕ **Origin.** A sleek, industrial space of exposed brick, spun-wire lamps, and charcoal-colored upholstery gives a suitably chic backdrop to this global food bar. Throughout the menu, ingredients are allowed to star without being overworked. Great examples of this include the Japanese-style tuna salad with Asian pear, avocado, and spicy ponzu dressing;

the fried calamari with caramelized peanut sauce; and 32-ounce rib eye with chimichurri. A cream soda soft-serve float awaits at the end. *Average main: C$17 ✉ 107 King St. E, Old Town ☎ 416/603–8009 🌐 www.origintoronto.com ✣ 1:H6.*

$$ IRISH ✕ **PJ O'Brien.** This traditional pub will make you feel like you're in Dublin the second you set foot on its wooden floors. And unlike the legions of cookie-cutter imitation Irish pubs, with token Irish beers, phony Irish names, and shamrocks galore, this is the real deal. Tuck into an authentic meal of Irish Kilkenny Ale–battered fish-and-chips, beef and Guinness stew, or corned beef and cabbage, ending with bread pudding steeped in whiskey and custard, just like Gran made. The bar upstairs is even cozier than the one on the main floor. *Average main: C$15 ✉ 39 Colborne St., Old Town ☎ 416/815–7562 🌐 www.pjobrien.com ⏲ Closed Sun. Ⓜ King ✣ 1:H6.*

ST. LAWRENCE MARKET

For a great place to nibble and sample a variety of yummy eats, head to the historic St. Lawrence Market building, a place where food connoisseurs go to acquire seasonal produce, fancy cuts of meat, and fresh seafood. Those who don't have time to cook can choose from a selection of baked goods like croissants or butter tarts; head to Carousel Bakery to try the iconic peameal bacon sandwich or Buster's Sea Cove for a scrumptious lobster roll. In the summer months, you will also find food trucks parked outside the Sony Centre, which rotate daily.

$$ JAPANESE ✕ **Toshi Sushi.** Toshi caters to lovers of both raw and cooked Japanese food in a simple, well-kept dining room with small tables, lightly colored walls, and hanging lanterns. The daily lunch special is an implausibly good deal: C$12.50 for a warming miso and a bento box loaded with al dente green beans in luscious sesame-mirin sauce, crunchy shrimp and vegetable tempura, ginger-tinged green salad, proper sticky rice topped with chicken teriyaki, and orange wedges to finish. Don't bypass the stellar sushi lineup, including European-influenced torched foie gras or tempura-battered crab croquette, and chef's specials such as tuna carpaccio and crispy flounder. **TIP→ Call ahead for the omakase (chef's choice) menu and join the in-the-know Japanese businesspeople at the eight-seat bar at the back.** *Average main: C$18 ✉ 565 King St. W, King West ☎ 416/260–8588 🌐 www.toshisushi.ca ⏲ Closed Sun. Ⓜ King ✣ 1:D6.*

DISTILLERY DISTRICT

Just a short distance away from Old Town, the Distillery District is a pedestrian-only shopping and dining oasis paved in cobblestone. Here you'll find one-of-a-kind vendors and great al fresco dining options.

$ BAKERY ✕ **Brick Street Bakery.** If the smell of fresh bread and buttery croissants doesn't draw you into this charming bakery, the decadent sweets on display—like the sticky ginger cake, Nanaimo bars, or French macaroons—certainly will. For heartier items, opt for a pulled pork sandwich or steak-and-stout pie. *Average main: C$4 ✉ 55 Mill St., Bldg. 45A, Distillery District ☎ 416/214-4949 🌐 www.brickstreetbakery.ca Ⓜ Union ✣ 2:C5.*

$$ MEXICAN Fodor's Choice ★ ✕ **El Catrin.** With a 5,000-square-foot patio and stunning and vibrant floor-to-ceiling murals by artist Oscar Flores, El Catrin is the hottest place to be in the Distillery District. And the food matches the setting. Delight in the traditional tacos *al pastor* with shaved pork and pineapple salsa or a foie gras *tostado,* which pays homage to chef Olivier Le Calvez's French roots. Tequila lovers have a long list of options to choose from—served straight up or in a refreshing margarita. Finish the evening on a sugar high with churros rolled in sugar served with a trio of chocolate, strawberry, and dulce de leche dipping sauces. $ *Average main: C$12* ✉ *18 Tank House Lane, Distillery District* ☎ *416/203-2121* 🌐 *www.elcatrin.ca* ✍ *Reservations essential* ⊙ *No lunch Mon.–Fri.* Ⓜ *Union* ✥ *2:C6.*

$$ CANADIAN ✕ **Mill Street Beer Hall.** One of the best spots to try bier schnapps (a traditional German-style spirit that is akin to tequila), this gastropub features classics with a twist such as crispy Cornish hen with Sriracha maple glaze, or ultrameaty chicken wings. Even salads are anything but boring, like the red quinoa salad with sweet and tangy sherry vinaigrette. Fondue is served up with a duo of Oka and aged cheddar with roasted beets, house-made bratwurst, apples, and mini potatoes. For dessert, opt for Nonna's sugar donuts; they're melt-in-your-mouth and pillowy soft. $ *Average main: C$18* ✉ *21 Tank House Lane, Distillery District* ☎ *416/681-0338* 🌐 *toronto.millstreetbrewpub.ca* Ⓜ *Union* ✥ *2:C6.*

DUNDAS SQUARE AREA

Hailed as Toronto's Times Square, Dundas Square has bright neon screens beaming down the newest fashions and trends. It's also home to one of the city's largest shopping centers. And the square hosts an array of events ranging from food to film.

$$$$ STEAKHOUSE ✕ **Barberian's.** A Toronto landmark where wheeling, dealing, and lots of eating have gone on since 1959, Barberian's is also romantic: Elizabeth Taylor and Richard Burton got engaged here (for the first time). The menu is full of steak-house classics, like starters of tomato and onion salad and jumbo shrimp cocktail. Mains are all about the meat, be it a perfectly timed porterhouse, New York strip loin, or rib steak. Fresh fish of the day and grilled free-range capon also hold their charms. One of the oldest steak houses in the city, Barberian's offers a selection of 3,000 labels in its underground two-story wine cellar. $ *Average main: C$40* ✉ *7 Elm St., Dundas Square Area* ☎ *416/597–0335* 🌐 *www.barberians.com* ✍ *Reservations essential* ⊙ *Closed for lunch weekends* Ⓜ *Dundas* ✥ *1:G4.*

$$ JAPANESE ✕ **Guu Izakaya.** Torontonians went crazy when Guu opened in 2009, and for good reason. There simply isn't another place like it here. The passionate staff shouts greetings at the top of their lungs before patrons sit down. It's noisy, rowdy, and ultra-friendly—very much in line with the traditional *izakaya* (bar with drinks and small plates), complete with an open space and communal tables. The salmon *natto yukke* (a mixture of chopped salmon, *natto*, wonton chips, garlic chips, and egg yolk wrapped in crunchy nori) makes the introduction to *natto* (fermented soybeans) a pleasant experience and offers amazing textural differences

among its elements. For a hot dish, the *kakimayo* (grilled oysters with spinach and garlic mayo topped with cheese) is savory and creamy. Even midst a menu of small plate items, you'll still find excellent rice dishes. Kinoko cheese *bibimbap*, rice and garlic sautéed mushrooms with seaweed sauce and cheese in a hot stone bowl, take this humble ingredient to new heights. Choose from an array of sake cocktails to sip. *Average main: C$16 ⊠ 398 Church St., Dundas Square Area ☎ 416/977–0999 ⊕ www.guu-izakaya.com/toronto.html ⊗ No lunch Saturday or Sunday. Ⓜ College ⊕ 1:H4.*

$$$$ CHINESE **Lai Wah Heen.** The service is formal in Lai Wah Heen's elegant dining room topped with a sculpted ceiling and surrounded with etched-glass turntables and silver serving dishes. Here mahogany-color Peking duck is wheeled in on a trolley and presented with panache as it's cut into paper-thin slices. Excellent choices from the 100-dish inventory include wok-fried shredded beef tenderloin with sundried chili peppers, and dried seafood delicacies like dried scallops with fried garlic on a bed of vegetables. Dim sum is divine for lunch: meat-filled morsels and translucent dumplings burst with juicy fillings of shark's fin sprinkled with bright-red lobster roe and in shrimp dumplings with green tops reminiscent of baby bok choy. *Average main: C$32 ⊠ Metropolitan Hotel, 108 Chestnut St., 2nd fl., Dundas Square Area ☎ 416/977–9899 ⊕ www.laiwahheen.com ✍ Reservations essential Ⓜ St. Patrick ⊕ 1:F4.*

CHINATOWN, KENSINGTON MARKET, AND QUEEN WEST

CHINATOWN

While urban sprawl has led to the creation of many mini-Chinatowns in the city, this is the historic original. University students and chefs alike gather here for cheap eats and late-night bites. Experience various regional Chinese cuisines from spicy Szechuan to exotic Cantonese. Or skip brunch and opt for dim sum—it's a great way to sample Chinese staples.

$$ CHINESE Fodor's Choice ★ **Lee Garden.** Always packed, this Cantonese eatery has printouts of recommended dishes taped up on its green walls, but truthfully it does everything well. Oysters steamed in black bean sauce are meaty and flavorful, Grandfather's smoked chicken is aromatic and moist, and flash-fried salt-and-pepper shrimp is addictive. Avoid lines by going early. *Average main: C$16 ⊠ 331 Spadina Ave., Chinatown ☎ 416/593–9524 ⊕ www.leegardenspadina.ca ⊗ No lunch. ⊕ 1:D4.*

$$ MALAYSIAN **Matahari Grill.** It's hard to pass up any of the Southeast Asian dishes here, so you might use size as a decision-making tool. If you have a taste for adventure, order the platter for two: a sampling of satays, spring rolls, deep-fried wontons, *keropok*, and *achar achar*. Then get into more exotic flavors with the *sambal udang*—grilled tamarind-scented prawns in sweet, sour-and-spicy tamarind-shallots *sambal*. The seafood curry grill is scallops, prawns, calamari, tomatoes, and okra served in a tantalizing coconut-curry broth. In summer there's a tiny outdoor patio, but most people prefer the sophisticated green-and-white decor inside. *Average main: C$16 ⊠ 39 Baldwin St., Chinatown ☎ 416/596–2832 ⊕ www.mataharigrill.com ✍ Reservations essential ⊗ Closed Mon. No lunch weekends Ⓜ St. Patrick ⊕ 1:E4.*

CLOSE UP

Vegetarian Restaurants

The days when a vegetarian had few menu options other than a limp iceberg salad are past.

Today meatless options in Toronto abound, and vegetarian restaurants are increasingly creative and delicious.

Fresh by Juice for Life. The Continental fare from Asian Buddha bowl to Middle Eastern starter plate, and great selection of energy elixirs and smart drinks at Fresh by Juice for Life will make meat look boring. ✉ *326 Bloor St. W, The Annex* ☎ *416/531-2635* 🌐 *www.freshrestaurants.ca.*

Kings Café. In Kensington Market, Kings Café is spacious and open. This Chinese vegetarian- and health-oriented center of calm in the bustling market offers vegan delights like mushroom, cabbage, and ginger dumplings, and eggplant and broccoli stir-fry. Hot ginger tea is a must. Pick up some quality tea leaves in the little shop inside the restaurant. ✉ *192 Augusta Ave.* ☎ *416/591-1340* 🌐 *www.kingscafe.com* 💳 *No credit cards.*

Live Organic Food Bar. If you want to try something completely different, check out "live food" at Live Organic Food Bar. Their vegetarian dishes are completely raw and free of dairy, wheat, and preservatives. Try the manicotti of zucchini noodles with cashew-spinach ricotta; the pizza with walnut and sweet potato crust, pesto, and almond Parmesan; and the chocolate avocado pie. Choose from a good selection of organic wines, cocktails, and beer to go with the meal. ✉ *264 Dupont St., at Spadina Ave., The Annex* ☎ *416/515-2002* 🌐 *www.livefoodbar.com* 💳 *No credit cards.*

Udupi Palace. If you visit the India Bazaar area, dine on authentic south Indian *dosas* (pancakes) at Udupi Palace. Paper-thin, and crisp on the outside and soft on the inside, they are stuffed with potato, onions, mustard seeds, and lentils. The mild spicing will appeal to all ages. Soups are loaded with veggies and sing of coconut and coriander. It's gently priced, with complete dinners for C$12 per person. ✉ *1460 Gerrard St. E, East Toronto* ☎ *416/405-8189* 🌐 *www.udupipalace.ca.*

Urban Herbivore. Tucked inside an old house with an exposed-brick open kitchen, Urban Herbivore serves up rustic daily soups or lets diners design their own salads and sandwiches on house-made flax bread, all eaten while perched on stools at a high table. ✉ *64 Oxford St., Kensington Market* ☎ *416/927-1231* 🌐 *www.herbivore.to.*

$ VIETNAMESE ✕ **Pho Pasteur.** Open 24/7, this is the place to hit when you're having a pho craving. Slurp up a bowl of rice noodles with your choice of beef cuts (flank, tendon, tripe). Standard pho condiments—hoisin sauce, Sriracha, and chili oil—are readily available to boost up the heat and flavor. For a lighter dish on a summer day, the shrimp summer rolls with a citrusy dipping sauce make a refreshing pit stop. Or swing by for a sour sop milk shake or a cup of slow-drip Vietnamese coffee; the dark roast sweetened with condensed milk beats Starbucks every time. $ *Average main: C$10* ✉ *525 Dundas St. W, Chinatown* ☎ *416/351-7188* 💳 *No credit cards* Ⓜ *St. Patrick* ✣ *1:D4.*

$ CHINESE FAMILY **Spadina Garden.** The Chen family has owned Spadina Garden for more than a decade, and the restaurant's dishes are Toronto classics. Start with barbecued honey-garlic spareribs or hot-and-sour soup before moving on to entrées like the chili chicken and the crispy ginger beef alongside steamed rice. This is largely the cuisine of inland northwest China, so there is no tank of finny creatures to peruse. And the dining room itself is peaceful, with standard black lacquer, high-back chairs, and red paper lanterns, leaving your focus on the plate. *Average main: C$10 114 Dundas St. W, Chinatown 416/977–3413 www.spadinagardenrestaurant.com No lunch Sun. St. Patrick or Dundas 1:G4.*

3

$ CHINESE **Swatow.** If there is an equivalent to a fast-paced, casual Hong Kong–style diner in Chinatown, this would be it; here you'll find cheap, honest, and authentic food. In bright and clean surrounds, communal diners enjoy heaping bowls of congee and customized noodle soups, including the best fish balls and shrimp dumpling bowls in town. Rice dishes are also a filling specialty, the best of which, *fuk-kin*, tosses fried rice together with shrimp, crab, scallops, chicken, and egg. The beef fried rice noodles and *lo-mein* are also must-eats. *Average main: C$12 309 Spadina Ave., Chinatown 416/977–0601 No credit cards Dundas 1:D4.*

$$ CHINESE **Wah Sing Seafood Restaurant.** Just one of a jumble of Asian eateries clustered on a tiny Kensington Market street, this meticulously clean and spacious restaurant has two-for-one lobsters (in season, which is almost always). They're scrumptious and tender, with black-bean sauce or ginger and green onion. You can also choose giant shrimp Szechuan-style or one of the lively queen crabs from the tank. Chicken and vegetarian dishes are good, too. *Average main: C$15 47 Baldwin St., Chinatown 416/599–8822 www.wahsing.ca College 1:E4.*

KENSINGTON MARKET

$ MEXICAN Fodor's Choice ★ **Seven Lives Tacos Y Mariscos.** Pop-up-vendor-turned-sensation, this small taco joint in Kensington Market brings in the crowds. A small eatery of only ten seats, Seven Lives doesn't have much space, but most are willing to forego the seats and take the food to go. Bringing the best of SoCal and Tijuana seafood, the menu features Baja fish tacos and *camarones a la diabla* (spicy shrimp and cheese). The tacos are made with 100% corn tortillas. And the daily ceviche is a must. Juices include refreshing, unexpected options like cucumber-lime. *Average main: C$5 69 Kensington Ave., Kensington Market 416/803-1086 www.sevenlives.ca Reservations not accepted No credit cards Closed Mon. and Tues. St. Patrick 1:D4.*

QUEEN WEST

Queen West is a boisterous 'hood of cafés, organic food shops, galleries, funky clothing stores, and lots of good restaurants at manageable price points. Urban, young, and laid-back bistros line the street, adding to the inviting atmosphere of the area.

$$ SUSHI **Aji Sai.** For great value, try the all-you-can-eat lunch at Aji Sai Japanese Restaurant. *Average main: C$19 467 Queen St. W, Queen West 416/603–3366 www.ajisai.com Spadina 1:D5.*

$ ASIAN FUSION ✕ **Banh Mi Boys.** Brothers David, Philip, and Peter Chau have banh mi in their blood—their parents opened one of the original Vietnamese sandwich shops in Chinatown—but they've taken the classic and decked it out with fillers such as melt-in-your-mouth pork belly, duck confit, and kalbi beef. Other offerings include Asian-inspired tacos and steamed buns. Make the meal complete with a side of kimchi fries—dare we call it Asian *poutine*? There's a second location at 399 Yonge Street in Dundas Square. *Average main: C$9 392 Queen St. W, Queen West 416/363-0588 www.banhmiboys.com Spadina 1:D5.*

$$$ FRENCH ✕ **La Palette.** Formerly in Kensington Market, this bright spot moved to the hip and trendy Queen West area, and continues to stake its claim as one of Toronto's truly authentic bistros. The updated location ditched old checkered tablecloths and vinyl chairs, and went for simple decor of exposed brick interior and wooden floors and chairs. Favorite dishes include luscious Camembert fritters with pickled cherries, garlicky escargots, good steak frites, rack of lamb, and many quaffable wines, including a long list of European choices. A three-course prix-fixe (C$35) is available; it's a great spot for brunch, too. *Average main: C$24 492 Queen St. W, Queen West 416/929–4900 www.lapalette.ca College 1:D3.*

$ INTERNATIONAL ✕ **Lisa Marie.** Beloved food truck Fidel Gastro's has brought creative street food to Queen West, combining Asian street vendor dishes with classic Italian cuisine. Now owner Matthew Basile has given his food a permanent home with his restaurant, Lisa Marie. The menu features small plates such as the delicious deep-fried pizza topped with hoisin sauce and duck breast that's been smoked for 12 hours; the divine mozzarella and bone marrow sandwich with house-made pineapple-chili ketchup; and Alabama tailgaters (grass-fed beef carpaccio wrapped in smoked bacon) that will have you shouting olé! And the signature Elvis in a Jar dessert—layers of peanut butter, mascarpone, rum-soaked brioche French toast, boozy maple syrup, and caramelized bacon—would make the King of Rock swoon. *Average main: C$7 638 Queen St. W, Queen West 416/999-6822 www.fidelgastro.ca No lunch Tues.–Fri. Closed Mon. Osgoode 1:C5.*

$$$ MODERN CANADIAN ✕ **Nota Bene.** Chef David Lee's pedigree is impressive, having worked in the kitchens of Centro and Splendido; but if that pedigree doesn't get you, the crispy duck salad with green papaya slaw will. Chef Lee turns out finely wrought Continental dishes with seasonal Canadian ingredients. Jalapeños add zip to a refreshing yellowtail ceviche, and the beef brisket burger with Stilton is substantial without being heavy. A stone's throw from the Four Seasons Opera House, the modern dining room is all clean lines in Brazilian cherrywood, chartreuse leather banquettes, and panels of contemporary art. *Average main: C$27 180 Queen St. W, Queen West 416/977–6400 www.notabenerestaurant.com Closed Sun. No lunch Sat. Osgoode 1:F5.*

$$ SUSHI ✕ **Omi.** Previously located on Church Street, Omi moved to Cabbagetown where the kitchen continues to whip up delicious sushi, using sustainable fish, in a narrow, brightly colored space. Start the meal with organic miso soup, then move onto appetizers like the sweet potato–wrapped catfish and mini torched Hokkaido scallop pizza. Sushi and sashimi are standard

mains. For those who like to be surprised, ask for the *omakase* option and let the chef have a little fun tailoring dishes just for you. *Average main: C$18* ✉ *243 Carlton St., Cabbagetown* ☎ *416/920–8991* 🌐 *www.omisushi.weebly.com* ⏲ *No lunch weekends* ✣ *2:C5.*

$$ SEAFOOD **Oyster Boy.** Whether you get them baked (in one of four different ways), fried, or raw, oysters are the thing at this casual neighborhood spot. A chalkboard spells out what's fresh and available, along with sizing and price for the beauties. There's a pleasing array of house condiments with which to slurp your choices. Other treats include beer-battered fish-and-chips, lobster rolls, and excellent onion rings. A nice selection of wines and beers, as well as cool, friendly servers, makes for a fun night out. *Average main: C$20* ✉ *872 Queen St. W, Queen West* ☎ *416/534–3432* 🌐 *www.oysterboy.ca* ⏲ *No lunch* Ⓜ *Queen* ✣ *1:A5.*

$$ JAPANESE **To-ne Sushi.** There may not be bells and whistles, but diners come here for beautifully presented fresh sushi and the seared tuna salad at a very reasonable price. *Average main: C$15* ✉ *414 Queen St. W, Queen West* ☎ *416/866–8200* 🌐 *www.tonesushi.com* *No credit cards* ⏲ *No lunch Sun.* Ⓜ *Queen West* ✣ *1:D5.*

$$$ MODERN CANADIAN **URSA.** URSA is modern Canadian cuisine and molecular gastronomy under one roof. But surprisingly, it's also health-conscious; in fact URSA takes pride in creating delicious, healthy dishes that break the mold of "diet" food. Case in point, the burrata salad with grilled apricot, wild foraged leaves, blossoms, and currants—a bounty of seasonal local ingredients and a riot of color. Another example, the lamb zaatar with a rye berry purée, asparagus, and béarnaise boasts rich flavors with healthy sides. And if you worry dessert will disappoint, end the meal with a deconstructed lemon meringue pie with yuzu lemon curd, blueberry preserves, spruce caramel, and duck fat sable. *Average main: C$25* ✉ *924 Queen St. W, Queen West* ☎ *4165368963* 🌐 *www.ursa-restaurant.com* ⏲ *No lunch* Ⓜ *Ossington* ✣ *1:A5.*

EAST AND WEST OF THE CITY CENTER

OSSINGTON

All along this narrow strip you'll find the city's best restaurants in a range of cuisines from classic French to Asian fusion, and all manner of other options. It is also a vibrant spot for local bars and watering holes west of the city.

$$$ FRENCH Fodor's Choice ★ **Delux.** This better-than-average neighborhood bistro is a worthwhile stop on Ossington. With its welcoming yet slightly edgy room, streamlined service, and a menu full of comforting French classics, it's a busy local favorite that's full every night. There are oysters on the half shell with a playful Granny Smith mignonette; steak frites; and ricotta ravioli with kale, roasted tomato sauce, and olives. Chef-owner Corinna Mozo's cubano sandwich is simplicity at its best with cider-cured pork, ham, Gruyère, and grainy mustard. Hot-from-the-oven sugar-rolled mini donuts are melt-in-your-mouth good and guarantee you'll come back for more. *Average main: C$23* ✉ *92 Ossington Ave., Ossington* ☎ *416/537–0134* 🌐 *www.deluxrestaurant.ca* ⏲ *Closed Mon.* Ⓜ *St. Patrick* ✣ *2:A5.*

$$ ASIAN FUSION Fodor's Choice ★

Foxley. Like the appealingly bare-bones aesthetic of its space (exposed brick, hardwoods, candlelight), this creative bistro offers unadorned dishes that are jammed with flavor. After traveling for a year, chef-owner Tom Thai returned to Toronto with newfound inspiration from places like Asia, Latin America, and the Mediterranean. There are daily ceviches like sea bream with yuzu and shiso, as well as a couple dozen other *tapas*-style offerings, including spicy blue crab and avocado salad, lamb and duck prosciutto dumplings, and grilled side ribs with sticky shallot glaze. All can be paired with an impressive list of red, white, and sparkling wine, sake and soju, from dry Hungarian Tokaji to a bold Barolo—most modestly priced. **TIP→ The restaurant doesn't take reservations, and it does get busy. Plan accordingly and go early or late.** *Average main: C$13* *207 Ossington St., Ossington* *416/534–8520* *Reservations not accepted* *No lunch. Closed Sun.* *Ossington* *2:A5.*

$$ PIZZA

Pizzeria Libretto. Authentic, thin-crust Neapolitan pizzas are fired in a wood-burning oven imported from Italy at this pizza joint on the Ossington strip. Amid the communal wood tables, exposed brick, chalkboard paint, and Banksy artwork, owner Max Rimaldi adheres to the rules of classic pizza set by the Associazione Verace Pizza Napoletana. Starters include charcuterie and cheeses like house-made duck prosciutto and four-year-old Parmigiano-Reggiano, but the pizza's the thing, pulled from the oven in ninety seconds flat. Try the pizza Margherita D.O.P. with San Marzano tomatoes, fresh basil, and local (nearby Ingersoll) Fiore di Latte Mozzarella, or the porchetta pizza with moist pork roast, rapini, truffle oil, and crackling (which combines two Italian classics—pizza and porchetta). Service is both speedy and charming. Also check out the Danforth location at 550 Danforth Avenue; they take reservations. *Average main: C$16* *221 Ossington Ave., Ossington* *416/532–8000* *www.pizzerialibretto.com* *Reservations not accepted* *St. Patrick* *2:A5.*

THE DANFORTH

Historically known as Greektown, The Danforth has gotten an infusion of non-Greek restaurants, which makes for more varied dining options. But you'll still find those classic Greek spots along with local watering holes and busy patios.

$$$ IRISH

Allen's. Slide into a well-worn wood booth or sit at a blue-and-white-checkered table at this New York–style saloon, complete with oak bar and pressed-tin ceiling. If the traditional interior isn't your style, perhaps the famous willow-shaded patio is. With 340 varieties of whiskey, it is home to one of the best selections in the city. The beer selection lags behind some, with 140 options in bottles and 16 on draft. All meats on the menu include their place of origin. The Guinness-braised lamb shanks and the liver and onions get raves. Servers may recommend the chocolate bread pudding with caramel sauce, bourbon, and pecans; trust them. *Average main: C$25* *143 Danforth Ave., Danforth* *416/463–3086* *www.allens.to* *Reservations essential* *Broadview* *2:C5.*

$$ GREEK FAMILY **Christina's.** Who doesn't have a foodie love affair with Greek dips? Here they're served individually or as a large platter combination, *pikilia mezedakia,* which comes with a warm pita. A bottle of Greek wine and specials like *saganaki* (an iron plate of Kefalograviera cheese flamed in brandy), and you may shout "*Opa*" with the waiters. Order a fish or mixed-meat grill, and the tray of food almost covers the table. This cheery place, with the colors of the Aegean Sea and sun on the walls, has live music and belly dancers on Friday and Saturday evenings. *Average main: C$20 492 Danforth Ave., Danforth 416/463–4418 www.christinas.ca Chester 2:D4.*

3

$$$ MODERN CANADIAN **Globe Bistro.** The motto here is "Think global. Eat local." Globe does justice to locally raised animals by letting the main ingredient shine in the international-inspired dishes, from head-to-tail, like Muscovy duck with seared duck breast and liver sausage, celeriac "risotto," kale, pickled grapes, and *verjus gastrique.* Ivory and taupe neutral tones and soft lights enhance the open dining room and give it a luxurious feel, but, weather permitting, you may want to skip out to the swanky rooftop patio. *Average main: C$27 124 Danforth Ave., Danforth 416/466–2000 www.globebistro.com Closed Mon. No lunch Tues.–Thurs. Broadview. 2:C4.*

LESLIEVILLE

Just a little east of the city, Leslieville is a quaint neighborhood of great local eateries, pastry shops, and coffee bars. Take a break from bustling downtown and spend an afternoon hopping from boutique stores to bakeries where you can indulge in *pain au chocolat* or cupcakes.

$ AMERICAN **Leslieville Pumps.** This is the ultimate place to fuel up, and we're not just talking about the gas tank. Leslieville Pumps is a 24/7, kitschy gas station and general store with a look straight out of a John Wayne western. But—surprise!—it serves some of the best barbecue in town. Slow and low is their cooking philosophy, which they show off in tender pulled pork and brisket sandwiches. Country sides such as BBQ corn salad and Southern coleslaw make the meal complete. At 9 pm every night, the joint is busy serving up their curry and butter chicken with rice. It is the go-to place for cab drivers looking for a late-night bite. *Average main: C$7 929 Queen St. E, Leslieville 416/465-1313 www.leslievillepumps.com Pape 2:D5.*

$$ PIZZA **Queen Margherita Pizza.** One of the best pizza places east of town, Queen Margherita is all about authenticity. Inside this small space with dark wooden floors and tables, the Neapolitan pizza oven, hauled in by crane prior to restaurant opening, pumps out daily selections like Margherita pizza made simply, with just tomato sauce, mozzarella, and basil; or burrata and Calabrese, made with tomato sauce, mozzarella, Italian sausage, and hot peppers. Each pizza is cooked quickly at an ultra-high heat to give it that beautifully blistering crust. Request a table in the bright loft upstairs for more comfortable seating. *Average main: C$15 1402 Queen St. E, Unit 8, Queen East 416/466–6555 2:D5.*

$ CANADIAN **Rashers.** For all things bacon, Rashers has no equal. The full bacon experience is represented, from the sizzling strips of American to the iconic Canadian peameal. The showstopper is definitely the Hogtown, the ultimate breakfast sandwich made from peameal bacon topped with an egg on a white butter-brushed bun. Those looking for a bit of English flair can opt for the Bacon Butty, featuring rashers (Irish/British style bacon) with beer mayo and brown butter sauce. Those willing to walk on the wild side can try the boar with cider glaze. $ *Average main: C$7* ✉ *948 Queen St. E, Leslieville* ☎ *416/710-8220* 🌐 *www.rashers.ca* Ⓜ *Pape* ✥ *2:D5.*

$$ MIDDLE EASTERN Fodor'sChoice ★ ✕ **Tabülè.** Bold Middle Eastern flavors and spices are showcased at Tabülè. Get hands-on as you dip warm flatbread into *baganüj*, hummus or *tabülè*. The falafels are fried to a deep golden brown and served with a tahini sauce that's thick and rich. Grilled lamb chops are a must-eat dish, grilled to a perfect medium-rare atop a bed of fragrant and savory rice with vegetables. And if you're feeling a little tired order a cup of Lebanese coffee—the small cup packs a punch! Drop in on Saturday evenings for a belly dancing performance. Check out their alternate location at 2009 Yonge Street. $ *Average main: C$17* ✉ *810 Queen St. E, Leslieville* ☎ *416/465-2500* 🌐 *www.tabule.ca* Ⓜ *Broadview* ✥ *2:D5.*

QUEEN'S PARK, THE ANNEX, AND LITTLE ITALY

QUEEN'S PARK

Steps away from the busy shopping hub that is Bloor/Yorkville, Queen's Park is also home to the provincial parliament. Pair your lunch with a public tour and learn about the province's political makeup or visit the Royal Ontario Museum.

$ ECLECTIC ✕ **7 West Cafe.** No late-night craving goes unsatisfied at this 24-hour haven for the hip and hungry. Snacks, pastas, sandwiches, soups, and drinks are all served in this eclectic, three-story, dimly lit café. Everything is homemade and comes with a green salad. Soups like Moroccan or vegetarian chili are comforting and filling, and dinner-size sandwiches like the grilled herbed chicken breast with honey mustard are huge. The menu of basic foods sets the tone for simple wine, beer, and cocktail choices. It's not fancy, but there's plenty to choose from. $ *Average main: C$12* ✉ *7 Charles St. W, Bloor/Yonge* ☎ *416/928–9041* 🌐 *www.7westcafe.com* Ⓜ *Bloor-Yonge* ✥ *1:G2.*

THE ANNEX

The Annex caters to a winning mix of students, professors, historic homes, and treed spaces, a kind of bookish kaffeeklatsch amid the hubbub of the city. Come here for everything from authentic fish-and-chips to a thriving new restaurant row along Harbord Street.

$ CAFÉ ✕ **Future Bakery & Café.** Aside from European-style baked goods, this spot also serves old-world recipes like beef borscht, buckwheat cabbage rolls, and potato-cheese pierogi slathered with thick sour cream. It's a place beloved by the pastry-and-coffee crowd, students wanting great value, and people-watchers, from 7 am to 2 am. Health-conscious foodies looking for fruit salad with homemade yogurt and honey get their sweet fix, while those who like to indulge order the *dulce de leche* cheesecake. A St. Lawrence Market branch at 95 Front St. East sells just bread and pastries and closes early in the evening. $ *Average main: C$5* ✉ *483 Bloor St. W, The Annex* ☎ *416/922–5875* ✍ *Reservations not accepted* Ⓜ *Bathurst* ✥ *1:C1.*

CLOSE UP

Alfresco Dining

From the first sign of warm weather until September's cool evenings, Torontonians hit the deck, the patio, the courtyard, and the rooftop terrace.

YORKVILLE

Amber. The patio at Amber rocks with cool, late-night people. ✉ *119 Yorkville Ave., Yorkville* ☎ *416/926-9037* 🌐 *www.amberinyorkville.com.*

Christina's. The sidewalk patio at Christina's is a good place to check out the scene. ✉ *513 Danforth Ave., Danforth* ☎ *416/465-1751* 🌐 *www.christinas.ca.*

MBCo. MBCo has gourmet sandwiches, pizza, and soups to eat on the patio or in the park. ✉ *100 Bloor St. W, Yorkville* ☎ *416/961-6226* 🌐 *www.mbco.ca.*

Summer's Ice Cream. Summer's Ice Cream is the spot to grab homemade ice cream in just-made waffle cones, then stroll in Yorkville Park. ✉ *101 Yorkville Ave., Yorkville* ☎ *416/944-2637* 🌐 *www.summersicecream.com.*

KENSINGTON MARKET

Jumbo Empanadas. Savor oversized empanadas and corn pie on the tented patio of Jumbo Empanadas. ✉ *245 Augusta Ave., Kensington Market* ☎ *416/977-0056.*

Supermarket. Supermarket has a boisterous patio and tasty Asian tapas. ✉ *268 Augusta Ave., Kensington Market* ☎ *416/840-0501* 🌐 *www.supermarkettoronto.com* ⏲ *Closed Mon. No lunch.*

Torito. One of the first authentic tapas restaurants in the city, Torito has excellent *patatas bravas* and sangria. Traditional dishes such as paella get a makeover in the form of *rossejat,* a paella-style pasta topped with succulent shrimp and aioli. Classic dishes such as piquillo peppers are stuffed with tender, braised oxtail, and crème catalana makes for a creamy and luscious dessert. In the summer months, people-watch in the front patio or grab a seat on the back patio for a little more privacy. ✉ *276 Augusta Ave., Kensington Market* ☎ *416/961-7373* 🌐 *www.toritotapasbar.com* ⏲ *Closed Mon.*

THE ENTERTAINMENT DISTRICT

Black Bull Tavern. One of the largest and most affordable local patios is the Black Bull Tavern. ✉ *298 Queen St. W, Queen West* ☎ *416/593-2766* 🌐 *www.blackbulltavern.ca.*

Drake Hotel. Way west, the Drake Hotel has a swanky rooftop prime for people-watching. ✉ *1150 Queen St. W, Queen West* ☎ *416/531-5042* 🌐 *www.thedrakehotel.ca.*

Queen Mother Café. The garden at the Queen Mother Café is a cool place for East–West dishes. ✉ *208 Queen St. W, Queen West* ☎ *416/598-4719* 🌐 *www.queenmothercafe.ca.*

Rivoli. The Rivoli is a hot outdoor spot for people-watching on hip and cool Queen St. ✉ *322 Queen St. W, Queen West* ☎ *416/596-1908* 🌐 *www.rivoli.ca.*

Trattoria Giancarlo. Trattoria Giancarlo has tasty grilled meats you can savor at outdoor picnic tables. ✉ *41 Clinton St., Little Italy* ☎ *416/533-9619* 🌐 *www.giancarlotrattoria.com* ⏲ *No lunch. Closed Sun.*

$$$ BISTRO Fodor's Choice ★ **ICI Bistro.** Chef Jean-Pierre Challet does classic French bistro fare proud by using locally sourced ingredients while showcasing his culinary finesse. Start with crusty slices of bread, baked in-house, and ease into one of three signature tartares, or get the whole lot as a trio sampler. Escargots, lobster bisque, or duck *magret* are at its best in Challet's talented hands. All dishes are available in appetizer or entrée size to suit any appetite. And cataloging some 30 wines by the glass, the carefully selected wine list has some of the best sips from local and French wineries. Check out Le Matin, Challet's bakery in Leslieville if you're in the area. *Average main: C$28 538 Manning Ave., The Annex 416/536-0079 www.jpco.ca Reservations essential Closed Sun.–Tues. No lunch. M Christie ↔ 1:B2.*

$$ VEGETARIAN **Live Organic Food Bar.** The sunny decor will charm you, but the real draw here is the imaginative (and enthusiastic) owners and the amazing raw foods they create. A manicotti of cashew-spinach ricotta, cherry tomatoes, almond Parmesan, and zucchini noodles is a crowd favorite. The stove is used ever so slightly for "roasting" root vegetables served over mixed greens with balsamic drizzle. A long list of seriously fresh–squeezed juices is served. Be aware: service is casual. *Average main: C$15 264 Dupont St., The Annex 416/515–2002 www.livefoodbar.com M Spadina ↔ 1:C1.*

$$ DINER FAMILY Fodor's Choice ★ **Rose and Sons.** Rose and Sons is the kind of neighborhood, family joint that strives to make both parents and kids happy. Forget run-of-the-mill, mediocre, greasy spoon diner fare; here diner classics get a modern twist, such as grilled romaine, a fresh take on the traditional Caesar salad with anchovy, toscano cheese, and garlic chicken or the patty tuna melt, a hybrid of a grilled cheese and burger with fried onions and mayo. Be sure to order a milkshake for the kids or spoil them with soft serve—or just order one for yourself. Check out the Big Crow (out back) for camping-inspired dishes. *Average main: C$18 176 Dupont St., The Annex (647) 748-3287 www.roseandsons.ca M Dupont ↔ 1:D1.*

$$ SOUTHERN **Southern Accent.** On a street lined with antiques shops, bookstores, and galleries sits this funky Cajun and Creole restaurant. Perch at the bar, order a martini and hush puppies, and chat with the resident psychic. Whimsical knickknacks adorn every inch of the place, and dining rooms on two floors offers a market-driven menu. Some constants are Bourbon Street chicken (blackened boneless chicken breast in lemon butter sauce), cracker catfish (a fillet coated with spiced crackers) served with jalapeño tartar sauce, and the Nawlins bread pudding with bourbon sauce. *Average main: C$20 595 Markham St., The Annex 416/536–3211 www.southernaccent.com Closed Mon. No lunch M Bathurst ↔ 1:C1.*

$$$ MODERN CANADIAN Fodor's Choice ★ **Splendido.** Chef Victor Barry, a disciple of former owner and superstar chef David Lee, ensures that even the hardest to please will be thrilled by the tasting menus here. The selection might include foie-gras-stuffed quail with lime creme fraiche or egg yolk raviolo with spinach and ricotta purée and black truffles. The kitchen is peerless, and the front of the house functions like a fine Swiss watch. A huge iron chandelier serves as the focal point in one of the city's most beautifully

balanced dining rooms. Luxe touches include a champagne trolley and purse stools for the ladies. The chef's daily four-course prix fixe menu is a steal for $65. *Average main: C$30* ✉ *88 Harbord St., The Annex* ☎ *416/929–7788* 🌐 *www.splendido.ca* *Reservations essential* *Closed Sun. and Mon.* Ⓜ *Spadina* ✣ *1:D2.*

LITTLE ITALY

Some of the city's best pastas and pizzas are served up in Little Italy, a place where chefs still strive to reproduce the taste of Nonna's cooking. Specialties like charcuterie and ceviche have local followings, as do the quaint patios and neighborhood bakeries.

3

$$ ITALIAN **Bar Italia.** A fixture in Little Italy, this is where the city's glitterati can be found getting their fix of the classics: well-prepared pasta, risotto, fish of the day, and a traditional favorite of sautéed mushroom salad with arugula and Parmesan. In the summer, sip a glass of wine on the patio and dig into a specialty, the Cubano sandwich of roasted pork, avocado, pancetta, and garlicky mayo on a huge Italian bun. Close your eyes and pretend you're in southern Italy; you'll still hear Italian spoken at many tables. *Average main: C$20* ✉ *582 College St., Little Italy* ☎ *416/535–3621* 🌐 *www.bar-italia.ca* Ⓜ *Bathurst, Queen's Park* ✣ *2:A5.*

$$$ MODERN CANADIAN **The Black Hoof.** A typical evening spent in this narrow head-to-tail cuisine hot spot features exotic meats and loving attention from owner Jen Agg. A chalkboard behind the bar lists the selection, and patrons can see the cooks hard at work at the tiny stove just to the left of the bar where hot foods are prepared. The must-have house-made charcuterie plates include bites of cured venison *bresaola* (air-dried, salted meat), and duck prosciutto, plus octopus salad and roasted bone marrow. A house specialty is tongue on brioche; smoked sweetbreads; and horse tartare, a first for many in Toronto and not available in the United States. The tartare is delicious: a clean, lean meat, not gamey at all, like the purest, lightest beef. Go over-the-top and end with a dessert of foie gras and Nutella. Monthly cocktails are listed on a huge mirror by the bar. **TIP→ It gets quite busy and seeing as reservations are not accepted, leave your name and head across the street to the Cocktail Bar to grab a drink.** *Average main: C$25* ✉ *928 Dundas St. W, Little Italy* ☎ *416/551–8854* 🌐 *www.theblackhoof.com* *Reservations not accepted* *No credit cards* *Closed Tues. and Wed. No lunch* Ⓜ *St. Patrick* ✣ *1:B4.*

$$ SEAFOOD **BENT.** BENT feels like a school cafeteria abuzz with Generation Y teens and twentysomethings looking to catch up on the latest gossip or trends. Vintage Pachinko machines line the walls alongside a great selection of sakes, and childhood figurines are displayed like a meticulous collectors' show-and-tell. Feast on the day's selections from the raw bar, be it sashimi or ceviche, or indulge in one of local celebrity chef Susur Lee's fusion creations such as the duck salad wrap. If that doesn't win you over, the daily selection of complimentary desserts will ensure your visit has a sweet ending. *Average main: C$14* ✉ *777 Dundas St. W, Little Italy* ☎ *6473520092* 🌐 *www.bentrestaurant.com* *Reservations essential* *Closed Sun. and Mon. No lunch* Ⓜ *St. Patrick* ✣ *1:C4.*

$$$ ITALIAN Fodor's Choice ★ **Campagnolo.** Praised as Toronto's best new restaurant when it opened, Campagnolo continues to serve its award-winning Italian-grandmother-inspired cooking in a cozy space of wooden tables and gold leaf–striped walls. Start with fresh burrata cheese and roasted grapes on crusty bread—the perfect play of sweet and savory. Lovers of curious cuts can opt for the roasted bone marrow with oxtail marmalade and plums, but traditional pasta dishes also satisfy. The menu changes daily to take advantage of market fresh ingredients, which guarantees that neither you nor the chef will get bored. *Average main: C$22 ✉ 832 Dundas St. W, Little Italy ☎ 416/364-4785 ⊕ www.campagnolotoronto.com ⚠ Reservations essential ⊗ No lunch. Closed Mon. and Tues. Ⓜ St. Patrick ⊕ 1:B4.*

$$$$ PORTUGUESE **Chiado.** It's all relaxed elegance here, beginning with the fine selection of appetizers at Senhor Antonio Tapas and Wine Bar and continuing through the French doors to the dining room, which has polished wood floors and plum-velvet armchairs. The exquisite fish, which form the menu's base, are flown in from the Azores and Madeira. You might have monkfish, grouper, or *peixe espada* (scabbard fish). Traditional Portuguese dishes include *assorda,* in which seafood is folded into a thick, custard-like soup made with bread and eggs. But there's much for meat eaters, too—like a roasted rack of lamb that sparkles with Douro wine sauce. *Average main: C$40 ✉ 864 College St. W, Little Italy ☎ 416/538–1910 ⊕ www.chiadorestaurant.com ⚠ Reservations essential ⊗ No lunch weekends Ⓜ Ossington, Queen's Park ⊕ 2:A5.*

$ ITALIAN Fodor's Choice ★ **Porchetta & Co.** Porchetta is a labor of love for Italian cooks: first, pork shoulder is marinated for 24 hours, then it's wrapped in slices of prosciutto, that's further wrapped in slices of bacon, and finally it's roasted in an oven to get a crispy crackling skin and slow-roasted several hours more. Is it any wonder why this spot, a porchetta wonderland, would have a fanatical following? Eat it wedged in between a bun or as is with roasted potatoes, rapini, or baked beans. Or skip the bun and dig in to pork heaven! Note: There isn't much sitting room (think lunch counter) so call ahead and grab it to go. *Average main: C$8 ✉ 825 Dundas St. W, Little Italy ☎ 647/352-6611 ⊕ www.porchettaco.com ▭ No credit cards ⊗ Closed Sun. and Mon. Ⓜ St. Patrick ⊕ 1:B4.*

YORKVILLE AND CHURCH-WELLESLEY

YORKVILLE

Home to the rich and fabulous, Yorkville is THE prime spot for celebrity sightings, especially during the Toronto International Film Festival. Posh bars and lively patios all provide a chance to do a little people-watching, and sample some of the city's best high-end cuisine.

$$ SUSHI **Asuka.** Among hip and often pretentious establishments, this sunken space stands out for its simplicity and coziness, and proves that celebrity spotting and fine Asian cuisine are not exclusive to upscale restaurants. You won't find any avant-garde dishes here, but you will find well-crafted and fresh sushi and sashimi at a reasonable price. *Average main: C$20 ✉ 108 Yorkville Ave., Yorkville ☎ 416/975–9084 Ⓜ Bay ⊕ 1:F1.*

$$$$ FRENCH Fodor's Choice ★ ✕ **Café Boulud.** Nestled in tony and fabulous Yorkville, Café Boulud, spearheaded by world-renown restaurateur Daniel Boulud, occupies the coveted dining room of the Four Seasons Toronto. Art lovers can study Andy Warhol-esque paintings by Mr. Brainwash and gourmands can savor the beautiful dishes crafted by executive chef Tyler Shedden. The menu, split into four sections, invites exploration. Classic French dishes like foie gras represent the Traditional portion of the menu, whereas appetizers like a decadent duck egg mark the Seasonal menu; Korean beef tartare highlights the Asian portion; and sweet corn risotto brings the Garden to light. It's the culinary equivalent of Choose Your Own Adventure all with a delicious conclusion. *Average main: C$34 ✉ 60 Yorkville Ave., Yorkville ☎ 416/963-6000 🌐 www.fourseasons.com/toronto/dining/cafe_boulud ⏲ No lunch Sun. Ⓜ Bay ✣ 1:G1.*

$$ ITALIAN ✕ **Ciao Wine Bar.** This 2010 addition to the Yorkville scene is swanky, yet soulful. A modern staircase greets you upon entrance to a dimly lighted space, filled with put-together patrons; you can sit either on the sleek upper level or the rustic lower level with wooden tables and exposed brick walls. The wine selection is extensive, dominated by European classics and many Italian regional choices. Regulars enjoy reliable and familiar choices like capellini with tomatoes, capers, anchovies, and olives; oven-baked whole fish with lemon and parsley; and the Caprese pizza with cherry tomatoes, *bocconcini* cheese, arugula, and shaved Grana Padano cheese. *Average main: C$17 ✉ 133 Yorkville Ave., Yorkville ☎ 416/925–2143 🌐 www.ciaowinebar.com Ⓜ Bay ✣ 1:F1.*

$ FRENCH FAMILY ✕ **Crêpes à GoGo.** In this casual bistro, proprietress Veronique and crew turn out simple sandwiches and buckwheat crepes, also known as galettes, using a technique that has been passed down for generations. Signature items include the cheese crepe, a crisped crepe folded around the sharpness of red onion, the fatty nuttiness of Swiss, a herbaceous hit of parsley, and a bit of tangy sour cream; and the Veronique, made of Brie, strawberries, baby spinach, and maple syrup. Limonana, a refreshing drink made of mint leaves, lemon juice, organic cane juice, and water is also served (hot or cold). Crepes are presented in the distinctive square Bretonne-style fold, whereupon Veronique tears down the paper bag's edges, looks you in the eye, and says, "*Bon appétit.*" *Average main: C$8 ✉ 18 Yorkville Ave., Yorkville ☎ 416/922–6765 🌐 www.crepesagogo.com Ⓜ Bay ✣ 1:G1.*

$$$ ASIAN FUSION ✕ **Dyne.** For an intimate and unexpected date night in Yorkville head to Dyne, where chef Julie Marteleira fuses Iberian and Asian cuisine. Dishes like succulent lobster salad with avocado, papaya, and roasted macadamians or flank steak with an Asian chimichurri of Thai basil and *nam pla* are unexpected delights. If you've come ravenous, the "Chef's Last Meal" featuring a 32-ounce rib eye, butter-poached lobster, foie gras, and sides of marrow fingerling potatoes and chili fried rice will ensure you die happy. Hardwood floors and exposed bulbs give a quaint yet inviting look to the dining room, and the service is always attentive. *Average main: C$26 ✉ 120 Avenue Rd., Yorkville ☎ 416/962-5655 🌐 www.dyneonavenue.com ⏲ No lunch Sat. Closed Sun. Ⓜ Bay ✣ 1:F1.*

3

$$ INDIAN

The Host. Dine in the garden room among flowering plants or in the handsome dining room at this well-established curry spot. Waiters rush around carrying baskets of hot naan. Fish *tikka* (white fish baked in a tandoor oven and served on a sizzling plate) is an excellent dish and tender sliced lamb is enfolded in a curry of cashew nuts and whole cardamom. End your meal with such classic Indian desserts as *golabjabun,* little round cakes soaking in rosewater-scented honey. *Average main: C$17 14 Prince Arthur Ave., Yorkville 416/962–4678 www.welcometohost.com Reservations essential Bay 1:F1.*

$$$$ SEAFOOD

Joso's. Artistic *objets*, sensuous paintings of nudes and the sea, and signed celebrity photos line the walls at this two-story seafood institution that might catch you off-guard with its eccentricity. The kitchen prepares dishes from the Dalmatian side of the Adriatic Sea, and members of the international artistic community who frequent the place adore the unusual and healthy array of seafood and fish. The black risotto with squid is a must. A dish of grilled prawns, their charred tails pointing skyward, is often carried aloft by speed-walking servers. *Average main: C$36 202 Davenport Rd., Yorkville 416/925–1903 No lunch Sat. Closed Sun. Dupont 2:B4.*

$$$ ITALIAN
Fodor's Choice ★

Mistura. Mistura's combination of comfort and casual luxury and its innovative menu make for an ongoing buzz. A bright dining room with wooden pillars, black chairs and curtains, and white tablecloths sets the tone for a straightforward meal without fuss or nonsense. Choose from more than a dozen delectable starters, like beef carpaccio with Parmesan shavings and black truffle over arugula. Balsamic glazed lamb ribs and boneless Cornish hen with onions and roasted vegetables are specialties. Daily whole fish is a carefully thought-out triumph. Vegetarians are given their due with signature dishes like beet risotto. **Sopra** ($$–$$$), a second-floor Italian lounge and jazz bar, offers full-sized meals as well as bite-size delights. Conceived as a million-dollar playroom for grown-ups, it's all zebrawood and onyx, complete with a grand piano. *Average main: C$30 265 Davenport Rd., ½ block west of Avenue Rd., Yorkville 416/515–0009 www.mistura.ca Closed Sun. No lunch Dupont 2:B4.*

$$$$ STEAKHOUSE

Morton's. Just when you thought this top-notch international chain couldn't possibly get better, it added glorious additional steak variations to its repertoire, including steak au poivre, with yummy peppercorn-cognac sauce. You can still dine on a New York strip or a 48-ounce porterhouse. All beef is shipped chilled, not frozen, from one Chicago supplier. The interior has a handsome, wood-panel clubbiness. *Average main: C$45 4 Avenue Rd., Yorkville 416/925–0648 www.mortons.com/toronto No lunch. Bay 1:F1.*

$$$ MODERN CANADIAN

One. In the buzzing Hazelton Hotel, One has become a celeb-spotting free-for-all during September's Film Festival. (It also has one of the hippest patio scenes any time of year.) The modern and elegant dining room—rich woods, smoked glass, cowhide, and onyx—is the brainchild of designer Yabu Puschelberg. But thankfully the food lives up to all the razzle-dazzle. Chef-owner Mark McEwan's ingredient-driven cuisine starts with playful appetizers such as a nicely caramelized and supple duck steam bun or the deeply satisfying Muscovy duck breast with foie gras and vanilla-stewed cherries. Many dishes, like the wild Atlantic halibut, arrive perfectly cooked but simply prepared and are meant to be accompanied by cauliflower purée and salsa verde. The all-Canadian cheese lineup is an especially proud menu moment. The chef ages his own beef, and many agree his steaks are the best in the city. $ *Average main: C$30* ✉ *The Hazelton Hotel Toronto, 118 Yorkville Ave., Yorkville* ☎ *416/963–6300* 🌐 *www.one.mcewangroup.ca* ✍ *Reservations essential* Ⓜ *Bay* ✣ *1:F1.*

$$$ ITALIAN ✕ **Sotto Sotto.** This coal cellar in a turn-of-the-20th-century home was dug out, its stone walls and floor polished, and what has emerged is a dining oasis for locals and international jet-setters alike. The menu of more than 20 pasta dishes gives a tantalizing tug at the taste buds. Gnocchi here is made daily. The orecchiette ("ear-shape" disks of pasta) tossed with prosciutto and mixed garden vegetables is a symphony of textures. Cornish hen is marinated, pressed, and grilled to a juicy brown, and the swordfish and fresh fish of the day are beautifully done on the grill. $ *Average main: C$30* ✉ *Lower Level, 116-A Avenue Rd., Yorkville* ☎ *416/962–0011* 🌐 *www.sottosotto.ca* ⏲ *No lunch Mon. or Sun.* Ⓜ *Bay* ✣ *1:F1.*

GREATER TORONTO

YONGE AND EGLINTON

This neighborhood used to be a haven for young professionals, but the demographic is evolving and briefcases have been replaced with strollers, as the area attracts more young families. The upside of all this is more kid-friendly restaurants. But there are also a few venues that cater to the couple on a date night.

$$ SPANISH Fodor's Choice ★ ✕ **Cava.** The flavors are as loud as the chatter at Cava, a gem that truly is hidden, as it's tucked away on a plaza terrace. This restaurant and wine bar is a great place to experience regional Spanish cuisines from the Basque country to Catalonia. Chris McDonald showcases bold flavors and rich textures with dishes such as roasted sablefish in a miso-cider glaze and veal sweetbreads on a bed of radicchio-poblano chile salad and walnut vinaigrette. And the gamay-poached foie gras or baked Alaska with sherry-poached pears shows that wine can be just as indulgent out of the glass and on the plate. $ *Average main: C$18* ✉ *1560 Yonge St., Yonge and Eglinton* ☎ *416/979–9918* 🌐 *www.cavarestaurant.ca* ✍ *Reservations essential* ⏲ *No lunch* Ⓜ *St. Clair* ✣ *2:B4.*

$$ JAPANESE

EDO. Aficionados of Japanese food may have to stop themselves from ordering everything on the menu at EDO. Even the uninitiated are mesmerized by the intriguing dishes here, including plates of black cod marinated in *saikyo* miso sauce, dynamite roll with giant shrimp and dynamite sauce, and miso-glazed eggplant. If soft-shell crab is on the menu, it's a worthy choice. The chef is an artist with sushi and sashimi, but if you can't decide, the kitchen menus give you a balanced and exciting array of dishes. *Average main: C$20 484 Eglinton Ave. W, Yonge and Eglinton 416/481–1370 www.edosushi.com No lunch Mon., Sat., or Sun. Eglinton 2:B3.*

$$$ MODERN CANADIAN

Globe Earth. Many restaurateurs believe this location is cursed, as predecessors always floundered, but not its current owner Ed Ho, who is passionate about knowing and sharing the origin of foods. Situated in the affluent Rosedale area, Globe Earth is a neighborhood bistro that's surprisingly laid-back, with cool black-and-gray furniture, wooden floors, and a marble bar. Many meat dishes are prepared in the wood-burning oven, like the BBQ platter featuring ribs, smoked chicken thighs, beef sausage, algonquin corn grits, and slaw which is succulent, not greasy or cloying. All in all, it's a great value. *Average main: C$21 1055 Yonge St., Rosedale 416/551–9890 www.earthrosedale.com Closed Mon. No lunch. Rosedale 2:C4.*

$$$$ MODERN CANADIAN

North 44. The lighting here creates a refined, sophisticated environment, and the appetizers match: medley of lobster; crab and prawns with spiced crème fraîche; and crispy soft-shell crab with white asparagus, grapefruit, and hollandaise awaken your taste buds. It's hard to choose from chef-owner Marc McEwan's creative and exciting main courses, including pan-seared Dover sole in brown butter, and roasted lamb loin with minted spring pea ravioli, and cauliflower purée. There are more than 50 wines sold by the glass, enough to complement any dish. *Average main: C$40 2537 Yonge St., 4½ blocks north of Eglinton Ave., Yonge and Eglinton 416/487–4897 www.north44.mcewangroup.ca Closed Sun. No lunch Eglinton 2:C3.*

$$$ FRENCH

Pastis. Menu items etched into the frosted-glass windows and plastered walls the color of the dawn in Provence bring a Gallic mood to Yonge Street. The food is good, but this place could run on the charm of owner George Gurnon alone. Expect pure bistro fare here, like mussels and foie gras terrine to start, traditional steak frites, and butter roasted lobster. The wine list is short and simple, with something for every palate. End the perfect meal with a crème brûlée or profiteroles. *Average main: C$22 1158 Yonge St., at Summerhill, Yonge and Eglinton 416/928–2212 Closed Sun. and Mon. No lunch Summerhill 2:B4.*

$$ ITALIAN FAMILY

Pizza Banfi. No matter what day or time, there's usually a line for two reasons: Pizza Banfi doesn't take reservations, and the classic Italian food is really good. The decor is slightly cliché, with wall paintings over light colored bricks, but the pizzas are the main attraction here. Thin-crust pies are tossed in full view, then baked with aplomb, especially the popular pesto, chicken, and roasted red pepper combo. Pastas, generously portioned, are just as good, and the stellar Caesar salad tops just about every table. *Average main: C$15 333B Lonsdale Rd., Forest Hill 416/322–5231 Reservations not accepted Closed Sun. Eglinton West 2:B3.*

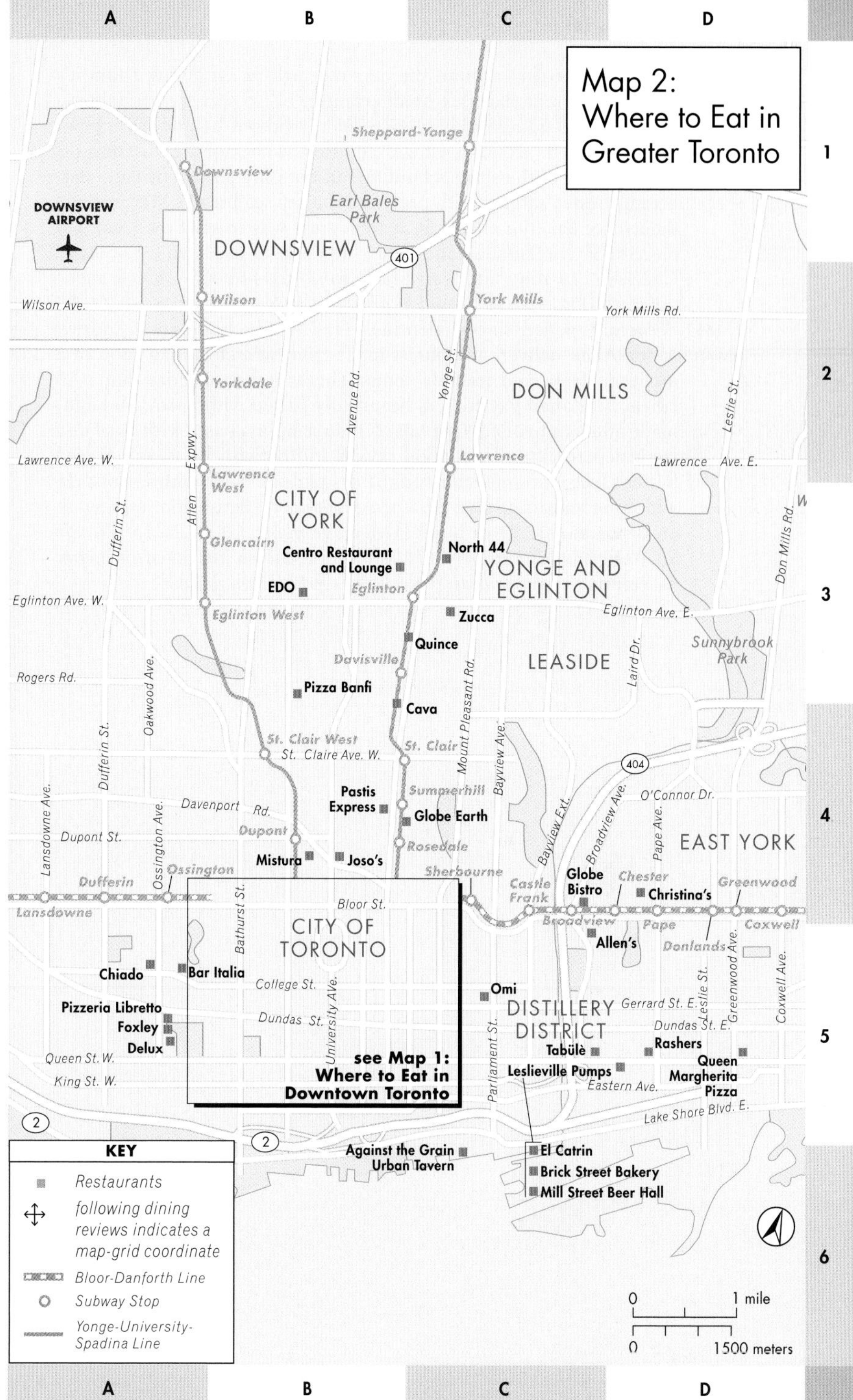

Map 2:
Where to Eat in
Greater Toronto
A
B
C
D
1
2
3
4
5
6
DOWNSVIEW AIRPORT
DOWNSVIEW
Earl Bales Park
Sheppard-Yonge
Downsview
Wilson
Wilson Ave.
York Mills
York Mills Rd.
401
Yorkdale
Avenue Rd.
Yonge St.
DON MILLS
Leslie St.
Lawrence Ave. W.
Allen Expwy.
Lawrence West
Lawrence
Lawrence Ave. E.
CITY OF YORK
Dufferin St.
Glencairn
Centro Restaurant and Lounge
North 44
YONGE AND EGLINTON
EDO
Eglinton
Don Mills Rd.
Eglinton Ave. W.
Eglinton West
Zucca
Eglinton Ave. E.
Quince
Sunnybrook Park
Davisville
LEASIDE
Laird Dr.
Rogers Rd.
Pizza Banfi
Mount Pleasant Rd.
Oakwood Ave.
Cava
Bayview Ave.
St. Clair West
St. Clair
St. Claire Ave. W.
404
Pastis Express
Summerhill
O'Connor Dr.
Lansdowne Ave.
Davenport Rd.
Globe Earth
Broadview Ave.
Pape Ave.
Dupont St.
Ossington Ave.
Dupont
Rosedale
Bayview Ext.
EAST YORK
Mistura
Joso's
Ossington
Sherbourne
Globe Bistro
Chester
Greenwood
Dufferin
Castle Frank
Christina's
Lansdowne
Bloor St.
Broadview
Pape
Coxwell
Bathurst St.
CITY OF TORONTO
Allen's
Donlands
Greenwood Ave.
Chiado
Bar Italia
College St.
Omi
Coxwell Ave.
Pizzeria Libretto
Foxley
Delux
Dundas St.
University Ave.
DISTILLERY DISTRICT
Gerrard St. E.
Leslie St.
Dundas St. E.
Parliament St.
Tabülè
Rashers
Queen St. W.
see Map 1: Where to Eat in Downtown Toronto
Leslieville Pumps
Queen Margherita Pizza
King St. W.
Eastern Ave.
Lake Shore Blvd. E.
2
Against the Grain Urban Tavern
El Catrin
Brick Street Bakery
Mill Street Beer Hall
KEY
Restaurants
following dining reviews indicates a map-grid coordinate
Bloor-Danforth Line
Subway Stop
Yonge-University-Spadina Line
0
1 mile
0
1500 meters

$$$ MEDITERRANEAN **Quince.** Looking around the narrow earth-toned dining room it's quickly apparent that this Mediterranean bistro serves a straightforward and candid assembly of ingredients, without fuss or any type of distraction. The wood-burning oven near the back of the restaurant is the highlight of the space, churning out not only pizza, but daily flatbread, roasted salmon with peas, and roasted sea bream. Martinis like the Lychee Saketini and Quince are a great way to start the meal. Go on Monday or Tuesday and there's no corkage fee. *Average main: C$22 2110 Yonge St., Yonge and Eglinton 416/488–2110 www.quincetoronto.com Closed Sun. No lunch Sat. Eglinton 2:C3.*

$$$ ITALIAN **Zucca.** Opened since Valentine's Day 1997, chef-owner Andrew Milne-Allan delivers the purest made-from-scratch Italian food in a modern, sleek, and friendly room. The wine list of more than 150 labels, all Italian varieties, is beautifully paired with pasta, all handmade and hand-rolled. Options include semolina pasta with basil and fresh peperoncino; half-moon ravioli stuffed with beets, poppyseed butter sauce, and smoked ricotta; and squid-ink pasta with seafood. In addition to meats, grilled fish is a specialty here. Finish your night with an Amaretto crème caramel. *Average main: C$24 2150 Yonge St., Yonge and Eglinton 416/488–5774 www.zuccatrattoria.com Reservations essential No lunch. Eglinton 2:C3.*

4

WHERE TO STAY

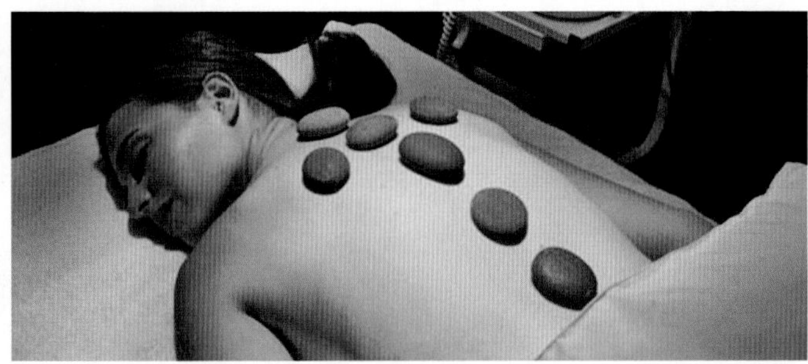

Updated by
Sarah Richards

Given that more than 100 languages and dialects are spoken in the Greater Toronto area, it's not surprising that much of the downtown hotel market is international-business-traveler savvy. Wi-Fi connections are standard at most high-end properties, and business services abound. But these same core hotels are close to tourist attractions—Harbourfront and the Toronto Islands, the cavernous Rogers Centre, the Air Canada Centre, the Four Seasons Centre for the Performing Arts, and the Royal Ontario Museum.

Not wanting to miss out on potential customers, hotels like the Delta Chelsea have instituted perks for the younger set, such as complimentary milk and cookies, kid-size bathrobes, and children's day camp. Another key trend in Toronto's downtown lodgings is the emergence of small, upscale boutique hotels, such as the Hotel Le Germain, the Pantages and Cosmopolitan hotels, and the swank SoHo Metropolitan. An explosion of ultraluxe chains has struck Toronto in recent years, and the city now boasts outposts of Shangri-La, Ritz-Carlton, and Trump International, plus a brand-new Four Seasons.

City-center accommodations are usually within a few minutes' walk of Yonge Street and the glittering lights of the Entertainment District, the soaring office towers of the Financial District, the shops of the Dundas Square Area, and the bars and art galleries of Queen West. Within a 15-minute drive west of downtown are the forested High Park and the meandering Humber River, an area where there are few major hotels but an ample array of B&Bs and the lovely Old Mill Inn. The growing West Queen West area has some unique places to stay, such as the restored Gladstone and Drake hotels, as well as funky restaurants and galleries. Lester B. Pearson International Airport is 29 km (18 miles) northwest of downtown; airport hotels are airport hotels, but staying in this area also means quick connections to cities beyond, such as Niagara Falls.

PLANNING

Where should you stay? With hundreds of Toronto hotels, it may seem like a daunting question. But fret not—our expert writers and editors have done most of the legwork. The 50-plus selections here represent the best the city has to offer—from the best budget motels to the sleekest boutique hotels. *Scan "Best Bets" on the following pages for top recommendations by price and experience. Or find a review quickly in the listings. Search by neighborhood, then alphabetically.* Happy Hunting!

RESERVATIONS

Hotel reservations are a necessity—rooms fill up quickly, so book as far in advance as possible. Summer is the busiest time, and if you plan on visiting during the Pride Festival (late June), Caribbean Carnival Toronto (late July), or Toronto International Film Festival (September), note that hordes of visitors will be joining you in search of a room, especially anywhere in the downtown area. At these times it doesn't hurt to search farther afield, but look for places along the subway lines to the north, west, or east, unless you have a car.

FACILITIES

Unless otherwise noted in individual descriptions, all the hotels listed have private baths, central heating, and private phones. Almost all hotels have Wi-Fi and phones with voice mail. Most large hotels have video or high-speed checkout capability, and many can arrange babysitting. Web TV, in-room video games, DVD players, iPod docks, and CD players are also provided in many hotels.

Driving a car in Toronto can be a headache unless your hotel provides free parking (which is extremely rare outside of airport hotels). Garages cost around C$25 per day, and street-side parking isn't available in most neighborhoods, but many city-owned parking lots have favorable rates on weekends and holidays.

WITH KIDS

Many of the downtown chain hotels offer free stays for kids under 12, but it would be best to check in advance when making reservations. Bed-and-breakfasts won't impose any rules against bringing children, but they will be considerably less accommodating. In recent years, boutique hotels have begun to embrace the "family-friendly" philosophy, and many now offer welcoming gifts for little ones such as cookies or teddy bears. *In the listings, look for the "Family" tag, which indicates a property that we recommend for when you're traveling with children.*

DISCOUNTS AND DEALS

When booking, remember first to ask about discounts and packages. Even the most expensive properties regularly reduce their rates during low-season lulls and on weekends. If you're a member of a group (senior citizen, student, auto club, or the military), you may also get a deal. Downtown hotels regularly have specials that include theater tickets, meals, or museum passes. It never hurts to ask for these kinds of perks up front.

WHERE SHOULD I STAY?

	Neighborhood Vibe	Pros	Cons
Harbourfront and the Financial District	This tourist hub includes the towering skyscrapers of the Financial District, and the many activities of Harbourfront.	Good eats in the historic Distillery District, close to island escapes in Lake Ontario, and surrounded by the city's top attractions.	Quiet at night and a bit removed from the action of Toronto's livelier neighborhoods.
Old Town	Toronto's first buildings crowd this leafy area, which extends to the historic Distillery District.	The St. Lawrence Market is here, and for a bustling night scene, you can hit the Esplanade.	Tourist-centric and local hangout, there's an interesting variety of lodgings available here.
Dundas Square Area	Dundas Square, Toronto's hottest new events center, faces the mammoth Eaton Centre shopping mall.	These areas have a festival-like atmosphere, and patios teem at sunset.	Things can get slightly sketchy late at night, and there aren't many recommended restaurants in the immediate vicinity.
Yorkville and Church-Wellesley	An area of superlatives: Canada's largest gay community is situated at Church-Wellesley, while upscale Yorkville houses the priciest boutiques.	Always busy and lively, and teeming with locals.	Yorkville can be painfully expensive and parts of Church-Wellesley can get sketchy late at night.
Queen West	Funky boutiques, cutting-edge design shops, and experimental restaurants and hotels.	This area sets the trends in Toronto, the restaurants and bars attract diverse clientele, and the Queen Street streetcar is frequent and runs 24 hours.	There aren't many parking options.

PRICES

The lodgings we list are the cream of the crop in each price category. Properties are assigned price categories based on the price of a standard double room during Toronto's busy summer season. When pricing accommodations, always ask what's included and what costs extra.

Although paying with U.S. dollars no longer gives you the advantage it has in the past, there are other ways to save money during a visit. Many hotels that cater to business travelers cut rates for weekends, and these hotels typically have special packages for couples and families. Toronto hotels usually slash rates a full 50% in January and February. Smaller hotels and apartment-style accommodations downtown are also moderately priced (and, therefore, popular in summer).

Prices in the reviews are the lowest cost of a standard double room in high season.

HOTEL REVIEWS

Listed alphabetically within neighborhoods.

Throughout the chapter, you'll see mapping symbols and coordinates (✣ F2) after property names or reviews. To locate the property on a map, turn to the Where to Stay Toronto map within this chapter. The numbers after the ✣ symbol indicate its coordinate on the map grid.

For expanded hotel reviews, visit Fodors.com.

HARBOURFRONT, ENTERTAINMENT DISTRICT, AND FINANCIAL DISTRICT

4

HARBOURFRONT

Situating yourself here is a good idea for exploring the greatest concentration of Toronto's must-see attractions—especially the kid-friendly ones—like the Rogers Centre, Ontario Place, and the CN Tower.

$$$$ HOTEL **Hôtel Le Germain Maple Leaf Square.** Inside the Maple Leaf Square complex, which includes a Starbucks, this ultra-stylish hotel is perfectly poised to receive traffic from the Air Canada Centre across the street and the Rogers Centre just minutes away. **Pros:** free welcome treats for kids and pets (mention when booking); great service; spacious lobby with free coffee; attached to PATH network; near Billy Bishop Toronto City Airport. **Cons:** area is boisterous when events are happening at nearby Air Canada Centre. *Rooms from: C$269 ✉ 75 Bremner Blvd., Harbourfront ☎ 416/649–7575, 888/940–7575 ⊕ www.germainmapleleafsquare.com 167 rooms Breakfast* Ⓜ *Union ✣ E6.*

$$ HOTEL FAMILY **Radisson Hotel Admiral Toronto–Harbourfront.** You can't get much closer to Toronto's waterfront, and unobstructed Lake Ontario and verdant Toronto Islands' vistas come standard. **Pros:** good value; easy access to Toronto Islands' ferries and convention center; free Wi-Fi. **Cons:** quiet and seems out of the way in winter and spring. *Rooms from: C$169 ✉ 249 Queen's Quay W, at York St., Harbourfront ☎ 416/203–3333, 800/395–7046 ⊕ www.radisson.com 157 rooms No meals* Ⓜ *Union ✣ E6.*

$$$ HOTEL FAMILY **Westin Harbour Castle.** On a clear day you can see the skyline of Rochester, New York, across the sparkling blue Lake Ontario from most rooms at this mid-range, kid-friendly hotel. **Pros:** very comfortable beds; great kids' programs. **Cons:** not right in downtown; hotel can feel overwhelmingly large; decor is dated. *Rooms from: C$229 ✉ 1 Harbour Sq., at Bay St., Harbourfront ☎ 416/869–1600, 800/937–8461 ⊕ www.westinharbourcastletoronto.com 977 rooms No meals* Ⓜ *Union ✣ F6.*

THE ENTERTAINMENT DISTRICT

It's hard to imagine the quiet, empty-looking warehouses in the Entertainment District spontaneously exploding with activity, but when the sun goes down this neighborhood is party central. The bustle and excitement generated by Toronto's clubbers, theatergoers, and night owls keep the action alive until 3 am most nights.

$$$ HOTEL **Hilton Toronto.** Everything that you'd expect from a Hilton, this central outpost near the entertainment and financial districts is decorated in golds and browns in the lobby with wooden floors and subtle earth tones. **Pros:** across the street from the Four Seasons Centre for the Performing Arts; popular on-site Ruth's Chris Steak House; safe and walkable neighborhood. **Cons:** rooms can be small; service lags at times; expensive Internet ($15 per device per day). *Rooms from: C$209 ✉ 145 Richmond St. W, at University Ave., Entertainment District ☎ 416/869–3456, 800/267–2281 🌐 www.hilton.com 601 rooms, 47 suites No meals Ⓜ Osgoode ✣ E5.*

WORD OF MOUTH

"Just stayed at the Hyatt and it is a very nice hotel, lots of bars and nightlife nearby (Second City with a rooftop bar is directly across the street and offers a 20% discount to those staying at the Hyatt)" —hlphillips2

$$$ HOTEL **Hilton Garden Inn Downtown.** Like the downtown entertainment hub that surrounds it, this brand-new hotel pulses with activity around the clock. **Pros:** free Wi-Fi; central downtown location; excellent service. **Cons:** some rooms on south side can get noisy; parking lot tends to fill up quickly. *Rooms from: C$229 ✉ 92 Peter St., Entertainment District ☎ 416/593–9200 🌐 hiltongardeninn.hilton.com 224 rooms No meals Ⓜ Osgoode, St. Andrew ✣ D5.*

$$$ Fodor's Choice ★ **Hôtel Le Germain Toronto.** The retro, redbrick exterior of this chic hotel—conveniently located near the TIFF Lightbox, site of the Toronto International Film Festival—blends seamlessly with the historic architecture of the surrounding theater district. **Pros:** complimentary Continental breakfast; free Wi-Fi; attentive staff; on a quiet street; pet-friendly with welcome gifts for four-legged friends; putting green and outdoor terrace on 11th floor. **Cons:** rooms fill up fast. *Rooms from: C$249 ✉ 30 Mercer St., at John St., Entertainment District ☎ 416/345–9500, 866/345–9501 🌐 www.germaintoronto.com 118 rooms, 4 suites Breakfast Ⓜ St. Andrew ✣ D6.*

$$$ HOTEL **Hyatt Regency Toronto.** Request views of Lake Ontario, the downtown skyline, or the Rogers Centre at this luxury hotel smack in the middle of the pulsating Entertainment District. **Pros:** closest large hotel to King Street West theaters; dozens of excellent restaurants and cinemas nearby. **Cons:** pricey restaurant; guest rooms on lower floors facing King Street may be noisy; expensive parking. *Rooms from: C$199 ✉ 370 King St. W, Entertainment District ☎ 416/343–1234, 800/633–7313 in U.S. 🌐 www.torontoregency.hyatt.com 394 rooms, 32 suites No meals Ⓜ St. Andrew ✣ D6.*

$$$ HOTEL **InterContinental Toronto Centre.** Attached to the Metro Toronto Convention Centre, this large but unassuming hotel is a good bet for visiting businesspeople, but leisure travelers can also find deals on weekends or during slow periods. **Pros:** atypical convention hotel; bright and airy lobby restaurant; pet-friendly. **Cons:** no shopping nearby. *Rooms from: C$209 ✉ 225 Front St. W, west of University Ave., Entertainment District ☎ 416/597–1400, 800/422–7969 🌐 www.torontocentre.intercontinental.com 440 rooms, 136 suites No meals Ⓜ Union ✣ E6.*

BEST BETS FOR TORONTO LODGING

Fodor's offers a selective listing of quality lodging experiences at every price, from the city's best budget motel to its most sophisticated luxury hotels. Here, we've compiled our top recommendations by price and experience. The very best properties—those that provide a particularly remarkable experience in their price range—are designated in the listings with a Fodor's Choice logo.

Fodor's Choice ★

Drake Hotel, $$$, p. 145

Four Seasons Toronto, $$$$, p. 147

Gladstone Hotel, $$, p. 145

Hazelton Hotel, $$$$, p. 147

Hôtel Le Germain Toronto, $$$, p. 136

Residence Inn Downtown, $$$, p. 140

Shangri-La Toronto, $$$$, p. 140

Suite Dreams, $$, p. 145

By Price

$

Annex Quest House, p. 145

Bonnevue Manor Bed & Breakfast Place, p. 143

$$

Gladstone Hotel, p. 145

Hilton Garden Inn City Centre, p. 143

Hotel Victoria, p. 141

$$$

Drake Hotel, p. 145

Fairmont Royal York, p. 141

Hôtel Le Germain Toronto, p. 136

One King West Hotel & Residence, p. 141

Residence Inn Downtown, p. 140

SoHo Metropolitan Hotel, p. 140

$$$$

Hazelton Hotel, p. 147

Hôtel Le Germain Maple Leaf Square, p. 135

Ritz-Carlton, Toronto, p. 141

Shangri-La Toronto, p. 140

By Experience

BEST FOR ROMANCE

Cosmopolitan Toronto Hotel, $$$, p. 141

Hazelton Hotel, $$$$, p. 147

Hôtel Le Germain Toronto, $$$, p. 136

Park Hyatt Toronto, $$$$, p. 147

BEST FOR BUSINESS

Fairmont Royal York, $$$, p. 141

InterContinental Toronto Centre, $$$, p. 136

Westin Harbour Castle, $$$, p. 135

Ritz-Carlton, Toronto, $$$$, p. 141

Shangri-La Toronto, $$$$, p. 140

BEST FOR FAMILIES

Eaton Chelsea Hotel, $$, p. 143

Radisson Hotel Admiral Toronto-Harbourfront, $$, p. 135

Renaissance Toronto Hotel Downtown, $$$, p. 140

Residence Inn Downtown, $$$, p. 140

BEST VIEWS

Four Seasons Toronto, $$$$, p. 147

Radisson Hotel Admiral Toronto–Harbourfront, $$, p. 135

Sheraton Centre, $$$, p. 140

One King West Hotel & Residence, $$$, p. 141

Westin Harbour Castle, $$$, p. 135

BEST CELEBRITY RETREAT

Four Seasons Toronto, $$$$, p. 147

Hazelton Hotel, $$$$, p. 147

Park Hyatt Toronto, $$$$, p. 147

Shangri-La Toronto, $$$$, p. 140

The King Edward, $$$, p. 142

BEST INTERIOR DESIGN

Drake Hotel, $$$, p. 145

Gladstone Hotel, $$, p. 145

Hazelton Hotel, $$$$, p. 147

Hôtel Le Germain Maple Leaf Square, $$$$, p. 135

Shangri-La Toronto, $$$$, p. 140

BEST SPA

Hazelton Hotel, $$$$, p. 147

Park Hyatt Toronto, $$$$, p. 147

Ritz-Carlton, Toronto, $$$$, p. 141

Where to Stay in Toronto
KEY
Hotels
Subway Stops
following lodging reviews indicates a map-grid coordinate
0 1/4 mile
0 400 meters
Suite Dreams
Alt Hotel Pearson
Old Mill Inn & Spa
Sandman Signature Toronto Airport
Sheraton Gateway Hotel
Islington Bed & Breakfast House
By the Park B&B
TO AIRPORT STRIP
The Drake Hotel
Gladstone Hotel
Bonnevue Manor Bed & Breakfast Place
Annex Quest House
Hilton Garden Inn Downtown
Hyatt Regency Toronto
Hôtel Le Germain Toronto
SoHo Metropolitan Hotel
Residence Inn
Renaissance Toronto Hotel Downtown
THE ANNEX
LITTLE ITALY
CHINATOWN
QUEEN WEST
UNIVERSITY OF TORONTO
ST. GEORGE
SPADINA
Alexandra Park
Grange Park
Bloor St. W.
Lennox St.
Herrick St.
Harbord St.
Ulster St.
College St.
Oxford St.
Nassau St.
Dundas St. W.
Robinson St.
Carr St.
Wolseley St.
Queen St. W.
Richmond St. W.
Adelaide St. W.
King St. W.
Wellington St. W.
Front St. W.
Sussex Ave.
Hoskin Ave.
Willcocks St.
Russell St.
Cecil St.
Baldwin St.
D'Arcy St.
Sullivan St.
Grange Rd.
Bulwer St.
Renfrew Pl.
Camden St.
Mercer St.
Clinton St.
Bathurst St.
Lippincott St.
Croft St.
Howland Ave.
Brunswick Ave.
Major St.
Robert St.
Sussex Mews
Spadina Ave.
Walmer Rd.
Huron St.
St. George St.
Devonshire Pl.
King's College
King's College Rd.
Ross St.
Henry St.
Euclid Ave.
Palmerston Blvd.
Markham St.
Leonard Ave.
Bellevue Ave.
Augusta Ave.
Denison Ave.
Ryerson Ave.
Grange Pl.
Beverley St.
Peter St.
John St.
Tecumseth St.
Brant St.
Brant Pl.
Widmer St.
Portland St.
Blue Jays Way
Windsor St.
A B C D
1 2 3 4 5 6

E
F
G
H
1
2
3
4
5
6
Novo Spa
The Hazelton Hotel
YORKVILLE
ROSEDALE
Park Hyatt Toronto
Four Seasons Toronto
Cumberland St.
Asquith Ave.
Avenue Rd.
BAY
BLOOR-YONGE
Bloor St. E.
InterContinental Toronto Yorkville
Windsor Arms
St. Thomas St.
Mt. Pleasant Rd.
Hayden St.
Au Petit Paris
MUSEUM
Queen's Park
Charles St. W.
Charles St. E.
St. Mary's St.
Sherbourne St.
QUEEN'S PARK
Isabella St.
St. Nicholas St.
Gloucester St.
Tower Rd.
Queen's Park
St. Joseph St.
Phipps St.
WELLESLEY
Church St.
Queen's Park Cir. W.
Queen's Park Cir. E.
Wellesley St. W.
Wellesley St. E.
CHURCH-WELLESLEY
Cir.
Breadalbane St.
Yonge St.
Maitland Ter.
Maitland Ave.
Jarvis St.
Homewood Ave.
ONTARIO LEGISLATIVE BUILDING
Grosvenor St.
Alexander St.
Grenville St.
Wood St.
COLLEGE
College St.
QUEEN'S PARK
Carlton St.
Elizabeth St.
Bay St.
Les Amis
Granby St.
Allan Gardens
Orde St.
McGill St.
Mutual St.
University Ave.
Murray St.
DUNDAS SQUARE AREA
Gerrard St. W.
Gerrard St. E.
Walton St.
Eaton Chelsea Hotel
Pembroke St.
George St.
Elm St.
Gould St.
ST. PATRICK
Edward St.
DUNDAS
Hilton Garden Inn City Centre
McCaul St.
St. Patrick St.
Chestnut St.
Dundas St. W.
O'Keefe St.
Toronto Downtown Marriott Eaton Centre
Dundas St. E.
Sherbourne St.
Simcoe St.
Armoury St.
CITY HALL
Bond St.
Grand Hotel and Suites
Pantages Hotel
Shuter St.
Nathan Phillips Square
James St.
Moss Park
Pullan Pl.
QUEEN
Victoria St.
Church St.
Jarvis St.
OSGOODE
Queen St. E.
Duncan St.
Sheraton Centre
York St.
Bay St.
Yonge St.
Berti St.
Shangri-La Toronto
Cambridge Suites
Richmond St. E.
Nelson St.
Hilton Toronto
Temperance St.
Lombard St.
Trump International Hotel & Tower Toronto
FINANCIAL DISTRICT
Adelaide St. E.
Pearl St.
ST. ANDREW
KING
Toronto St.
Cosmopolitan Toronto Hotel
King St. E.
ENTERTAINMENT DISTRICT
One King West Hotel & Residence
Colborne St.
King Edward
Leader La.
Front St. E.
OLD TOWN
Wellington St. W.
The Fairmont Royal York
Wellington St. E.
Scott St.
Front St. E.
Ritz-Carlton
Heenan Pl.
Piper St.
The Esplanade
Hotel Victoria
Wilton St.
InterContinental Toronto Centre
Radisson Hotel Admiral Toronto-Harbourfront
Novotel Toronto Centre
Station St.
York St.
TORONTO CONVENTION CENTER
The Westin Harbour Castle
Hôtel Le Germain Maple Leaf Square
E
F
G
H

$$$ HOTEL FAMILY **Renaissance Toronto Hotel Downtown.** Where else can you watch a baseball game, pop-star concert, or monster-truck rally from the comfort of your room? **Pros:** likable staff; free lobby Internet; guest rooms best place to watch Blue Jays baseball games. **Cons:** very long hallways; little natural light in guest rooms overlooking field; hotel's public spaces and rooms due for a makeover. *Rooms from: C$199 ✉ 1 Blue Jays Way, at Front St. W, Entertainment District ☎ 416/341–7100, 800/237–1512 www.renaissancehotels.com 313 rooms, 35 suites No meals M Union ✣ D6.*

$$$ HOTEL FAMILY Fodor's Choice ★ **Residence Inn Downtown.** A big hit with families and long-term visitors to Toronto, the modern suites at the Residence Inn come with full kitchens, spacious living and dining rooms, and comfortable bedrooms. **Pros:** close to Toronto's major attractions; a smart choice for large families; no minimum stay. **Cons:** valet parking only; breakfast buffet gets extremely crowded during peak season. *Rooms from: C$229 ✉ 255 Wellington St. W, at Windsor St., Entertainment District ☎ 416/581–1800 www.marriott.com 256 suites Breakfast M Union ✣ D6.*

$$$$ HOTEL Fodor's Choice ★ **Shangri-La Toronto.** This hotel, opened in 2012, embodies the attention to service for which the Shangri-La brand is beloved while putting an art-focused twist on its traditional East-meets-West aesthetic. **Pros:** stellar service; noted art collection; appealing vibe. **Cons:** pricey. *Rooms from: C$355 ✉ 188 University Ave., Entertainment District ☎ 647/788–8888 www.shangri-la.com/toronto/shangrila 197 rooms, 5 suites No meals M Osgoode, St. Andrew ✣ E5.*

$$$ HOTEL **Sheraton Centre.** Views from this hotel in the city center are marvelous—to the south are the CN Tower and the Rogers Centre; to the north, both new and old city halls. **Pros:** underground access to PATH network; pool open late; walk to Four Seasons Centre for Performing Arts. **Cons:** slightly sterile; expensive parking and Internet; hotel is overwhelmingly large. *Rooms from: C$249 ✉ 123 Queen St. W, at Bay St., Entertainment District ☎ 416/361–1000, 800/325–3535 www.sheratontoronto.com 1,302 rooms, 75 suites No meals M Osgoode ✣ E5.*

$$$ HOTEL **SoHo Metropolitan Hotel.** Saturated in pampering detail, the SoHo Met conjures luxury with Frette linens, down duvets, walk-in closets, heated bathroom floors, and Molton Brown bath products. **Pros:** no detail left to chance, including electric do-not-disturb signs and curtains; stylish but not showy. **Cons:** lap pool only three feet deep; located slightly away from main streets. *Rooms from: C$225 ✉ 318 Wellington St. W, east of Spadina Ave., Entertainment District ☎ 416/599–8800, 800/668–6600 www.soho.metropolitan.com 72 rooms, 19 suites No meals M St. Andrew ✣ D6.*

FINANCIAL DISTRICT

While the sidewalks are brimming with suits and cell phones during the day, this area really quiets down after the sun sets. On the weekend, it can feel almost eerie. Still, there are a few notable attractions here that appeal to diverse palettes, such as the Hockey Hall of Fame and the Design Exchange.

$$$ HOTEL **Cambridge Suites.** With just 12 suites per floor, this self-dubbed boutique hotel focuses on service: rooms are cleaned twice daily, and there's same-day dry cleaning and laundry, free access to a downtown fitness club, and complimentary Wi-Fi. **Pros:** central location; extras like free shoe shines; "social hour" with discounted drinks at on-site bar; late checkout. **Cons:** some services, such as parking, can be expensive. *Rooms from: C$199* ✉ *15 Richmond St. E, at Victoria St., Financial District* ☎ *416/368–1990* *www.cambridgesuitestoronto.com* *229 suites* *No meals* *Queen* *F5.*

$$$ HOTEL **Cosmopolitan Toronto Hotel.** Tucked away on a side street in the heart of Toronto, this überboutique, all-suite hotel seamlessly blends an Eastern aesthetic with typical Western hotel amenities. **Pros:** private and quiet; hipness factor. **Cons:** side streets dark at night; "Zen" philosophy may not appeal to all; charge for Wi-Fi. *Rooms from: C$219* ✉ *8 Colborne St., at Yonge St., Financial District* ☎ *416/945–5455, 800/958–3488* *www.cosmotoronto.com* *95 suites, 2 penthouse suites* *No meals* *King* *F6.*

$$$ HOTEL **Fairmont Royal York.** Like a proud grandmother, the Royal York stands serenely on Front Street in downtown Toronto, surrounded by gleaming skyscrapers and the nearby CN Tower. **Pros:** royal experience; excellent health club; environmentally conscious; extensive Canadian wine list. **Cons:** immense hotel with small rooms; charge for in-room Internet access; expensive parking. *Rooms from: C$249* ✉ *100 Front St. W, at York St., Financial District* ☎ *416/368–2511, 800/441–1414* *www.fairmont.com/royalyork* *1,304 rooms, 61 suites* *No meals* *Union* *E6.*

$$ HOTEL **Hotel Victoria.** A local landmark built in 1909, "the Vic" is Toronto's second-oldest hotel, with a long-standing reputation for service excellence. **Pros:** gym privileges at nearby health club; complimentary newspapers; free Wi-Fi. **Cons:** inconvenient, off-site parking; second-floor rooms noisy from street; slow elevator. *Rooms from: C$139* ✉ *56 Yonge St., at Wellington St., Financial District* ☎ *416/363–1666, 800/363–8228* *www.hotelvictoria-toronto.com* *56 rooms* *No meals* *King* *F6.*

$$$ HOTEL **One King West Hotel & Residence.** Made up entirely of suites, this 51-story tower is attached to the old Dominion Bank of Canada (circa 1912) in the city's downtown business and shopping core. **Pros:** great views from upper floors; self-catering facility; central locale; excellent service. **Cons:** some rooms have small TVs; valet parking only. *Rooms from: C$229* ✉ *1 King St. W, at Yonge St., Financial District* ☎ *416/548–8100, 866/470–5464* *www.onekingwest.com* *340 suites* *No meals* *King* *F6.*

$$$$ HOTEL **Ritz-Carlton, Toronto.** This Ritz has a great location—across from Roy Thompson Hall and smack-dab in the center of the Financial District—and a solid elegance, embellished with a Canadian motif of brass maple leaves and local woods. **Pros:** reliable Ritz service; top-of-the-line amenities; access to the Club Lounge and its free open bar, buffets, business center, and TV room for C$100. **Cons:** five-star prices; expensive valet parking. *Rooms from: C$525* ✉ *181 Wellington St. W, Financial District* ☎ *416/585–2500* *www.ritzcarlton.com/toronto* *208 rooms, 59 suites* *No meals* *St. Andrew, Union* *E6.*

$$$$ HOTEL **Trump International Hotel & Tower Toronto.** The new darling of the Financial District, this 65-story, hotel-and-condo tower from the well-known luxury hotelier has taken Toronto by storm. **Pros:** free Wi-Fi; if you can score a corporate rate, it's actually affordable; little surprises abound, such as free chocolates in room. **Cons:** area gets quiet at night; business-oriented; cautious, if restrained decor. *Rooms from: C$545 ✉ 325 Bay St., Financial District ☎ 416/306–5800, 855/888–7867 reservations ⊕ www.trumphotelcollection.com/toronto 261 rooms No meals Ⓜ Queen or King ⊕ F5.*

WORD OF MOUTH

"Closer to the Distillery District and Harbourfront are the Cosmopolitan (a boutique style suite hotel, I've also stayed here) and the Novotel. These are also walking distance to the St. Lawrence Market which is popular and vibrant, especially Saturday mornings (great breakfast sandwiches at Carousel Bakery)."

—mat54

OLD TOWN

A pleasant mix of Toronto's oldest buildings, modern coffee shops and restaurants hiding behind historic redbrick facades, and newish condo developments fill the leafy streets in this evolving neighborhood. Staying here puts you near some of the city's oldest landmarks, such as the St. Lawrence Market, the historic Distillery District, and St. James Cathedral.

$$$ HOTEL **Grand Hotel and Suites.** A gorgeous 30-foot facade leads into a lobby of gleaming marble and granite pillars peppered with plush furnishings. **Pros:** complimentary Wi-Fi throughout the property; close to Eaton Centre, St. Lawrence Market, and Yonge Street. **Cons:** the neighborhood is a bit run-down; breakfast is the same every day. *Rooms from: C$249 ✉ 225 Jarvis St., Old Town ☎ 416/863–9000, 877/324–7263 ⊕ www.grandhoteltoronto.com 177 suites Breakfast Ⓜ Dundas ⊕ G4.*

$$$ HOTEL **The King Edward.** Toronto's landmark "King Eddy" Hotel, which has hosted the well-heeled for over a century, continues to be a favorite choice for special occasions and a nod to grand hotels of the past. **Pros:** great location; historic; friendly service. **Cons:** no mirror above sink in some rooms; high daily Internet fee; furniture shows wear and tear. *Rooms from: C$199 ✉ 37 King St. E, east of Yonge St., Old Town ☎ 416/863–9700, 800/543–4300 ⊕ www.thekingedwardhotel.com 292 rooms, 29 suites No meals Ⓜ King ⊕ G6.*

$$ HOTEL **Novotel Toronto Centre.** A good-value, few-frills, modern hotel, the Novotel is in the heart of the animated, bar-lined Esplanade area, near the St. Lawrence Market, the Air Canada Centre, Union Station, and the Entertainment District. **Pros:** excellent location; good value; laptop-size in-room safes. **Cons:** small in-hotel parking spaces; spotty service and housekeeping; noisy neighborhood. *Rooms from: C$175 ✉ 45 The Esplanade, at Church St., Old Town ☎ 416/367–8900, 800/668–6835 ⊕ www.novotel.com 262 rooms No meals Ⓜ Union ⊕ F6.*

DUNDAS SQUARE AREA

This tourist-centric area feels like the heart of Toronto with the ginormous Eaton Centre as its anchor. The sprawling Dundas Square bustles every day with an open-air market, an impromptu concert, a mini festival, or, on those rare days when no events are scheduled, kids leaping around water fountains.

$$ HOTEL FAMILY **Eaton Chelsea Hotel.** Canada's largest hotel has long been popular with families and tour groups, so be prepared for a flurry of activity. **Pros:** all-inclusive atmosphere; good service; extremely family-friendly. **Cons:** busy and noisy lobby at times; can be long lines for check-in/checkout; slow elevators. *Rooms from: C$169 33 Gerrard St., at Yonge St., Dundas Square Area 416/595–1975, 800/243–5732 chelsea.eatonhotelscom 1,590 rooms, 46 suites No meals College F3.*

$$ HOTEL **Hilton Garden Inn City Centre.** Suites at this hotel, an incarnation of the popular Hilton chain, are modern and simple with basic furniture and spacious bathrooms. **Pros:** close to the Eaton Centre; advance reservations are heavily discounted. **Cons:** run-down neighborhood with panhandlers. *Rooms from: C$169 200 Dundas St. E, Dundas Square Area 416/362–7700 416/362–7706 hiltongardeninn.hilton.com 151 suites No meals Dundas G4.*

$$$ HOTEL **Pantages Hotel.** Clean lines, gleaming hardwood flooring, and brushed-steel accents exude contemporary cool at this hotel. **Pros:** quiet but central location for shopping; excellent spa; great for long stays. **Cons:** smallish TVs; lobby can be noisy; dark hallways; some rooms in need of upgrading. *Rooms from: C$199 200 Victoria St., at Shuter St., Dundas Square Area 416/362–1777, 866/852–1777 www.pantageshotel.com 95 suites No meals Queen F4.*

$$$ HOTEL **Toronto Downtown Marriott Eaton Centre.** Guest rooms at the Marriott's flagship hotel in Canada are connected to Eaton Centre through an aboveground walkway. **Pros:** knowledgeable employees; good value; large guest rooms. **Cons:** may be noisy; parking area fills up quickly. *Rooms from: C$199 525 Bay St., at Dundas St. W, Dundas Square Area 416/597–9200, 800/905–0667 www.marriotteatoncentre.com 435 rooms, 24 suites No meals Dundas F4.*

QUEEN WEST

In this trend-setting neighborhood, along Queen Street West beyond Bathurst Street, the hotels get more experimental and cutting-edge the farther west you go. Many highlight local art and music, and have noteworthy restaurants that practice sustainability.

$ B&B/INN **Bonnevue Manor Bed & Breakfast Place.** True craftsmen created this 5,000-square-foot house, and it shows in every enchanting nook and cranny, in the high plastered ceilings, and in the richly aged hardwood floors. **Pros:** safe and comfortable neighborhood; excellent breakfasts; free Wi-Fi. **Cons:** not downtown; petite rooms; not all rooms have private bathrooms. *Rooms from: C$125 33 Beaty Ave., south of Queen St. W, Queen West 416/536–1455 www.bonnevuemanor.com 4 rooms Breakfast Osgoode, then streetcar 501 west A5.*

CLOSE UP

Toronto Lodging Alternatives and Resources

APARTMENT RENTALS

If you want a home base that's roomy enough for a family and comes with cooking facilities, consider a furnished rental. Home-exchange directories sometimes list rentals as well as exchanges.

Hideaways International. A four-month membership is US$49. ☎ *603/430-4433* 🌐 *www.hideaways.com.*

LOCAL AGENTS

Apartments International Inc. Provides upper-end furnished apartments for executives visiting for a month or more. ☎ *416/410-2400, 888/410-2400* 🌐 *www.apts-intl.com.*

BED-AND-BREAKFASTS

Au Petit Paris. A great alternative to big chain hotels in this area, this B&B is southeast of Yorkville, west of the Church-Wellesley district, and north of the Dundas Square neighborhood. ✉ *3 Selby St., Church-Wellesley* ☎ *416/928-1348* 🌐 *www.bbtoronto.com/aupetitparis.*

By the Park B&B. This B&B is the brainchild of a couple who happen to be alumni of the Ontario College of Art and Design; their attention to design is evident. ✉ *92 & 89 Indian Grove., at Bloor St. W, Greater Toronto* ☎ *416/761-9778, 416/520-6102* 🌐 *www.bythepark.ca.*

The Downtown Toronto Association of Bed & Breakfast Guest Houses. This organization represents privately owned B&Bs. ☎ *416/410-3938* 🌐 *www.bnbinfo.com.*

Islington Bed & Breakfast House. At this good-value B&B, paintings and tapestries reflect the local landscape. ✉ *1411 Islington Ave., Greater Toronto* ☎ *416/236-2707* 🌐 *www.islingtonhouse.com.*

Les Amis. The charming Parisian host Paul-Antoine fills Les Amis with beautiful photos of his travels through South America and Africa and the tantalizing aromas of his legendary fruit crepes and Belgian-style waffles. ✉ *31 Granby St., at Yonge St., Dundas Square Area* ☎ *416/928-1348* 🌐 *www.bbtoronto.com.*

Toronto Bed & Breakfast. A free registry, this organization lists more than a dozen private homes, all in and around downtown Toronto. ☎ *705/738-9449, 877/922-6522* 🌐 *www.torontobandb.com.*

HOSTELS

With some 4,000 locations in more than 90 countries, Hostelling International (HI), the umbrella group for a number of national youth-hostel associations, has single-sex, dorm-style beds and, at many hostels, including those in Toronto, rooms for couples and accommodations for families. Membership in any HI national hostel association, open to travelers of all ages, allows you to stay in HI-affiliated hostels at member rates; one-year membership is C$28 for adults (C$35 for a two-year membership in Canada); hostels charge about C$15 to C$35 per night.

ORGANIZATIONS

Hostelling International—USA ✉ *8401 Colesville Rd., Ste. 600, Silver Spring, Maryland, USA* ☎ *240/650-2100* 🌐 *www.hiusa.org.*

WORD OF MOUTH

"Eaton Chelsea in Toronto is the best kids' hotel, and has a good waterslide and other stuff for children."

—BAK

$$$ HOTEL Fodor's Choice ★ **The Drake Hotel.** Once a notorious flophouse, this 19th-century building is now an ultra-hip hotel peppered with contemporary art and attracting a chic, creative crowd. **Pros:** attracts Toronto's hippest crowd; excellent food; complimentary access to off-site gym. **Cons:** can be noisy at night; not great for children; hard to get a room. *Rooms from: C$189 ✉ 1150 Queen St. W, at Beaconsfield Ave., Queen West ☎ 416/531–5042, 866/372–5386 www.thedrakehotel.ca 19 rooms, 1 suite No meals* Ⓜ *Osgoode, then streetcar 501 west ✣ A5.*

$$ HOTEL Fodor's Choice ★ **Gladstone Hotel.** An intimate size and focus on local art and products helped this hotel earn raves as the "anti chain-hotel Toronto experience"—really, it's a sort of community event space, with artist-designed guest rooms and an emphasis on everything that is one-of-a-kind. **Pros:** local flavor; intimate service and setting; every guest room has a different, playful design; friendly, bohemian place; truly a one-of-a-kind property and experience. **Cons:** rooms are on the smaller side; long walk or transit ride to downtown core. *Rooms from: C$175 ✉ 1214 Queen St. W, at Gladstone Ave., Queen West ☎ 416/531–4635 www.gladstonehotel.com 34 rooms, 3 suites No meals* Ⓜ *Osgoode, then streetcar 501 west ✣ A5.*

THE ANNEX

The Annex may bustle along Bloor Street West, but the long residential streets running north hide quiet B&Bs that lend a small-town feel to the middle of the city.

$ B&B/INN **Annex Quest House.** Ecologically friendly and following the eastern design rules of *Vastu* (a sort of Hindu feng shui), the eighteen rooms at this Victorian house are decked out in colorful Asian textiles, wooden sculptures and furniture, and splashes of sequined silk. **Pros:** Free Wi-Fi and all-day snacks; good value; excellent location. **Cons:** Vastu decor not for everyone; no breakfast. *Rooms from: C$105 ✉ 83 Spadina Rd., The Annex ☎ 416/922–1934 www.annexquesthouse.com 18 rooms No meals ✣ D1.*

$$ B&B/INN Fodor's Choice ★ **Suite Dreams.** At the western end of the Annex, almost bordering the trendy area dubbed "Little Korea," this elegant B&B has four lovely suites that remain in high demand among B&B enthusiasts. **Pros:** interesting location; owner is wealth of tourist information. **Cons:** only four rooms means reserve well in advance. *Rooms from: C$149 ✉ 390 Clinton St., at Bloor St. W, The Annex ☎ 416/538–0417 www.suitedreamstoronto.com 4 rooms, 3 with bath Breakfast* Ⓜ *Christie ✣ B1.*

4

CLOSE UP

Toronto's Best Spas

The spa scene in Toronto is both established and ever evolving, with a wrap, massage, and facial to match every mood and personality type. The problem with spa-hopping in Toronto isn't about finding a good spa but more a matter of choosing one.

All of the city's best boutique hotels offer high-end spa treatments, often with added perks like an infrared sauna or saltwater pool. The **Hyatt's Stillwater Spa** has been touted as the city's best by Toronto's choosiest spa connoisseurs, although a dip in the Bissaza mosaic-tile lap pool after a Copper Relaxation Body Scrub at the **Hazelton** is an experience you won't soon forget. For the royal treatment, book at the **Ritz-Carlton** spa: its aromatherapy massages, purifying facials, and attentive service live up to the luxury brand's reputation.

Here are a few of our favorite independent spas:

Elmwood. Since 1982, the Elmwood, hidden inside a historic redbrick building, has been offering classic spa packages including hot stone massages, anti-aging facials, microdermabrasion treatments, and exfoliating wraps. ✉ *18 Elm St., Dundas Square Area* ☎ *416/977-6751* 🌐 *www.elmwoodspa.com* ⏲ *Mon. -Thurs. 10-9, Fri. 9-9, Sat. 9-8, Sun. 10:30-6:30* Ⓜ *Dundas.*

Hammam Spa. At Hammam Spa devoted Entertainment District clients come to soak up eucalyptus-scented steam in a 500-square-foot marble-tile Turkish bath following a Reiki massage or detoxifying algae wrap. ✉ *602 King St. W, at Portland, Entertainment District* ☎ *416/366-4772* 🌐 *www.hammamspa.ca* ⏲ *Mon. -Fri. 11-9, Sat. 9-8, Sun. 11-7* Ⓜ *Spadina or St. Andrew.*

Lush & Lavish. Toronto's only certified Eminence Green Spa, Lush & Lavish delivers organic skin care and wraps, vegan nail polishes, and eco-conscious products for massages, facials, and makeup to the discerning clientele of the new hotter-than-hot Ossington district. ✉ *200 Ossington Ave., at Dundas St. W, Ossington* ☎ *647/343-6001* 🌐 *lushandlavish.com* ⏲ *Tues.-Fri. 11-8, Sat. 9-6* ⏲ *closed Mon. and Sun.*

Novo Spa. A perennial favorite among Toronto's day-spa enthusiasts, this Yorkville hideaway offers massages (couples, prenatal), facials, manicures, pedicures, and various waxing treatments. The calming staff members always have soothing refreshments on hand. ✉ *66 Avenue Rd., Yorkville* ☎ *416/926-9303* 🌐 *www.novospa.ca* ⏲ *Mon.-Fri. 10-8, Sat. 9:30-8, Sun. 10-6* Ⓜ *Bay.*

Ten Spot. If you end up in West Queen West with a sudden desire for a Brazilian wax, the attractive Ten Spot has got you covered. It also carries Dermalogica and Exuberance (vegan) skincare products for its inexpensive facials (from $45). ✉ *749 Queen St. W, Queen West* ☎ *416/915-1010* 🌐 *www.the10spot.com* ⏲ *Sun.-Wed. 8-8, Thurs.-Sat. 8-9.*

YORKVILLE

In keeping with its lofty image as Toronto's most upscale neighborhood, Yorkville boasts a handful of glamorous, ultradecadent hotels. This is a great destination for shopaholics and style gurus who want to take in designer boutiques, visit see-and-be-seen cafés and restaurants, and stargaze during the Toronto International Film Festival.

$$$$ HOTEL Fodor's Choice ★ **Four Seasons Toronto.** Opened in late-2012, this gleaming, 55-story tower in the leafy Yorkville neighborhood is the long-awaited new Toronto home for the luxury brand, with interiors by noted hospitality design firm Yabu Pushelberg and two restaurants overseen by chef Daniel Boulud. **Pros:** on-site dining hot spots; excellent spa and gym; central location; on-point service. **Cons:** free Wi-Fi limited to one device; hefty price tag. *Rooms from: C$545 ✉ 60 Yorkville Ave, at Bloor St. W, Yorkville ☎ 416/964–0411, 800/819–8053 ⊕ www.fourseasons.com/toronto 217 rooms, 42 suites No meals Ⓜ Bay ⊕ E1.*

$$$$ HOTEL Fodor's Choice ★ **Hazelton Hotel.** Stepping through a discreet check-in area, guests are personally ushered through plush hallways to palatial guest rooms with sumptuous furnishings, floor-to-ceiling windows, individual doorbells, and electronic housekeeping controls. **Pros:** excellent service; Toronto's Hollywood hangout; well-equipped gym; on-site spa. **Cons:** high quality with prices to reflect it; next to impossible to get a reservation during the Toronto International Film Festival. *Rooms from: C$525 ✉ 118 Yorkville Ave., at Avenue Rd., Yorkville ☎ 416/963–6300, 866/473–6301 ⊕ www.thehazeltonhotel.com 62 rooms, 15 suites No meals Ⓜ Bay ⊕ E1.*

$$$ HOTEL **InterContinental Toronto Yorkville.** Handsome and intimate, this outpost of the respected InterContinental chain is a two-minute walk from the Yorkville shopping area and directly across from the Royal Ontario Museum's stunning Crystal addition. **Pros:** close to the Royal Ontario and Gardiner museums; feels like a boutique hotel; ultracool lobby bar; Keurig coffeemakers in all rooms. **Cons:** some front-desk staff inexperienced; expensive Internet. *Rooms from: C$250 ✉ 220 Bloor St. W, west of Avenue Rd., Yorkville ☎ 416/960–5200, 800/267–0010 ⊕ www.toronto.intercontinental.com 185 rooms, 23 suites No meals Ⓜ Museum ⊕ E1.*

$$$$ HOTEL **Park Hyatt Toronto.** The experience here is *très* New York Park Avenue, with elegant, 400-square-foot guest rooms overlooking Queen's Park and Lake Ontario. **Pros:** large marble baths; Le Labo toiletries; free Internet; impeccably appointed. **Cons:** breakfast is pricey. *Rooms from: C$329 ✉ 4 Avenue Rd., at Bloor St. W, Yorkville ☎ 416/925–1234, 800/778–7477 ⊕ www.parktoronto.hyatt.com 291 rooms, 45 suites No meals Ⓜ Museum ⊕ E1.*

$$$$ HOTEL **Windsor Arms.** With a guest-to-staff ratio of 5:1 and 24-hour butler on duty, the Windsor Arms places high importance on personalized service. **Pros:** high repeat business due to privacy and personalized service; ultracomfortable beds; complimentary Continental breakfast; Molton Brown toiletries. **Cons:** high service standards mean high prices; some fourth-floor rooms noisy due to downstairs functions. *Rooms from: C$356 ✉ 18 St. Thomas St., at Bloor St. W, Yorkville ☎ 416/971–9666, 877/999–2767 ⊕ www.windsorarmshotel.com 2 rooms, 26 suites Breakfast Ⓜ Bay ⊕ E1.*

4

GREATER TORONTO

A breath of fresh air, the Old Mill Inn is closer to natural beauty but still well-situated on the subway line.

$$$ B&B/INN **The Old Mill Inn & Spa.** Tucked into the Humber River Valley, the Old Mill is the only country inn within the city limits of Toronto. **Pros:** whirlpool tubs; subway and bus stop very close; live jazz Friday and Saturday. **Cons:** residential neighborhood is too quiet for some; you must reserve by telephone; gets busy with weddings. *Rooms from: C$239 21 Old Mill Rd., at Bloor St. W, Greater Toronto 416/236–2641, 866/653–6455 www.oldmilltoronto.com 44 rooms, 13 suites Breakfast Old Mill A1.*

NEAR PEARSON INTERNATIONAL AIRPORT

If you have an early-morning departure or late-night arrival at Pearson International Airport, staying nearby might be the best option, considering the drive from downtown Toronto can take up to two hours when traffic is at its worst.

$$ HOTEL **Alt Hotel Pearson.** Not your average airport hotel, this hip boutique hotel offers a convenient location adjacent to long-term parking and a LINK station, as well as plush digs at affordable prices. **Pros:** great value; year-round rate (C$129); free Wi-Fi; convenient location; interesting decor. **Cons:** some noise from hallways and highway. *Rooms from: C$129 6080 Viscount Rd., Mississauga 905/362–4337, 855/855–6080 pearson.althotels.ca 153 No meals A1.*

$$ HOTEL FAMILY **Sandman Signature Toronto Airport.** Reasonable prices, great parking deals, and quiet, modern rooms are the advantages of this Sandman property just down the road from Pearson International Airport. **Pros:** best value along the Airport Strip; excellent service; free Internet. **Cons:** on-site restaurant gets extremely busy. *Rooms from: C$149 55 Reading Ct., Airport Strip 416/798–8840 www.sandmansignature.com/toronto.html 256 rooms No meals A1.*

$$ HOTEL **Sheraton Gateway Hotel.** For business travelers and quick layovers, it's hard to beat the location of this mid-range hotel right inside Pearson International Airport. **Pros:** inside the airport; totally soundproof. **Cons:** room service prices don't match quality of food; Internet is pricey (C$15 per day). *Rooms from: C$174 Terminal 3, Toronto AMF, PO Box 3000, Airport Strip 905/672–7000 www.starwoodhotels.com 474 rooms No meals A1.*

5

NIGHTLIFE

Updated by Andrew Dobson

The nightlife scene in Toronto is as varied as the neighborhoods. Downtown—in the Entertainment and Financial districts and Old Town—bars and pubs cater to theatergoers and weekday worker bees. They can be dead on weekends after dark, however—especially in the Entertainment District—until 11 pm rolls around and the big loft-style dance clubs get going. To hang with locals at their neighborhood joints, head to Little Italy or the Annex, where university students mix with residents of the surrounding Victorian-lined streets.

Gay nightlife centers around Church and Wellesley streets northeast of the downtown core. Everyone under 40 ends up on Queen West at some point, patronizing the once-bohemian, now-established arty bars and cafés. Ladies who lunch meet for midday martinis in swanky Yorkville and later clink glasses at the tony lounges. Throughout the city are dedicated music venues, bars, and supper clubs that specialize in jazz, Latin, blues, rock, hip-hop, and everything in between.

Most recently Toronto has emerged as a food-obsessed city with late-night restaurants (from hole in the walls to the crème de la crème in fine dining), offering sips and nibbles to those who wish to feast past the usual dinner hour. Other emerging trends include a flourish of local brewpubs and luxury hotels offering unique evening programs which have locals and tourists swarming. In this section, we've covered the places that have cemented their place in the city's scene, but new hot spots are always emerging. Check local news outlets *(see "What's On Now" in the Planning section)* to get the latest.

PLANNING

BARS

Establishments in Toronto that serve alcohol must also serve some kind of food. This might account for the fact that many bars in the city are also restaurants. (If they have to build a kitchen anyway, they might as well put it to good use.) Getting just drinks is within your rights at any hour, but at these resto-bars you may be asked to sit at the bar rather than at a table before 10 or 11 pm. This is not to say that all bars serve proper meals: some get around the law with meager offerings like chips and microwavable cups of Mr. Noodles, or by striking a deal with a neighboring pizza joint.

Several bars are also music venues that either have a separate space (with cover only for that space) or charge a cover for the bar (maybe C$5–C$10) on performance nights.

It's not unusual for smaller bars to be cash-only.

DANCE CLUBS

The majority of Toronto's big dance clubs are in the Entertainment District, specifically along Richmond and Adelaide between University and Spadina. But you can find more intimate spaces on Ossington, Queen West, and in the Church-Wellesley area (the "Gay Village"). Always call ahead or check websites to get on the guest list to avoid a wait at the door. Doors at clubs usually open at 10 but don't get busy until after 11 or midnight. Cover charges of C$10–C$20 are standard. Most clubs are open until 2 or 3 am. Dress codes are usually in effect but aren't over the top; avoid sneakers, shorts, and casual jeans and you should be fine. Some of the classier lounges in the theater and business districts cater to suit- and stiletto-clad clientele.

The club scene can be fickle, with new venues opening and closing all the time. Our choices have been going strong for years, but for the flavor of the month, special events, and DJ bookings, check weekly papers.

MUSIC VENUES

Toronto is a regular stop for top musical performers from around the world. Most venues have covers that range from C$5 to C$10. Tickets are often available on **Ticketmaster** (🌐 *www.ticketmaster.ca*). Record shops **Rotate This!** (✉ *801 Queen St. W* ☎ *416/504–8447* 🌐 *www.rotate.com*) and **Soundscapes** (✉ *572 College St.* ☎ *416/537–1620* 🌐 *www.soundscapesmusic.com*) also sell tickets.

North by Northeast (*NXNE*). Each June, Toronto hosts North by Northeast, an annual festival that brings more than 1,000 musicians to the indoor and outdoor venues around the city. Affiliated with the similar South by Southwest festival in Austin, Texas, NXNE also presents film, comedy, art, and a digital interactive media conference as part of the weeklong event. Massive free outdoor concerts anchor NXNE downtown, but the heart of the festival is the lineup at more than 50 club venues across the city. Tickets and passes are available on the website and go on sale as early as mid-January. (Significant early-bird discounts apply.) **■ TIP→ Front-of-the-line access is given to those with a Priority Pass (C$200)–others may have to line up for highly anticipated bands, sometimes hours in advance.** ☎ *416/863–6963* 🌐 *www.nxne.com*.

CLOSE UP

Beer: The National Drink

Torontonians love their beer, which is evidenced by the plethora of craft breweries opening throughout the city. Each is worth visiting for a sip, nibble, and tour.

See full reviews under neighborhoods.

Amsterdam BrewHouse recently opened its doors in the summer of 2013 offering tours and tastings of its on-site brewery located in the heart of the Harbourfront. Locals swarm here in the summer for their phenomenal patio, which offers fantastic views of the lake. Tours and tastings weekdays at 2 and 6 pm and weekends at 12, 3 and 6.

Bar Volo is a classy, relaxed place for a beer on busy Yonge Street.

Beer Bistro has a long beer list and also a brew-inspired menu.

Bier Markt has an awe-inspiring keg room and a loyal after-five clientele.

Bellwoods Brewery is a restaurant, bar, and on-site brewery located on Ossington Avenue in the heart of the city's hipster West End. Beer fans line up for a chance to plop themselves into coveted street-side patio seats. The building is petite so it's likely you'll see the brewmaster preparing his next batch while you sip and nibble your way through their menu.

Mill Street Brew Pub, in the Distillery District, makes Ontario's only certified organic lager and seasonal Helles Bock. It is open for sampling daily, with free tours on weekends at 3 pm and weekends at 3 and 5. A brewpub is on-site.

Mill Street Beer Hall is a recently launched concept by the team at Mill Street that is attached to their much-loved Brew Pub. Freshly brewed beer from the brewpub is piped across the walls and served up at the bar. The center of the dining room features an imported copper still that brews a rare trio of Bierchnaps (Tankhouse, Framboise, and Coffee Porter).

Mill Street Brewery, in the Distillery District, makes Ontario's only certified organic lager and a seasonal Helles Bock. It is open for sampling daily, with free tours weekdays at 3 pm and weekends at 3 and 5. A brewpub is on-site.

Steam Whistle Brewery, in the Harbourfront, brews an authentically crafted pilsner and offers tours of its historic premises Monday–Thursday 1–5, Friday and Saturday noon–5, and Sunday noon–4. A great spot to pop by before or after a Blue Jays Game at the Rogers Centre. Their annual Oktoberfest party is a hoot.

Toronto's major arena venues are the Air Canada Centre (home of the Maple Leafs and Raptors), the Rogers Centre (home of the Blue Jays; formerly the SkyDome), and the outdoor summer-only Molson Canadian Amphitheatre on the waterfront with city skyline views. *For large-venue shows see Major Venues in Performing Arts.*

GAY AND LESBIAN NIGHTLIFE

Much of Toronto's gay and lesbian nightlife is centered on Church and Wellesley streets. You can easily cruise up Church from Alexander to a couple of blocks north of Wellesley and pop into whichever bar is most happening that night.

There are plenty of LGBT-friendly places outside the Church Street strip. Queen Street West, for example, is sometimes called Queer West, due to the number of not-exclusively-gay-but-gay-friendly bars and restaurants like the Beaver, the Drake, the Gladstone, and Mitzi's Sister.

Check out *X-Tra* (🌐 *www.xtra.ca*) available for free at various venues and at paper boxes around town. It has information on nightlife, community issues, and events.

Nightlife listings are organized by neighborhood.

HARBOURFRONT, ENTERTAINMENT DISTRICT, AND THE FINANCIAL DISTRICT

The historic brick buildings of Toronto's oldest district mingle with office towers in this downtown neighborhood, popular for weeknight drinks with coworkers and midday power-broker lunches. Many of the city's hotels are concentrated here.

5

HARBOURFRONT

In general, this area is quiet after dark, but a nightlife scene is slowly emerging as more condos are erected and the waterfront is developed. Waterfront concerts take place here in summer, dinner cruises leave from the Harbourfront, and this is the location of Toronto's largest dance club: the Guvernment.

BARS, PUBS, AND LOUNGES

Amsterdam BrewHouse. This brewpub, which opened its doors in July 2013, is the newest addition to Toronto's lakeside dining scene. Originally used as a boat freight storage house, the interior of the 1930s building features two massive bars with more than 10 brews on tap, an open-concept kitchen with an imported Italian wood-burning pizza oven, and a sprawling patio with stunning views of the Toronto Islands. Brewery tours and beer tastings are available on weekdays at 2 and 6 pm and weekends at noon, 3, and 6 pm. ✉ *245 Queens Quay W, Harbourfront* ☎ *416/504–1020* 🌐 *amsterdambrewhouse.com* Ⓜ *Union.*

Real Sports Bar & Grill. No hole-in-the-wall sports bar, this sleek 25,000-square-foot space adjacent to the Air Canada Centre lights up with 199 high-definition flat-screen TVs, and amazing sightlines from every club-style booth, table, or stool at one of the three bars. Head to the second floor to watch a game on the two-story high HD TV. For popular sporting events, or any day or night the Leafs or Raptors play, it's best to get a reservation (accepted up to three weeks in advance), though the bar does reserve a third of its seats for walk-in traffic an hour before face-off. ✉ *15 York St., at Bremner Blvd., Harbourfront* ☎ *416/815–7325* 🌐 *www.realsports.ca* Ⓜ *Union.*

DANCE CLUBS

The Guvernment. If you want to get your grind on in a sea of revelers, this is the place. Each of the eight lounges and dance clubs in this mega-complex has its own themed decor and DJ. In the main club pulsing lasers and thumping electronic beats permeate the 22,000 square feet of dance space. The chic rooftop Skybar has one of the city's best skyline views. The complex is generally open Friday and Saturday nights, but access might be limited by ticketed concerts or events—Deadmau5, Justin Bieber, Prince, Armin Van Burren, Drake, and the Rolling Stones have performed here. All the spaces are usually accessible for one cover (C$10–C$25) on Saturday. Take a taxi to this one—it's a desolate after-hours walk. ✉ *132 Queen's Quay E, at Jarvis, Harbourfront* ☎ *416/869–0045* 🌐 *www.theguvernment.com* Ⓜ *Union.*

THE ENTERTAINMENT DISTRICT

Traditionally this was Toronto's center for dance clubs cranking out house music. A few of the more popular clubs are still going strong (especially along Richmond), but this area is transitioning as condos are erected and professionals in their 30s and 40s move in. It's also home to three of the big Broadway-style theaters and tourist-oriented pre-show restaurants with bars. The King West neighborhood has experienced a surge of swanky lounges, bars, and restaurants ever since the Toronto International Film Festival moved its headquarters to the area from Yorkville.

BARS, PUBS, AND LOUNGES

Lobby Lounge at Shangri-La. The Shangri-La Hotel has become wildly popular with the refined 20–30 something set keen for live music, top-notch cocktails, and bar bites. From Wednesday through Saturday the hotel's spacious Lobby Lounge serves up trendy Fig Sours and a to-die-for Gin Basil Smash while live musical talent performs everything from classic Sinatra to modern house tracks. **TIP→ The Fazioli piano sitting in the lounge is signed by Canadian-born Joni Mitchell.** ✉ *188 University Ave., Entertainment District* ☎ *647/788–8888* 🌐 *www.shangri-la.com* Ⓜ *Osgoode.*

Momofuku Nikai. Located across the street from the Four Seasons Centre for the Performing Arts, those looking for a cocktail before or after the ballet and opera will find comfort in this funky space outfitted with living-room-style leather couches and coffee tables as well as bar and high-top seating. You may even find yourself pondering the Zhang Huan sculpture entitled "Rising," which features a flock of birds flying across the Nikai window, while you enjoy one of the playful Asian fusion cocktails such as a Momoiro Sour and Pok Pok Tai. ✉ *190 University Ave., 2nd flr., Entertainment District* ☎ *N/A* 🌐 *momofuku.com* ⏲ *Closed Sundays* Ⓜ *Osgoode.*

Wayne Gretzky's Toronto. The pregame Jays and Leafs fans and the post-comedy-club crowd from Second City next door flock to this sports bar. When he's in town, the eponymous hockey icon and owner can often be seen in the crowd. The sports bar downstairs has Gretzky memorabilia, 40 flat-screen TVs (broadcasting all sports, not just hockey) and pub-style grub. On the cabana-chic rooftop patio (open from 11 am May through September), considered one of the best in town, a faux waterfall babbles, strings of white lights twinkle, and partygoers order barbecue and buckets of mini Coronas and make themselves heard over the blasting music. ✉ *99 Blue Jays Way, at Mercer St., Entertainment District* ☎ *416/979–7825* 🌐 *www.gretzkys.com* Ⓜ *St. Andrew.*

COMEDY CLUBS

Fodor's Choice ★ **The Second City.** Since it opened in 1973, Toronto's Second City—the younger sibling of the Second City in Chicago—has been providing some of the best comedy in Canada. Regular features are sketch comedy, improv, and revues. Seating is cabaret-style with table service and is assigned on a first-come, first-served basis. **TIP→ Arrive 30 minutes prior to show time.** Weekend shows tend to sell out. Tickets are C$14–C$29. ✉ *51 Mercer St., 1 block south of King, Entertainment District* ☎ *416/343–0011* 🌐 *www.secondcity.com* Ⓜ *St. Andrew.*

A PRE- OR POST-SHOW TIPPLE

The strip of lounges and restaurants on Wellington Street East, just west of Church Street (of which Pravda is one), are all ideal stop-ins before or after theater, symphony, or opera performances downtown. They have an air of sophistication, and as you're already dressed for the occasion, why not?

Yuk Yuk's. Part of a Canadian comedy franchise, this venue headlines stand-up comedians on the rise (Jim Carrey and Russell Peters performed here on their way up), with covers usually between C$12 and C$25. Admission is C$4 on Tuesday, for amateur night. The small space is often packed; getting cozy with your neighbors and sitting within spitting distance of the comedians is part of the appeal. Booking a dinner-and-show package guarantees better seats. ✉ *224 Richmond St. W, 1½ blocks west of University Ave., Entertainment District* ☎ *416/967–6425* 🌐 *www.yukyuks.com* Ⓜ *Osgoode.*

THE FINANCIAL DISTRICT

After happy hour, this business- and high-rise-dense part of town quiets down. Bars and restaurants here are tony affairs, equally suited to schmoozing clients and blowing off steam after a long day at the office.

BARS, PUBS, AND LOUNGES

Bymark. Located in the heart of the Financial District, this culinary oasis is popular with the business suits that work in the area. Don't let that keep you away though, because this downtown hot spot offers a sun-filled patio that's hidden from the hustle and bustle of Wellington Street. Bartenders whip up phenomenal cocktails while the kitchen creates harmonious textures and flavors on your plate. ✉ *66 Wellington St. W., Financial District* ☎ *416/777–1144* 🌐 *www.bymark.mcewangroup.ca* Ⓜ *King.*

Fodor's Choice ★ **Canoe.** Though it's primarily a restaurant, Canoe, on the 54th floor of the Toronto-Dominion Bank tower, is worth a trip just for a drink at the bar and a panoramic view of the lake. It has what might be the city's best Niagara wine selection and an extensive list of international bottles, as well as cocktails and beer. It's popular with finance types from the neighboring towers, who suit the swank surroundings. Go just before sunset to make the most of the view. ✉ *66 Wellington St. W, between York and Bay Sts., Financial District* ☎ *416/364–0054* 🌐 *www.oliverbonacini.com* ⏲ *Mon.–Fri. 11:45 am–10:30 pm* ⏲ *Closed Sat. and Sun.* Ⓜ *King, Union.*

OLD TOWN AND THE DISTILLERY DISTRICT

OLD TOWN

On weeknights, an after-work crowd frequents the easygoing bars and restaurants in Toronto's historic district. Weekends see a fair number of suburbanites living it up.

BARS, PUBS, AND LOUNGES

Bier Markt. With more than 150 beers from 30 countries, including 50 on tap, this enormous restaurant/bar has a corner on the international beer market, but the best thing about it is the oversized sidewalk patio on the Esplanade, ideal for an afternoon brew. **TIP→ The lines are ridiculous on weekends—do as the locals do and go midweek instead.** ✉ *58 The Esplanade, just west of Church St., Old Town* ☎ *416/862–7575* 🌐 *www.thebiermarkt.com* Ⓜ *Union, King.*

Pravda Vodka Bar. A deliberately faded elegance, like a Communist-era club gone rough around the edges, permeates Pravda. Huge paintings of Mao Tse-tung adorn the brick walls, and crystal chandeliers run the length of the two-story room with exposed ductwork. Weekday happy-hour specials draw after-work clientele to lounge on well-worn leather sofas, around low wooden tables, or in a red-velvet-curtained VIP bottle-service area upstairs. Some 75 to 100 vodkas from around the globe are always on the menu, as are vodka flights, martinis, Czech and Russian beers, and caviar, smoked fish, and pierogi. ✉ *44 Wellington St. E, between Church and Yonge Sts., Old Town* ☎ *416/863–5244* 🌐 *www.pravdavodkabar.com* Ⓜ *King.*

Steam Whistle Brewery. The Steam Whistle Brewery brews an authentically crafted pilsner and offers tours (C$10) of its historic premises Monday–Thursday 1–5, Friday and Saturday noon–5, and Sunday noon–4. It has tastings and hosts other special events, like the not-to-be-missed Oktoberfest. It's also a great place to stop before or after a Blue Jays Game. ✉ *The Roundhouse, 255 Bremner Blvd., Old Town* ☎ *416/362–2337* 🌐 *www.steamwhistle.ca* Ⓜ *Union.*

The Sultan's Tent and Cafe Moroc. Not far from the historic St. Lawrence Market, the Sultan's Tent re-creates a traditional Moroccan banquet atmosphere complete with belly dancers, plush divans, beautiful lantern lit tents, and classic North African dishes—be sure to sample the addictive *maftoul*, a hand rolled pastry suffed with spiced beef, cashews and rasins. There's live music and belly dancers every evening. If you're keen to extend your evening after the show, head downtstairs to Berber for an intimate North African bar vibe. **TIP→ This is a great spot for brunch, lunch, and dinner as well as a cocktail.** ✉ *49 Front St E, Old Town* ☎ *416/961–0601* 🌐 *www.thesultanstent.com* Ⓜ *King.*

DISTILLERY DISTRICT

A visit to Toronto isn't complete without a stroll along the cobblestone streets of the city's iconic Distillery District. Originally the heart of Toronto's spirit production in the late 1800s—the Gooderham and Worts Distillery produced whisky here—stunning heritage buildings now house art galleries, bars, restaurants, and cafés.

BARS, PUBS, AND LOUNGES

Mill Street Beer Hall. Opened in early 2013, this German beer hall–inspired space features long wooden tables and high-top bar stools. The outside patio seats 200 comfortably and features plush couches and a roaring fireplace. There's also Bavarian pub grub perfect for sharing; standouts include a generous charcuterie board and potato and ricotta dumplings. In the center of the beer hall, a beautiful German-imported copper still produces their signature Bierchnaps; this classic German spirit distilled from the brewpubs' very own Coffee Porter, Tankhouse Ale, and Framboise is a must-try! ✉ *21 Tank House Ln., Distillery District* ☎ *416/681–0338* 🌐 *www.millstreetbrewpub.ca* Ⓜ *501 Queen Streetcar.*

Mill Street Brew Pub. There may not be a better place in the city for a brewery and pub than in the brick-laned pedestrian-only Distillery District. Sixteen house-brewed beers are on tap; be sure to sample the signature trilogy: Organic, Tank House Ale and Wit. After a proper tasting, head to the on-site beer boutique where you can purchase some of your favorites. The pub serves dressed-up fare: beer-braised ribs, lobster grilled cheese and beer-steamed mussels. Alfresco tables are prime real estate in warm weather. ✉ *21 Tankhouse Ln., Distillery District* ☎ *416/681–0338* 🌐 *www.millstreetbrewpub.ca* Ⓜ *504 King streetcar to Parliament St.*

5

DUNDAS SQUARE AREA

With more neon lights than anywhere else in the city, and a big central square used for outdoor concerts and films, Yonge–Dundas Square is decidedly commercial. But remnants of its past remain in Victorian houses on side streets, and there are some worthwhile bars ideal for a drink before or after a show at Massey Hall and the Canon and Elgin theaters.

BARS, PUBS, AND LOUNGES

Bar Volo. Despite its location on a busy thoroughfare, classy Bar Volo has a relaxed, brick-walled, wood-beamed, old-world atmosphere. A side patio is ideal for people-watching. It has one of the cities most celebrated craft beer lists, wines from around the globe and a dinner menu featuring pizza, pasta, sandwiches, and cheese and charcuterie boards. ✉ *587 Yonge St., Dundas Square Area* ☎ *416/928–0008* 🌐 *www.barvolo.com* Ⓜ *Wellesley or Bloor.*

Jazz Bistro. Finding a quiet place to relax and listen to great music is a rarity in busy Dundas Square (the Times Square of Toronto). Luckily, there's the Jazz Bistro. In the busiest part of the city, it's the perfect spot to sit back and relax while sipping on a glass of red wine or snacking on bistro fare such as wild boar terrine, beef tartare, or crispy duck confit. It features a state-of-the-art sound system and a beautiful Steinway piano that's affectionately referred to by regulars as The Red Pops. Blues, Jazz, and Latina bands perform nightly Wednesday to Saturday. ✉ *251 Victoria St., Dundas Square Area* ☎ *416/363–5299* 🌐 *jazzbistro.ca* Ⓜ *Dundas.*

The Queen and Beaver Public House. Toronto's British heritage thrives at this classy bar with a full restaurant that opened in 2009. The black-and-white photos on the walls reveal its true passion: soccer. A Manchester United game is never missed, though NHL and other sporting events are also shown in the library-like "sports bar." On weekend mornings when an early game is on, they'll open—sometimes as early as 7 am. The wine list is admirable for a pub; the beer selection is surprisingly small and focused on Ontario microbrews. Dressed-up British staples—available in the bar or ground-floor dining room—range from Scotch eggs to a killer hand-chopped-beef burger. ✉ *35 Elm St., between Yonge and Bay Sts., Dundas Square Area* ☎ *647/347–2712* 🌐 *www.queenandbeaverpub.ca* Ⓜ *Dundas.*

CHINATOWN, KENSINGTON MARKET, AND QUEEN WEST

CHINATOWN AND KENSINGTON MARKET

Chinatown bustles along Spadina Avenue offering lots of late night cheap and cheerful Hong Kong–style restaurants while the bohemian Kensington Market bustles during the day as locals pick up groceries and hipsters shop vintage. The zone is slowly picking up speed at night and worth strolling through after dark.

BARS, PUBS, AND LOUNGES

Cold Tea. Located in the heart of Kensington Market and just a stone's throw from the heart of Chinatown, Cold Tea has an intimate, but rowdy bar scene and cozy back patio. It's also *the* place to go for late-night dancing. Rotating DJs play everything from hip-hop and funk to rock and electronic (Wednesday to Sunday nights). A clear nod to its neighborhood, cocktail-clamoring dance fans can order dim sum from a cart at the bar's entrance; Sunday BBQs feature guest chefs. **TIP→ There is no phone number, website, or sign so be sure to ask locals if you are having a hard time finding the place.** You literally have to march off the beaten path to find this nightspot, which—truth be told—is part of its charm. ✉ *60 Kensington Ave., Chinatown* ☎ *N/A* 🌐 *N/A* Ⓜ *506 College Streetcar.*

MUSIC

The Silver Dollar Room. Some of the top blues acts around play here, as well as rock bands. The bar is dark and the viewing area narrow, but the blues-loving clientele is friendly, and you may strike up a conversation with the musicians between sets. ✉ *486 Spadina Ave., at College St., Chinatown* ☎ *416/763–9139* 🌐 *www.silverdollarroom.com* Ⓜ *505 Spadina or 506 College streetcar.*

QUEEN WEST

To an outsider, Queen West, with its mix of young owner-operated clothing boutiques, decades-old appliance and antiques stores, dive bars, and hipper-than-thou establishments, might seem to be a neighborhood undergoing a metamorphosis. But it has arrived, firmly grounded in bohemian chic.

JAZZ FESTIVALS

Toronto Jazz Festival. Late June and early July bring music lovers to Toronto for the Toronto Jazz Festival. The 2013 bill included Smokey Robinson, Trombone Shorty, and Willie Nelson. Performances are at various venues around town. Concerts are priced individually, but you can buy a three- or five-show pass for a 15% or 20% discount on Mainstage shows. ☎ *416/928–2033* 🌐 *www.torontojazz.com.*

The Beaches International Jazz Festival. Held in late July, the 10-day Beaches International Jazz Festival in the east Toronto Beach neighborhood showcases jazz, Latin, R&B, funk, soul, and world-music performers like eclectic R&B-pop-reggae group Jay Douglas and the All Stars and "blusion" pianist-saxophonist Deanna Bogart at its Woodbine Park and Kew Gardens stages. Musicians and food vendors also line 2 km (1¼ miles) of Queen Street East, which is closed to traffic for the event. All performances are free. ☎ *416/698–2152* 🌐 *www.beachesjazz.com* Ⓜ *501 Queen streetcar to Woodbine.*

5

BARS, PUBS, AND LOUNGES

Bar Chef. The dark interior features dimly lit chandeliers and tabletop candles, which set the stage for Chef Frankie Solarik's wild and wonderful concoctions that force patrons to reimagine classic cocktails. Each cocktail is "gastro," meaning liquid nitrogen is used; so when it's poured into the glass the contents foam over like a foggy mist onto the table or turn into ice shards. Small dishes accompany each beverage that contain wee bits of food (like foams in a spoon, gels, or truffle dust), which create a complete sensory experience. Fans of whisky should order their signature Vanilla and Hickory Smoked Manhattan which clocks in at C$45. ✉ *472 Queen St. W., Queen West* ☎ *416/868–4800* 🌐 *www.barcheftoronto.com* Ⓜ *501 Queen Streetcar.*

MUSIC

JAZZ, LATIN, AND FUNK

The Rex Hotel Jazz & Blues Bar. Legendary on the Toronto jazz circuit since it opened in the 1980s, the Rex has two live shows every night plus afternoon shows on weekends. Shows range from free to C$10. The kitchen serves diner fare and there are affordable hotel rooms available. ✉ *194 Queen St. W, at St. Patrick St., Queen West* ☎ *416/598–2475* 🌐 *www.therex.ca* Ⓜ *Osgoode.*

POP AND ROCK

Horseshoe Tavern. Since 1947, this club has evolved from a legendary country-music venue (Charlie Pride, Tex Ritter, Hank Williams, and Loretta Lynn) to a just-as-legendary club that welcomes an eclectic mix of new alternative rock, roots, blues, punk, and rockabilly bands six nights a week. This is the place to catch young bands on the rise. ✉ *370 Queen St. W, at Spadina Ave., Queen West* ☎ *416/598–4753* 🌐 *www.horseshoetavern.com* Ⓜ *Osgoode.*

Rivoli. Along the Queen Street strip, the Rivoli has long been a major showcase for more daring entertainment in Toronto. A back room functions as a performance space, with progressive and indie rock, improvisational comedy troupes, and more. Bands have a cover charge, usually C$5–C$10. Asian-influenced cuisine and good steak are served in the dining room. The walls are lined with work (all for sale) by up-and-coming local artists. There's also a bar and, upstairs, a pool hall. Big-name acts that have played here include Blue Rodeo, Arcade Fire, Feist, Nora Jones, Adele, John Mayer, and Tori Amos. ✉ *332 Queen St. W, at Spadina Ave., Queen West* ☎ *416/596–1908, 416/597–0794* 🌐 *www.rivoli.ca* Ⓜ *Osgoode.*

EAST AND WEST OF CITY CENTER

WEST QUEEN WEST AND OSSINGTON

Originally a residential area for Portuguese immigrants and a home to Vietnamese karaoke bars and restaurants, Ossington and West Queen West are now *the* place for bohemian artists to set up shop, young chefs to take risks, and hipsters to party until the sun comes up.

BARS, PUBS, AND LOUNGES

Bellwoods Brewery. This restaurant, bar, and on-site brewery has been a smash hit since it opened in 2012; expect a line if the sun is shining because the spacious patio is a great spot to sample the always evolving craft beer selection. Be sure to sip the White Picket Fence Belgian Wit, which pairs perfectly with a plate of fresh oysters. The cheese and charcuterie board is perfect for sharing with a group. ✉ *126 Ossington Ave., Ossington* ☎ *N/A* 🌐 *bellwoodsbrewery.com* Ⓜ *501 Queen Streetcar.*

The Drake. A hotel, restaurant, art gallery, café, and music venue all in one, the Drake is high-style hip that appeals to ages 20 to 50, depending on the entertainment. The Underground, downstairs, fills with a younger crowd for indie bands. The sound system is great, and the stark walls are usually decorated with art or projections. Live jazz is performed in the main-floor Drake Lounge, where scenesters sip cocktails and order snacks or dinner. Escape to the rooftop Sky Yard, with potted plants and heat lamps, year-round. ✉ *1150 Queen St. W, 2 blocks east of Gladstone Ave., West Queen West* ☎ *416/531–5042* 🌐 *www.thedrakehotel.ca* Ⓜ *501 Queen streetcar.*

Gladstone Hotel. In a restored Victorian hotel, the Gladstone draws a young, stylish Toronto crowd who appreciate a multitude of creative events: karaoke (every Friday and Saturday); indie, jazz, and bluegrass bands; spoken word; burlesque; queer nights; and art shows. The Ballroom is the main event space—and frequent wedding venue—with tall ceilings, exposed brick walls, and a long, dark wood bar. The Melody Bar hosts karaoke and bands and serves dinner until 10 pm; a late-night menu is available from 10 to midnight, but there's always cocktail service. The tiny Art Bar has exhibitions, performances, and private events; there are art galleries on the 2nd, 3rd, and 4th floors; and there are rotating exhibits throughout the hotel's public spaces. ✉ *1214 Queen St. W, at Dufferin, Queen West* ☎ *416/531–4635* 🌐 *www.gladstonehotel.com* Ⓜ *501 Queen streetcar to Dufferin St.*

Reposado Bar. The Toronto bar buzz is officially centered on Ossington Avenue, where watering holes, shops, and galleries have sprung up like wildflowers over the past few years. One of the first (in 2007) and still going strong is this classy tequila bar. The dark wood, large windows, big back patio, and live jazz (most nights no cover) set the tone for a serious list of tequilas meant to be sipped, not slammed, and Mexican nibbles like tequila-cured salmon with crostini. ✉ *136 Ossington Ave., between Queen and Dundas Sts., Ossington* ☎ *416/532–6474* 🌐 *www.reposadobar.com* Ⓜ *505 Dundas or 501 Queen streetcars, or Ossington Subway/Bus.*

DANCE CLUBS

LATIN DANCE CLUBS

Lula Lounge. Latin-music lovers of all ages dress up to get down to live Afro-Cuban, Brazilian, and salsa music at this Little Portugal hot spot. Pop and rock musicians also perform occasionally. Dinner-and-a-show tickets are available on weekends and include a salsa lesson on Saturday. Lula is also an arts center, with dance and drumming lessons and a multitude of festivals and cultural events. No running shoes on weekends. ✉ *1585 Dundas St. W, 1½ blocks west of Dufferin St., West Queen West* ☎ *416/588–0307* 🌐 *www.lula.ca* Ⓜ *505 Dundas streetcar.*

Wrong Bar. This is your go-to spot to dance yourself silly in the West End. Opened in 2007, the venue has hosted notable acts such as Hot Chip, Claude Von Stroke, Flosstradamus, Crystal Castles, and Peaches. It's a popular weekend spot for pretty twenty- to thirtysomethings ready to rage on the dance floor. If you're having a hard time finding signage for the bar, and you're asking yourself, "Am I at the wrong bar?" Don't worry. You're probably there. ✉ *1279 Queen St. W., West Queen West* ☎ *416/516–8677* 🌐 *www.wrongbar.com* Ⓜ *501 Queen Streetcar.*

LESLIEVILLE

This area of Queen Street was up-and-coming for years, and is now a bonafide reason to cross the DVP (Don Valley Parkway), thanks to a flurry of small but excellent restaurants, artisanal food shops, niche design stores, and relaxed labor-of-love bars catering to a discerning and artistic local community.

BARS, PUBS, AND LOUNGES

The Céilí Cottage. Owned and operated by an oyster-loving Irishman, locals rave about the cottage's authentic pub vibe, sun-filled patio, and inventive Emerald Isle–inspired food. The Whiskey Wall has won numerous awards and features more than 80 whiskeys—you'll find Irish, Scotch, American, and Canadian. There's nightly live music that ranges from traditional Irish folk or jazz to blues and Motown. **TIP→ End your night (or meal) with the Sticky Toffee Pudding.** ✉ *1301 Queen St. E., Leslieville* ☎ *416/406–1301* 🌐 *www.ceilicottage.com* Ⓜ *501 Queen Streetcar.*

Rasputin Vodka Bar. The Russian Empire is a streetcar ride away at this no-pretenses vodka bar whose mismatched barware, chandeliers, and well-worn Victorian sofas create the illusion that the entire place was smuggled out of the old country. More than 40 varieties of the clear stuff are on the menu, as are creative cocktails and Eastern European nosh (latke, cabbage rolls). DJs spin dance music on weekends. ✉ *780 Queen St. E, Leslieville* ☎ *416/469–3737* 🌐 *www.rasputinvodkabar.com* Ⓜ *501 Queen Streetcar.*

5

Skin and Bones. The name is a coy indicator of the playful atmosphere offered up at this East End wine bar and restaurant—Skin refers to grape skins and the owners' passion for wine, and Bones refers to the menu's focus on meat-centric dishes. There are anywhere from 120–150 bottles on the wine list at any given time with a rotating selection of at least 40 bottles available by the glass. Opened in late 2012, this has quickly become the perfect spot for oenophiles to spend an evening discovering a few new vintages. ✉ *980 Queen St. E., Leslieville* ☎ *416/524–5209* 🌐 *skinandbonesto.com* Ⓜ *501 Queen Streetcar.*

Swirl. This itty-bitty, bespoke wine bar with flirty Parisian flair was carved out of a petite second-story one-bedroom apartment. The pretty decor is quirkily shabby-chic, with wooden farmhouse chairs set at reclaimed antique sewing tables. Everything is compact, including the well-chosen, reasonably priced wine list (glasses start at $6; bottles are C$30–C$40 on average), the handful of interesting beers, and the food (pâté, pickled quail eggs, chocolate cake), most of it pre-made and served in pickling jars. ✉ *946½ Queen St. E(2nd fl.), near Carlaw Ave., Leslieville* ☎ *647/351–5453* 🌐 *www.swirltoronto.com* Ⓜ *501 Queen Streetcar.*

MUSIC

POP AND ROCK

Opera House. This late-19th-century vaudeville theater retains some of its original charm, most notably in its proscenium arch over the stage. The 850-capacity venue hosts internationally touring acts of all genres. Past performers include K-OS and French pop-princess Yelle. ✉ *735 Queen St. E, 1 block east of Broadview, Leslieville* ☎ *416/466–0313* 🌐 *www.theoperahousetoronto.com* Ⓜ *504 Queen Streetcar.*

THE ANNEX

Along Bloor between Spadina and Bathurst, the Annex is an established neighborhood of leafy side streets with large Victorian houses that attracts university students and young professionals to its mix of true-blue pubs and well-loved lounges.

BARS, PUBS, AND LOUNGES

Guu Izakaya SakaBar. An original concept imported from Vancouver, Guu has wowed local audiences with its rowdy Izakaya atmosphere—every guest is greeted with a cheerful hello in Japanese by both kitchen and serving staff when you walk through the door—gaining it quite a cult-like following. A few shots of sake are a must-try, but don't miss the imported plum wine or Japanese vodka-infused cocktails. The food is delicious and perfect for sharing; signature dishes include Gyu Carpaccio, Kabocha Karokke, and Carbonara Udon. ✉ *559 Bloor St. W, The Annex* ☎ *647/343–1101* 🌐 *www.guu-izakaya.com/sakabar* Ⓜ *Bathurst.*

Playa Cabana Hacienda. One of the city's favorite Tequilerias, Playa Cabana, opened this sister property in July 2013. The Hacienda, as it's fondly known, offers a small second-floor patio that overlooks Dupont, as well as a massive outdoor patio behind the restaurant—it may be the largest outdoor space to sip a margarita north of Bloor. The interior wows with a wild and wonderful assortment of glowing bar signs, hanging pulleys, industrial lamps, leather horse saddles, and endless bottles of booze. The kitchen stays open as late as the bar, so you can plan to sip your margaritas and munch on tacos until 2 am with DJ beats to boot. ✉ *14 Dupont St., The Annex* ☎ *647/352–6030* 🌐 *www.playacabana.ca* Ⓜ *Dupont.*

HOTEL BARS

Don't want to stray far from your home away from home at night? Opt for a hotel with nightlife in-house, like the hip bar-and-live-music combo at the Drake or the Gladstone, on Queen West, or the classy martini lounges at the Four Seasons (dBar) or the Park Hyatt (the Roof Lounge), both in Yorkville.

MUSIC

POP AND ROCK

Lee's Palace. Some of the most exciting young bands in rock, indie, and punk are served up at this midsize club with a psychedelic graffiti facade on the edge of the University of Toronto campus. Grab a table or watch the show from the sunken viewing area. ✉ *529 Bloor St. W, 1½ blocks east of Bathurst St., The Annex* ☎ *416/532–1598* 🌐 *www.leespalace.com* Ⓜ *Bathurst.*

5

LITTLE ITALY

College Street between Bathurst and Ossington isn't so much an old-school Italian neighborhood these days as it is a prime destination for bars and restaurants of all cuisines. Casual (but rarely rowdy) student-friendly pubs mix with candlelit martini bars. The party often spills out onto the streets on weekends.

BARS, PUBS, AND LOUNGES

Café Diplomatico. Holding court over a central Little Italy corner since 1968, Diplomatico is popular for one reason: its big sidewalk patio with umbrella-shaded tables, one of the best in the city for people-watching. "The Dip," as it's locally known, serves up middle-of-the-road Italian fare and affordable beer and wine. It's really all about the outdoor space, which is open from 8 am daily and has one of the few neighborhood kitchens serving after midnight. ✉ *594 College St., at Clinton St., Little Italy* ☎ *416/534–4637* 🌐 *www.diplomatico.ca* Ⓜ *506 College streetcar.*

La Carnita. It may seem odd that this wildly popular Mexican spot is in Little Italy, but don't let it deter you. Originally started as a pop-up taco stand, La Carnita became a permanent fixture when lines started forming well into the late evening. The tacos, handcrafted cocktails, and sweet churros are well worth the wait. The space is filled with funky graffiti and the sounds of vintage beats, hip-hop, and DJ mixes. ✉ *501 College St., at Palmerston Ave., Little Italy* ☎ *416/964–1555* 🌐 *www.lacarnita.com* Ⓜ *506 College Streetcar.*

MUSIC

FOLK AND BLUES

Free Times Cafe. This casual restaurant specializes in Jewish, Middle Eastern, and Canadian food, with many vegetarian and organic options. There's live acoustic and folk music every night of the week on its back-room stage, plus a highly popular traditional Jewish brunch called "Bella! Did Ya Eat?" complete with live klezmer and Yiddish music every Sunday. ✉ *320 College St., at Major St., Queen's Park* ☎ *416/967–1078* 🌐 *freetimescafe.com* Ⓜ *Queen's Park.*

PATIO FEVER

Torontonians are patio-mad once warm weather hits. Can you blame them, after a long, often-brutal winter where they wait outside for streetcars in the path of Arctic-fed winds? Patios open in April or May as weather permits or by Victoria Day (May 24) weekend at the latest. Here are some favorites:

Bier Markt (✉ *58 The Esplanade*): A downtown location near most of the city's office buildings, a low-key vibe, a big sidewalk patio, and a long beer list make this a sweet spot during happy hour.

Café Diplomatico (✉ *594 College St.*): Perfect for soaking up *la bella vita* on Little Italy's main strip is Diplomatico's sidewalk patio, open from morning until last call.

The Drake (✉ *11 S. Queen St. W*): Even jaded hipsters who criticize the Drake's trendy-lounge-in-the-'hood persona can't resist this swish rooftop patio overlooking Queen Street with throw pillows and potted palms.

Wayne Gretzky's (✉ *99 Blue Jays Way*): The roof patio atop the NHL star's restaurant juxtaposes love seats, palm trees, and sparkling lights with a boisterous crowd decompressing after Blue Jays games or comedy shows at next door's Second City.

Also see full reviews.

POP AND ROCK

Mod Club Theatre. Excellent indie shows occasionally appear in this sexy black-on-black midsize space with great sight lines and killer acoustics and lighting. Past shows have included Lana Del Ray and Digitalism, but upstart Canadian indie rockers are frequent guests. ✉ *722 College St., at Crawford St., Little Italy* ☎ *416/588–4663* 🌐 *www.themodclub.com* Ⓜ *506 College streetcar.*

YORKVILLE AND CHURCH-WELLESLEY

YORKVILLE

The trendy bars of Yorkville tend to draw a well-heeled clientele for excellent drinks, food, and views.

BARS, PUBS, AND LOUNGES

dBar. This high-end lounge in the new flagship Four Seasons Toronto is modern and subdued. The bartender serves up some of the city's best hand-crafted cocktails—Flower Mojito, Neo-Negroni, and the Atwood, which pays homage to one of the city's most famous writers and features Havana Club anejo, grapefruit juice, nepitella syrup and crispy basil leaf—but there are also craft beers and a complete wine list. French Chef Daniel Boulud has his hand in the kitchen, and menu highlights include perfectly crisp falafel; a selection of sausages; signature Boulud classics like "The Yankee Burger" prepared with freshly ground Cumbrae beef; and freshly baked madeleines. ✉ *21 Avenue Rd., Yorkville* ☎ *416/964-0411* 🌐 *www.fourseasons.com* Ⓜ *Bay.*

Hemingways. One of the few Toronto pubs that isn't overtaken by rowdy sports fans or students, Hemingways is a homey bastion in a sea of Yorkville swank. The three-story complex, with indoor and outdoor spaces—front and back—is a mishmash of booths, tables, several bars, mirrors, artsy posters, and books. It has a full pub menu, and free appetizers are doled out most nights at around 6. About three-quarters of the over-30 professionals who frequent this place are regulars. ✉ *142 Cumberland St., just east of Avenue Rd., Yorkville* ☎ *416/968–2828* 🌐 *www.hemingways.to* Ⓜ *Bay.*

Fodor's Choice ★ **The Roof Lounge.** Such Canadian literary luminaries as Margaret Atwood and Mordecai Richler have used the 18th-floor Roof Lounge as a setting in their writings. The tiny bar is chic and refined without stuffiness or pretension and has dark wood and leather accents. Martinis and cosmopolitans are the specialties, though the menu also includes a nice selection of single malts and tequilas, small plates, and tapas. In warm weather you can choose a Cuban cigar from the menu of eight south-of-the-border stogies ranging in price from C$5 to C$100 and smoke on the adjoining patio, which affords lovely views of the downtown skyline and lake. The bar is cozily petite and does not accept reservations, so arrive in the late afternoon on weekends to avoid a wait. ✉ *Park Hyatt Hotel, top fl., 4 Avenue Rd., Yorkville* ☎ *416/925–1234* 🌐 *www.parktoronto.hyatt.com* Ⓜ *Bay or St. George.*

TORONTO COMEDIANS

Since the Second City opened, Toronto has been a comedic hub. Gilda Radner, John Candy, Dan Aykroyd, Dave Thomas, Martin Short, Eugene Levy, Catherine O'Hara, and Rick Moranis all cut their teeth here or on SCTV, a TV offshoot of the theater and precursor to *Saturday Night Live.* Toronto native Lorne Michaels cast Aykroyd and Radner in the first season of *SNL.* Mike Myers, Dave Foley, Bruce McCulloch, and Mark McKinney started at the Bad Dog Theatre. Jim Carrey and Howie Mandel debuted at Yuk Yuk's, and Samantha Bee frequented the Rivoli before joining *The Daily Show.*

La Societe. This French-inspired space features a chic dining room that boasts a 20-foot-by-30-foot illuminated stained-glass ceiling, a Parisian-style bar top, and the best patio Yorkville has to offer. Guests can sip on a variety of French wines, champagne, and carefully crafted cocktails while people-watching on one of two European-style terraces that overlook Bloor Street glamour. Nights are filled with always-changing DJs who offer up French house music to well-heeled fashion fans. ✉ *131 Bloor St. W, Yorkville* ☎ *416/551–9929* 🌐 *www.lasociete.ca* Ⓜ *Bay.*

CHURCH-WELLESLEY

The "Gay Village," the "gayborhood," or just plain old "Church and Wellesley"—whatever you call it, this strip of bars, restaurants, shops, and clubs is a fun, always-hopping hangout for the LGBT crowd or anyone with an open mind.

GAY AND LESBIAN NIGHTLIFE

BARS, PUBS, AND LOUNGES

Woody's. A predominantly upscale, professional male crowd (20s to 40s) frequents this cavernous pub. DJs mix every night. Check out weekly events like the Best Chest and Best Butt contests, which are hosted by some of the city's most beloved drag queens. The exterior of Woody's was used on the television show *Queer as Folk.* ✉ *467 Church St., at Maitland St., Church-Wellesley* ☎ *416/972–0887* 🌐 *www.woodystoronto.com* Ⓜ *Wellesley.*

CABARET For queer-positive theater, check out **Buddies in Bad Times.** ⇨ *See the Performing Arts chapter.* It offers entertaining cabaret, comedy, and award-winning performances throughout the year.

DANCE CLUBS **CHURCH on Church.** CHURCH, which opened in the summer of 2012, is the newest spot to open its doors in the Village. This queer bar and lounge is a popular spot for 20- to 40-year-olds with a penchant for well-crafted cocktails and a rowdy dance floor. The space is best described as a refined boutique club where DJs spin and well-dressed professional gays come to mix and mingle late at night. ✉ *504 Church St., Church-Wellesley* ☎ *647/352–5223* 🌐 *www.churchonchurch.com* Ⓜ *Wellesley.*

Crews & Tangos. Downstairs is Crews, a gay and lesbian bar with a stage for karaoke or drag shows (depending on the night), a dance floor in back with a DJ spinning house beats, and a sizable back patio. Tangos, upstairs, has a bar and a small dance floor that gets packed with twenty- to thirtysomething guys and gals kicking it to old-school hip-hop and '80s beats. The male–female ratio is surprisingly balanced and the drag shows lots of fun. Usually a C$5 cover on weekends. ✉ *508 Church St., Church-Wellesley* ☎ *416/972–1662* 🌐 *crewsandtangos.com* Ⓜ *Wellesley.*

Fly. Some of the biggest and best DJs from around the world have spun records at the original "Babylon" from television's *Queer as Folk.* An impressive sound system, light show, and 10,000 square feet have won this queer-positive club several Best Dance Club in Toronto awards. The hot—and generally young—clientele doesn't hurt, either. It's one of the best dance spots in the city, gay club or not. Cover ranges from C$10 to C$20. ✉ *8 Gloucester St., just east of Yonge St., Church-Wellesley* ☎ *416/410–5426* 🌐 *www.flynightclub.com* Ⓜ *Wellesley.*

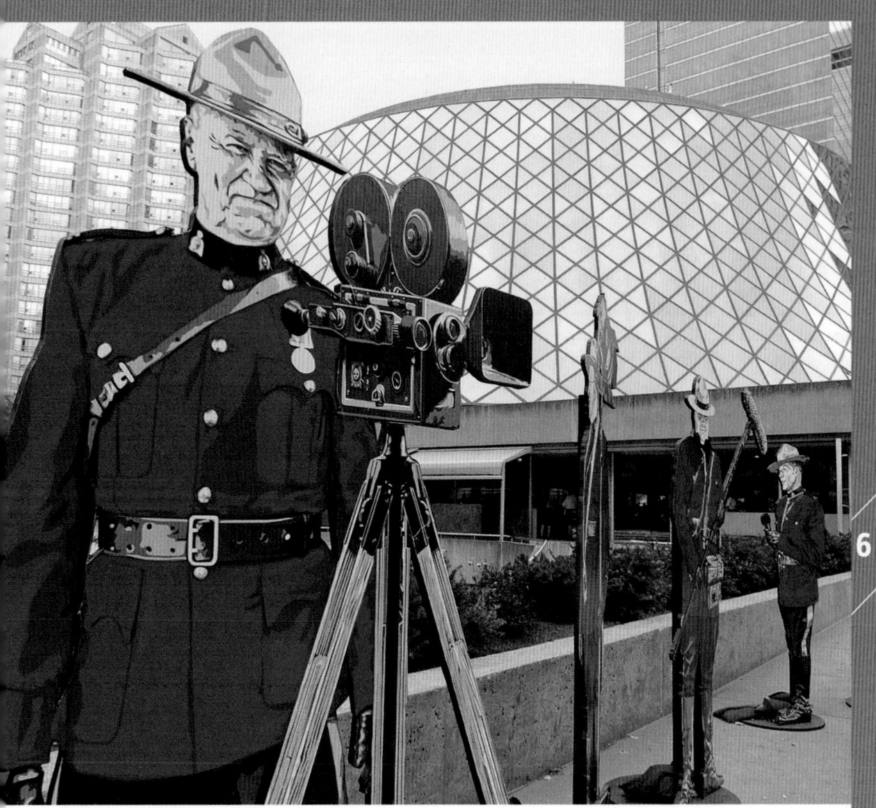

6

THE PERFORMING ARTS

Updated by Kathryn Lane

In terms of culture, Toronto truly is Canada's New York—the city to which artists immigrate to make a name for themselves. And the rest of us reap the rewards. With all the options available, these days the biggest obstacle to arts and culture in Toronto is deciding what to experience while you're here. The capital of the performing arts in English-speaking Canada, Toronto has world-class resident symphony, opera, and ballet companies.

But the arts scene wasn't always this lively. Before 1950, Toronto had no opera company, no ballet, and very little theater worthy of the title "professional." Then came the Massey Report on the Arts, and money began to pour in from government grants. The Canada Council, the Canadian Opera Company, CBC television, and the National Ballet of Canada were born. A number of small theaters began to pop up as well, culminating in an artistic explosion throughout the 1970s in every aspect of the arts. (This was also when the Toronto International Film Festival was born.) Adding fuel to the fire was a massive spike in immigration, a recognition that if Canadians did not develop their own arts the Americans would do it for them, and a severing of the political apron strings tying Canada to England, resulting in a desire to cement Canada's independence and to encourage homegrown talent.

Now Toronto is growing, with new performance venues opening and old ones being refurbished. The current flurry of artistic activity shows no signs of abating. The city has more than 50 dance companies; film festivals and retrospectives overtake screens year-round; and the numerous theatrical troupes and big-budget musicals staged here have earned it the nickname "Broadway North." Theater is where it really shines, from spit-and-chewing-gum new works to Broadway-style, no-expenses-spared extravaganzas. In fact, Toronto is the largest center for English-speaking theater in the world after New York and London—not bad for a city that's only the fifth largest in North America by population.

PLANNING

WHAT'S ON NOW?

Check free alternative newsweeklies *NOW* (🌐 *www.nowtoronto.com*) and *The Grid* (🌐 *www.thegridto.com*) and monthly magazine *Toronto Life* (🌐 *www.torontolife.com*) for reviews, concerts, movie times, and events. *Whole Note* (🌐 *www.thewholenote.com*) publishes classical, jazz, opera, and world music concert dates and news online and in its free monthly print publication.

LATE-NIGHT TRANSPORTATION

Subway and streetcar service ends at 1 am, so for late-night outings, hailing a cab is your best bet. Some streetcars and buses along major streets (including Queen, Bloor, and Yonge) run 24 hours but pick up only every half hour.

TOP EXPERIENCES

Rub elbows with Hollywood types at the Toronto International Film Festival. See star-studded premieres and discover the next big thing with independent films.

Laugh it up. In Canada's breeding ground for comedy, Second City is the cream of the crop, and there are about a dozen stand-up venues around town.

See a major musical. Catch a performance of *War Horse* or *Sister Act* at one of the grand, historic theaters in Toronto—the next best thing to Broadway.

Partake in patio life. Torontonians are notorious in Canada for being cold, but when the sun comes out, they're giddy, and come 5:15 on a warm-weather weekday April through October, bar and restaurant patios are teeming.

Root for your team. Sports fans run rampant in the T-Dot; if you can't get to the pitch, catch NHL matches, Premier League games, or even cricket and curling at Hemingways, Wayne Gretzky's, the Queen and Beaver, or the mother of them all, Real Sports Bar.

TICKETS

Ticketmaster. Tickets for almost any event can be obtained through Ticketmaster. ☎ *855/985–5000* 🌐 *www.ticketmaster.ca.*

StubHub. Check ticket reseller StubHub for sold-out events or last-minute deals. ☎ *866/788–2482* 🌐 *www.stubhub.com.*

T.O. Tix booth. For discounted theater, dance, music, and comedy tickets on the day of a performance, visit the T.O. Tix booth (tickets for Sunday and Monday performances are sold on Saturday). **TIP→ Arrive before noon for the best chance of getting the same-day tickets you want; they go off-sale at 5.** T.O. Tix is a fully fledged Ticket Master outlet, so you can pick up tickets for just about anything here. Discounted advance tickets are also available. Pay cash, by debit card, or by credit card—Visa or MasterCard are accepted. ✉ *Yonge and Dundas Sts., Dundas Square Area* 🌐 *www.totix.ca* ⏲ *Tues.–Sat. noon–6:30* Ⓜ *Dundas.*

TORONTO'S FILM SCENE

Toronto loves the movies, and the feeling is mutual. So many films are shot here (the city has posed as everywhere from Paris to Vietnam) that Toronto has earned the nickname "Hollywood North." The highlight of the cinematic year is the world-renowned Toronto International Film Festival.

North America's third-largest film production center after L.A. and New York, Toronto keeps cameras rolling with its excellent local crews and production facilities and plenty of filmmaker tax credits. It helps, too, that Toronto's chameleonic streets easily impersonate other cities and time periods. Credits include: Yonge Street as Harlem (*The Incredible Hulk*), the Distillery District as Prohibition-era Chicago (*Chicago*), Casa Loma as the school for young mutants in *X-Men,* and the U of T campus as Harvard (*Good Will Hunting*). Spotting Toronto "tells" in films is fun, but locals get even more jazzed when the city represents itself for a change, as in 2010's *Scott Pilgrim vs. the World.*

MORE FESTIVALS

Hot Docs. This is North America's largest documentary film festival. *www.hotdocs.ca* *late April.*

Inside Out Toronto LGBT Film Festival. This major event features films made by and about lesbian, gay, bi, and transgender people. *www.insideout.ca/torontofestival* *late May.*

TIFF Kids International Film Festival. TIFF Kids features new and classic films aimed at the 2-to-13-year-old crowd. *www.tiff.net* *April.*

Toronto After Dark. This festival is dedicated to horror, sci-fi, and thriller films. *www.torontoafterdark.com* *late October.*

TORONTO INTERNATIONAL FILM FESTIVAL

Widely considered the most important film festival in the world after Cannes, TIFF is open to the public with even star-studded galas accessible to the average joe. More than 300 of the latest works of great international directors and lesser-known independent-film directors from around the world are shown. Movies premiered at TIFF have gone on to win Academy Awards and launch the careers of emerging actors and directors. In recent years, TIFF audiences have been among the first in the world to see *The King's Speech, Slumdog Millionnaire,* and *Juno,* to mention just a few. The red carpet is rolled out, and paparazzi get ready for big-budget, star-studded premieres ("galas"), for which actors and directors may be on hand afterward for Q&As. Along with the serious documentaries, foreign films, and Oscar contenders, TIFF has fun with its Midnight Madness program, screening campy horror films, comedies, and action movies into the wee hours. ✉ *TIFF Bell Lightbox, 350 King St. West, at John St., Harbourfront* ☎ *416/968–3456, 877/968–3456* 🌐 *www.tiff.net.*

DOING THE FESTIVAL

When: The 11-day festival begins in early September

Where: Screenings are at movie theaters and concert halls throughout the city, as are ticket booths, but the festival HQ is the TIFF Bell Lightbox building, at ✉ *350 King St. W (at John St.).*

Tickets: If you plan to see 10 or more films, consider a festival pass or package, which go on sale in July; you can choose screenings on the website. Individual tickets go on sale four days before the start of the festival. You may not get your first choice, but discovering something new is part of the fun. (No, really!) Ticket prices are about C$25 per film and $45 for red-carpet premiers. If you have your heart set on a particular film and you don't get a ticket, keep checking each morning at 7 am—TIFF releases extra tickets each day of the festival. Tickets are almost always available for *something,* even at the last minute, and even sold-out shows have a rush line.

TIPS

- Book a hotel as early as possible: some hotels near the theaters are booked by May.
- Read ticket-buying instructions carefully; you'll need to call TIFF to fix anything and there's a fee to exchange tickets.
- Pick up your order at least an hour before your screening to ensure you don't get stuck in a long line and miss the best seats.
- Arrive at least two hours early if you're trying to get a rush ticket. They're released ten minutes before the start of a film.

WHERE TO WATCH

Oddball series and theme nights: Revue

Documentaries: Bloor Cinema

Pure cinephelia: TIFF Bell Lightbox

IMAX: Ontario Science Centre Omnimax Theatre (Toronto's only 70 mm celluloid IMAX); Cineplex Odeon Yonge & Dundas Cinemas; Scotiabank Theatre

3-D: Scotiabank Theatre; TIFF Bell Lightbox; Varsity and Varsity VIP; Cineplex Odeon Yonge & Dundas

Summer films al fresco: Harbourfront Centre (🕒 *Wed.* 🎫 *Free* ✉ *235 Queens Quay W*); Polson Pier Drive-In (🕒 *Fri. & Sat.,* 🎫 *C$15; Sun., C$25 per car load* ✉ *176 Cherry St., Harbourfront*); TIFF in the Park (🕒 *Wed.* 🎫 *Free* ✉ *King and Simcoe Sts., next to Roy Thompson Hall*); City Cinema (🕒 *Tues.,* 🎫 *Free.* ✉ *Yonge-Dundas Square*). Most screenings start at sunset (usually 8:30 to 9 pm) and run through July and August.

6

CLASSICAL MUSIC AND OPERA

CLASSICAL MUSIC

Fodor's Choice ★ **Glenn Gould Studio.** A variety of classical, folk, jazz, and world-music companies perform at this 341-seat shoebox concert hall named for the famed Torontonian pianist and designed for the Canadian Broadcasting Centre (CBC). Studio recordings are done here as well, a testament to its excellent acoustics. Gould would have expected nothing less. ✉ *Canadian Broadcasting Centre, 250 Front St. W, at John, Entertainment District* ☎ *416/205–5000* 🌐 *www.glenngouldstudio.com* Ⓜ *Union, St. Andrews.*

FREE CONCERTS

The Canadian Opera Company's Free Concert Series takes place September through June with music and dance performances most Tuesdays and Thursdays at noon in the Four Seasons Centre's Richard Bradshaw Amphitheatre. Check the calendar on the COC website to see what's on. ✉ *145 Queen St. W., Queen West* ☎ *416/363–8231* 🌐 *www.coc.ca* Ⓜ *Osgoode Station.*

Fodor's Choice ★ **Koerner Hall.** Artists and audiences quickly fell in love with this handsome 1,135-seat concert hall with rich acoustics and undulating wood "strings" floating overhead when it opened in 2009. Performers have included such greats as Yo-Yo Ma, Chick Corea, Ravi Shankar, Midori, Taj Mahal, and Savion Glover. The hall is part of the Royal Conservatory's arts-education facility, the TELUS Centre for Performance and Learning. ✉ *273 Bloor St. W, at Avenue Rd., Yorkville* ☎ *416/408–0208* 🌐 *www.rcmusic.ca* ⏲ *Box Office open Mon.–Fri. 10–6, Sat. noon–6* Ⓜ *St. George.*

Tafelmusik. Internationally renowned as one of the world's finest period ensembles, Tafelmusik presents baroque and classical music on original instruments. Most performances are in the recently revitalized Trinity–St. Paul's Church; the pews have been replaced by seats, and the acoustics are much improved. The Sing-Along *Messiah* at ⇨ *Massey Hall* is a rollicking Christmas season highlight where the audience is invited to join in; tickets start at C$30 and they usually sell out. ✉ *Trinity–St. Paul's United Church, 427 Bloor St. W, The Annex* ☎ *416/964–6337* 🌐 *www.tafelmusik.org* Ⓜ *Spadina.*

Toronto Mendelssohn Choir. This group of more than 120 choristers was formed in 1894 and performs major classical choral works at various venues including the Royal Conservatory's lovely Koerner Hall and Yorkminster Park Baptist Church at Yonge and St. Clair. The choir often performs with the Toronto Symphony Orchestra, including its annual Christmas performance of Handel's *Messiah.* ✉ *Yorkminster Park Baptist Church, 1585 Yonge St., north of St. Clair, Rosedale* ☎ *416/598–0422* 🌐 *www.tmchoir.org.*

Toronto Symphony Orchestra. Since 1922 this orchestra has achieved world acclaim with music directors such as Seiji Ozawa, Sir Thomas Beecham, and Sir Andrew Davis. Canadian-born Peter Oundjian helped return the ensemble to an international level when he took over as musical director in 2003. Guest performers have included

With its circular shape and striking glass canopy, Roy Thomson Hall is a classic of Toronto architecture.

pianist Lang Lang, violinist Itzhak Perlman, and singer-songwriter Rufus Wainwright. Each season the orchestra screens a classic film, such as *Casablanca* or *West Side Story,* and plays the soundtrack as it runs. The TSO presents about three concerts weekly at Roy Thomson Hall from September through June. ✉ *Roy Thomson Hall, 60 Simcoe St., Entertainment District* ☎ *416/598–3375 TSO information and tickets, 416/593–4828 Roy Thomson Hall ticket line* 🌐 *www.tso.ca* Ⓜ *St. Andrew.*

University of Toronto. Performances by professors and students of the University of Toronto Faculty of Music and visiting artists, ranging from symphony to jazz to full-scale operas, take place September through May, at little or no cost, in two spaces: the 815-seat **MacMillan Theatre** and the 490-seat **Walter Hall.** ✉ *University of Toronto Faculty of Music, Edward Johnson Bldg., 80 Queen's Park Crescent, Queen's Park* ☎ *416/408–0208* 🌐 *www.music.utoronto.ca* Ⓜ *Museum.*

CONTEMPORARY AND EXPERIMENTAL MUSIC

Fodor's Choice ★ **The Music Gallery.** Toronto's go-to spot for experimental music, the self-titled "center for creative music" presents an eclectic selection of avant-garde and experimental music from world and classical to jazz and avant-pop in a relaxed environment. ✉ *St. George the Martyr Church, 197 John St., 2 blocks north of Queen St. at Stephanie St., Queen West* ☎ *416/204–1080* 🌐 *www.musicgallery.org* Ⓜ Osgoode.

OPERA

Canadian Opera Company. Founded in 1950, the COC has grown into the largest producer of opera in Canada, and has proven innovative and often daring with presentations that range from popular operas to more modern or rarely performed works. The COC maintains its international reputation for artistic excellence and creative leadership by presenting new productions from a diverse repertoire, collaborating with leading opera companies and festivals, and attracting the world's foremost Canadian and international artists. It often hosts world-renowned performers, and it pioneered the use of scrolling surtitles, which allow the audience to follow the libretto in English in a capsulized translation that appears above the stage. Tickets sell out quickly. Tours (C$20 for adults; C$15 for seniors/students) of the COC's opera house, the magnificent **Four Seasons Centre for the Performing Arts,** are given when the performance schedule allows (usually on Sundays); check the website for times and dates. ✉ *Four Seasons Centre for the Performing Arts, 145 Queen St. W, at University Ave., Queen West* ☎ *416/363–8231, 1–800/250–4653* 🌐 *www.coc.ca* Ⓜ *Osgoode.*

HARBOURFRONT CENTRE

When looking for cultural events in Toronto, always check the schedule at the Harbourfront Centre. A cultural playground, it has an art gallery (the Power Plant), two dance spaces, a music garden co-designed by Yo-Yo Ma, and chockablock festivals and cultural events, some especially for kids and many of them free. ✉ *235 Queen's Quay W, at Lower Simcoe St., Harbourfront* ☎ *416/973–4000* 🌐 *www.harbourfrontcentre.com* Ⓜ *Union, then 510 streetcar.*

Opera Atelier. Since its opening in 1985, Opera Atelier has been dedicated to staging 17th- and 18th-century baroque operas, with extravagant sets and costumes and original instruments. The two annual productions are stage at the ⇨ *Elgin Theatre* each fall and spring. ✉ *Elgin Theatre, 189 Yonge St., just north of Queen St.* ☎ *416/703–3767* 🌐 *www.operaatelier.com.*

MAJOR VENUES

It's not uncommon for a concert hall to present modern dance one week, a rock- or classical-music concert another week, and a theatrical performance the next. Arenas double as sports stadiums and venues for the biggest names in music and the occasional monster-truck rally or other spectacle.

Air Canada Centre. Most arena shows are held here rather than at the larger Rogers Centre due to superior acoustics. Past performances at the 20,000-capacity arena have included Beyoncé, Rod Stewart, American Idol Live!, and Nine Inch Nails. ✉ *40 Bay St., at Gardiner Expressway, Harbourfront* ☎ *416/815–5500* 🌐 *www.theaircanadacentre.com* Ⓜ *Union.*

Fodor's Choice ★ **Elgin and Winter Garden Theatre Centre.** This jewel in the crown of the Toronto arts scene consists of two former vaudeville halls, built in 1913, one on top of the other. It is the last operating double-decker theater complex in the world and a Canadian National Historic Site. Until

1928, the theaters hosted silent-film and vaudeville legends like George Burns, Gracie Allen, and Edgar Bergen with Charlie McCarthy. Today's performances are still surrounded by magnificent settings: Elgin's dramatic gold-leaf-and-cherub-adorned interior and the Winter Garden's *A Midsummer Night's Dream*–inspired decor, complete with tree branches overhead. These stages host Broadway-caliber musicals, comedians, jazz concerts, operas, and Toronto International Film Festival screenings. The Elgin, downstairs, has more than 1,500 seats; the 992-seat Winter Garden is upstairs. Guided tours (C$12) are given Thursday at 5 pm and Saturday at 11 am. ✉ *189 Yonge St., at Queen St., Dundas Square Area* ☎ *855/622–2787 tickets, 416/314–2871 tours* 🌐 *www.heritagetrust.on.ca/ewg* Ⓜ *Queen.*

TORONTO ARTS ILLUMINATED

Every June, Luminato packs in 100 or more events spanning the arts from plays to tango lessons, from puppetry to poetry, and from art installations to funk bands. The festival attracts some big names such as Joni Mitchell, the Mark Morris Dance Group, and Marina Abramović. ☎ *416/368–3100* 🌐 *www.luminato.com.*

Fodor's Choice ★ **Massey Hall.** Near-perfect acoustics and handsome, U-shape tiers have made Massey Hall a great place to enjoy music since 1894, when it opened with a performance of Handel's *Messiah*. It's always been a venerable place to catch big-time solo acts like Neil Young and Gilberto Gil, comedians, indie bands, and occasional dance troupes. However, this grand old venue is a bit cramped, and at last plans are under way to expand the interior, modernize the amenities, and scrub up the façade. The hall is anticipated to remain open throughout the renovations, but check the website for the latest on scheduled performances. ✉ *178 Victoria St., at Shuter St., Dundas Square Area* ☎ *416/872–4255* 🌐 *www.masseyhall.com* Ⓜ *Queen.*

Rogers Centre. Toronto's largest performance venue, with seating for up to 55,000, is the spot for the biggest shows in town—Rolling Stones, Bruce Springsteen, Justin Bieber—though the acoustically superior Air Canada Centre is the more widely used arena venue. ✉ *1 Blue Jays Way, at Spadina Ave., Harbourfront* ☎ *855/985–5000 concert and event tickets* 🌐 *www.rogerscentre.com* Ⓜ *Union.*

Fodor's Choice ★ **Roy Thomson Hall.** Toronto's premier concert hall, home of the ⇨ *Toronto Symphony Orchestra* (TSO), also hosts visiting orchestras, popular entertainers, and Toronto International Film Festival red-carpet screenings. The 2,630-seat auditorium opened in 1982 and is named after Roy Thomson, who was born in Toronto and founded the publishing empire Thomson Corporation (now Thomson Reuters). ✉ *60 Simcoe St., at King St., Entertainment District* ☎ *416/872–4255 tickets, 416/593–4822 tours* 🌐 *www.roythomson.com* Ⓜ *St. Andrew.*

Sony Centre for the Performing Arts. This cavernous 3,191-seat hall boasts an international program of diverse yet mostly mainstream artists such as the Merchants of Bollywood, Russell Brand, the Dance Theater of Harlem, and Hong Kong power duo Adam Cheng and Liza Wang. When this theater opened in 1960 as the O'Keefe Centre, it showcased

In addition to producing numerous works by Canadian artists, the Toronto Dance Theatre collaborates with choreographers from throughout the United States and Europe.

the world premiere of *Camelot,* starring Julie Andrews, Richard Burton, and Robert Goulet. A 2010 renovation restored original elements of the design and made technological improvements. ✉ *1 Front St. E, at Yonge St., Old Town* ☎ *855/872–7669 tickets, 416/368–6161* 🌐 *www.sonycentre.ca* Ⓜ *Union, King.*

DANCE

Toronto's rich dance scene includes pretty *Giselle* interpretations and edgy, emotionally charged modern-dance performances.

The National Ballet of Canada. Canada's internationally recognized classical-ballet company was founded in 1951 and is made up of 70 dancers and its own orchestra. It's the only company in Canada to perform a full range of traditional full-length ballet classics, including frequent stagings of *Swan Lake* and *The Nutcracker*. The company also performs contemporary works and is dedicated to the development of Canadian choreography. The season runs fall through spring at the Four Seasons Centre for the Performing Arts, Canada's first purpose-built ballet opera house, which the ballet shares with the Canadian Opera Company. ✉ *Four Seasons Centre for the Performing Arts, 145 Queen St. W, Queen West* ☎ *416/345–9595, 866/345–9595 outside Toronto* 🌐 *www.national.ballet.ca* Ⓜ *Osgoode.*

Harbourfront Centre. This venue has two theaters for dance and two renowned dance series: Next Steps, which runs from September through the spring, and World Stage, which also includes theatre and begins in January. The **Fleck Dance Theatre** was built specifically for modern dance in 1983. The proscenium stage hosts some of the best local and Canadian modern and contemporary companies, in addition to some international acts. The **Enwave Theatre** welcomes these same types of dance performances as well as plays and concerts. It has excellent acoustics. Both theaters are small (446 and 422 seats, respectively) so you're never far from the stage. ✉ *Harbourfront Centre, 207 Queen's Quay W, at Lower Simcoe St., Harbourfront* ☎ *416/973–4000* 🌐 *www.harbourfrontcentre.com* Ⓜ *Union.*

MORE LISTINGS TO PERUSE

Toronto has many more theaters, festivals, and film events than we're able to fit within these pages. A great source for what's new and interesting in alternative cinema and festivals is the online magazine *Toronto Film Scene* (🌐 *thetfs.ca*).

Fodor's Choice ★ **Toronto Dance Theatre.** The oldest contemporary dance company in the city, TDT has created more than 100 original works since its beginnings in the 1960s, over a third of which use original scores by Canadian composers. Two or three pieces are performed each year in its home theater in Cabbagetown, and one major production is performed at the Harbourfront Centre's ⇨ *Fleck Dance Theatre.* ✉ *80 Winchester St., 1 block east of Parliament St., Greater Toronto* ☎ *416/967–1365* 🌐 *www.tdt.org* Ⓜ *Castle Frank.*

6

FILM

Toronto has a devoted film audience. The result is a feast of riches—commercial first- and second-run showings, independent films and documentaries, cult classics, myriad festivals, and lecture series for every taste. For movie times, contact the theaters directly, or check CinemaClock (🌐 *www.cinemaclock.com*) or newsweeklies *NOW* (🌐 *www.nowtoronto.com*) and *The Grid* (🌐 *www.thegridto.com*), online or free on newsstands. Advance tickets are sold through the larger theaters' websites.

FIRST-RUN AND MAINSTREAM MOVIES

Cineplex Odeon Yonge & Dundas. This 24-screen stadium-seated multiplex shows first-run blockbusters, as well as 3D and digital IMAX movies. Once you have your ticket, it's five escalators up to the screens themselves. If you want to catch the trailers, take the elevator. ✉ *Ste. 402, 10 Dundas St. E, at Yonge St., Dundas Square Area* ☎ *416/977–9262* 🌐 *www.cineplex.com* Ⓜ *Dundas.*

Polson Pier Drive-in Theatre. For an old-fashioned treat, park your car at this downtown drive-in that locals still refer to by its former name, the Docks. Open Victoria Day weekend in May to Labour Day in September (except for major electrical storms), it shows first-run double features on Friday, Saturday, and Sunday evenings. The gates open at 8:30pm, and films start at sundown, usually around 9:30. Purchase tickets on-site (C$15); on Sunday, admission is C$25 per carload. ✉ *11 Polson St., south of Lakeshore Blvd., Harbourfront* ☎ *416/465–4653* 🌐 *www.polsonpier.com.*

Scotiabank Theatre. In the heart of the Entertainment District, this megaplex with 14 screens shows all the latest blockbusters and is the place to see films with impressive special effects. Tickets are C$13; a few dollars more for 3-D and digital IMAX movies. ✉ *259 Richmond St. W, at John St., Entertainment District* ☎ *416/368–5600* 🌐 *www.cineplex.com* Ⓜ *Osgoode.*

The Varsity and Varsity VIP. The 12 screens here show new releases. The smaller, licensed VIP screening rooms (ages 19 and up, C$20) have seat-side waitstaff ready to take your concession-stand orders. There's a licensed lounge for pre-screening drinks as well. Regular movie tickets start at C$13. ✉ *Manulife Centre, 3rd fl., 55 Bloor St. W, at Bay St., Yorkville* ☎ *416/961–6303* 🌐 *www.cineplex.com* Ⓜ *Bay or Bloor.*

INDEPENDENT, FOREIGN, AND REVIVAL FILMS

The Bloor Hot Docs Cinema. If you like your films factual, informative, and inspiring then the Bloor is for you. Come here for documentaries on political movements, such as *A Fierce Green: The Battle for a Living Planet*, or perhaps something more esoteric like *Mussels in Love*. The only documentary-focused cinema in the world, the Bloor is the permanent home of the annual Hot Docs festival; numerous other festivals, including TIFF, have screenings here, too. There are occasional showings of good old classics and rep-cinema favorites, such as *Fitzcaraldo* or the *Rocky Horror Picture Show*. Tickets are C$11. Festival screenings and some special presentations are pricier. ✉ *506 Bloor St. W, at Bathurst St., The Annex* ☎ *416/637–3123* 🌐 *www.bloorcinema.com* Ⓜ *Bathurst.*

Harbourfront Centre. In July and August, free movies are screened outdoors as part of the Free Flicks program. Documentaries, frequently accompanying summer festivals, cultural events, and retrospectives, are presented ad hoc throughout the year. ✉ *235 Queen's Quay W, at Lower Simcoe St., Harbourfront* ☎ *416/973–4000* 🌐 *www.harbourfrontcentre.com* Ⓜ *Union.*

The Revue. This beloved neighborhood movie house is operated by the nonprofit Revue Film Society. Onscreen are documentaries, classics (cult and non-), foreign films, some first-run movies, silent films, and the occasional oddity like *Giant Killer Shark: The Musical.* Admission is C$11, or buy a C$6 six-month Star Card for benefits that include C$8 tickets. ✉ *400 Roncesvalles Ave., at Howard Park Ave., Greater Toronto* ☎ *416/531–9959* 🌐 *www.revuecinema.ca* Ⓜ *Dundas West, then 504 streetcar to Howard Park Ave.*

The Royal. This fully restored 1939 single-screen theater shows indie documentaries, features, and art films on a state-of-the-art digital projector. ✉ *608 College St., at Clinton St., Little Italy* ☎ *416/466–4400* 🌐 *www.theroyal.to* Ⓜ *506 streetcar across College St.*

TIFF Bell Lightbox. Operated by the Toronto International Film Festival (TIFF) organization, this state-of-the-art five-screen, five-story complex, opened in 2010, shows classic and avant-garde films, director retrospectives, actor tributes, national cinema spotlights, exclusive limited runs, and new documentaries and artistic films. Tickets are C$13. ✉ *350 King St., at John St., Entertainment District* ☎ *416/968–3456* 🌐 *www.tiff.net/tiffbelllightbox* Ⓜ *St. Andrew.*

SUMMER THEATER

Summer is the off-season for non-commercial theaters, but—lucky for us—there's no rest for the weary thespians. To avoid getting stuck with a stinker, read reviews for individual festival plays in local newspapers.

Shakespeare in High Park. Every summer, Shakespeare's most popular plays are performed under the stars at this outdoor amphitheater. Productions are usually knockouts and run from July through August, weather permitting. Performances are pay what you can, with a suggested C$20 donation, and regular seating is on a first-come, first-served basis. To ensure you get a spot, reserve a cushion in the Premium Zone online for C$25. Performances are Tuesday through Sunday at 8; gates open at 6 pm. It gets cold in this leafy park, so bring layers and a blanket to sit on; picnicking is encouraged. ✉ *High Park, High Park Ave., main entrance off Bloor St. W., Greater Toronto* ☎ *416/368–3110* 🌐 *www.canadianstage.com* 🎫 *Pay what you can; free for children under 14* Ⓜ *High Park.*

SummerWorks Performance Festival. More than 50 plays, performances, concerts, and happenings deemed sufficiently forward-thinking and provocative are staged at the Factory Theatre, Theatre Passe Muraille, and other venues around Queen West for the 11-day SummerWorks Performance Festival in August. Tickets are about C$15 per show. ✉ *Queen West* ☎ *416/628–8216* 🌐 *www.summerworks.ca.*

Toronto Fringe Festival. The city's largest theater festival, with more than 140 shows taking place in 35 venues (including a Laundromat, storage space, and a back alley), takes place over 10 days in late June/early July. Raw and untested works by emerging (and some established) artists are the norm. Tickets are C$11 or less per show. The most popular shows are given extended runs in the Best of the Fringe Festival. ☎ *416/966–1062* 🌐 *www.fringetoronto.com.*

6

THEATER

Toronto has the third-largest theater scene in the world, following London and New York. Here you can see Broadway shows as well as a range of smaller Canadian and international productions from reproduced "straight" plays to experimental performances.

For reviews, news, and schedules, check 🌐 *www.stage-door.com* (a wealth of information—this is where industry types browse), the *Globe and Mail* Arts section (🌐 *www.theglobeandmail.com/arts*), and the free newsweeklies *Now* (🌐 *www.nowtoronto/stage*) and *The Grid* (🌐 *www.thegridto.com/culture/theatre*).

COMMERCIAL THEATERS

For more large-theater venues see Major Venues.

Ed Mirvish Theatre. This 1920 vaudeville theater has had a checkered history—it was chopped up into six cinemas in the '70s—and has had numerous names over the year, including the Pantages, the Imperial, and most recently the Canon. Now named after local businessman and theater impresario Ed Mirvish, the theater is one of the most architecturally and acoustically exciting live theaters in Toronto. Today it hosts big-budget musicals, such as *Wicked* and *Billy Elliot,* and occasional short runs by dance troupes and other performances. The theater itself is one of the most beautiful in the world and was refurbished in 1989 in preparation for the Canadian debut of *The Phantom of the Opera*, Canada's longest-running stage musical, which closed in 1999. Designed by world-renowned theater architect Thomas Lamb, it has columns, a grand staircase, gold leaf detailing, and crystal chandeliers. ✉ *244 Victoria St., 1 block south of Dundas St. E, Dundas Square Area* ☎ *416/364–4100 theater, 416/872–1212 tickets, 800/461–3333 tickets* 🌐 *www.mirvish.com* Ⓜ *Dundas.*

Princess of Wales. State-of-the-art facilities and wonderful murals by American artist Frank Stella grace this 2,000-seat theater, built by father-and-son producer team Ed and David Mirvish in the early 1990s to accommodate the technically demanding musical *Miss Saigon*. Big-budget musicals like *Lion King* and *The Book of Mormon* and plays such as *War Horse* are showcased. ✉ *300 King St. W, at John St., Entertainment District* ☎ *416/351–9011 theater, 416/872–1212 tickets, 800/461–3333 tickets* 🌐 *www.mirvish.com* Ⓜ *St. Andrew.*

Royal Alexandra. The most historic of the Mirvish theaters, the "Royal Alex" has been the place to be seen in Toronto since 1907 and is the oldest continuously operating legitimate theater in North America. The 1,500 plush red seats, gold plasterwork, and baroque swirls and flourishes make theatergoing a refined experience. Charleston Heston made his debut here and Lawrence Olivier, Edith Piaf, Mary Pickford, Alan Bates, and John Gielgud have also graced the stage. Programs are a mix of blockbuster musicals and dramatic productions, some touring before or after Broadway appearances. Second-balcony seats are firmer than those in the first balcony. ✉ *260 King St. W, Entertainment District* ☎ *416/593–1840 theater, 416/872–3333 tickets, 800/461–3333 tickets* 🌐 *www.mirvish.com* Ⓜ *St. Andrew.*

SMALL THEATERS AND COMPANIES

Seasons at most of these smaller theaters are September or October through May or June, though some special performances might be scheduled in summer. Soulpepper is open year-round.

Buddies in Bad Times. Canada's largest LGBT theater company presents edgy plays and festivals, as well as specialty after-hours events (burlesque, stand-up). Tickets bought day-of for Sunday's show are pay-what-you-can. ✉ *12 Alexander St., just east of Yonge St., Church-Wellesley* ☎ *416/975–8555* 🌐 *www.buddiesinbadtimes.com* Ⓜ *Wellesley.*

Canadian Stage. Canadian- and European-inspired plays that incorporate dance, photography, video, and other media are at the heart of this company's mission, but it is known also for its excellent Shakespeare in High Park productions. ⇨ *See Summer Theater box.* The **Bluma Appel Theatre** at the St. Lawrence Centre for the Arts seats 867, while the more intimate **Berkeley Street Theatre** has a capacity of 250. ✉ *Bluma Appel Theatre, 27 Front St. East, Old Town* ☎ *416/368–3110 box office, 877/399–2651 toll free* 🌐 *www.canadianstage.com.*

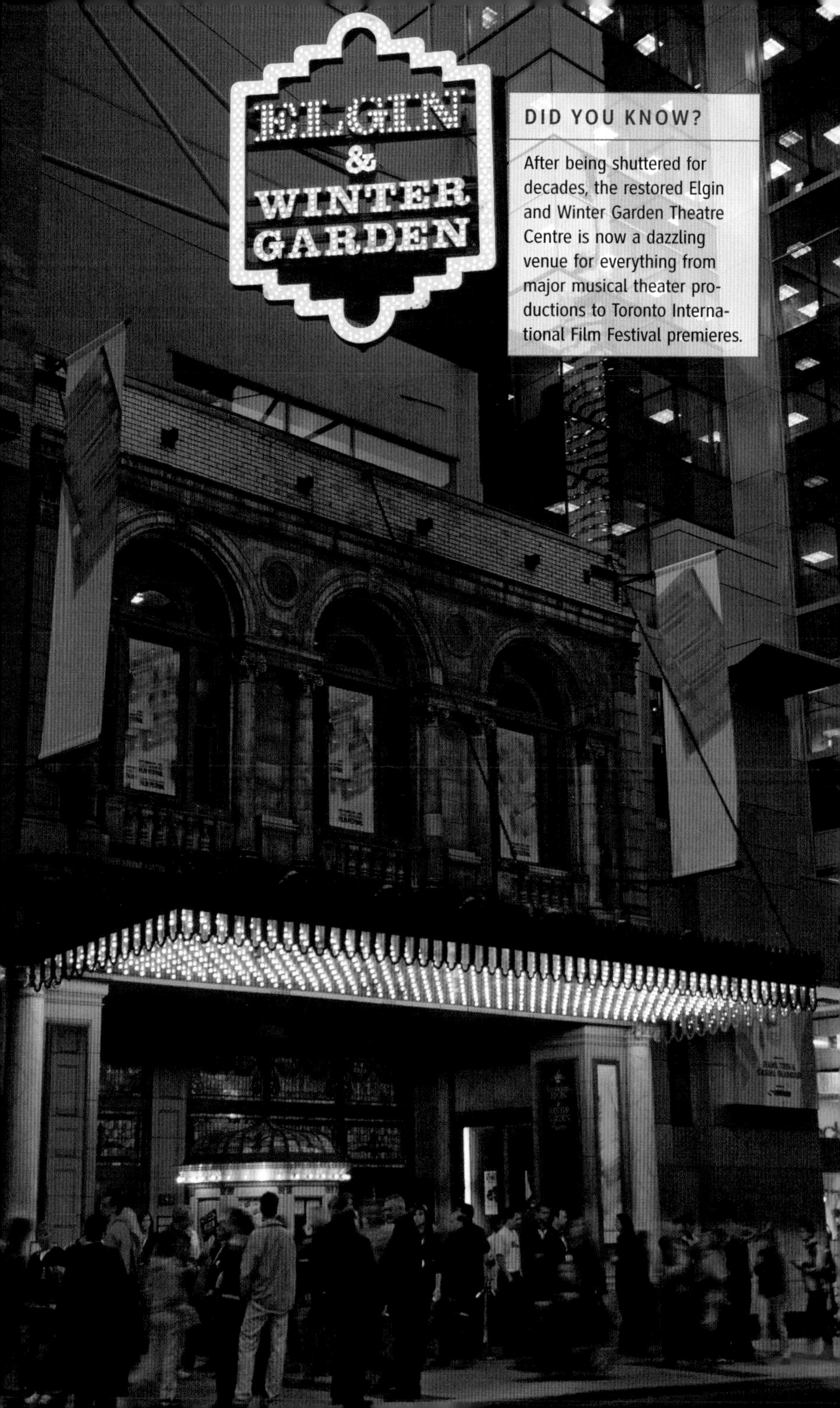

DID YOU KNOW?

After being shuttered for decades, the restored Elgin and Winter Garden Theatre Centre is now a dazzling venue for everything from major musical theater productions to Toronto International Film Festival premieres.

Factory Theatre. This is the country's largest producer of exclusively Canadian plays. Many of the company's shows are world premieres that have gone on to tour Canada and win prestigious awards. An extensive renovation to the Factory's century-old heritage building to improve accessibility will be taking place over the summer of 2014, but the season will continue as usual in the spring and fall. ✉ *125 Bathurst St., at Adelaide St., Entertainment District* ☎ *416/504–9971* 🌐 *www.factorytheatre.ca* ⏲ *Box office open daily, 1–7 pm* Ⓜ *511 Bathurst streetcar to Adelaide St., 501 Queen or 504 King streetcars to Bathurst St.*

FAMILY **Young People's Theatre.** Plays are contemporary, relevant, and kid-focused at YPT, whether a heavily interactive romp, such as *Where the Wild Things Are* which is based on Maurice Sendak's classic book, or a dramatic thought-provoker, *Hana's Suitcase,* the story of a young girl orphaned in the Holocaust. Productions aren't condescending nor do they compromise on dramatic integrity. They are as entertaining for adults as for kids. ✉ *165 Front St. E, between Jarvis and Sherbourne Sts., Old Town* ☎ *416/862–2222* 🌐 *www.youngpeoplestheatre.ca* Ⓜ *King.*

Fodor's Choice ★ **Soulpepper Theatre Company.** Established in 1997 by 12 of Canada's leading theater actors and directors, this repertory theater company produces classic plays year-round, reimagining the works of Henrik Ibsen, Anton Chekhov, and Samuel Beckett. The company makes its home in the Young Centre for the Performing Arts in the Historic Distillery District. ✉ *50 Tank House Lane, Historic Distillery District, Old Town* ☎ *416/866–8666* 🌐 *www.soulpepper.ca* Ⓜ *504 King streetcar to Parliament St.*

Tarragon Theatre. The natural habitat for indigenous Canadian theater is in this old warehouse and railroad district. The main stage is 205 seats and presents plays by new and established Canadian playwrights. Maverick companies often rent the smaller of the Tarragon's theaters (100 seats) for interesting experimental works. ✉ *30 Bridgman Ave., 1 block north of Dupont St., The Annex* ☎ *416/531–1827* 🌐 *www.tarragontheatre.com* Ⓜ *Dupont.*

Théâtre Français de Toronto. High-quality French-language drama—with English supertitles—is performed at this theater, whose French and French-Canadian repertoire ranges from classical to contemporary. A children's play and a teen show are part of the seven-play season. ✉ *Berkeley Street Theatre, 26 Berkeley St., 2nd fl., at Front St. E, Old Town* ☎ *416/534–6604* 🌐 *www.theatrefrancais.com* Ⓜ *King then 504 King streetcar eastbound to Ontario.*

Theatre Passe Muraille. Toronto's oldest alternative theater company, established in 1968, has long been the home of fine Canadian collaborative theater and has launched the careers of many Canadian actors and playwrights. ✉ *16 Ryerson Ave., near Queen and Bathurst Sts., Queen West* ☎ *416/504–7529* 🌐 *www.passemuraille.on.ca* Ⓜ *Osgoode, 501 Queen streetcar west to Bathurst; or Bathurst, then 511 streetcar to Queen.*

7

SHOPPING

Updated by Kathryn Lane

Toronto prides itself on having some of the finest shopping in North America. Indeed, most of the world's name boutiques have branches here, especially in the Yorkville area, where you can find such luxury labels as Chanel, Prada, and Cartier. For those a little leaner of wallet, you can join in one of Torontonians' favorite pastimes: bargain hunting. Locals wear discount threads like badges of honor and stretch their dollar at Winners—where overstocked and liquidated designer pieces and last-season fashions are slashed to a fraction of their original retail prices.

Toronto has a large arts-and-crafts community, with numerous art galleries, custom jewelers, clothing designers, and artisans. Sophisticated glass sculpture and Inuit art are ideal as gifts or for your own home. A few record stores are still going strong despite the dominance of digital music. The survivors' trump card has been focused inventory and knowledgeable staff—head to Rotate This for alterative and indie music or Atelier Grigorian for classical and jazz. Bookstores such as Indigo have lounge areas where you can sip a coffee from the in-store café while perusing books by Canadian authors such as Alice Munro, Ann-Marie MacDonald, and Rohinton Mistry; don't miss favorite independent Book City.

When it comes to department stores, all roads lead to Holt Renfrew on Bloor Street West, the epicenter of Toronto's designer shopping. A mere block east is the more mid-price department store The Bay. A second Bay can be found across from Eaton Centre, a sprawling shopping complex with multilevel parking in the heart of the city.

PLANNING

HOURS

Most shops open by 10 am Monday to Saturday and close at 6 or 7 pm Monday to Thursday, 8 or 9 pm Friday, and as early as 6 pm Saturday. On Sunday, most downtown shops open noon to 5 pm. There are, however, exceptions. Large chain stores downtown often stay open weeknights until 9 or 10 pm.

SALES

The biggest sale day of the year is Boxing Day, the first business day after Christmas, when nearly everything in the city is half price. In fact, clothing prices tend to drop even further as winter fades. Summer sales start in late June and continue through August.

SHIPPING

Nearly all stores that sell larger items like sculpture and furniture will ship to anywhere in the United States or Canada.

TAXES

A hefty rate of 13% Harmonized Sales Tax is levied on most goods and services.

Shopping listings are organized by neighborhood.

HARBOURFRONT, ENTERTAINMENT DISTRICT, AND THE FINANCIAL DISTRICT

HARBOURFRONT

Shopping in the Harbourfront area is somewhat limited but there are plenty of tourist-oriented shops in Queen's Quay Terminal, where you can find some unique gifts, albeit at elevated prices. The Harbourfront Centre complex is also worth a look for crafts and design items.

DEPARTMENT STORES AND SHOPPING CENTERS

Queen's Quay Terminal. Incoming ships once unloaded their fishy cargo at the terminal, which now hosts a collection of unique boutiques, crafts stalls, food stores, and more. This is a great place to buy gifts, though you won't find any deals. The Museum of Inuit Art sells prints and soapstone sculptures, and Canadian travel-wear company Tilley Endurables makes those familiar wide-brimmed khaki hats. It's an easy walk from Union Station in summer, and a quick streetcar ride in winter. Parking is expensive, but there are some free spots in the area. ✉ *207 Queen's Quay W, at York St., Harbourfront* ☎ *416/203–0510 security desk/main number* 🌐 *www.qqterminal.com* ⏲ *Daily 10–6; June–Aug., Thurs.–Fri. and Sat. 10–8* Ⓜ *Union.*

SPECIALTY GIFTS

The Centre Shop. You'll find plenty of locally made crafts and very clever design objects, including glass pieces blown in Harbourfront's own studios, textiles, ceramics, and wood carvings. The shop also carries design classics, such as the Fink anodized water jug, and innovative objects, including Plog-its lighting system of filament bulbs and brightly colored wiring, and O Bags' self-assembled mix-and-match purses and

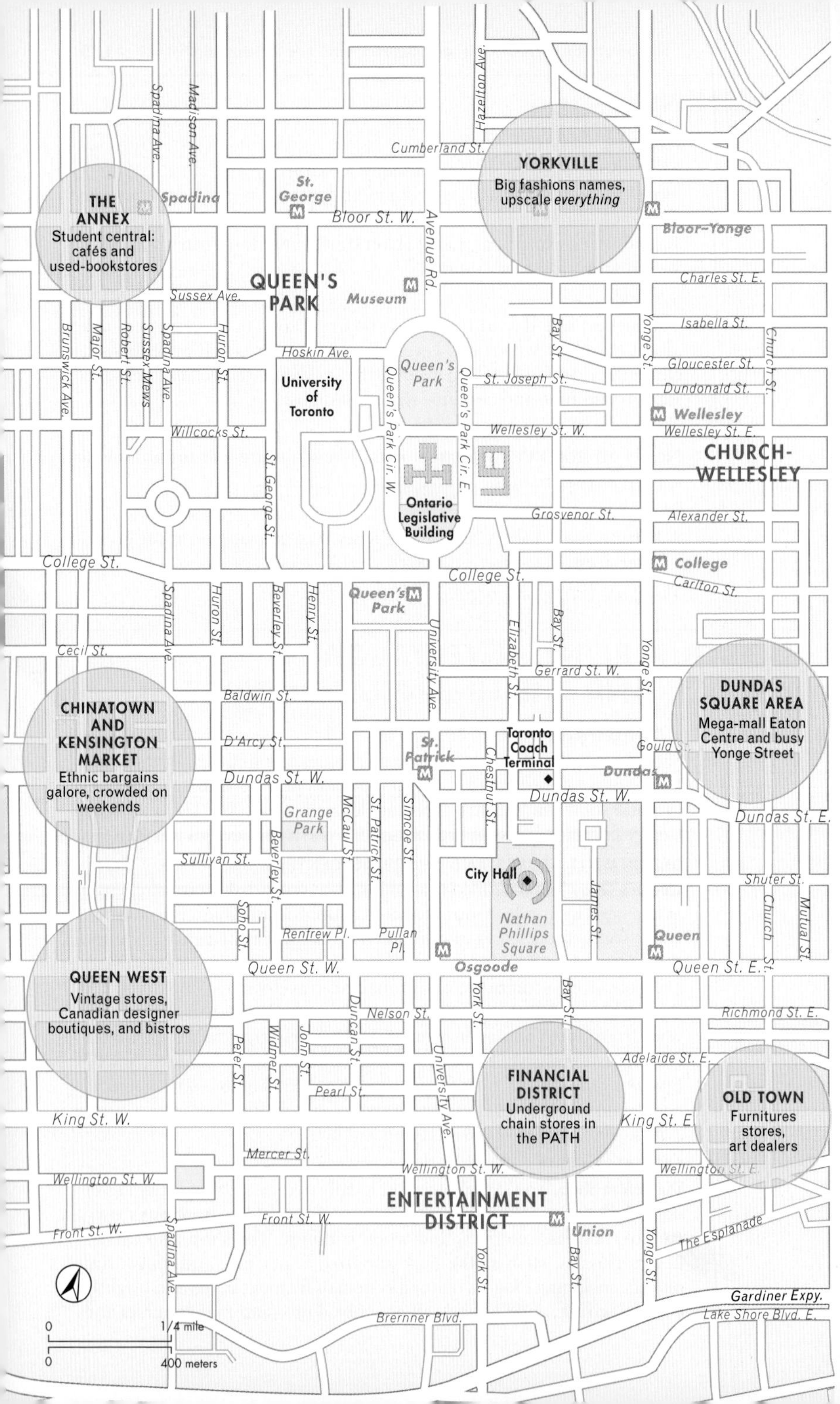

Hazelton Ave.
Spadina Ave.
Madison Ave.
Cumberland St.
YORKVILLE
Big fashions names, upscale everything
THE ANNEX
Student central: cafés and used-bookstores
Spadina
St. George
Bloor St. W.
Avenue Rd.
Bloor–Yonge
QUEEN'S PARK
Museum
Charles St. E.
Sussex Ave.
Isabella St.
Brunswick Ave.
Major St.
Robert St.
Sussex Mews
Spadina Ave.
Huron St.
Hoskin Ave.
Queen's Park
Bay St.
Yonge St.
Church St.
Gloucester St.
University of Toronto
Queen's Park Cir. W.
Queen's Park Cir. E.
St. Joseph St.
Dundonald St.
Wellesley
Willcocks St.
Wellesley St. W.
Wellesley St. E.
CHURCH-WELLESLEY
St. George St.
Ontario Legislative Building
Grosvenor St.
Alexander St.
College St.
College
College St.
Carlton St.
Spadina Ave.
Huron St.
Beverley St.
Henry St.
Queen's Park
University Ave.
Elizabeth St.
Bay St.
Yonge St.
Ceci St.
Gerrard St. W.
DUNDAS SQUARE AREA
Mega-mall Eaton Centre and busy Yonge Street
CHINATOWN AND KENSINGTON MARKET
Ethnic bargains galore, crowded on weekends
Baldwin St.
Toronto Coach Terminal
D'Arcy St.
St. Patrick
Chestnut St.
Gould St.
Dundas St. W.
Dundas
Dundas St. W.
Grange Park
McCaul St.
St. Patrick St.
Simcoe St.
Dundas St. E.
Beverley St.
Sullivan St.
City Hall
James St.
Shuter St.
Soho St.
Nathan Phillips Square
Church St.
Mutual St.
Renfrew Pl.
Pullan Pl.
Queen
QUEEN WEST
Vintage stores, Canadian designer boutiques, and bistros
Queen St. W.
Osgoode
Queen St. E.
York St.
Bay St.
Duncan St.
Nelson St.
Richmond St. E.
Peter St.
Widmer St.
John St.
University Ave.
Adelaide St. E.
FINANCIAL DISTRICT
Underground chain stores in the PATH
OLD TOWN
Furnitures stores, art dealers
Pearl St.
King St. W.
King St. E.
Mercer St.
Wellington St. W.
Wellington St. W.
Wellington St. E.
ENTERTAINMENT DISTRICT
Front St. W.
Front St. W.
Union
The Esplanade
Spadina Ave.
York St.
Bay St.
Yonge St.
Gardiner Expy.
Brenner Blvd.
Lake Shore Blvd. E.
0
1/4 mile
0
400 meters

accessories. ✉ *Harbourfront Centre, 235 Queen's Quay W, Harbourfront* ☎ *416/973–4993* 🌐 *www.harbourfrontcentre.com* ⏲ *Sat.–Wed. 11–6; Thurs.–Fri. 11–8* Ⓜ *Union.*

THE ENTERTAINMENT DISTRICT

While there aren't a ton of shops between the theatres and restaurants of King Street West between Bay and Spadina, those that are there are best in class.

ANTIQUES

Fodor's Choice ★ **Toronto Antiques on King.** The 7,000 square feet of this shop provide ample opportunity for browsing pre- or post-show (the Princess of Wales theater is next door) among the cabinets, shelves, and bins overflowing with porcelain, silver tea sets, majolica pottery, Lalique vases, collectibles, and antique maps. It's also Toronto's leading purveyor of vintage and estate jewelry, making it a popular stop for those seeking out engagement rings. Take the stairs beside Dunn's Deli. ✉ *284 King St. W (2nd fl.), at John St., Entertainment District* ☎ *416/260–9057* 🌐 *www.cynthiafindlay.com* ⏲ *Tues.–Sun. 10–6* Ⓜ *St. Andrew.*

BOOKS

TheatreBooks. An astounding collection of performing-arts books spans theater, film, opera, dance, and television. ✉ *101 Spadina Ave., just south of Adelaide St. West, Entertainment District* ☎ *416/922–7175, 800/361–3414* 🌐 *www.theatrebooks.com* ⏲ *Weekdays 10–7, Sat. 10–6, Sun. noon–5* Ⓜ *St Andrew, then 504 King streetcar west; or Spadina, then 510 streeetcar.*

OUTDOOR EQUIPMENT AND CLOTHING

Fodor's Choice ★ **Mountain Equipment Co-op.** MEC (rhymes with "check"), the much-beloved Toronto spot for anyone remotely interested in camping, sells wares for minor and major expeditions. It's also a go-to spot for cycling gear. A baffling assortment of backpacks allows you to choose anything from a schoolbag to a globetrotting sack. For $5, you get lifetime membership to the co-op. **TIP→ Try out the rappelling goods on the climbing wall.** ✉ *400 King St. W, at Charlotte St., Entertainment District* ☎ *416/340–2667* 🌐 *www.mec.ca* ⏲ *Mon.–Wed. 10–7 (until 9 in summer), Thurs. and Fri. 10–9, Sat. 9–6, Sun. 11–5* Ⓜ *St. Andrew.*

SPECIALTY GIFTS

Fodor's Choice ★ **TIFF Shop.** This sleek little gift shop, located at the cinematic HQ of the Toronto International Film Festival, the TIFF Bell Lightbox, stocks an ever-changing selection of cinematic paraphernalia linked to TIFF's current program (James Bond, Chinese cinema, etc.). The exhaustive inventory of film books includes many difficult-to-find titles, biographies of just about every director you can think of, and studies of even the most obscure film movements. Other unusual gifts range from Jonathan Adler laptop sleeves to lomographic cameras, and there's fun children's stuff, too—think Sesame Street enviro sacks and Pantone flash cards (orangutan orange, pancake brown, and of course, lobster red). ✉ *TIFF Bell Lightbox, 350 King St. W, at John St., Entertainment District* ☎ *416/934–7959* 🌐 *tiff.net/tiffshop* ⏲ *Sun.–Thurs. 11–8, Fri.–Sat. 11–9* Ⓜ *St Andrew.*

THE FINANCIAL DISTRICT

Toronto's Financial District has a vast underground maze of shopping warrens that burrow between and underneath its office towers. The tenants of this Underground City are mostly the usual assortment of chain stores, with an occasional surprise. Marked PATH, the walkways (the underground street system) make navigating the subterranean mall easy. The network runs roughly from the Fairmont Royal York hotel near Union Station north to the Atrium at Bay and Dundas.

CLOTHING

Moores the Suit People. Browse through thousands of discounted Canadian-made dress pants, sport coats, and suits, including many famous labels. Sizes run from extra short to extra tall and from regular to oversize; the quality is solid and the service is good. ✉ *100 Yonge St., at King St., Financial District* ☎ *416/363–5442* 🌐 *www.mooresclothing.com* ⏲ *Weekdays 9:30–8, Sat. 9–6, Sun. 11–5* Ⓜ *King.*

OLD TOWN AND THE DISTILLERY DISTRICT

OLD TOWN

Regal, historic buildings housing upscale businesses dominate this area, but if you're into furniture, design, high-end antiques, or discerning galleries, walking King Street east of Yonge will be an afternoon well spent. **TIP→ Satiate your appetite at the enormous St. Lawrence Market.**

ART AND CRAFTS GALLERIES

Feheley Fine Arts. Browse contemporary and even avant-garde Canadian Inuit art—a far cry from the traditional whale carvings and stone-cut prints you may expect—at this family-owned gallery founded in 1964. ✉ *65 George St., at King St. East, Old Town* ☎ *416/323–1373* 🌐 *www.feheleyfinearts.com* ⏲ *Tues.–Sat. 10–5:30* Ⓜ *King, then 504 streetcar east.*

BOOKS

Open Air Books and Maps. More than 10,000 travel books, oodles of atlases and road maps, and titles on nature, history, and food has made this jam-packed jumble of a bookshop the ideal place to feed your wanderlust since 1974. The entrance is below street level, through an unmarked black door. ✉ *25 Toronto St., at Adelaide St. E, Old Town* ☎ *416/363–0719* 🌐 *www.openairbooksandmaps.com* ⏲ *Weekdays 10–6, Sat. 10–5:30* Ⓜ *King.*

CLOTHING

Stagioni. This 2,000-square-foot store has great deals on Italian designer suits, which the proprietors buy in bulk from factories in Italy. ✉ *20 Toronto St., at Adelaide St. E, Old Town* ☎ *416/365–7777* 🌐 *www.stagionimens.com* ⏲ *Weekdays 9:30–5:30, Sat. 10–2 (after hours by appointment)* Ⓜ *King.*

HOME DECOR

UpCountry. This 44,000-square-foot store holds a unique mix of furniture collections that reflect leading-edge design principles. Well-made and reasonably priced, many of the upholstered sofas and chairs are built in small runs by Canadian manufacturers; there are European designers too. ✉ *310 King St. E, at Parliament St., Old Town* ☎ *416/366–7477* ⊕ *www.upcountry.com* ⏲ *Mon.–Wed. and Sat. 10–6, Thurs.–Fri. 10–7, Sun. noon–5* Ⓜ *King, then 504 streetcar east.*

MARKETS

Fodor's Choice ★ **St. Lawrence Market Complex.** Nearly 70 vendors occupy the historic permanent indoor market and sell items such as fish, meats, produce, caviar, and crafts. The building, on the south side of Front Street, was once Toronto's first city hall. **TIP→ The best time to visit is early on Saturday from 5 am, when there's a farmers' market in the building on the north side. Get there after 9 and it quickly becomes the worst time to visit.** ✉ *91 Front St. E, at Jarvis St., Old Town* ☎ *416/392–7219* ⊕ *www.stlawrencemarket.com* ⏲ *Tues.–Thurs. 8–6, Fri. 8–7, Sat. 5–5; farmers' market Sat. 5–3* Ⓜ *Union or King.*

DISTILLERY DISTRICT

The Distillery District's pedestrianized brick alleyways and Victorian industrial buildings boast some of the city's best shopping. Come here for one-of-a-kind crafts, artisanal food, stylish urban threads, and art to hang on your walls. Restaurants and cafés abound—as do tourists—and there's a brewpub to quench your thirst. A once neglected pocket, the Distillery District sits on its own east of downtown. Take a streetcar along King or a bus down Parliament, and then walk south from where the two roads intersect.

ART AND CRAFTS GALLERIES

Corkin Gallery. With work by contemporary artists such as Iain Baxter& and David Urban, this gallery is one of the most fascinating in town. See hand-painted photos, documentary photos, fashion photography, and mixed-media art. ✉ *7 Tank House Ln., Distillery District* ☎ *416/979–1980* ⊕ *www.corkingallery.com* ⏲ *Tues.–Sat. 10–6, Sun. noon–5* Ⓜ *King, then streetcar 504 east.*

CLOTHING

Fodor's Choice ★ **GotStyle.** This Torontonian start-up has hit the nail on the head, providing stylish clothes—Tiger of Sweden, Ted Baker, and John Varvatos—to the thousands of career-boys occupying the city's downtown condos. This huge airy branch carries ladies' as well, including Montreal's Mackage outerware and Malene Birger dresses. Head up to the lush purple-carpeted mezzanine level for business and evening wear and a round on the purple pool table. Another branch can be found in the Entertainment District at 62 Bathurst Street. ✉ *21 Trinity St., Distillery District* ☎ *416/260–9696* ⊕ *gotstylemenswear.com* ⏲ *Mon.–Sat. 10–8, Sun. 11–6; Winter: Mon.–Fri. 11–8, Sat. 11–6, Sun., noon–5* Ⓜ *King, then 504 streetcar east to Parliament; or Castle Frank, then bus 65 to King.*

Lileo. Part emporium, part gallery, this is the place to go for men's and women's forward-looking fashion and lifestyle accessories—many of which are exclusive or were created in limited edition for the store. **TIP→ Stop by the juice bar/restaurant Livia to keep your energy up while you shop.** ✉ *12 Trinity St., Distillery District* ☎ *416/413–1410* ⊕ *www.lileo.ca* ⏲ *Mon.–Sat. 10–7, (10–8 in summer), Sun. 11–6* Ⓜ *King, then streetcar 504 east to Parliament; Castle Frank, then 65 bus to King.*

7

JEWELRY AND ACCESSORIES

Corktown Designs. Seventy percent of the reasonably priced jewelry at this Distillery District shop is Canadian-designed, and all of it is unique and handmade. Pieces range from inexpensive glass-and-silver pendants to Swiss-made stainless steel rings and pricier pieces set with pearls and other semiprecious stones. ✉ *5 Trinity St., Distillery District* ☎ *416/861–3020* 🌐 *www.corktowndesigns.com* ⏲ *Mon.–Wed. 10–7, Thurs.–Sat. 10–9, Sun. 11–6 (shorter hours in winter)* Ⓜ *508 Lakeshore or 504 King streetcar.*

SHOES, HANDBAGS, AND LEATHER GOODS

Fodor's Choice ★ **John Fluevog.** Fluevog's funky shoes look their best in this barely converted high-ceilinged industrial space. The building was once the distillery boiler house, which would explain the three-story brick oven that accounts for a third of the floor-space, and the safety ladder leading to an overhead catwalk. Take a seat on the stunning embossed leather couch when trying on the fun, cutting-edge merchandise—some shoes can be custom colored right in the shop. The Vancouver native's original Toronto outlet is in Queen West at 242 Queen Street West. ✉ *4 Trinity St., Distillery District* ☎ *416/583–1970* 🌐 *www.fluevog.com* ⏲ *Mon.–Sat. 10–8, Sun. 11–6 (winter hours are shorter)* Ⓜ *King, then 504 streetcar east to Parliament; or Castle Frank, then 65 Parliament to King (the walk south).*

WINE AND SPECIALTY FOOD

Soma Chocolatemaker. Satisfy your sweet tooth just by inhaling the delicate wafts of chocolate, dried fruits, and roasted nuts in this gourmet chocolate shop that specializes in microbatch, fair-trade chocolate. Big sellers include crystallized Australian ginger tumbled in dark Peruvian chocolate, spiced chai tea truffles, and gelato. For something different, try the Bicarin, a thick mixture of melted chocolate, espresso, and whipped cream. Another branch can be found in the Entertainment District at 443 King Street West. ✉ *32 Tank House Ln., Distillery District* ☎ *416/815–7662* 🌐 *www.somachocolate.com* ⏲ *Mon.–Sat. 10–8, Sun. 11–6* Ⓜ *King, then streetcar 508 east.*

A Taste of Quebec. You'll find gorgeous woodwork and ceramics from a select group of Québécois artisans including fine wooden serving bowls and cutting boards; crackly, naked raku serving bowls and vases; burnt-orange Japanese-style bowl sets; and intricate pewter jewelry. The adjoining Thompson Landry Gallery sells fine paintings and sculptures. ✉ *52 Gristmill Ln., Distillery District* ☎ *416/364–5020* 🌐 *www.atasteofquebec.com* ⏲ *Tues.–Sat. 11–6, Sun. noon–5* Ⓜ *King, then 504 streetcar east to Parliament; or Castle Frank, then bus 65 to King.*

DUNDAS SQUARE AREA

Dundas Square is the go-to place for chain stores like Gap, Zara, Roots, and Aritzia, electronics giants Future Shop and Best Buy, and cheap souvenir shops, which line Yonge Street to the north. The mammoth Eaton Centre shopping mall, which opens up into the square, has more than 230 stores (Coach, Banana Republic, and the Apple Store, to name a few) and is anchored by The Bay and Sears at either end.

CLOTHING

Danier Leather. Suede and leather street wear and dressy attire, made in Canada from the finest hides, are the draw here. The latest trends are up front but bargains can be found in the back. ✉ *in the Eaton Centre, 2nd floor,Dundas Square Area* ☎ *416/598–1159* 🌐 *www.danier.com* ⏲ *Mon.–Fri. 9–9, Sat. 9:30–7, Sun. 11–6* Ⓜ *Queen.*

Urban Outfitters. The young and trendy scan the racks here for the latest "it" piece. Prices are comparatively high considering the clothes' often-low quality. Don't miss the quirky, modern housewares and oddball coffee-table books. There is another location in Queen West at 481 Queen Street West. ✉ *235 Yonge St. W, north of Queen St., Dundas Square Area* ☎ *416/214–1466* 🌐 *www.urbanoutfitters.com* ⏲ *Mon.–Sat. 10–10, Sun. 11–8 pm* Ⓜ *Dundas, Queen.*

DEPARTMENT STORES AND SHOPPING CENTERS

Eaton Centre. This block-long complex with exposed industrial-style ceilings is anchored at its northern end (Dundas Street) by Sears, and a Times Square–style media tower on top of a gigantic anchor store, Sweden's popular H&M. Across the street from the southern end is Canadian department store The Bay. **■ TIP→ Prices at Eaton Centre increase with altitude—Level 1 offers popularly priced merchandise, Level 2 is directed to the middle-income shopper, and Level 3 sells more expensive fashion and luxury goods.** The complex is bordered by Yonge Street on the east and James Street and Trinity Square on the west. ✉ *220 Yonge St., Dundas Square Area* ☎ *416/598–8560* 🌐 *www.torontoeatoncentre.com* ⏲ *Weekdays 10–9, Sat. 9:30–7, Sun. 11–6* Ⓜ *Dundas, Queen.*

7

CHINATOWN, KENSINGTON MARKET, AND QUEEN WEST

CHINATOWN

While Chinese-Canadians have made Spadina Avenue their own from Queen Street north to College Street, Spadina's basic bill of fare is still "bargains galore." Its collection of inexpensive Chinese clothing stores, Chinese restaurants, ethnic food and fruit shops, and eateries (not only Chinese, but also Vietnamese, Japanese, and Thai) give you your money's worth. A cluster of galleries surrounds the Art Gallery of Ontario (AGO) just east of the area. Take the (north–south) Spadina streetcar or the (east–west) College or Dundas streetcars to Spadina Avenue, or walk from St.Patrick.

ART AND CRAFTS GALLERIES

Bau-Xi Gallery. Paul Wong, an artist and dealer from Vancouver, started this gallery, which is directly across the street from the Art Gallery of Ontario. The paintings and sculpture are a window into contemporary Canadian art, with both emerging and established artists featured. Just a few block down Dundas is Bau-Xi Photo, which shows both Canadian and international fine art photography. ✉ *340 Dundas St. W, at McCaul St., Chinatown* ☎ *416/977–0600* 🌐 *www.bau-xi.com* ⏲ *Daily 10–5:30* Ⓜ *St. Patrick.*

HOME DECOR

Tap Phong Trading Co. Inc. The mops, brooms, and multicolored bins and buckets stacked outside make this kitchenware and restaurant equipment store appear much like all the other Chinese knick-knack shops along Spadina. However, once you're inside you'll find endless aisles stacked to the rafters with rice bowls and bamboo steamers, and restaurateurs piling up their shopping trolleys with glasses and serving ware to feed the masses. **■ TIP→ A gap halfway along the north wall leads to the industrial-scale equipment.** ✉ *360 Spadina Ave., south of Baldwin St., Chinatown* ☎ *416/977–6364* 🌐 *www.tapphong.com* ⏲ *Daily 10:30–8* Ⓜ *Spadina, then streetcar 510.*

MUSEUM STORES

shopAGO. The store attached to the Art Gallery of Ontario has an overwhelming selection of curiosities, from books on maximal architecture to colorful dollhouses to prints of celebrated paintings. Adults and kids can shop side by side among the books and fun educational toys. ✉ *317 Dundas St. W, at McCaul St., Chinatown* ☎ *416/979–6610* 🌐 *www.ago.net/shop* ⏲ *Tues., Thurs–Sun. 11:30–6, Wed. 11:30–9* ⏲ *Mon.* Ⓜ *St. Patrick.*

Fodor's Choice ★ **Textile Museum Shop.** Tucked away on the second floor of the already hidden Textile Museum, this shop is one of the city's best-kept secrets and an absolute treasure trove. It overflows with textile-based art from more than 50 Canadian artisans, as well as works by craftspeople from around the world keeping traditional, and often disappearing, skills alive. There are loads of books, scarves galore, unusual bags and hats, and crafty stuff for kids, too; many items are accessibly priced. **■ TIP→ Check out the changing exhibition on the second and third floor while you're here (admission charge) to develop a taste for the shop's featured items; past exhibits have included Finnish designer Marimekko and Afghan war rugs.** ✉ *55 Centre Ave., at Dundas St. W and University Ave., Chinatown* ☎ *416/599–5321* 🌐 *www.textilemuseum.ca* ⏲ *Thurs.–Tues. 11–5, Wed. 11–8* Ⓜ *St. Patrick.*

KENSINGTON MARKET

Tucked behind Spadina west to Bathurst Street, between Dundas and College streets to the south and north, is this hippie-meets-hipster collection of inexpensive vintage-clothing stores, cheap ethnic eateries, coffee shops, head shops, and specialty food shops specializing in cheeses, baked goods, fish, dry goods, health food, and more. **■ TIP→ Be warned—this area can be extraordinarily crowded on weekends; do not drive.** Take the College streetcar to Spadina or Augusta, or the Spadina streetcar to College or Nassau.

CLOTHING

Fodor's Choice ★ **Courage My Love.** The best and longest-running vintage store in Kensington Market is crammed with the coolest retro stuff, from sunglasses to sundresses, plus an ample supply of cowboy boots for guys and gals, all at low prices. Not everything is secondhand here: there's a wall of sparkly Indian-inspired clothing, lots of costume jewelry, and a selection of unique buttons. ✉ *14 Kensington Ave., at Dundas St. W, Kensington Market* ☎ *416/979–1992* ⏲ *Weekdays 11:30–6, Sat. 11–6, Sun. 1–5* Ⓜ *St. Patrick, then streetcar 504 west.*

TORONTO'S GALLERIES

Toronto is Canada's cosmopolitan art center, with a few hundred commercial art galleries carrying items as varied as glass sculpture, Inuit designs, and multimedia pieces. Galleries have always been on Queen West, but as rents rise, galleries move farther west—many are now clustered around the intersection with Ossington and show emerging and established artists. **TIP→ If you're really dedicated, it's worth heading up Ossington to Dundas West, where a few galleries have opened up, and then farther west to Morrow to the fixtures of Olga Korper and Christopher Cutts.** The galleries in Yorkville and the historic Distillery District tend to show well-established artists. Head to 401 Richmond for a smattering of cutting-edge galleries under one roof. Naturally, the area around the Art Gallery of Ontario is saturated with contemporary art galleries, too, most of which offer affordable pieces by Canadian artists.

To find out about special art exhibits, check *NOW* and *The Grid*—free weekly local newspapers on culture distributed on Thursday—or *Toronto Life* magazine. You can pick up a copy of *Slate* (🌐 *www.slateartguide.com*) at most galleries; the listings are very comprehensive. The website of *Canadian Art* magazine (🌐 *www.canadianart.ca*) is also a good source of information on gallery happenings. **TIP→ Most galleries are open Tuesday through Saturday from 10 to 5 or 6, but call to confirm.**

7

Tom's Place. Find bargains aplenty on brand-name suits like Calvin Klein, Armani, and DKNY. Tom Mihalik, the store's owner, keeps his prices low and carries some women's clothes as well. ✉ *190 Baldwin St., at Augusta Ave., Kensington Market* ☎ *416/596–0297* 🌐 *www.tomsplace.com* ⏲ *Mon.–Wed. 10–6, Thurs.–Fri. 10–7, Sat. 9–6, Sun. noon–5* Ⓜ *St. Patrick, then streetcar 505 west.*

SPECIALTY GIFTS

Fodor's Choice ★ **Kid Icarus.** At this old-school printing company, you'll find a range of very cool retro designs including band posters (Devo!) and event commemorations (Mars Rover landing), and one-of-a-kind creations. You'll also find screen-printed Greetings-from-Toronto postcards, art supplies, out-there books, and contemporary indie crafts in the gift shop, as well as handmade toys, key chains, and wallets. ✉ *205 Augusta Ave., Kensington Market* ☎ *416/977–7236* 🌐 *www.kidicarus.ca* ⏲ *Mon.–Thurs. noon–7, Fri.–Sat. 11–7, Sun. 11–6 (hours may be shorter in winter)* Ⓜ *Spadina, then streetcar 510 to Baldwin or Dundas.*

QUEEN WEST

In the 1980s, the strip of Queen from University to Spadina was synonymous with all things hip—it was a vibrant area filled with students. After years of gentrification, the area is now dominated by chains, but it's still busy, buzzy, and a great place to shop. **TIP→ Come summer, street vendors and buskers around Spadina create a carnival atmosphere.** West of Spadina, a few gems are mixed in with textile shops clinging on from earlier days and a couple of incongruous newcomers.

ANTIQUES

Abraham's Trading Inc. Indicative of a Queen West long gone, the most remarkable thing about Abraham's is that somehow it survives. Handwritten signs snarl "don't even think about it" amid a jumble of haphazardly piled rusty props and dusty "antiques" from doctor's bags and deer trophies to worn church doors, creepy clown shoes, and a sparkling collection of 1950s microphones. Purchasing anything will take some guts—few prices are marked, although everything, they say, is for sale. ✉ *635 Queen St. W, at Bathurst St., Queen West* ☎ *416/504–6210* 🌐 *www.abrahamstrading.com* ⏲ *Mon.–Fri. 11–6, Sat. 11–7* Ⓜ *Osgoode, then 501 Queen streetcar west; Bathurst, then 511 streetcar.*

ART AND CRAFTS GALLERIES

Fodor's Choice ★ **401 Richmond.** Packed with galleries, a couple of interesting shops and a decent café, this beautifully refurbished industrial building is an essential component of an exploration of Toronto's contemporary art scene. Check out **YYZ Artists' Outlet,** which holds consistently engaging shows in its two rooms, or **Gallery 44** for contemporary photography. There's also the respected artist collective **Red Head Gallery.** Pick up a Ukranian zither or South African kora at temple-to-world-music **Musideum**; concerts are also held in the space. Make sure you don't miss well-stocked ⇨ *Swipe* for books on all things design. ✉ *401 Richmond Ave., at Spadina, Queen West* ☎ *416/595–5900* 🌐 *www.401richmond.net* ⏲ *Closed Sundays* Ⓜ *Spadina, then 510 streetcar; or Osgoode, then 501 streetcar west.*

BOOKS

Fodor's Choice ★ **Swipe Design Books & Objects.** Books on advertising, art, and architecture—from green homes to an ode to sans-serif typefaces—pack the shelves of this aesthetically pleasing store, fittingly located in the arty 401 Richmond heritage building. Part of the store is devoted to modern gifts, including exquisitely carved and painted toy blocks, and coveted items such as Crevasse, a high-rise-like vase designed by architect Zaha Hadid. Swipe DX, another branch of this store, can be found in the Design Exchange at 234 Bay Street in the Financial District. ✉ *Ste. 121, 401 Richmond St. W, at Spadina Ave., Queen West* ☎ *416/363–1332, 800/567–9473* 🌐 *www.swipe.com* ⏲ *Weekdays 11–7, Sat. 11–6* Ⓜ *Osgoode then 501 streetcar west; or Spadine, then 510 streetcar.*

CLOTHING

Black Market. Determined vintage buffs hunt through the racks of band T-shirts, faded jeans, worn shoes, and biker jackets in this cavernous basement. There are more cheap sunglasses than you can imagine. Penguin Music, a CD and record store, is also located here, but its hours are unpredictable. ✉ *256A Queen St. W, at John St., Queen West* ☎ *416/599–5858* 🌐 *www.blackmarkettoronto.com* ⏲ *Mon–Wed 11–7, Thurs.–Fri. 11–8, Sun. 11–6* Ⓜ *Osgoode, then streetcar 501 west.*

Boomer. One of the best-kept secrets of Toronto men brings together tasteful yet trendy slim-fitting suitings and separates that appeal to fashion-forward guys who eschew stuffy, old-school business attire. Tiger of Sweden, J. Lindeberg, and Boss Orange populate the racks. ✉ *309 Queen St. W, at John St., Queen West* ☎ *416/598–0013* ⏲ *Weekdays 10:30–7, Sat. 10:30–6, Sun. 1–5* Ⓜ *Osgoode, then streetcar 501 west.*

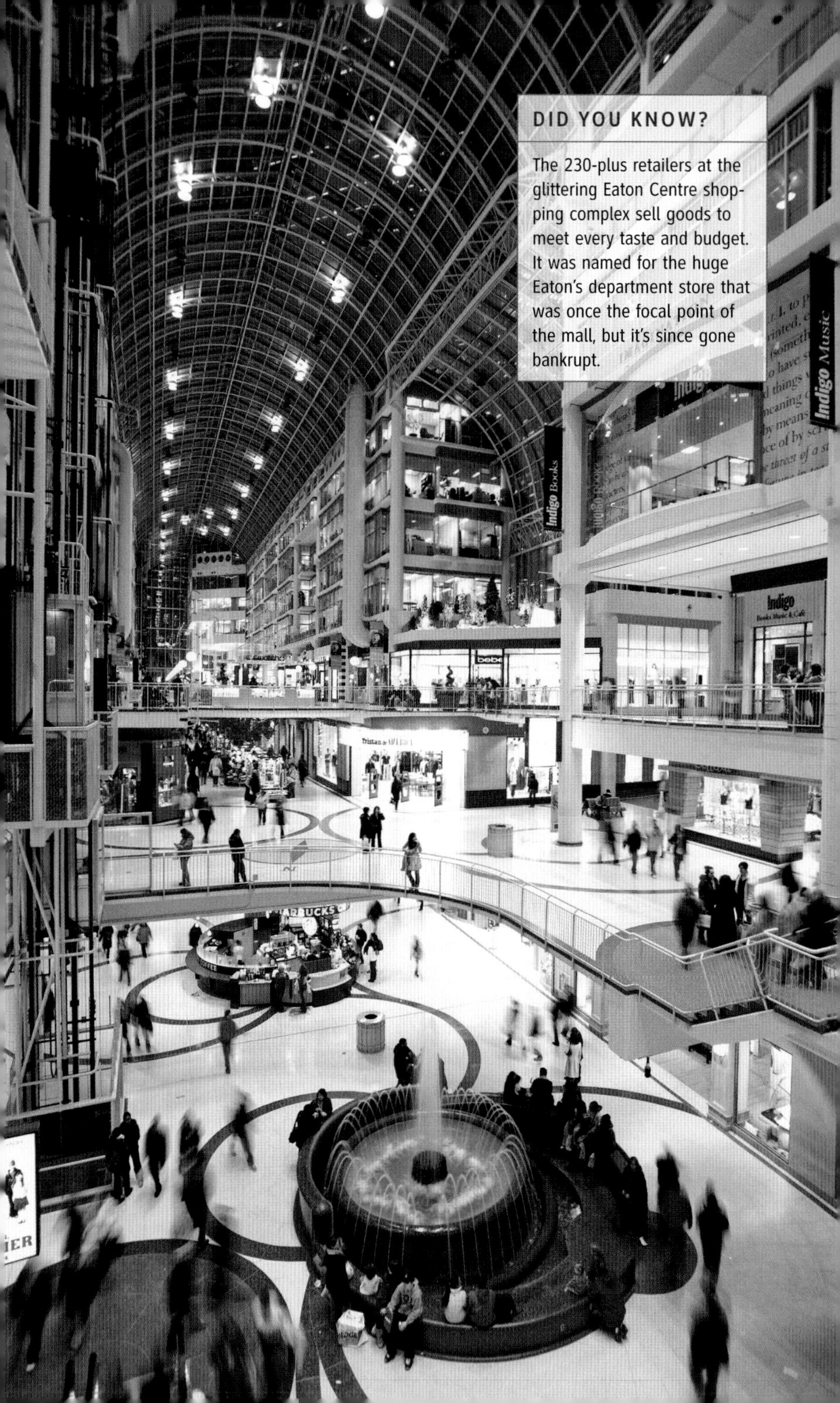

DID YOU KNOW?

The 230-plus retailers at the glittering Eaton Centre shopping complex sell goods to meet every taste and budget. It was named for the huge Eaton's department store that was once the focal point of the mall, but it's since gone bankrupt.

Fodor's Choice ★ **Durumi and Chocolate Shoes.** Delicate, pretty, and totally *with-it*, the two-boutique combo of Durumi Apparel and Chocolate Shoes makes for a perfect browsing and buying environment. Durumi has modern and feminine Korean-inspired styles such as floral hair ties, lacey socks, pocket watches on chains, blousy tops, and Capri pants. Chocolate Shoes adds ballet flats and baseball caps to the mix. ✉ *416 Queen St. W, west of Spadina* ☎ *647/727–2591* 🌐 *facebook.com/durumiapparel* ⏲ *Mon.–Sat. 11–8, Sun 11–7* Ⓜ *Osgoode, then streetcar 501 west; Spadina, then streetcar 510.*

Fashion Crimes. Part romantic, part funk, this Queen West haven of glam party dresses and dreamy designs has a display case packed full of elegant baubles and sparkling tiaras. ✉ *322½ Queen St. W, at Spadina Ave., Queen West* ☎ *416/592–9001* 🌐 *www.fashioncrimes.ca* ⏲ *Mon.–Thurs. 11–7, Fri. 11–8, Sat. 10–7, Sun. noon–6* Ⓜ *Osgoode, then streetcar west 501.*

lululemon athletica. This bright and airy store is a perfect match for yoga-centric items from this coveted Canadian brand such as specialized yoga sports bras, top-of-the-line yoga mats, and stretchy yoga and gym togs. Check out other Toronto-area branches online. ⚠ **Hours are subject to change to accommodate lessons.** ✉ *342 Queen W, at Spadina Ave., Queen West* ☎ *416/703–1399* 🌐 *www.lululemon.com* ⏲ *Mon. 11–8, Tues. 11–7, Wed.–Fri. 11–8, Sat. 10–8, Sun. 11–7* Ⓜ *Osgoode, then streetcar 501 west.*

Original. A blaze of rainbow colors, Original is glamorous, life-affirming, and more than a little outrageous. If you're heading to a gala, or after a crinoline dress (in fuchsia), you *need* to come here. The endless selection of platforms, pumps, and wedges (in every shade and size you can imagine) is only outdone by the dress-level, up a multicolored flight of stairs. Dresses by Vivienne Westwood, Sue Wong, Stop Staring, and just about anyone else you can think of are here. And, if you're getting married or walking the red carpet, they might let you into the back room with the *really* exclusive pieces. ✉ *515 Queen St. W, at Augusta Ave., Queen West* ☎ *416/603–9400* 🌐 *www.originaltoronto.com* ⏲ *Mon.–Fri. 11–7, Sat. 10–7, Sun. noon–6* Ⓜ *Osgoode, then 501 streetcar west.*

Tribal Rhythm. A few vintage gems and pretty silk scarves may be found among the army jackets, Cub Scout uniforms, and '70s polyester shirts and cowgirl attire, but most of the inventory is simply fun, kitschy, and kooky. Imported Thai and Indian trinkets, rows of body jewelry, tiaras, and wigs are part of the charming and eclectic mix. ✉ *248 Queen St. W, below street level, at John St., Queen West* ☎ *416/595–5817* 🌐 *www.tribalrhythm.ca* ⏲ *Mon.–Sat. 11–7, Sun. 11–6* Ⓜ *Osgoode; 501 Queen streetcar.*

JEWELRY AND ACCESSORIES

eko. Jewelry boutique eko's award-winning minimalist design pulls you in. Its whiter-than-white walls hide panels of glass, which compel the eye to gaze at each display separately. It's an effective, if slightly intimidating, way to get the shopper to consider the international one-of-a-kind jewelry designs carefully. Prices aren't displayed, but some really are accessible at well below $100, so work up some courage to ask. ✉ *288 Queen St. W, at Peter St., Queen West* ☎ *416/593–0776* 🌐 *www.ekojewellery.com* ⏲ *Mon.–Wed. 11–7, Thurs.–Fri. 11–8, Sat 11–7* Ⓜ *Osgoode.*

Goorin Bros. Look no further than this suitably traditional hat shop for wide-brim fedoras, panamas, Gatsbies, and pork pies. The Goorin Bros. have been making hats in the States for four generations, and many of the hats on display were handmade in Pittsburgh; this is their first foray into Canada. For the ladies, you'll find 1920s felt cloches, fascinators, and sunhats. ✉ *320 Queen St. W, east of Spadina, Queen West* ☎ *416/408–4287* 🌐 *www.goorin.com* ⏲ *Mon.–Wed. 11–7, Thurs.–Sat. 11–8, Sun. noon–6* Ⓜ *Osgoode.*

A SHOE THING

If you've literally worn out your shoe leather, consider hitting up Queen Street West between John and Spadina for a new pair of kicks. This strip is packed with shoe and sneaker stores for ladies and gents that stock a wide variety of styles at mostly mid-range prices. In winter consider uber-comfy Canadian-made Sorel boots, designed to keep tootsies toasty; in summer browse La Canadienne sandals. Our favorite shops are those covered in this chapter (Getoutside, John Fleuvog, and—a bit farther west—Heel Boy), but you can also find a Crocs shop and boutiques stocked with Camper, Vans, Tsubo, and more.

New Era Cap Co. Here's your chance to officially "wear your allegiance." Mounted with reverence, the caps that cover New Era's walls represent every Major League Baseball team, all teams in the National Football League and Canadian Football League, as well as numerous National Basketball League and National Hockey League teams. Caps come in every team color combo you can imagine, and some are emblazoned with beloved old logos. Sizing is paramount—you won't find a plastic hat adjuster in this shop. And, if your own cap is looking a little past its prime, you can bring it in to have it steamed and reshaped. ✉ *202A Queen St. W, at St Patrick St., Queen West* ☎ *416/597–2277* 🌐 *www.neweracap.com* ⏲ *Mon.–Sat. 10–8, Sun. 11–5* Ⓜ *Osgoode.*

SHOES, HANDBAGS, AND LEATHER GOODS

Getoutside. There are styles for men and women, including Hunter Wellies, Birkenstock sandals, Sperry Top-Siders, and a great selection of Laurentian Chief and Minnetonka street moccasins and mukluks. There are loads of Converse and Van sneakers, too. ✉ *437 Queen St. W, at Spadina Ave., Queen West* ☎ *416/593–5598* 🌐 *www.getoutsideshoes.com* ⏲ *Mon.–Sat. 10–9, Sun. 11–8* Ⓜ *Osgoode, then streetcar 501 west; or Spadina, then streetcar 510.*

SPECIALTY GIFTS

Malabar Ltd. If you're in the market for fake blood or eyelashes, a '50s wig, or a prosthetic nose, then look no further than Malabar. However, the real treasures are found in the costume rental department. Whether you're after a bishop's cassock, caveman's hides, a dirndl, or Edwardian frock and parasol, the costume maker upstairs has pieced one together, which you can check out on the racks groaning under decades' worth of designs. Dance wear for adults and children can be found as well, from pointe ballet shoes and tutus to leotards and leg warmers. ✉ *14 McCaul St., Queen West* ☎ *416/598–2581* 🌐 *www.malabar.net* ⏲ *Mon.–Fri. 10–6, Sat 10–5* Ⓜ *Osgoode.*

QUEEN'S PARK, THE ANNEX, AND LITTLE ITALY

THE ANNEX

In a neighborhood near the University of Toronto campus populated by academics, students, and '60s hippies, a mix of restored and run-down Victorians and brick low-rises house cafés and bistros, used-book and music stores, and the occasional fashion boutique, like Risqué.

BOOKS

Bakka Phoenix. Canada's oldest science fiction and fantasy bookstore, opened in 1972, Bakka Phoenix has several thousand new and used titles for adults, young adults, and children, as well as some graphic novels and DVDs (*Doctor Who* and the like). Knowledgeable staff is always on hand to give advice. ✉ *84 Harbord St., at Spadina Ave., The Annex* ☎ *416/963–9993* 🌐 *www.bakkaphoenixbooks.com* ⏲ *Weekdays 11–7, Sat. 11–6, Sun. noon–5* Ⓜ *Spadina; 510 Spadina streetcar.*

BMV. An impressive selection of new and used books is shelved side by side over two floors at BMV (which stands for "Books Magazines Video"). The staff is knowledgeable and helpful. Another branch is located in the Dundas Square Area at 10 Edward Street. ✉ *471 Bloor St. W., at Brunswick Ave., The Annex* ☎ *416/967–5757* ⏲ *Mon.–Wed. 10 am–11pm, Thurs.–Sat. 10 am–midnight, Sun. 11–8* Ⓜ *Spadina.*

Book City. Find good discounts—especially on publishers' remainders—a knowledgeable staff, and a fine choice of magazines at branches of this late-night Toronto chain, usually open until 10 or 11. Five locations are scattered around the city. ✉ *501 Bloor St. W, at Brunswick Ave., The Annex* ☎ *416/961–4496* 🌐 *www.bookcity.ca* ⏲ *Mon.–Sat. 9:30 am–11 pm, Sun. 11–10* Ⓜ *Bathurst, Spadina.*

CLOTHING

Risqué. Trendy young dresses, blouses, jumpers, and jeans by primarily Canadian designers as well as inexpensive accessories fill this boutique. The colorful, of-the-moment selections change weekly. ✉ *404 Bloor St. W, at Brunswick Ave., The Annex* ☎ *416/960–3325* ⏲ *Weekdays 11–7, Sat. 11–6, Sun. noon–6* Ⓜ *St. George.*

Secrets From Your Sister. The art of the brassiere is taken seriously at this bra-fitting boutique. Knowledgeable (but pretension-free) staff are on hand for advice. Fittings can be arranged on the spot at least one hour before closing and must be reserved in person. A session usually lasts from 30 minutes to an hour. Or simply peruse the massive selection of prêt-à-porter undergarments, including sports, fashion, strapless, seamless, and nursing bras in wide-ranging sizes and fits. ✉ *560 Bloor St. W, at Bathurst St., The Annex* ☎ *416/538–1234* 🌐 *www.secretsfromyoursister.com* ⏲ *Weekdays 11–7, Sat. 10–6, Sun. noon–6.*

HOME DECOR

Nella Cucina. Shop alongside Toronto chefs for quality kitchen novelties and supplies: cheese knives, seafood shears, cast-iron cookware, espresso machines and parts, or unique showpieces like locally made salvaged-wood platters. A teaching kitchen upstairs hosts classes, from Italian cooking to knife skills. ✉ *876 Bathurst St., at London St., The Annex* ☎ *416/922–9055* 🌐 *nellacucina.ca* ⏲ *Weekdays 9–6, Sat. 10–6* Ⓜ *Bathurst.*

LITTLE ITALY

Despite the waning Italian influence, Little Italy is a likeable neighborhood and you'll find a few genuine cafés and gelato shops among the restaurants and bars. You'll also find a mix of small boutiques, book and record shops, and trendy lifestyle and housewares stores.

BOOKS

Balfour Books. This hushed, but cozy secondhand bookshop has a tempting selection of coffee table–sized art and photography books. There's also more "luggage-friendly" fiction, too. ✉ *468 College St., west of Bathurst St., Little Italy* ☎ *416/531–9911* 🌐 *balfourbooks.squarespace.com* ⏲ *Daily 11–8* Ⓜ *Bathurst, then streetcar 511 to College.*

JEWELRY AND ACCESSORIES

Lilliput Hats. Wide-brimmed hats decorated with silk orchids in vibrant shades, fascinators, close-fitting cloches, a practical straw hat that packs flat, outrageous or tailored hats—all can be found in handmade, custom-fit head coverings. For the men there are trilbies, wide-brimmed fedoras, and pork pies. Karyn Ruiz, who has a huge following, works away with her team of milliners in the back half of the shop. Brides-to-be and their moms will have a field day. ✉ *462 College St., at Bathurst St., Little Italy* ☎ *416/536–5933* 🌐 *www.lilliputhats.com* ⏲ *Weekdays 10–6, Sat. 11–6, Sun. by appt.* Ⓜ *Bathurst, then streetcar 511 to College; or Queen's Park, then 506 streetcar west.*

MUSIC

Fodor's Choice ★ **Soundscapes.** Crammed with pop, rock, jazz, blues, folk, ambient, psychedelic, garage, avant-garde, and electronic titles, this shop satisfies hipsters as well as fans of early Americana. Selections and organization reflect a love of music and its ever-expanding history. ✉ *572 College St., at Manning Ave., Little Italy* ☎ *416/537–1620* 🌐 *www.soundscapesmusic.com* ⏲ *Daily 10 am–11 pm* Ⓜ *Bathurst, then 511 streetcar; or College or Queen's Park, then streetcar 506 west.*

YORKVILLE AND ROSEDALE

YORKVILLE

In the 1960s Yorkville was Canada's hippie headquarters. Today it's a well-heeled shopping and dining destination: the place to find high-end everything. North of Bloor, west of Bay, is the heart of Yorkville—pedestrian-friendly streets with tony cafés and designer stores that are fun to browse even if you're not buying. From Yonge Street to Avenue Road, Bloor Street is a virtual runway for fashionistas, with world-renowned designer shops like Bulgari, Prada, Chanel, and quality chains (Williams Sonoma, Roots).

7

Stanley Wagman Antiques. Stanley Wagman carries a large selection of art-deco pieces and lighting, as well as Louis XVI furniture and accessories. This is the place to find exquisite marble fireplaces, and it reputedly has the biggest selection of lighting in Canada. It also ships worldwide. ✉ *224 Davenport Rd., at Avenue Rd., Yorkville* ☎ *416/964–1047* ⏲ *Weekdays 10–6, Sat. noon–4 (closed summer Saturdays)* Ⓜ *Dupont, St George.*

ART AND CRAFTS GALLERIES

Fodor's Choice ★ **The Guild Shop.** An essential stop on any visitor's tour around Yorkville, the Guild Shop displays the best in Canadian craft. The shop is run by the Ontario Crafts Council and all exhibitors are members of OCC. You'll find stunning examples of blown glass, fine woodwork, textiles, jewelry, and pottery—from earthy stoneware to contemporary ceramics. There's also a gallery of Inuit and native art, including sculpture, beadwork, and prints. When you buy a handcrafted item here, you're supporting a local artist. ✉ *118 Cumberland St., Yorkville* ☎ *416/921–1721* 🌐 *www.theguildshop.ca* ⏲ *Mon.–Wed. 10–6, Thurs.–Fri. 10–7, Sat. 10–6, Sun. noon–5* Ⓜ *Bay.*

Loch Gallery. This intimate gallery in an old Victorian house almost exclusively exhibits representational historic and contemporary Canadian painting and sculpture. Artists include bronze sculptor Leo Mol and painters Jack Chambers and John Boyle. ✉ *16 Hazelton Ave., at Yorkville Ave., Yorkville* ☎ *416/964–9050* 🌐 *www.lochgallery.com* ⏲ *Tues.–Sat. 10–5* Ⓜ *Bay.*

BOOKS

Cookbook Store. This store has the city's largest selection of books and magazines on cooking and wine and holds frequent book signings. Owners and staff are so knowledgeable they seem to have read every book on the shelves. ✉ *850 Yonge St., at Yorkville Ave., Yorkville* ☎ *416/920–2665, 800/268–6018* 🌐 *www.cook-book.com* ⏲ *Weekdays 10–7, Sat. 10–6, Sun. noon–5* Ⓜ *Bloor-Yonge.*

CLOTHING: CHILDREN'S

Chanel. Coco would have loved the largest Chanel boutique in Canada. The lush surroundings showcase most of the line, including the bags and accessories. ✉ *131 Bloor St. W, at Avenue Road, Yorkville* ☎ *416/925–2577* 🌐 *www.chanel.com* ⏲ *Mon.–Sat. 10–6, Sun. noon–5* Ⓜ *Bay.*

Club Monaco. The bright and airy flagship store of this successful chain, now owned by Ralph Lauren, has homegrown design basics: mid-price sportswear and career clothes. ✉ *157 Bloor St. W, at Avenue Rd., Yorkville* ☎ *416/591–8837* 🌐 *www.clubmonaco.com* ⏲ *Mon.–Wed. 10–8, Thurs.–Fri. 10–8, Sat. 10–6, Sun. noon–6* Ⓜ *Museum or Bay.*

Escada. The spacious store carries the designer Escada line of chic Italian creations. ✉ *131 Bloor St. W, at Avenue Rd., Yorkville* ☎ *416/964–2265* 🌐 *www.escada.com* ⏲ *Mon.–Wed. 10–6, Thurs.–Fri. 10–7, Sat. 10–6, Sun. noon–5* Ⓜ *Bay.*

Free People. Yorkville is not generally the stomping ground of hippie chicks, but if you've dropped down at Bay in error, well, head here for beaded jewelry, jean cutoffs, kaftans, floppy hats, maxi dresses, and all things faded, layered, and '70s. Owned by Urban Inc. who also brings us Urban Outfitters and ⇨ *Anthropologie*, this shop—festooned with macramé wall hangings and plant holders—is one of the few in Canada and the only one in Toronto. ✉ *79 Yorkville Ave., Yorkville* ☎ *416/515–1555* 🌐 *www.freepeople.com* ⏲ *Mon.–Sat. 10–7, Sun. noon–5* Ⓜ *Bay.*

Fodor's Choice ★ **George C.** If you're put off by the anonymous uniformity of the big designers along Bloor, but you have some money to spend and want a touch of originality, head to this three-story Victorian refurb. Inside you'll find an inspired selection of sophisticated shoes, bags, and clothes from French, Italian, American, and Australian designers that you won't find anywhere else—replica 1930s bags from Numero 10 by Alberto Mondini; delicate laser-cut leather tops from Drome; and gorgeous chunky Rocco P. heels and boots that can be (you may not want to know this) custom ordered in your choice of color and material. ✉ *21 Hazelton Ave., Yorkville* ☎ *416/962–1991* 🌐 *georgec.ca* ⏲ *Mon.–Wed. 10–6, Thurs.–Fri. 10–7, Sat. 10–6, Sun. 1–5* Ⓜ *Bay.*

Fodor's Choice ★ **Harry Rosen.** This miniature department store is dedicated to the finest men's fashions, with designers such as Hugo Boss, Armani, and Zegna. The casual section stocks preppy classics. ✉ *82 Bloor St. W, at Bellair St., Yorkville* ☎ *416/972–0556* 🌐 *www.harryrosen.com* ⏲ *Mon.–Wed. 10–7, Thurs.–Fri. 10–9, Sat. 10–6, Sun. noon–6* Ⓜ *Bloor-Yonge.*

Hermès. The Parisian design house caters to the upscale horse- and hound-loving set, selling its classic sportswear, handbags, and accessories. ✉ *130 Bloor St. W, at Avenue Rd., Yorkville* ☎ *416/968–8626* 🌐 *www.hermes.com* ⏲ *Mon.–Sat. 10–6, Sun. noon–5* Ⓜ *Bay.*

Fodor's Choice ★ **Hugo Nicholson.** The selection of evening wear by Oscar de la Renta, Christian Dior, Alaia, Carolina Herrera, Alexander McQueen and more is vast and exclusive. The service offered by the owners, the Rosenstein sisters, is old school, with exacting alterations, a selection of accessories, and home delivery. ✉ *43 Hazelton Ave., Yorkville* ☎ *416/927–7714* 🌐 *www.hugonicholson.com* ⏲ *Mon.–Sat. 10–6, Sun. by appointment* Ⓜ *Bay.*

James Perse. This California-based company specializes in comfy cotton clothing in muted tones. There are T-shirts of course, but you'll also find fatigues, fleeces, and button-down shirts as well as ankle-length, striped sundresses and drapey long-sleeve shirts for women. The collection is spread over two floors of this Victorian Hazelton house; there's a Ping-Pong table on the second floor if you're up for a game. ✉ *18 Hazelton Ave., Yorkville* ☎ *416/513–0926* 🌐 *www.jamesperse.com* ⏲ *Mon.–Sat. 10–6, Sun. noon–5* Ⓜ *Bay.*

Fodor's Choice ★ **Kate Spade.** Bright, optimistic, and youthful, Spade's sophisticated, fun designs really "pop" in this whitewashed, rehabbed property at the corner of Old York Lane. Step through the turquoise door and feast your eyes on party dresses, sparkling pumps, and sweet bags to match. The cheerful atmosphere will put a spring in your step and, with the help of the smiling staff, you'll blithely depart with a hole in your wallet. Don't say we didn't warn you. ✉ *138 Cumberland Ave., Yorkville* ☎ *416/927–8282* 🌐 *www.katespade.com* ⏲ *Mon.–Wed. 10–6, Thurs.–Fri. 10–7, Sat. 10–6, Sun. noon–5* Ⓜ *Bay.*

Motion. This Toronto-based boutique features unique, comfortable clothing in crumpled cottons, linens, and wool. Many pieces are designed and made in-house, but outside designers such as Noriem and Cauliflower by Issey Miyake and Oksa are also featured. Bold, chunky accessories compliment the earthy, arty look perfectly. ✉ *106 Cumberland St., Yorkville* ☎ *416/968–0090* 🌐 *www.motionclothing.com* ⏲ *Mon.–Wed. 10–6, Thurs.–Fri. 10–8, Sat. 10–6, Sun. noon–6* Ⓜ *Bay.*

m0851. If you're looking for a good leather jacket, or perhaps a coat that's weatherproof, head to this industrial-scale shop. Full-grain, durable leather coats and bags—made in neighboring Québec—follow utilitarian designs. Gorgeous leather bags and accessories, such as wallets and toiletry bags, in bright primary colors also line the shelves. Weatherproof jackets in polyurethane-coated cotton twill are also here. ✉ *38 Avenue Rd., across from Yorkville Ave., Yorkville* ☎ *416/920–4001* 🌐 *www.m0851.com* ⏲ *Mon.–Wed. and Sat. 10–6, Thurs.–Fri. 10–7, Sun. noon–5* Ⓜ *Bay or St George.*

Over the Rainbow. This denim center carries every variety of cut and flare: the trendy, the classic, and the questionable fill the shelves. ✉ *101 Yorkville Ave., at Hazelton Ave., Yorkville* ☎ *416/967–7448* 🌐 *www.rainbowjeans.com* ⏲ *Mon.–Wed. 10–6, Thurs.–Fri. 10–8, Sat. 10–7, Sun. noon–6; summer extended hours on Tues. and Wed. 10–8* Ⓜ *Bay.*

Perry's. These are the suit professionals. Have one custom-made from a broad range of fabrics, or buy off the rack from a collection of some of the finest ready-to-wear suits, which are made by Samuelsohn and Jack Victor (both from Montréal). ✉ *1250 Bay St., at Cumberland St., Yorkville* ☎ *416/923–7397* 🌐 *www.perrysmenswear.com* ⏲ *Mon.–Wed. 9–6, Thu.–Fri. 9–7* Ⓜ *Bay.*

Fodor's Choice ★ **Pink Tartan.** Ontario-born designer Kimberly Newport-Mimran opened this, her flagship store, in 2011 after selling her sophisticated sportswear in high-end shops around the globe. Expect tailored Oxford shirts, classic little black dresses, and crisp, snug-fitting trousers in expensive fabrics, as well as objets d'art, shoes, and accessories hand-picked by the designer. ✉ *77 Yorkville Ave.(entrance on Bellair St.), Yorkville* ☎ *416/976–7700* 🌐 *www.pinktartan.com* ⏲ *Mon.–Wed. and Sat. 10–6, Thurs.–Fri. 10–7, Sun. noon–5* Ⓜ *Bay.*

Prada. The avant-garde designs are overshadowed only by the brilliant celadon interior of the store and the traffic-stopping window displays. ✉ *131 Bloor St. W, Unit 5, at Bellair St., Yorkville* ☎ *416/513–0400* 🌐 *www.prada.com* ⏲ *Mon.–Wed. 10–6, Thurs. 10–7, Fri.–Sat. 10–6, Sun. noon–5* Ⓜ *Bay.*

Fodor's Choice ★ **Roots.** Canadians' favorite leather jackets, bags, and basics come from this two-story flagship store. With the Olympic notoriety and the fact that the beaver is Canada's national animal, the company's beaver logo has become something of a national icon. ✉ *100 Bloor St. W, at Bellair St., Yorkville* ☎ *416/323–3289* 🌐 *www.roots.com* ⏲ *Mon.–Wed. 10–7, Thurs.–Sat. 10–8, Sun. 11–6* Ⓜ *Bay.*

Second Time Around. If you're after a designer handbag but can't bear to pay retail, head to this dark, little consignment shop. The selection is extensive without being overwhelming, and you might find that perfect, lightly used Fendi, Dior, or Dooney & Bourke at an accessible

CLOSE UP

City Chains

Below are some of the city's most interesting national and international chains.

Aritzia. Young urban women come here for modern funky pieces by lines such as TNA, Wilfred, and the house line Talula. There are other locations throughout the city. ✉ *280 Queen St. W, at Beverley St., Queen West* ☎ *416/977-9919* 🌐 *www.aritzia.ca* ⏱ *Weekdays 11–8, Sat. 11–7, Sun. noon–7* Ⓜ *Osgoode, then streetcar 501 west Osgoode* ✉ *Eaton Centre, 220 Yonge St., Dundas Square Area* ☎ *416/204-1318* 🌐 *www.aritzia.com* ⏱ *Weekdays 10–9, Sat. 9:30–7, Sun. 11–6* Ⓜ *Queen Dundas or Queen Street* ✉ *50 Bloor St. W, at Yonge and Bloor St., Yorkville* ☎ *416/934-0935* 🌐 *www.aritzia.com* ⏱ *Mon.–Fri. 10–9, Sat. 10–8, Sun. noon–7* Ⓜ *Bay Bloor-Yonge.*

Indigo. A huge selection of books, magazines, and CDs is stocked at this store, which has a Starbucks and occasional live entertainment. ✉ *55 Bloor St. W, Yorkville* ☎ *416/925-3536* 🌐 *www.chapters.indigo.ca* ⏱ *Sun.–Thurs. 9 am–10 pm, Fri. and Sat. 9 am–11 pm* Ⓜ *Bay* ✉ *Eaton Centre, 220 Yonge St., Dundas Square Area* ☎ *416/591-3622* 🌐 *www.indigo.ca* ⏱ *Mon.–Fri. 10–9:30, Sat. 9:30–7, Sun. 11–6* Ⓜ *Dundas, Queen.*

Winners. Toronto's best bargain outlet has designer lines at rock-bottom prices. The Yonge Street branch, below the elegant Carlu event center, is enormous, but there's a dozen branches of this store scattered all over the city. ✉ *57 Spadina Ave., at King St. W, Entertainment District* ☎ *416/585-2052* 🌐 *www.winners.ca* ⏱ *Mon.–Sat. 9:30–9, Sun. 11–8* Ⓜ *St. Andrew* ✉ *College Park, 444 Yonge St., Dundas Square Area* ☎ *416/598-8800* 🌐 *www.winners.ca* ⏱ *Mon.–Fri. 9 am–9:30 pm, Sat. 9:30 am–9 pm, Sun. 11–8* Ⓜ *College* ✉ *110 Bloor St. W, at Bay St., Yorkville* ☎ *416/920-0193* 🌐 *www.winners.ca* ⏱ *Weekdays 9:30–9, Sat. 9:30–9, Sun. 11–7* Ⓜ *Bay.*

Zara. The Spanish chain consistently attracts crowds craving gorgeous knockoffs of the hottest runway trends. ✉ *50 Bloor St. W, at Yonge St., Yorkville* ☎ *416/916-2401* 🌐 *www.zara.com* ⏱ *Mon.–Wed. and Sat. 10–8, Thurs.–Fri. 10–9, Sun. 11–6* Ⓜ *Bloor* ✉ *Eaton Centre, 220 Yonge St., Dundas Square Area* ☎ *647/288-0333* 🌐 *www.zara.com* ⏱ *Mon.–Fri. 10–9, Sat. 9:30–7, Sun. 11–6* Ⓜ *Queen, Dundas* ✉ *341 Queen St. W, Queen West* ☎ *647/288-0545* 🌐 *www.zara.com* ⏱ *Mon.–Wed. and Sat. 11–8, Thurs.–Fri. 11–9, Sun. noon–6* Ⓜ *Osgoode.*

7

price. High-fashion pre-owned clothes, including Chanel, Gucci, Vuitton and Vivienne Westwood, and loads of shoes are here, too. ✉ *99 Yorkville Ave., Yorkville* ☎ *416/916-7669* 🌐 *www.facebook.com/SecondTimeAroundToronto* ⏱ *Mon.–Sat. 1–6* Ⓜ *Bay.*

Shan. Montreal designer Chantal Levesque founded this label in 1985, and now stocks locations in more than 25 countries with her creative couture swimwear, swimwear accessories and wraps. There's a separate collection for men. ✉ *38 Avenue Rd., at Yorkville Ave., Yorkville* ☎ *416/961-7426* 🌐 *www.shan.ca* ⏱ *Mon.–Wed. and Sat. 10–6, Thurs. and Fri. 10–7, Sun. noon–5* Ⓜ *Bay or St. George (Bedford exit).*

Uncle Otis. Cool, casual, and ever so slightly street (UO was once the preferred shop of skaters), this purveyor of with-it menswear carries the wearable-when-you're-over-thirty styles of Fred Perry, Oliver Spencer, Made and Crafted by Levi's, and Rag & Bone. There are Filson bags, too, and even a few ties. ✉ *26 Bellair St., Yorkville* ☎ *416/920–2281* 🌐 *www.uncleotis.com* ⏲ *Mon.–Fri. 11:30–7, Sat. 11:30–6, Sun. noon–5* Ⓜ *Bay.*

DEPARTMENT STORES AND SHOPPING CENTERS

The Bay. The modern descendant of the Hudson's Bay Company, which was chartered in 1670 to explore and trade in furs, the Bay carries mid-price clothing, furnishings, housewares, and cosmetics, including designer names as well as The Bay's own lines. Another store is located on Yonge Street, connected to Eaton Centre by a covered skywalk over Queen Street. ✉ *44 Bloor St. E, at Yonge St., Yorkville* ☎ *416/972–3333* 🌐 *www.thebay.com* ⏲ *Mon.–Wed. 10–7, Thurs.–Fri. 10–9, Sat. 10–7, Sun. 11–6* Ⓜ *Bloor-Yonge.*

Fodor's Choice ★ **Holt Renfrew.** This multilevel national retail specialty store is the style leader in Canada. It is the headquarters for Burberry, Canali, Chanel, Donna Karan, Armani, and Gucci as well as cosmetics and fragrances from London, New York, Paris, and Rome. **TIP→ Concierge service and personal shoppers are available, but just browsing makes for a rich experience.** ✉ *50 Bloor St. W, at Bay St., Yorkville* ☎ *416/922–2333* 🌐 *www.holtrenfrew.com* ⏲ *Mon.–Wed. and Sat. 10–7, Thurs.–Fri. 10–8, Sun. noon–6* Ⓜ *Bay.*

FOOD AND TREATS

Pusateri's. From humble beginnings as a Little Italy produce stand, Pusateri's has grown into Toronto's deluxe supermarket, with in-house-prepared foods, local and imported delicacies, and desserts and breads from the city's best bakers. ✉ *57 Yorkville Ave., at Bay St., Yorkville* ☎ *416/785–9100* 🌐 *www.pusateris.com* ⏲ *Mon.–Wed. and Sat. 7:30 am–8 pm, Thurs.–Fri. 7:30–9, Sun. 7:30–7* Ⓜ *Bay.*

HOME DECOR

William Ashley. Ashley's has an extensive collection of china patterns that range from Wedgwood to Kate Spade and can often secure those it doesn't carry. Crystal and china are beautifully displayed. Prices are decent—and sales frequent—on expensive names such as Waterford. The store is happy to pack and ship all over the world. ✉ *55 Bloor St. W, at Bay St., Yorkville* ☎ *416/964–2900* 🌐 *www.williamashley.com* ⏲ *Mon.–Wed. 10–7, Thurs.–Fri. 10–7:30, Sat. 10–6, Sun. noon–5* Ⓜ *Bay.*

JEWELRY AND ACCESSORIES

Cartier. The famous jewel box caters to Toronto's elite and has a good selection of the jewelry designer's creations, including the triple-gold-band Trinity Ring and the diamond-studded Tortue Watch. ✉ *131 Bloor St. W, at Avenue Rd., Yorkville* ☎ *416/413–4929* 🌐 *www.cartier.com* ⏲ *Mon.–Sat. 10–6, Sun. noon–5* Ⓜ *Bay.*

Royal De Versailles. Don't let the front-door security scare you away from some of the most innovatively classic jewelry designs in town. ✉ *101 Bloor St. W, at St. Thomas St., Yorkville* ☎ *416/967–7201* 🌐 *www.royaldeversailles.com* ⏲ *Tues.–Fri. 10:30–5, Sat. 10:30–5:30* Ⓜ *Bay.*

Tiffany & Co. Tiffany & Co. Tiffany is perfect for breakfast or any other time. It's still the ultimate for variety and quality in classic jewelry. ✉ *150 Bloor St. W, at Avenue Rd., Yorkville* ☎ *416/921–3900, 800/265–1251* 🌐 *www.tiffany.ca* ⏲ *Mon.–Wed. 10–7, Thurs.–Fri. 10–8, Sat. 10–6, Sun. noon–5* Ⓜ *Bay.*

MUSIC

L'Atelier Grigorian. Since 1980, L'Atelier Grigorian has been specializing in classical, opera, jazz, and world music, making it Toronto's must-visit destination for music lovers from around the globe. More than 50,000 selections are in stock on CD, DVD, Blu-ray, and vinyl. Collectors and audiophiles will find rare recordings and high-end audio formats that will make them smile. ✉ *70 Yorkville Ave., Yorkville* ☎ *416/922–6477* 🌐 *www.grigorian.com* ⏲ *Mon.–Thur. 10–6, Fri. 10–7, Sat.10–6, Sun. noon–5* Ⓜ *Bay.*

SHOES, HANDBAGS, AND LEATHER GOODS

Davids. The collection is always elegant, if somewhat subdued—designers usually include Marc Jacobs, Kate Spade, Salvatore Ferragamo, Lorenzo Banfi, Christian Louboutin, Manolo Blahnik, Jimmy Choo, and Chloe. ✉ *66 Bloor St. W, at Bay St., Yorkville* ☎ *416/920–1000* 🌐 *www.davidsfootwear.com* ⏲ *Mon.–Wed. and Sat. 9:30–6:30, Thurs.–Fri. 9:30–8, Sun. noon–6* Ⓜ *Bay.*

Specchio. This is the place for fine Italian shoes and boots on the cutting edge of style, for every season. The store always seems to have your size in the back. ✉ *1240 Bay St., at Cumberland St., Yorkville* ☎ *416/961–7989* 🌐 *www.specchioshoes.com* ⏲ *Mon.–Wed. 10:30–6:30, Thurs.–Fri. 10:30–8, Sat. 10–6, Sun. noon–6 (winter hours may be shorter)* Ⓜ *Bay.*

SPECIALTY GIFTS

redLetter. Pretty tea sets and tiered pastry stands lure romantics into this gift shop, but push past the china and you'll find cool desk sets, quirky novelties, and plenty of stationery. Designs are fun, funky, and colorful, from Cath Kidston's rural-retro housewares to modern Pantone color-block mugs. ✉ *128 Cumberland St., Yorkville* ☎ *647/340–7294* 🌐 *www.redletterstore.ca* ⏲ *Mon.–Wed. 11–6, Thurs.–Fri. 11–7, Sat. 10–6, Sun. noon–5 (hrs change seasonally)* Ⓜ *Bay.*

ROSEDALE

One of Toronto's most exclusive neighborhoods, Rosedale has a strip of upscale antiques and interiors shops. If the thought of freight charges dissuades you from serious spending, you can take home packable gourmet food from All the Best or accessories from Putti.

ANTIQUES

Absolutely Inc. Curios, from porcupine quills to vertabrae walking sticks, are sold at this fascinating interiors shop; its sister branch is just a few blocks north. You'll also find an array of vintage jewelry; antique boxes made of materials ranging from horn to shagreen (ray or shark skin); English campaign furniture; and French architects' drafting tables. Absolutely North is at 1236 Yonge Street in Rosedale. ✉ *1132 Yonge St., at MacPherson Ave., Rosedale* ☎ *416/324–8351* 🌐 *www.absolutelyinc.com* ⏲ *Mon.–Sat. 10–6* Ⓜ *Rosedale.*

7

Fodor's Choice ★ **Putti.** This housewares shop is very romantic, and very turn-of-the-century. Everywhere you look, you'll see antiques, reproduction furniture, and home accessories piled so high that they scrape the chandeliers. There's also an impressive array of French toiletries as well as frilly frocks and fairy wings for little girls' flights of fancy. ✉ *1104 Yonge St., at Roxborough St., Rosedale* ☎ *416/972–7652* 🌐 *www.putti.ca* ⏲ *Mon.–Sat. 10–6, Sun. noon–5* Ⓜ *Rosedale.*

CLOTHING

Fodor's Choice ★ **Haute Classics.** If you're craving a bit of Blahnik or D&G, some Chanel, Dior or even von Furstenberg, head north to this selectively curated consignment shop. Yes, the designer shoes, bags, jeans, and dresses are secondhand but these pieces are so lightly worn no one will ever know. Someone else's impulse buy may become your fashion find! ✉ *1454 Yonge St., at St. Clair Ave., Rosedale* ☎ *416/922–7900* 🌐 *www.hauteclassics.com* ⏲ *Mon.–Fri. 11–7, Sat. 11–6* Ⓜ *St. Clair.*

SHOES, HANDBAGS, AND LEATHER GOODS

Mephisto. These walking shoes have been around since the 1960s and are made entirely from natural materials. Passionate walkers swear by them and claim they never, ever wear out—even on cross-Europe treks. ✉ *1177 Yonge St., at Summerhill Ave., Rosedale* ☎ *416/968–7026* 🌐 *www.mephisto-toronto.com* ⏲ *Mon.–Wed., Sat. 10–6, Thurs.–Fri., 10–7, Sun. noon–5* Ⓜ *Summerhill.*

WINE AND SPECIALTY FOOD

All the Best Fine Foods. Stop here for imported cheeses and good local breads and pastries, as well as high-quality prepared foods and condiments. Locally made goodies include Summer Kitchen preserves, Soma chocolate, and Kozlick's mustard. **TIP→ One of Toronto's largest LCBOs (the province-controlled liquor store) is a half-block north, making this an especially convenient picnic-supply stop.** ✉ *1099 Yonge St., at Marlborough Ave., Rosedale* ☎ *416/928–3330* 🌐 *www.allthebestfinefoods.com* ⏲ *Mon.–Wed 9–6:30, Thurs. 9–7, Fri. 8:30–7, Sat. 8:30–6, Sun. 9–6* Ⓜ *Summerhill.*

EAST AND WEST OF THE CENTER

THE BEACH

Relaxed and upper-middle-class, this strip of Queen East is just a few blocks from the boardwalk and Lake Ontario's sandy shore. It's packed with casual-clothing stores, gift and antiques shops, and bars and restaurants. It's a long ride to Woodbine on the Queen streetcar, but you'll pass through Riverside and Leslieville on the way.

FOOD AND TREATS

Nutty Chocolatier. A Beach institution, the Nutty Chocolatier serves up hand-scooped ice cream and handmade molded chocolates and truffles from Port Perry, just northeast of Toronto. Even more popular is the old-school candy—Charleston Chew and Tootsie Rolls—and British imports like Irn Bru, Walker's Crisps, Flakes, and Yorkshire Tea. ✉ *2179 Queen St. E, at Lee Ave., The Beach* ☎ *416/698–5548* 🌐 *thenuttychocolatier.com* ⏲ *Daily 9–9* Ⓜ *Queen 501 streetcar; or Woodbine station, then bus 92.*

Davids Tea. When you step into Davids Tea, you're faced with a wall of up to 150 stainless steel cannisters. Thankfully, the teas have been categorized and color-coded (blue for oolong, purple for maté, black for black), the names are printed large (Countess of Seville, mango diablo, jumpy monkey), and the staff is energetic and helpful. Sleek tea accessories are available for purchase, and the airy atmosphere is the perfect place to sit and sip. There are additional locations throughout the city. ✉ *2010 Queen St. E, across from Kew Gardens, The Beach* ☎ *416/698–6036* 🌐 *www.davidstea.com* 🕒 *Sat.–Wed. 9–8, Thurs.–Fri. 9–9* Ⓜ *Queen 501 streetcar; or Woodbine station, then bus 92.*

HOME DÉCOR

Nesters. French-country wares in creamy tones dominate this white-floored housewares and furnishings shop. Nineteen-twenties-inspired chandeliers clink above refurbished fireplace surrounds, garden statuary, and Provincial dressers. You'll also find beautiful bed linens, lavender sachets, and French soaps and toiletries. ✉ *2207 Queen St. E, east of Lee Ave., The Beach* ☎ *416/698–2207* 🌐 *www.nestershome.com* 🕒 *Mon.–Sat. 11–6, Sun. 11–5* Ⓜ *Queen streetcar 501; or Woodbine station, then bus 92.*

SHOES, HANDBAGS, AND LEATHER GOODS

Nature's Footwear. Established in 1978, this tiny, family-run shoe shop specializes in comfortable walking shoes. The store carries an impressive selection of styles, sizes, and widths by Birkenstock, Crocs, Keds, and Sperry Top-Siders, as well as moccasins, Sorel and Kamik boots, and Padraigs—toasty hand-knit baby booties. ✉ *1971a Queen St. E, at Waverley Rd., The Beach* ☎ *416/691–6706* 🌐 *naturesfootwear.com* 🕒 *Mon.–Fri. 10:30–7, Sat.–Sun. 11–5* Ⓜ *Queen 501 streetcar; or Woodbine station, then bus 92.*

THE DANFORTH

Often called Greektown, the Danforth is best known as a place to eat, and appropriately there's a fair amount of culinary retail to go along with the grazing. Carrot Common, just east of Chester subway, houses New Age businesses like the Big Carrot and its juice bar, yoga and massage studios, and a rock and crystal shop, along with a few independent boutiques.

FOOD AND TREATS

Big Carrot Natural Food Market. This large health-food supermarket carries good selections of organic produce, health and beauty aids, and vitamins. There's a vegetarian café on-site and freshly prepared foods for takeout. ✉ *348 Danforth Ave., at Hampton Ave., Danforth* ☎ *416/466–2129* 🌐 *www.thebigcarrot.ca* 🕒 *Weekdays 9–9, Sat. 9–8, Sun. 11–6* Ⓜ *Chester.*

Suckers Candy Co. It's like stepping into a comic book. More than 500 different suckers; retro and novelty candy from Canada, the United States, and the United Kingdom; 50 different Jelly Belly flavors; and custom-made loot bags and baskets will assuage any sweet tooth. This place is fun for all ages and open until midnight on Saturday. ✉ *450 Danforth Ave., at Chester Ave., Danforth* ☎ *416/405–8946* 🌐 *www.suckerscandyco.com* 🕒 *Sun.–Wed., 10:30–9, Thurs. 10:30–10, Fri. 10:30–11, Sat. 10:30–midnight (winter hours vary)* Ⓜ *Chester.*

HOME DÉCOR

IQ Living. This is a fun kitchen shop for those who take their cooking seriously. Every hue of Emile Henry ceramic cookware is available, as is the refined dinnerware by Sophie Conran for Portmeirion and bright nesting bowls and utensils by the innovative Joseph Joseph. A huge selection of insulated lunch boxes and bags, including take-along bento boxes can be found, along with funky popsicle molds and that '70s throwback, the Soda Stream. ✉ *542 Danforth Ave., at Carlaw Ave., Danforth* 🌐 *www.iqliving.com* ⏲ *Weekdays 10–9, weekends 10–6* Ⓜ *Pape or Chester.*

SHOES, HANDBAGS, AND LEATHER GOODS

Balisi. A feminie shoe shop with a distinctly European aesthetic, you'll find a range of shoes in every style including clunky wedges, strappy stilletos, funky, off-kilter boots, and Kamik Wellies in swirly prints and unusual colors. There are even hard-to-find European, Canadian, and Brazilian designers. Bright bags from Co-lab of Montreal, plus stylish outfits and a selection of cute dresses are also available. Additional branches can be found at 711 Queen Street West in West Queen West and at 650 College Street in Little Italy. ✉ *439 Danforth Ave., just east of Chester Ave., Danforth* ☎ *416/463–4848* 🌐 *www.balisi.com* ⏲ *Mon–Wed 10–8, Thurs–Sat 10–9, Sun 11–7 (shorter hrs in winter)* Ⓜ *Chester.*

LESLIEVILLE

Head east to Leslieville—a newly gentrified slice of Queen East stretched between Carlaw and Greenwood, once noted for antiques and junk shops, but now where hip clothing boutiques and brunch spots are the norm. Keep your eyes peeled as you trundle east over the DVP bridge; neighboring Riverside is catching up fast, and if you're seriously into interior design, just get off the tram and walk.

ANTIQUES

Fodor's Choice ★ **Gadabout.** This antique shop is a rummager's paradise. The walls groan under 1950s salt n' pepper shakers, snakeskin handbags, costume jewelry, Hudson's Bay blankets, and racks of vintage clothing that range from the 1800s to the 1970s and includes an extensive section for men. You can rifle through the scores of carefully labeled drawers to find magicians' business cards, Nana Mouskouri specs, and creepy vintage curling irons. Display cases burst with curios—medicinal bottles, a collection of eggshell-faced Japanese dolls, and a feng shui compass. As the owner says, "If it's odd, it's here!" ✉ *1300 Queen St. E, east of Leslie St., Leslieville* ☎ *416/463–1254* 🌐 *www.gadabout.ca* ⏲ *Mon.–Fri. 11:30–6:30, Sat. 10–6:30, Sun. 10–5* Ⓜ *Queen streetcar 501; Greenwood, then bus 31 to Queen.*

ARTS AND CRAFTS GALLERIES

Arts Market. More than 50 artisans and purveyors display their wares in mini 4-by-4 spaces where vintage collections rub shoulders with meditation beads, hand-knit baby booties, mixed-media paintings, and rhubarb jam. Another branch is located in Little Italy at 846 College Street. ✉ *1114 Queen St. E, east of Pape Ave., Leslieville* ☎ *647/997–7616* 🌐 *www.artsmarket.ca* ⏲ *Mon.–Fri. noon–6, Sat.–Sun. 11–6* Ⓜ *Queen streetcar 501; or Pape, then bus 72 to Carlaw and Queen.*

CLOTHING

Any Direct Flight. Sitting at the eastern edge of Leslieville, Any Direct Flight is worth the streetcar ride, if you're after retro-inspired, yet contemporary designs for women. Its spacious, exposed-brick rooms have comfy couches encouraging leisurely browsing of its feminine, yet slightly off-kilter collection of hats, luxurious sweaters, asymetric dresses, El Naturalista boots, and Sanita clogs. You can even mull over your clothing options at the in-store café. ✉ *1382 Queen St. E, east of Greenwood Ave., Leslieville* ☎ *416/504–0017* 🌐 *www.anydirectflight.com* 🕑 *Mon. noon–6, Tues.–Fri. 11–7, Sat. 11–6, Sun. noon–5* Ⓜ *Queen streetcar 501; Greenwood, then bus 31.*

Fodor's Choice ★ **Bergstrom Originals.** The wearability and quality of Christina Bergstrom's bold and bright designs is so evident, that the items practically leap off the racks. Slip on an ankle-length dress in multicolored stripes, or an open-weave bright orange tunic, and you'll see what we mean. Graphic and contrasting, fun and occasionally bohemian, Bergstrom outfits cloak many a Torontonian female. There's also a great selection of chunky heels by Fly London and El Naturalista. ✉ *781 Queen St. E, east of Broadview Ave. at Saulter St., Leslieville* ☎ *416/595–7320* 🌐 *www.bergstromoriginals.com* 🕑 *Tues.–Wed. 11–7, Thurs.–Fri. 11–8, Sat. 11–7, Sun. noon–6* Ⓜ *501 Queen streetcar; or Broadview, then 504 streeetcar to Queen.*

Doll Factory by Damzels. The Doll Factory has 1950s pin-up looks from Toronto designers Damzels in this Dress, including their own gingham and sailor-inspired numbers, and other rock n' roll retro designs from across the continent. Chunky heels and sweet polka-dot wedges are on the shelves, as are covertible high-waisted bikinis perfect for flattering those curves. Don't miss the Bright Chinese parasols or I Lava Tiki totem mugs. Another branch can be found in Roncesvalles at 394 Roncesvalles Avenue. ✉ *1122 Queen St. E, east of Pape Ave., Leslieville* ☎ *416/598–0509* 🌐 *www.damzels.com* 🕑 *Tue.–Sat. 11–6, Sun. noon–5* Ⓜ *Queen streetcar 501; Pape, then bus 72 to Carlaw and Queen.*

HOME DECOR

Love the Design. This warehouse-like space has concrete floors and a wall plastered with pages from the *Farmers' Almanac*. Fittingly, you'll find rough-luxe housewares and furniture such as worn filing cabinets and plan chests, galvanized-steel maple-sap buckets, stag hooks, industrial cage lights, and filament bulbs in every size and wattage available. The owner, Christine Flynn, is an artist and photographer whose muted, resin-covered photos are scattered around the store. Another branch can be found in Rosedale at 1226 Yonge Street. ✉ *1362 Queen St. E, just west of Greenwood Ave., Leslieville* ☎ *416/408–1727* 🌐 *www.lovethedesign.com* 🕑 *Tue.–Fri. 11–6, Sat. 11–5* Ⓜ *Queen streetcar 501; or Greenwood then bus 31.*

WEST QUEEN WEST

West of Bathurst, Queen is packed with cool boutiques, slick interiors stores, and shoe shops galore. Even farther west, beyond Trinity Bellwoods Park, the cool quotient is stepped up, with mid-century modern antiques and cutting-edge galleries and a sudden flurry of big name designers—think Stussy, Fred Perry, and Tiger of Sweden—elbowing their way in amongst the quirky boutiques at Ossington.

ART AND CRAFTS GALLERIES

OCC Gallery. The gallery hosts frequently changing exhibitions of contemporary craft that include cutting-edge decorative pieces handcrafted by Ontario artists. ✉ *990 Queen St. West, at Ossington Ave., West Queen West* ☎ *416/925–4222* 🌐 *www.craft.on.ca* ⏲ *Mon.–Sat. 11–6* Ⓜ *Ossington, then bus 63 south; or Osgoode, then streetcar 501 west.*

Stephen Bulger. This gallery focuses on historical and contemporary Canadian photography, with Canadian and international artists such as André Kertész and Larry Towell. ✉ *1026 Queen St. W, at Brookfield St., West Queen West* ☎ *416/504–0575* 🌐 *www.bulgergallery.com* ⏲ *Tues.–Sat. 11–6* Ⓜ *Osgoode, then streetcar 501 west; or Ossington, then bus 63 south.*

CLOTHING

Annie Aime. Bright comfy threads with a European aesthetic and a splash of street style are the focus here. There are plenty of French pieces for men and women, but Canadian designers are featured, too, such as locals Outclass and Montreal's Mylene B. The walls have been painted by Toronto grafitti artist Pascal Paquette, aka Chou. ✉ *42 Ossington Ave., West Queen West* ☎ *416/840–5227* 🌐 *www.annieaime.com* ⏲ *Mon.–Sat. 11–7, Sun. noon–5* Ⓜ *Osgoode then streetcar 501 west; or Ossington then bus 63 south.*

Cabaret. Classic Hollywood and mid-century-Parisian-style gowns (1920s–1970s), handbags, and jewelry fill this sweet little checkerboard-floored shop. For men there's a selection of dapper bowties, hats, and jackets and vintage suits and tuxedos. Popular with brides are the store's own line of vintage-inspired couture dresses. ✉ *672 Queen St W, at Palmerston Ave., West Queen West* ☎ *416/504–7126* 🌐 *www.cabaretvintage.com* ⏲ *Mon.–Wed. and Sat. 11–6, Thurs. and Fri. 11–7, Sun 1–5* Ⓜ *501 Queen or 511 Bathurst streetcar.*

Fred Perry. Classic mod style from this iconic British clothing company fills the store, the only one in Canada. Originated by 1940s Wimbledon champion Fred Perry, the brand has been associated with British youth culture for decades. ✉ *964 Queen St. W, at Givins St., West Queen West* ☎ *416/538–3733* 🌐 *www.fredperry.com* ⏲ *Mon.–Fri. 11–7, Sat. 11–6, Sun. noon–5* Ⓜ *Ossington, then 63 bus south; or Osgoode, then 501 streetcar west.*

Girl Friday. Designer Rebecca Nixon sells sweet and stylish designs with a retro glam look. Most of the clothing and accessories are by Canadian designers, including Dish jeans, and most of the jewelry is by Toronto artisans. ✉ *740 Queen St. W, at Claremont St., West Queen West* ☎ *416/364–2511* 🌐 *www.girlfridayclothing.com* ⏲ *Mon.–Tues. noon–7, Wed.– Sat. 11–7, Sun. noon–6* Ⓜ *Osgoode then 501 Queen streetcar; or Bathurst, then 511 streetcar.*

Fodor's Choice ★ **Gravity Pope.** This Canadian chain, frequented by dressers-in-the-know, has an impressive selection that includes Paul Smith, Comme des Garçons, and Reigning Champ. A massive selection of more than 2,000 pairs of shoes including See by Chloe, Camper, Hunter, Rag & Bone, and Vans. ✉ *1010 Queen St. W, at Ossington Ave., West Queen West* ☎ *647/748–5155* 🌐 *www.gravitypope.com* ⏲ *Mon.–Wed. 11–8, Thurs.–Fri. 10–9, Sat. 10–7, Sun. noon–6* Ⓜ *Osgoode then 501 streetcar west; or Ossington then bus 63 south.*

I Miss You Boutique. Julie Yoo's immaculately restored picks in this upscale consignment shop include familiar names such as Pucci, Dior, and Yves Saint Laurent. Head next door to the Emporium for more rustic pieces, including loads of brown leather bags and belts. Pieces from the 1960s and '70s can be found up the road on Dundas at I Miss You Vintage. ✉ *63 Ossington Ave., at Queen St. W, West Queen West* ☎ *416/916–7021* 🌐 *www.facebook.com/EmporiumByIMissYou* ⏲ *Mon.–Wed. and Sat.–Sun. noon–6, Thurs.–Fri. noon–7* Ⓜ *Queen 501 streetcar to Ossington Ave; or Ossington station, then bus 64 south.*

Preloved. Designers at this local favorite scour recycled textile facilities for secondhand, unfaded pieces to pull apart and reconstruct into entirely new dresses, tops, and more. You can be sure each item you buy is unique. ✉ *881 Queen St. W, at Trinity Bellwoods Park, West Queen West* ☎ *416/504–8704* 🌐 *www.preloved.ca* ⏲ *Mon.–Sat. 11–7, Sun. noon–6* Ⓜ *Osgoode, then streetcar 501 west; or Bathrust, then streetcar 511.*

HOME DECOR

Morba. Mad for teak? This double-fronted shop is stuffed with Scandinavian furniture and lighting (especially white, papery Le Klint from Denmark), but there's loads of vintage pieces and retro knock-offs, too. A great place for gifts, Morba has a huge selection of quirky desk accessories, alarm clocks, and martini shakers for your friends stuck in the 1950s. There's a wonderful collection of colorful Scandinavian glass, too. ✉ *665 Queen St. W, at Bathurst, West Queen West* ☎ *416/364–5144* 🌐 *www.morba.ca* ⏲ *Mon.–Fri. 11–6, Sat. 10–6, Sun. noon–5* Ⓜ *Bathurst, then streetcar 511; or Osgoode then streetcar 501 west.*

Quasi Modo. Design classics such as Herman Miller lounge chairs and Noguchi lamps are just a sampling of the high-end design pieces you'll find here—there's not a knock-off in sight. There are also sleek modern housewares for the kitchen and bathroom as well. ✉ *789 Queen St. W, at Manning Ave., West Queen West* ☎ *416/703–8300* 🌐 *www.quasimodomodern.com* ⏲ *Mon.–Sat. 10–6, Sun. noon–5* Ⓜ *Osgoode, then streetcar 501 west; or Bathurst, then streetcar 511.*

Urban Mode. Modern and trend-oriented furniture and home decor include the playful furniture designs of Blu Dot and 20th-century classics such as the Arturo lounge chair. ✉ *145 Tecumseth St., at Queen St. W, West Queen West* ☎ *416/591–8834* 🌐 *www.urbanmode.com* ⏲ *Mon.–Fri. 11–7, Sat. 10–6* Ⓜ *Osgoode, then streetcar 501 west; or Bathurst, then streetcar 511.*

GIFTS

Drake General Store. Only-in-Canada gifts like Mountie napkins, Hudson Bay Company wool blankets, totem-pole stacking mugs, supersoft Toronto-made Shared tees, and poutine bowls are tucked into every nook and cranny of this offbeat shop. Giftware extends from the unusual but beautiful (whimsical Rob Ryan dishware and pewter-and-ceramic moosehead shot glasses) to the singularly strange (preserved lemons, knitted mustache pins). Additional locations are in the Dundas Square Area at 176 Yonge Street and in Yonge and Eglinton at 2607 Yonge Street. ✉ *1144 Queen St. W, at Beaconsfield Ave., West Queen West* ☎ *416/531–5042* 🌐 *www.drakegeneralstore.ca* ⏲ *Mon.–Wed. 11–7, Thurs.–Sat. 11–9, Sun. 11–6.*

JEWELRY AND ACCESSORIES

Fodor's Choice ★ **Lady Mosquito.** Chunky necklaces in eye-popping colors cover the walls of this Peruvian accessories shop. Bright felt brooches, dangly earrings, and embroidered handbags—all made from recycled or sustainable materials—don't have a hint of shabby about them. Everything is festive, contemporary, and very, very South American. Cynthia Villegas chooses the work of Peruvian artisans you'll see in the store, and she also creates many of the striking pieces herself, many made from the tagua seed of the Amazonian rain forest. ✉ *1022 Queen St. W, at Ossington Ave., West Queen West* ☎ *647/344–3266* 🌐 *www.ladymosquito.ca* ⏲ *Tues. and Sat. 11–6, Wed.–Fri. 11–7, Sun. noon–4* Ⓜ *Ossington, then bus 63 south; or Osgoode then streetcar 501 west.*

Rue Pigalle. This bright and breezy shop boasts mostly French accessories—jewelry, bags, and scarves—that will add a certain "je ne sais quoi" to your wardrobe. Display drawers hide precious pieces that are worth exploring, and prints and paintings by local artists adorn the walls. ✉ *927 Queen St. W, across from Trinity Bellwoods Park, West Queen West* ☎ *647/352–8115* 🌐 *www.ruepigalle.ca* ⏲ *Mon.–Wed. and Fri.–Sat. 11–6, Thurs. 11–7* Ⓜ *Bathurst, then streetcar 511; or Osgoode then streetcar 501 west.*

Zane. This is the place to come for less obvious, on-trend items from designers such as Rebecca Minkoff, Vlieger and Vandam, and Issey Miyake. Fine luggage, including Rimowa hard-cases; a great line of Karen Walker tortoiseshell sunglasses; and fine jewelry are available. Men will find handsome satchels and handmade belts in The Den towards the back. ✉ *753 Queen St. W, at Euclid Ave., West Queen West* ☎ *647/352–9263* 🌐 *www.visitzane.com* ⏲ *Mon.–Wed. and Sat. 11–7, Thurs.–Fri. 11–8, Sun. noon–6* Ⓜ *Osgoode, then 501 streetcar west; or Bathurst, then 511 streetcar.*

MUSIC

Fodor's Choice ★ **Rotate This.** Music buyers in the know come here for underground and independent music from Canada, the United States, and beyond. It has CDs, LPs, some magazines, concert tickets, and other treats. ✉ *801 Queen St. W, at Manning Ave., West Queen West* ☎ *416/504–8447* 🌐 *www.rotate.com* ⏲ *Mon.–Thurs. 11–7, Fri. 11–8, Sun. noon–6:30* Ⓜ *Osgoode, then streetcar 501 west; or Bathurst, then streetcar 511.*

SHOES, HANDBAGS, AND LEATHER GOODS

Heel Boy. A tried and true spot for cool and cute footwear for both sexes, Heel Boy stocks the most unique styles by well-known brands like Camper, Ugg, TOMS, Colcci, and Dolce Vita, as well as eco-chic bags by Canadian company Matt and Nat. ✉ *773 Queen St. W, at Euclid Ave., West Queen West* ☎ *416/362–4335* 🌐 *www.heelboy.com* ⏲ *Mon.–Fri. 11–9, Sat. 10–7, Sun. noon–6* Ⓜ *501 Queen or 511 Bathurst streetcar.*

SPECIALTY GIFTS

Town Moto. True bikers and Sunday-riders alike will love this crowded shop that has all types of gear for your bike lining the walls. Push to the back to find biker jackets, an impressive selection of helmets and goggles, and natty biker boots. There's posters and biker Ts, too. ✉ *132 Ossington Ave., south of Dundas St. W, West Queen West* ☎ *416/856–8011* 🌐 *www.townmoto.com* ⏲ *Mon.–Wed. noon–7, Thurs.–Sat. noon–8, Sun. noon–5* Ⓜ *Ossington, then bus 64 south.*

GREATER TORONTO

RONCESVALLES VILLAGE AND LITTLE PORTUGAL

The main drag in Roncesvalles Village, an upper-middle-class neighborhood near High Park, is lined with unique bookstores, clothing shops, restaurants, and cafés, and vestiges of a once-dominant Polish community. Little Portugal, at Dundas West and Ossington, is evolving, with hip vintage stores and galleries popping up monthly.

7

ARTS AND CRAFTS GALLERIES

LE Gallery. Work by contemporary and edgy emerging and "mid-career" artists are on display here. Owner/director Wil Kucey's taste for graffiti and street art is apparent in many of the shows. ✉ *1183 Dundas St. W, Roncesvalles Village and Little Portugal* ☎ *416/532–8467* 🌐 *le-gallery.ca* ⏲ *Tues.–Sat. noon–6* Ⓜ *505 Dundas streetcar, or Ossington station, then bus 63 south.*

Olga Korper Gallery. Many important Canadian and international artists, such as Lynne Cohen, Paterson Ewen, John McEwen, and Reinhard Reitzenstein, are represented by this trailblazing yet accessible gallery, which displays art from the 1960s on. It's a good place for contemporary collectors and art enthusiasts alike. ✉ *17 Morrow Ave., off Dundas St. W., Roncesvalles Village and Little Portugal* ☎ *416/538–8220* 🌐 *www.olgakorpergallery.com* ⏲ *Tues.–Sat. 10–6* Ⓜ *Dundas West, then streetcar east.*

CLOTHING

Red Canoe. Canadian and aviation-themed clothing and accessories at the headquarters of this local brand include RCAF (Royal Canadian Air Force) messenger bags; '70s retro CBC (Canadian Broadcasting Corporation) tees; Cessna ball caps; and practical, but not-too-bulky, goose-down jackets. Red Canoe merchandise is also sold in Pearson Airport, Kensington Market's Blue Banana, Queen West's Design Republic, and the Drake General Store. ✉ *1356 Dundas St. W, at Rusholme Rd., Roncesvalles Village and Little Portugal* ☎ *416/205–1271* 🌐 *www.redcanoebrands.com* ⏲ *Mon.–Fri. 9–5* Ⓜ *505 Dundas streetcar.*

YONGE AND EGLINTON

Jokingly called "Young and Eligible," this northerly nabe is a somewhat sterile but lively high-rise hot spot for chain stores, movie megaplexes, and Irish pubs.

CLOTHING: CHILDREN'S

Hatley. This company began as a cottage business in rural Quebec 20 years ago, with a line of aprons depicting cute farm animals. Now this mainly children's boutique is stocked with quirky, nature-inspired clothing covered in insects, animals, trees, and flowers—designs inspired by the Canadian wilderness. ✉ *2648 Yonge St., at Craighurst Ave., Yonge and Eglinton* ☎ *416/486–4141* 🌐 *www.hatleystore.com* ⏲ *Mon.–Sat. 10–6, Sun. 11–5* Ⓜ *Lawrence or Eglington, then 97 Bus.*

HOME DECOR

The Art Shoppe. The block-long, two-story shop is chock-full of eclectic highbrow furniture ranging from antique Louis XV armoires to modern Italian leather sofas, artfully arranged in multiple museumlike showrooms. ✉ *2131 Yonge St., just south of Eglinton Ave., Yonge and Eglinton* ☎ *416/487–3211* 🌐 *www.theartshoppe.com* ⏲ *Mon.–Wed., Fri., and Sat. 9:30–6, Thurs. 9:30–9* Ⓜ *Eglinton.*

OUTDOOR EQUIPMENT AND CLOTHING

Sporting Life. The first off the mark with the latest sportswear trends, this is the place to get couture labels like Juicy, La Coste, and Burberry—or to snag snowboard gear and poll the staff for advice on where to use it. A second "bikes and boards store" (that's snow boards) is down Yonge Street. ✉ *2665 Yonge St., north of Eglinton Ave., Yonge and Eglinton* ☎ *416/485–1611* 🌐 *www.sportinglife.ca* ⏲ *Weekdays 9:30–9, Sat. 9–6, Sun. 10–6* Ⓜ *Eglinton.*

8

SIDE TRIPS FROM TORONTO

SIDE TRIPS FROM TORONTO

TOP REASONS TO GO

★ **The Falls:** Niagara Falls' amazing display of natural power is Ontario's top attraction. See them from both the U.S. and Canadian sides.

★ **Shakespeare and Shaw:** A couple of long-dead British playwrights have managed to make two Ontario towns boom from May through October with the Shakespeare Festival in Stratford and the Shaw Festival in Niagara-on-the-Lake.

★ **Wineries:** The Niagara Peninsula has an unusually good microclimate for growing grapes; most of the more than 60 wineries have tastings.

★ **The great outdoors:** Ski at resorts north of Toronto; canoe backcountry rivers in Algonquin Provincial Park; hike or bike the Niagara-to-Lake-Huron Bruce Trail or the Niagara Parkway along the Niagara River.

★ **Edible Ontario:** Niagara-on-the-Lake and Stratford are both renowned for their skilled chefs who serve culinary masterpieces created with farm-fresh ingredients.

1 Niagara Falls. South of Toronto near the U.S. border, the thundering falls are an impressive display of nature's power.

2 The Niagara Wine Region. The temperate Niagara region bordering Lake Ontario is the ideal growing climate for all kinds of produce, including grapes. Wineries stretch along the shores of Lake Ontario south of Toronto to the pretty Victorian-style town of Niagara-on-the-Lake, at the junction of Lake Ontario and the Niagara River.

3 Stratford. An acclaimed Shakespeare Festival brings this rural town alive from April through October. Overwhelmingly popular, it has become Stratford's raison d'etre, with a multitude of inns and locavore restaurants growing up around it. Frequent outdoor music and arts festivals color the squares and parks all summer.

4 Southern Georgian Bay. North of Toronto is a series of lakes and summer homes, ski resorts, and the small towns that serve them.

5 The Muskokas. This area north of the city is known for its lakes and vacation cottages. Tackle the four-hour drive to Algonquin Provincial Park and you're rewarded with pristine forested land for canoeing, camping, and moose-spotting.

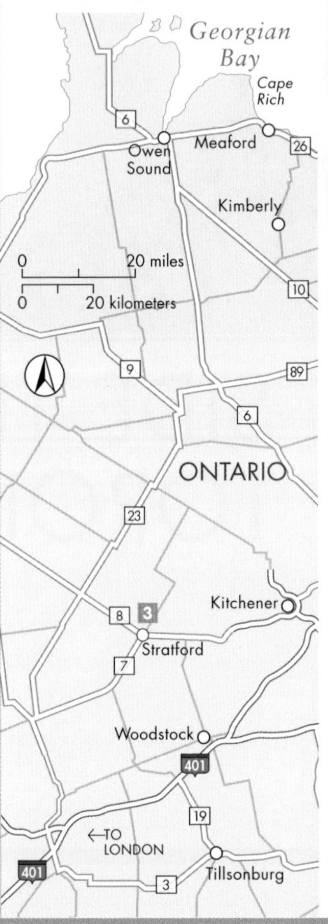

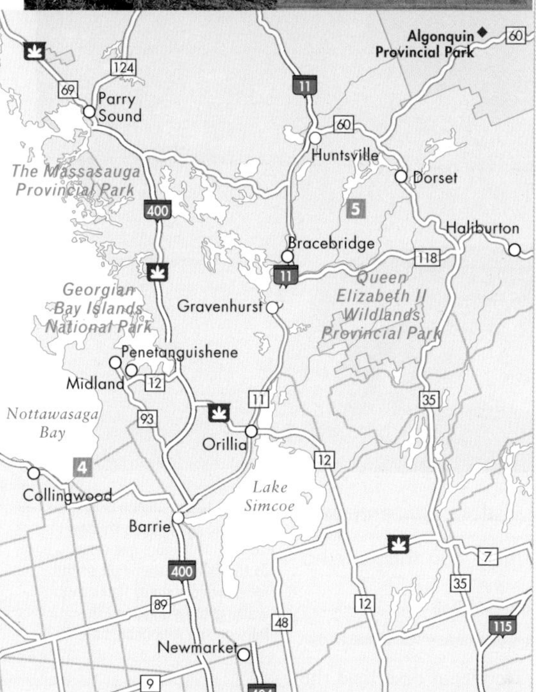

GETTING ORIENTED

Wedged between three Great Lakes—Ontario, Huron, and Erie—and peppered with thousands of smaller lakes, Southern Ontario is a fertile area of farmland, wineries, forests, and waterways. Within a two-to-four-hour drive north, west, or southwest of Toronto are small towns, beaches, ski resorts, and rural farmland that feel light-years away from the city lights. Toronto sits at the eastern edge of Southern Ontario, a region that makes up no more than 15% of the province but is home to nearly 95% of the population and most of its major attractions. Head north and you hit the Muskokas and Algonquin, west for Stratford, and south–southwest to Niagara Falls and the Niagara Wine Region.

NIAGARA FALLS

Niagara Falls has inspired visitors for centuries, and the allure hasn't dimmed for those who want to marvel at this natural wonder.

(above) Niagara Falls is as dramatic by night as by day. (top right) Visitors get close to the falls on the *Maid of the Mist*. (bottom right) Parks and walking trails surround the falls on the American side.

Missionary and explorer Louis Hennepin described the falls in 1678 as "an incredible Cataract or Waterfall which has no equal." Nearly two centuries later, Charles Dickens declared, "I seemed to be lifted from the earth and to be looking into Heaven."

Countless daredevils have been lured here. In 1859, 100,000 spectators watched as the French tightrope walker Charles Blondin successfully crossed Niagara Gorge, from the American to the Canadian side, on a three-inch-thick rope. From the early 18th century, dozens went over in boats and barrels. Nobody survived until 1901, when schoolteacher Annie Taylor emerged from her barrel and asked, "Did I go over the falls yet?" Stunts were outlawed in 1912.

The depiction of the thundering cascades in the 1953 Marilyn Monroe film *Niagara* is largely responsible for creating modern-day tourism. And though the lights of the arcades, tacky souvenir shops, and casinos shine garishly bright for some, views of the falls themselves are unspoiled.

NIGHT LIGHTS

See **Fireworks Over the Falls** on Fridays, Sundays, and holidays at 10 pm from mid-May to early September (and on Friday during the Winter Festival of Lights).

Between early November and late January, the **Winter Festival of Lights** illuminates the Niagara Parkway, with 125 animated lighting displays and 3 million tree and ground lights. *www.wfol.com.*

WAYS TO EXPLORE

By Air: Niagara Helicopters Ltd. Niagara Helicopters Ltd. does 12-minute sightseeing flights over the whirlpool, gorge, and all three falls, plus winery trips. ✉ *3731 Victoria Ave., Niagara Falls* ☎ *905/357–5672, 800/281–8034* 🌐 *www.niagarahelicopters.com* 🎫 *C$139/person.*

The **Whirlpool Aero Car** cable car crosses the gorge over the Niagara River whirlpool.

By Boat: The **Maid of the Mist** is an oldie but a goody, and still pulls in huge crowds. Adrenaline-fueled Whirlpool Jet Boat Tours in Niagara-on-the-Lake plow headfirst into the Class-V Niagara River rapids on an hour-long ride.

By Bus: Double Deck Tours. Take an authentic, red London double-decker bus tour with Double Deck Tours. Fares include admission to Journey Behind the Falls, *Maid of the Mist,* and the Whirlpool Aero Car; the four-hour tour also includes the Floral Clock and Niagara Glen. Tickets and departures are next to the *Maid of the Mist* building. ☎ *905/374–7423* 🌐 *www.doubledecktours.com* 🎫 *C$79* ⏲ *Apr–Oct. at 11 am; also 10:15 am and 1:15 pm in July and Aug.*

By Foot: Stroll the Niagara Parkway promenade, stand on the Table Rock Centre terrace, and walk over the Rainbow Bridge. The **White Water Walk** is the closest you'll get to the rapids from land; **Journey Behind the Falls** is a walk through tunnels behind the falls.

Cave of the Winds. Worth a border crossing, Cave of the Winds takes you 175 feet into the gorge to an observation deck less than 20 feet from thundering Bridal Veil falls. **TIP→ You will get drenched; you are provided with a poncho and footwear for a reason.** ✉ *Departures from Goat Island, Niagara Falls State Park, Niagara Falls, New York, USA* ☎ *716/278–1730* 🌐 *www.niagarafallsstatepark.com* 🎫 *$11* ⏲ *May–Oct. 9 am–7:30 pm.*

IN ONE DAY

If you have only a day in Niagara Falls, walk the waterfront promenade and go on a *Maid of the Mist* tour. (Plan for wet shins and shoes.) Also consider the Whirlpool Aero Car, a cable-car ride over the whirlpool, or the Whitewater Walk, to see the rapids up close. Dinner within view of the falls, which are colorfully lit at night, is a relaxing end to a full day.

THE AMERICAN SIDE

Canada has the superior views and a more developed waterfront, with better restaurants. In contrast, the American waterfront is lined with parks, ideal for hiking and picnicking. Because you're behind the falls here, rather than facing them, views are limited. Stick to Canada for most of your visit, but if you have more time, cross the Rainbow Bridge on foot to get close to Bridal Veil Falls on a Cave of the Winds tour from Goat Island.

WINE REGION KNOW-HOW

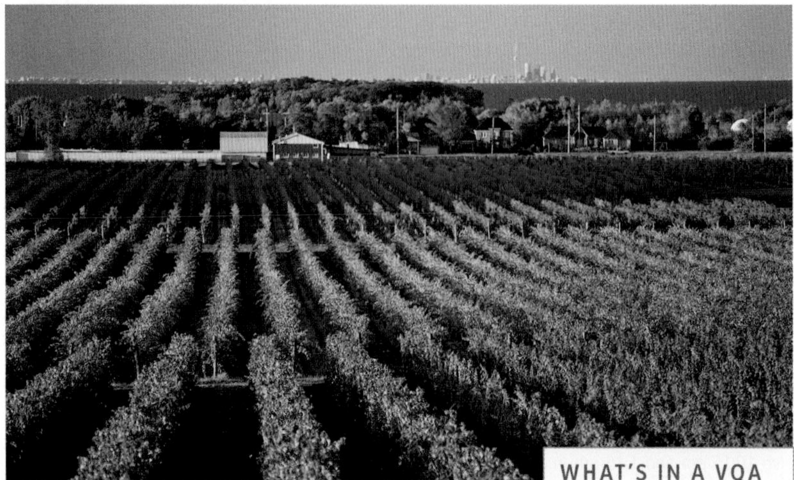

Ontario may not be famed for its wines—yet—but the Niagara Peninsula alone has around 75 wineries and has been producing wine commercially since the early 1970s. Four decades on, the region is coming into its own with some of the world's best wines of origin.

The position of the Niagara appellation, wedged between Lake Ontario and the Niagara Escarpment, creates a microclimate that regulates ground and air temperature and allows for successful grape-growing (today more than 30 varietals) in an otherwise too-cold province. Winds off Lake Ontario are directed back by the escarpment, preventing cold air from settling. Heat stored in lake waters in summer keeps ground temperatures warmer longer into winter. In spring, the cold waters keep the grounds from warming too fast, protecting buds from late-spring frosts. Some say that the slightly colder climate means a more complex-tasting grape. Indisputably it *does* provide perfect conditions for producing some of the world's best ice wine.

WHAT'S IN A VQA

Canadian wine is regulated by the Vintners Quality Alliance, a government-sanctioned wine authority whose strict standards are on par with regulatory agencies in France and Italy. Many Niagara wineries proudly declare their vintages VQA; in fact, 65% of all VQA wines in Ontario are Niagara wines. To be deemed VQA is no small honor: Wines must meet rigorous standards—including being made entirely from fresh, quality-approved Ontario-grown grapes (no concentrates) and approved grape varieties, passing laboratory testing, and approval by an expert tasting panel prior to release. Look for the VQA stamp on the label.

NIAGARA WINE TOURING BASICS

THE ONTARIO WINE ROUTE

Ontario Wine Route. Niagara wineries along the Ontario Wine Route are well marked by blue signs between Grimsby and Niagara Falls. **TIP→ For a full map of the wine route, pick up the free Wine Country Ontario Travel Guide, updated annually and available at wineries and tourist attractions or directly from the Wine Council.** ✉ *Niagara-on-the-Lake* ☎ *905/684-8070* 🌐 *www.winecountryontario.ca.*

TIMING AND COSTS

Most wineries are open year-round, with limited hours in winter. Tastings begin between 10 and noon. Reservations may be needed for tours in summer.

Tastings usually cost C$1–C$2 per wine, or up to C$7 for more expensive wines. The larger wineries do regular public tours; at smaller operations you may be able to arrange a tour in advance. Tasting and/or tour fees are often waived if you buy a bottle of wine.

ORGANIZED TOURS

Crush on Niagara. Crush on Niagara wine-tour packages include overnight stays, meals, and winery tours. ✉ *4101 King St., Beamsville* ☎ *905/562-3373, 866/408-9463* 🌐 *www.crushtours.com.*

Grape and Wine Tours. Grape and Wine Tours runs day trips and one- or two-night wine-tour packages from Toronto and Oakville. Pick-up and drop-off at Niagara-on-the-Lake and Niagara Falls hotels is included. ✉ *758 Niagara Stone Rd., Niagara-on-the-Lake* ☎ *905/562-9449, 866/562-9449* 🌐 *www.grapeandwinetours.com.*

Niagara Wine Tours International. Niagara Wine Tours International leads guided bike, van, and coach tours along the Wine Route and has bike rentals. ✉ *92 Picton St., Niagara-on-the-Lake* ☎ *905/468-1300, 800/680-7006* 🌐 *www.niagaraworldwinetours.com.*

EVENTS

Niagara Wine Festival. The Niagara Wine Festival group organizes three big events in Niagara. The largest, with an annual half million attendees is the eponymous, 10-day **Niagara Wine Festival**, in September, celebrating the grape harvest. The three-week **Niagara Ice Wine Festival**, in January, is a nod to Niagara's specialty, ice wine. The three-weekend **Niagara New Vintage Festival**, in June, is a wine-and-culinary event. ✉ *Montebello Park, 64 Ontario St., St. Catharines* ☎ *905/688-0212* 🌐 *www.niagarawinefestival.com.*

ONTARIO'S ICE WINES: SWEET SIPPING

Ontario is the world's leading producer of ice wine. It's produced from ripe grapes left on the vine into the winter. When grapes start to freeze, most of the water in them solidifies, resulting in a fructose-laden, aromatic, and flavorful center. Ice-wine grapes must be picked at freezing temperatures before sunrise and basket-pressed immediately. By nature ice wine is sweet, and when well made it smells of dried fruits, apricots, and honey and has a long, refreshing finish. Vidal grapes are ideal for ice wine, due to their thick skin and resistance to cracking in subzero temperatures. The thin-skinned Riesling yields better results but is susceptible to cracking and ripens much later than Vidal. Drink ice wine after dinner, with a not-too-sweet dessert, or alongside a strong cheese. Here in Niagara it also appears in unexpected places such as tea, martinis, chocolate, ice cream, French toast, and glazes for meat and seafood.

Updated by Sarah Richards

The rush of 700,000 gallons of water a second. The divinely sweet, crisp taste of ice wine. The tug of a fish hooked under a layer of ice. Sure, the big-city scene in Toronto delivers the hustle and bustle you came for, but escaping the city can transport you to another world. The struggle is choosing which world to visit first.

There's Niagara Falls, acres of local vineyards in Niagara-on-the-Lake and the surrounding wine region, or the whimsical "cottage country," with its quiet towns, challenging ski slopes, and lakefront resorts. Two major theater events have long seasons with masterfully orchestrated plays. Or you can hit the outdoors on Bruce Trail, Canada's oldest and longest footpath, which winds from Niagara Falls to Tobermory 885 km (550 miles) north.

If superlatives are what you seek, the mesmerizing and deservedly hyped Niagara Falls, one of—or more technically, three of—the most famous waterfalls in the world, is Ontario's most popular attraction. Worth seeing at least once, it is truly beautiful (say what you will about the showy town behind it).

Oenophile trailblazers should consider Niagara's rapidly developing wine trail. The Niagara Escarpment, hugging Lake Ontario's western shores, is one of the most fertile growing areas in Canada. A lakeshore drive southwest of Toronto yields miles of vineyards and farm-to-table restaurants, culminating in the Victorian white-picket-fence town of Niagara-on-the-Lake, known for its amazing five-star restaurants and hotels and nearly-as-luxurious B&Bs.

Nourish your appreciation for the arts in and around Stratford. Two major theater events, the Stratford Festival and the Shaw Festival (in Niagara-on-the-Lake), have long seasons with masterfully orchestrated plays by William Shakespeare and George Bernard Shaw.

Both outdoors enthusiasts who want to "rough it" and soft-adventure seekers who yearn for a comfortable bed with the glow of a fireplace at night feel the lure of the nearly 3,000-acre Algonquin Provincial Park. Sunday drivers find solace near Georgian Bay and in the Muskokas, part of Ontario's lake-smattered cottage country.

PLANNING

WHEN TO GO

With the exception of destinations like wineries and ski resorts, June through September is prime travel season: Stratford and Shaw festivals are in full swing, hours of operation are longer for most attractions, the mist coming from Niagara Falls is at its most refreshing, and patios are open almost everywhere, not to mention the obvious abundance of water activities and amusement parks.

That said, there's fun to be had in wintertime as well. While Muskoka cottage country, Stratford, and some parks in Algonquin become inaccessible ghost towns between November and April (the time most resorts schedule renovations and maintenance), ski resorts and wineries offer many packages and activities. Enjoy tours on and tastings of one of Ontario's most prized exports during Niagara's Icewine Festival, or enjoy the Canadian winter by snowboarding, skiing, ice fishing, and snowmobiling. Travel around the holiday season to take in the beautiful decorations, lights, and special events.

GETTING HERE AND AROUND

AIR TRAVEL

Toronto's Pearson International Airport, 30 km (18 miles) north of downtown, is the obvious choice. Downtown Toronto's smaller Billy Bishop Toronto City Airport serves mostly Porter Airlines; it gets you Niagara-bound on the Gardiner Expressway in a matter of minutes. Hamilton International Airport is about halfway between Toronto and Niagara Falls. Buffalo Niagara International Airport is 30 miles from Niagara Falls, Ontario, but border crossings can add time to your trip. Or, if you are fortunate enough to have a private plane, some resorts in Muskoka have their own landing strip.

Air Travel Contacts **Billy Bishop Toronto City Airport** ☎ *416/203–6942* 🌐 *www.torontoport.com/airport.aspx.* **Buffalo Niagara International Airport** ☎ *716/630–6000* 🌐 *www.buffaloairport.com.* **Hamilton International Airport** ☎ *905/679–1999* 🌐 *www.flyhi.ca.* **Toronto Pearson International Airport** ☎ *866/207–1690, 416/776–3000* 🌐 *www.torontopearson.com.*

CAR TRAVEL

You can get by without a car in downtown Niagara Falls and Stratford if you book a hotel close to the action.

Avoid Toronto-area highways during weekday rush hours (6:30 to 9:30 am and 3:30 to 6:30 pm). Traffic between Toronto and Hamilton might crawl along at any hour.

Ontario's only toll road is the east–west Highway 407, north of Toronto. It's expensive (22¢–25¢ per kilometer) and has no tollbooths; you will be billed via mail if the system has your state's license plate information on file.

The Ministry of Transportation has updates for roadwork and winter road conditions.

Car Contacts **Ministry of Transportation** ☎ *416/235–4686, 800/268–4686* 🌐 *www.mto.gov.on.ca.*

8

PLANNING YOUR TIME

Toronto is a great base to begin your explorations of Ontario.

One Day: In a long day you could see a matinee at the Shakespeare festival, hit a ski resort north of Toronto, visit a few Niagara Escarpment wineries, or—with some stamina—see Niagara Falls. All these destinations require about four hours of driving time round-trip, not accounting for rush-hour traffic jams.

Two Days: A couple of days are sufficient to get a feel for Niagara Falls, Niagara-on-the-Lake, Stratford, or a Muskoka town or two. Alternatively, head up to Collingwood for an overnight snowboarding or skiing trip.

Four Days: You can decide between an intensive outdoorsy trip in the Algonquin area hiking, biking, camping, canoeing, and exploring; or, a relaxing tour of Niagara Falls and Niagara-on-the-Lake, with some time spent at spas and wineries, biking, and hitting culinary hot spots.

One Week: Combine Stratford and Niagara, or really delve into the Niagara region. (A week is probably too much for just Niagara Falls or just Niagara-on-the-Lake.) Alternatively, you could spend some serious time communing with nature in Algonquin Park and meandering through quaint Muskoka and Georgian Bay towns.

TRAIN TRAVEL

VIA Rail connects Toronto with Niagara Falls and Stratford. GO Transit, Toronto's commuter rail, has summer weekend service to Niagara Falls. Ontario Northland's Northlander line travels between Toronto and Bracebridge, Gravenhurst, Huntsville, and other northern points.

Train Contacts GO Transit ☎ *888/438–6646, 416/869–3200* 🌐 *www.gotransit.com.* **Ontario Northland** ☎ *800/461–8558, 705/472–4500* 🌐 *www.ontarionorthland.ca.* **VIA Rail** ☎ *888/842–7245* 🌐 *www.viarail.ca.*

RESTAURANTS

The dining in Stratford and Niagara-on-the-Lake is enough to boost a whole other genre of tourism, as there are a number of outstanding restaurants thanks to the area's many chefs being trained at the area's reputable culinary schools, and impeccably fresh ingredients from local farms. Produce, meats, cheeses, beers, and wine are all produced in Ontario, and some restaurants even have their own gardens, vineyards, or farms. In the immediate areas surrounding Niagara Falls, the dining is a little more lackluster, as views, convenience, and glamour take precedence over food, but there are some great pubs and upscale restaurants to be found among the tourist traps. Reservations are always encouraged, if not essential.

HOTELS

Make reservations well in advance during summer and at ski areas in winter. Prices are higher in peak season and nearer to the tourist centers. In Niagara Falls, for example, hotel rates are determined by proximity to the falls. Taxes are seldom included in quoted prices, but rates sometimes include food, especially in more remote areas such as Muskoka, where many resorts offer meal plans.

At the Cottage. Cottage rentals are available through local tourism boards or At the Cottage. ☎ *416/466–1452, 888/394–8884* 🌐 *www.atthecottage.com.*

BBCanada.com. BBCanada.com can help you locate a B&B and reserve a room. ☎ *800/239–1141* 🌐 *www.bbcanada.com.*

Federation of Ontario Bed & Breakfast Accommodations. A comprehensive B&B guide listing about 250 establishments is published by the Federation of Ontario Bed & Breakfast Accommodations. 🌐 *www.fobba.com.*

Camping, in campgrounds or backcountry, is popular in summer and early fall, especially in the provincial parks to the north of Toronto.

VISITOR INFORMATION

Niagara Falls Tourism ☎ *800/563–2557* 🌐 *www.niagarafallstourism.com.*

Ontario Parks ☎ *800/668–2746, 905/754–1958* 🌐 *www.ontarioparks.com.*

Ontario Tourism ☎ *800/668–2746, 905/754–1958* 🌐 *www.ontariotravel.net.*

Tourism Niagara ☎ *905/945–5444, 800/263–2988* 🌐 *www.tourismniagara.com.*

NIAGARA FALLS

130 km (81 miles) south of Toronto via the QEW (Queen Elizabeth Way).

Fodor's Choice ★ **Niagara Falls.** Although cynics have had a field day with Niagara Falls (most memorably, Oscar Wilde called it "the second major disappointment of American married life"), most visitors are truly impressed. The falls are actually three cataracts: the American and Bridal Veil Falls in New York State, and the Horseshoe Falls in Ontario. In terms of sheer volume of water—more than 700,000 gallons per second in summer—Niagara is unsurpassed in North America.

On the Canadian side, you can get a far view of the American Falls and a close-up of the Horseshoe Falls. You can also park your car for the day in any of several lots and hop onto one of the WEGO buses, which run continuously to all the sights along the river. If you want to get close to the foot of the falls, the *Maid of the Mist* boat takes you near enough to get soaked in the spray.

After experiencing the falls from the Canadian side, you can walk or drive across Rainbow Bridge to the U.S. side. On the American side you can park in the lot on Goat Island near the American Falls and walk along the path beside the Niagara River, which becomes more and more turbulent as it approaches the big drop-off of just over 200 feet.

The amusement parks and tacky souvenir shops that surround the falls attest to the area's history as a major tourist attraction. Most of the gaudiness is contained on Clifton Hill, Niagara Falls' Times Square. Despite these garish efforts to attract visitors, the landscaped grounds immediately bordering the falls are lovely and the beauty of the falls remains untouched.

Clifton Hill's food, shopping, games, rides, and other attractions will keep the whole family entertained.

One reason to spend the night here is to admire the falls illumination, which takes place every night of the year, from dusk until at least 10 pm (as late as 1 am during the summer). Even the most contemptuous observer will be mesmerized as the falls change from red to purple to blue to green to white, and finally all the colors of the rainbow in harmony.

WHEN TO GO

Water-based falls tours operate only between mid-May and mid-September, and the summer weather combats the chilly falls mist. Fewer events take place in other seasons, and it's too cold in winter to linger on the promenade along the parkway next to the falls, but it's much easier to reserve a window-side table for two at a falls-view restaurant. Clifton Hill and most indoor attractions are open year-round. At any time of year it feels a few degrees cooler on the walkway near the falls.

GETTING HERE AND AROUND

Niagara Falls is easily accessible by car and train from Toronto. VIA Rail and GO (summer only) trains serve Niagara Falls, both stopping at the main rail station, not far from the falls. The nearest airports are in Toronto, Hamilton, and Buffalo, New York. It is possible to use public transportation and cabs to get around, but a car is more flexible and is recommended. There is no public transport between Niagara Falls and Niagara-on-the-Lake, 20 km (12 miles) north.

The four- to eight-lane Queen Elizabeth Way—better known as the QEW—runs from the U.S. border at Fort Erie through the Niagara region to Toronto.

PARKING In Niagara Falls, parking prices increase closer to the falls. It can be triple the price to park along the Niagara Parkway (C$15/day) than it is up the hill near Victoria Street (usually C$5/day). If you park up top, know that the walk down to the falls is a steep one. You might want to take a taxi back up, or hop aboard the Falls Incline Railway, a funicular that operates between the Table Rock Centre and Portage Road behind the Konica Minolta Tower. The trip takes about one minute and costs C$2.50 (day passes are available for C$6).

SHUTTLE Available year-round, climate-controlled WEGO buses travel on a loop route on the Niagara Parkway between the Table Rock Centre and the Whirlpool Aero Car parking lot (9 km [6 miles] north) and as far north as Queenston Heights Park, 15 km (9 miles) downriver. A day pass, available from Welcome Centres and at any booth on the system, is C$7 per person per day (get the second day free from late October to mid-April). You can get on and off as many times as you wish at well-marked stops along the route, and buses pick up frequently (every 20 minutes).

FIRST THINGS FIRST

Start at the **Table Rock Centre** (✉ *6650 Niagara Pkwy., about 500 meters south of Murray Hill*) for a close-up of Horseshoe Falls. Here you can buy a Niagara Parks Great Gorge Adventure Pass, tickets for the WEGO buses, and do the Journey Behind the Falls and Niagara's Fury. At the end of the WEGO line, it's easy to hop aboard and do all the falls-front sights in a northward direction. Starting with the *Maid of the Mist* or a Jet Boat Tour when you arrive is also a good way to get your feet wet—literally.

BORDER CROSSINGS Everyone—including children and U.S. citizens—must have a passport or other approved travel document (e.g. a New York State–issued "enhanced" driver's license) to enter the United States. Go to the Department of Homeland Security website (🌐 *www.dhs.gov*) for the latest information. Avoid crossing the border at high-traffic times, especially Friday and Saturday nights. The Canada Border Agency and the U.S. Customs and Border Protection list border wait times into Canada and into the U.S., respectively, online at 🌐 *www.cbsa-asfc.gc.ca/bwt-taf* and 🌐 *apps.cbp.gov/bwt*. Crossings are at the Peace Bridge (Fort Erie, ON–Buffalo, NY), the Queenston–Lewiston Bridge (Queenston, ON–Lewiston, NY), and the Rainbow Bridge (Niagara Falls, ON–Niagara Falls, NY).

DISCOUNTS AND DEALS

Pick up the free Save-A-Buck coupon booklet for discounts on various tours, attractions, and restaurants. **TIP→ Many attractions have significant online discounts and combination tickets.** Bundled passes are available through the tourism board, at Welcome Centres (foot of Clifton Hill and Murray Hill, near *Maid of the Mist* ticket booth, Table Rock Centre), and at most attractions' ticket windows.

The **Clifton Hill Fun Pass** incorporates entry to six of the better Clifton Hill attractions (including the SkyWheel and the Midway Combo Pass rides) for C$29.95 plus tax. The Midway Combo Pass (C$9.99 plus tax) includes two indoor thrill rides: Ghost Blasters and the FX Ride Theatre.

The **Niagara Falls and Great Gorge Pass** (C$46.95; available mid-April–late October) covers admission to Journey Behind the Falls, *Maid of the Mist*, White Water Walk, and Niagara's Fury, plus a number of discounts and two days of unlimited use of both the WEGO buses and the Falls Incline Railway. It's available from Niagara Parks, as is the **Winter Magic Pass** (C$28; available late October–mid-April), which includes Niagara's Fury, the Butterfly Conservatory, Journey Behind the Falls, and discount coupons.

TOURIST INFORMATION

The main Niagara Falls Tourism center is on Robinson Street near the Skylon Tower.

Open June through August, Welcome Centres are run by Niagara Parks and have tickets for and information about Niagara Parks sights, including WEGO and Falls Incline Railway passes and the Niagara Falls and Great Gorge Adventure Pass. Welcome Centre kiosks are at the foot of Clifton Hill, foot of Murray Hill, and near the *Maid of the Mist* ticket booth; a Welcome Centre booth is inside the Table Rock Centre.

ESSENTIALS

Discounts and Deals **Clifton Hill Fun Pass** ⊕ *www.cliftonhill.com.* **Save-A-Buck coupon booklet** ⊕ *www.saveabuck.com.*

Transportation Contacts **GO Transit** ☎ *888/438–6646, 416/869–3200* ⊕ *www.gotransit.com.* **Niagara Falls VIA Rail Canada Train Station** ✉ *4267 Bridge St.* ☎ *888/842–7245.***VIA Rail** ☎ *888/842–7245* ⊕ *www.viarail.ca.* **WEGO** ☎ *905/356–1179* ⊕ *www.wegoniagarafalls.com.*

Visitor Information **Niagara Falls Tourism** ✉ *5400 Robinson St.* ☎ *905/356–6061, 800/563–2557* ⊕ *www.niagarafallstourism.com.* **Niagara Parks** ☎ *905/371–0254, 877/642–7275* ⊕ *www.niagaraparks.com.*

EXPLORING

TOP ATTRACTIONS

FAMILY **Clifton Hill.** This is undeniably the most crassly commercial district of Niagara Falls, with haunted houses, more wax museums than one usually sees in a lifetime, and fast-food chains galore (admittedly, the Burger King here is unique for its gigantic Frankenstein statue towering above). For kids the entertainment is endless—especially kids who enjoy arcade games—and the SkyWheel is interesting for all ages. Attractions are typically open late (midnight–2 am in summer, 11 pm off-season), with admission ranging from about C$10 to C$16. The most popular attractions include: The 175-foot **SkyWheel** (✉ *4950 Clifton Hill* ☎ *905/358–4793 C$10.99*) has enclosed, climate-controlled compartments. Next door, **Dinosaur Adventure Golf** (✉ *4960 Clifton Hill* ☎ *905/358–3676 C$9.99*) combines mini golf, ferocious mechanical dinosaurs, and an erupting mini volcano. The **Great Canadian Midway** (✉ *4950 Clifton Hill* ☎ *905/358–3676*) is a 70,000-square-foot entertainment complex with arcade games, a bowling alley, air hockey, and food. **Ripley's Believe It or Not! Museum** (✉ *4960 Clifton Hill* ☎ *905/356–2261* ripleysniagara.com) is creepily fascinating. **Movieland Wax Museum** (✉ *4960 Clifton Hill*

NIAGARA FALLS: PAST AND FUTURE

The story begins more than 10,000 years ago as a group of glaciers receded, diverting the waters of Lake Erie north into Lake Ontario. The force and volume of the water as it flowed over the Niagara Escarpment created the thundering cataracts. Erosion has been considerable since then, more than 7 miles in all, as the soft shale and sandstone of the escarpment have been washed away and the falls have receded. Diversions of the water for power generation have slowed the erosion somewhat, spreading the flow more evenly over the entire crestline of Horseshoe Falls. The erosion is now down to 1 foot or less per year.

At this rate—given effects of power generation and change in riverbed composition—geologists estimate it will be some 50,000 years before the majestic cascade is reduced to rapids somewhere near present-day Buffalo, 20 miles to the south.

☎ *905/358–3061*) has such lifelike characters as Harry Potter and Barack and Michelle Obama. The **Hershey Store** (✉ *5685 Falls Ave.* ☎ *800/468–1714*) is 7,000 square feet of truffles, fudge, and the trademark Kisses, marked by a six-story chocolate bar at the base of the hill, on the other side of Casino Niagara. ✉ *Clifton Hill* ☎ *905/358–3676* 🌐 *www.cliftonhill.com.*

Fallsview Casino Resort. Canada's largest gaming and resort facility crowns the city's skyline, overlooking the Niagara Parks with picture-perfect views of the falls. Within the 30-story complex are Canada's first casino wedding chapel, a glitzy theater, spa, shops, plenty of restaurants and, for the gaming enthusiasts, more than 100 gaming tables and 3,000 slot machines on one of the largest casino gaming floors in the world. The Las Vegas–style Avalon Ballroom showcases a wide array of talents, from Al Pacino to Jon Stewart. ✉ *6380 Fallsview Blvd.* ☎ *888/325–5788, 905/371–7505* 🌐 *www.fallsviewcasinoresort.com.*

FAMILY Fodor's Choice ★ ***Maid of the Mist.*** Boats have been operating for *Maid of the Mist* since 1846, when they were wooden-hulled, coal-fired steamboats. Today, double-deck steel vessels tow fun-loving passengers on 30-minute journeys to the foot of the falls, where the spray is so heavy that ponchos must be distributed. From the observation areas along the falls, you can see those boarding the boats in their blue slickers. **TIP→ Unless you cower in the center of the boat, your shoes and pants will get wet: wear quick-drying items or bring spares.** ✉ *Tickets and entrance at foot of Clifton Hill on falls side of Niagara Pkwy.* ☎ *905/358–0311* 🌐 *www.maidofthemist.com* 🎫 *C$19.75* 🕙 *May–late Oct. 9 am–7:45 pm, departs every 15 mins.*

FAMILY **Marineland.** A theme park with a marine show, wildlife displays, rides, and aquariums—including a beluga whale habitat with underwater viewing areas where you can pet and feed the whale—Marineland is 1½ km (1 mile) south of the falls. The daily marine shows include performing killer whales, dolphins, harbor seals, and sea lions.

Children can pet and feed deer at the Deer Park. Among the many rides are Dragon Mountain, the world's largest steel roller coaster, and Ocean Odyssey. ✉ *7657 Portage Rd., off Niagara Parkway or QEW (McLeod Rd. exit)* ☎ *905/356–9565* 🌐 *www.marinelandcanada.com* 🎫 *C$42.96* ⏲ *Mid-May–late June and early Sept.–mid-Oct., daily 10–dusk (ticket booths close at 5); late June–early Sept. daily 9:30–dusk (ticket booths close at 6).*

Niagara Parks Botanical Gardens and School of Horticulture. Professional gardeners have graduated from here since 1936; 100 acres of immaculately maintained gardens are open to the public. Within the Botanical Gardens is the **Niagara Parks Butterfly Conservatory,** housing one of North America's largest collections of free-flying butterflies—at least 2,000 butterflies from 50 species around the world are protected in a climate-controlled, rain forest–like conservatory. **TIP→ Between May and mid-October, for C$18.50 per person, you can tour the gardens in a horse and carriage.** ✉ *2565 Niagara Pkwy* ☎ *905/356–8554, 877/642–7275* 🌐 *www.niagaraparks.com* 🎫 *parking C$5* ⏲ *Gardens daily dawn–dusk; Butterfly Conservatory daily, hrs vary.*

FAMILY **Skylon Tower.** Rising 775 feet above the falls, this is the best view of the great Niagara Gorge and the entire city. The indoor-outdoor observation deck has visibility up to 130 km (80 miles) on a clear day. Other reasons to visit include amusements for children, a revolving dining room, a gaming arcade, and a 3-D theater that lets you experience the falls up close. Tickets are sometimes as much as 50% off if purchased online. ✉ *5200 Robinson St.* ☎ *905/356–2651, 800/814–9577* 🌐 *www.skylon.com* 🎫 *C$11.99* ⏲ *Mid-June–early Sept., daily 8 am–midnight; early Sept.–mid June, 9 am–10 pm most days.*

Whirlpool Aero Car. In operation since 1916, this antique cable car crosses the Whirlpool Basin in the Niagara Gorge. This trip is not for the faint-hearted, but there's no better way to get an aerial view of the gorge, the whirlpool, the rapids, and the hydroelectric plants. ✉ *3850 Niagara Pkwy., 4½ km (3 miles) north of falls* ☎ *905/371–0254, 877/642–7275* 🌐 *www.niagaraparks.com* 🎫 *C$13.50* ⏲ *Mid-Mar.–late Jun. and early Sept.–early Nov. 10–5; late Jun.–early Sept. 9–8.*

White Water Walk. A self-guided route involves taking an elevator to the bottom of the Niagara Gorge, the narrow valley created by the Niagara Falls and River, where you can walk along a 1,000-foot boardwalk beside the Class VI rapids of the Niagara River. The gorge is rimmed by sheer cliffs as it enters the giant whirlpool. ✉ *4330 Niagara Pkwy., 3 km (2 miles) north of falls* ☎ *905/371–0254, 877/642–7275* 🌐 *www.niagaraparks.com* 🎫 *C$10.95* ⏲ *Early Apr.–mid-Nov. daily 10–4:30, weather permitting.*

WORTH NOTING

FAMILY **Bird Kingdom.** A tropical respite from the crowds and Las Vegas–style attractions, Bird Kingdom is the world's largest indoor aviary, with over 400 free-flying birds and more than 35 exotic-bird species in the 50,000-square-foot complex. For creepy-crawly lovers, there are also spiders, lizards, and snakes—including a 100-pound python that you can hold. Check online for a schedule of feeding times. Parking

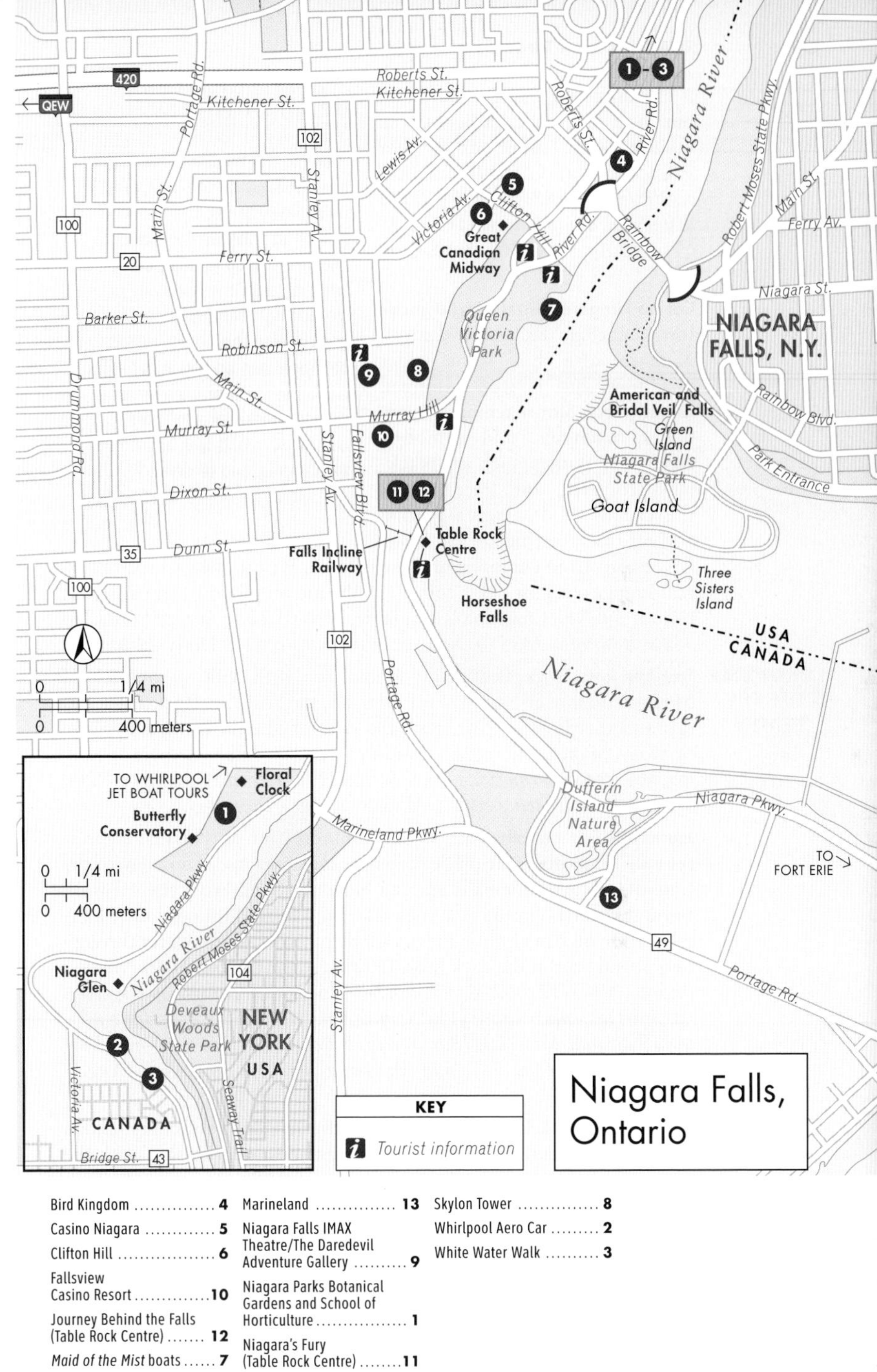

Bird Kingdom **4**
Casino Niagara **5**
Clifton Hill **6**
Fallsview Casino Resort **10**
Journey Behind the Falls (Table Rock Centre) **12**
Maid of the Mist boats **7**
Marineland **13**
Niagara Falls IMAX Theatre/The Daredevil Adventure Gallery **9**
Niagara Parks Botanical Gardens and School of Horticulture **1**
Niagara's Fury (Table Rock Centre) **11**
Skylon Tower **8**
Whirlpool Aero Car **2**
White Water Walk **3**

is an additional C$2 per half hour, but there's a public lot behind the building (on Hiram Street) that is C$5 per day. ✉ *5651 River Rd.* ☎ *905/356–8888, 866/994–0090* 🌐 *www.birdkingdom.ca* 🎫 *C$16.95* ⏲ *Jul.–Aug. 9–6:30; Sept.–Jun. 9:30–5.*

WORD OF MOUTH

"Cave of the Winds—loved loved loved this. By far the best, most unique way to see the falls. It is a winding stairway down and up, and you end up at one point on what is called the hurricane deck. No kidding! Walking up the stairs approaching the American Falls pouring down on you, it is hard to climb the stairs or even breathe with the sheer force of water coming at you. It was amazing, exhilarating, and terrifying!"
—LizaMarie

Casino Niagara. Smaller and more low-key than Fallsview, Casino Niagara also has some older machines, but is well equipped nonetheless. Slot machines, video-poker machines, and gambling tables for games such as blackjack, roulette, and baccarat fill this casino. Multisports wagering and off-track betting are available. Diversions from gambling are also offered. Within the casino are several lounges, a Yuk Yuk's comedy club, and an all-you-can-eat buffet restaurant. Valet parking is available. ✉ *5705 Falls Ave.* ☎ *905/374–3598, 888/946–3255* 🌐 *www.casinoniagara.com* ⏲ *Daily 24 hrs.*

OFF THE BEATEN PATH

Fort Erie Race Track. Beautifully landscaped with willows, manicured hedges, and flower-bordered infield lakes, the Fort Erie Race Track has dirt and turf horse racing, with the year's highlight being the Prince of Wales Stakes, the second jewel in Canada's Triple Crown of Racing. ✉ *230 Catherine St., off QEW Exit 2, Fort Erie* ☎ *905/871–3200* 🌐 *www.forterieracing.com* ⏲ *May–Nov., Sat.–Tues. 9–3.*

Journey Behind the Falls. This 30-to-45-minute tour starts with an elevator ride to an observation deck that provides an eye-level view of the Canadian Horseshoe Falls and the Niagara River. From there a walk through tunnels cut into the rock takes you behind thunderous waterfalls, and you can glimpse the back side of the crashing water through two portals cut in the rock face. ✉ *Table Rock Centre, 6650 Niagara Pkwy.* ☎ *905/371–0254, 877/642–7275* 🌐 *www.niagaraparks.com* 🎫 *Mid-Dec.–mid-Apr. C$11.25, mid-Apr.–Dec. C$15.95* ⏲ *Jan.–mid-May 9–5; mid-Mar.–late Mar. and mid-Oct.–Dec. 9–6; Apr.–mid-May and Sept.–mid-Oct. 9–7; mid-May–mid-June 9–8; mid-June–Aug. 9 am–10 pm.*

Niagara Falls IMAX Theatre/The Daredevil Adventure Gallery. Get the human story behind the falls, from local native tribes' relationship with the waters to the foolhardy folks who went over the edge, with *The Falls Movie: Legends and Daredevils* on the six-story IMAX screen. The Daredevil Adventure Gallery chronicles the expeditions of those who have tackled the falls and has some of the actual barrels they used on display. ✉ *6170 Fallsview Blvd.* ☎ *905/358–3611, 866/405–4629* 🌐 *imaxniagara.com* 🎫 *Movie C$12.50; exhibit C$8* ⏲ *Shows on the hr Nov.–Apr., daily 10–4; May, Sept., and Oct., daily 9–8; June–Aug., daily 9–9.*

Rides on the *Maid of the Mist* have been thrilling visitors to Niagara Falls since 1846.

FAMILY **Niagara's Fury.** Learn how Niagara Falls formed over thousands of years on this 20-minute simulation ride. Standing on a mesh platform surrounded by an uninterrupted 360-degree viewing screen, you feel snow falling, winds blowing, the floor rumbling, and waves crashing as you watch glaciers form, collide, and melt, creating the falls as we know them today. **TIP→ In certain spots you will get wet; ponchos are provided.** ✉ *Table Rock Centre, 6650 Niagara Pkwy.* ☎ *905/371–0254, 877/642–7275* 🌐 *www.niagaraparks.com* 🎟 *C$15* ⏲ *July and Aug. 9–9, shows every 15 mins; Sept.–June 10:30–4, shows every 30 mins.*

8

WHERE TO EAT

Dining in Niagara Falls is still a bit disappointing because of the lack of sophistication that usually comes with a highly touristic area (especially when compared with the neighboring foodie paradise Niagara-on-the-Lake). A view of the falls and convenient location don't come cheap, so prices are rarely what one would consider reasonable. Thankfully, the landscape is slowly changing, and some falls-view restaurants, such as 21 Club, are hiring creative chefs who are stepping up the quality—though still at a pretty penny. But with views like these, it might be worth it.

$$$$ STEAKHOUSE ✕ **21 Club.** The best fine-dining-with-a-view in town, 21 Club plays up its casino locale without being kitschy. The tall-ceilinged, modern space is inspired by roulette, in a profusion of red, black, and gold, and juxtaposes the traditional steak house menu. More secluded seating areas wind around the perimeter next to huge windows overlooking the falls, on a raised, illuminated floor on a patio. The menu is seasonal,

but you might start out with fresh oysters or roasted beet salad, then move on to Canadian or USDA Prime steak, Arctic char with warm potato salad, or a rack of lamb with parsnip purée and minted *jus*. The decadent chocolate mousse—with espresso and mocha *anglaise*—is a memorable dessert. Because 21 Club is accessible only via the casino floor, all diners must be at least 19. $ *Average main: C$40 ✉ Fallsview Casino Resort, 6380 Fallsview Blvd., Niagara Falls ☎ 905/358–3255, 888/325–5788 ⊕ www.fallsviewcasinoresort.com/dining ✍ Reservations essential ⊗ Closed Tues. and Wed. No lunch.*

$$$$ ITALIAN Fodor's Choice ★ ✕ **Casa Mia Ristorante.** Fresh, quality ingredients done simply and in generous portions are what make this off-the-beaten-path restaurant, about a 10-minute drive from the falls. A free shuttle service from Niagara Falls hotels whisks guests to this labor of love, owned and operated by the Mollica family. Modern Amalfi Coast–inspired decor brings a seaside terrace indoors, and it all feels miles, not minutes, away from the city's tourist attractions. To start, try a delectable *bresaola* (air-dried salted beef) served with arugula, Parmigiano-Reggiano shavings, and fragrant truffled dwarf peaches, drizzled with balsamic vinegar and truffle oil. Move on to tender pieces of shredded duck confit over linguine in a white-truffle–duck-broth reduction. A sommelier is on hand with suggestions from the 300-plus-label cellar. $ *Average main: C$35 ✉ 3518 Portage Rd. ☎ 905/356–5410, 888/956–5410 ⊕ www.casamiaristorante.com ✍ Reservations essential ⊗ No lunch Sat.–Sun.*

$$ AMERICAN ✕ **Edgewaters Restaurant.** Inside a former refectory building, this second-floor restaurant operated by Niagara Parks has a huge veranda overlooking the falls, across Niagara Parkway. Secondary to the view, the decor and menu are reflective of those in a diner—standard options of burgers, salads, pasta, and steaks served to small wooden tables. The location is prime and the patio is the perfect place to enjoy the view. Reservations are taken online, and you should make one if you want one of the coveted patio tables closest to the falls. Live amplified music often accompanies dinner in summer. $ *Average main: C$17 ✉ 6345 Niagara Pkwy., at Murray St. ☎ 905/356–2217 ⊕ www.niagaraparks.com/dining ⊗ Closed mid-Oct.–early May.*

$$ CANADIAN ✕ **Elements on the Falls.** Most tourists end up at the Table Rock Centre, where you can buy tickets for most of the attractions in Niagara Falls and peer over the brink of Horseshoe Falls. There are a fair number of fast-food restaurants—Burger Town, Tim Horton's, and a sushi takeout station—but upstairs, you can find casual fine dining in Elements on the Falls. The menu includes everything from seasonal Canadian fare, such as bison in wild-mushroom sauce and pork medallions with braised red cabbage, to Angus sirloin steak, which isn't terribly overpriced. The decor is simple but modern, and your meal can be enjoyed next to tall windows overlooking the falls or from the terrace. $ *Average main: C$20 ✉ Table Rock Centre, 6650 Niagara Pkwy., 2nd fl. ☎ 905/354–3631 ⊕ www.niagaraparks.com/dining.*

$$ JAPANESE ✕ **Hotei Sushi.** In a tourist area of mostly gaudy steak houses and themed restaurants sits this renovated sushi restaurant showing simplicity and refinement. The decor, donimated by wood in the floors,

chairs, and tables, and set off by dark walls, gives the space a sense of relaxation and sets the mood for the forthcoming plates of beautifully presented, fresh sushi and sashimi. The tempura-battered Shibuki roll of shrimp, avocado, and spicy sauce is a popular item, as are other rolls and standard sushi dishes. *Average main: C$20 ✉ 6175 Dunn St., Niagara Falls ☎ 905/371–2227 🌐 www.hoteisushi.com ⏲ No lunch Sat.–Sun.*

WORD OF MOUTH

"Yes, you can do *Maid of the Mist*, Cave of the Winds, Journey Behind the Falls, etc., all in one day. Many people do—I have done it. It's doable. But, that does mean that you are spending all your time rushing around from one activity to the next without being able to just soak up the mist. If you've got the time, spread it out and enjoy it."

—toedtoes

$$$ STEAKHOUSE ✕ **Lucky's Steakhouse.** Heavy soundproof doors insulate this classy 1920s-style steak house from the less glamorous and very loud Casino Niagara where it's located. Inside the intimate second-story dining room, all is quiet and comfortably chic, with gleaming hardwood floors, a floor-to-ceiling wine cabinet along one wall, semicircular leather booths, and music provided by some of the greats (Ella Fitzgerald, Frank Sinatra) whose black-and-white portraits adorn the brick walls. Tall windows provide lots of light but, alas, only street views. The menu includes a wide range of choices and prices, from garlic-rubbed thin-crust pizza to surf and turf, but the house specialties are the chops and steaks: filet mignon, prime rib, T-bone, and more. *Average main: C$30 ✉ Casino Niagara, 5705 Falls Ave., 2nd. flr. ☎ 905/374–3598 🌐 www.casinoniagara.com ⏲ No lunch. Closed Mon. and Tues.*

8

$$ ITALIAN ✕ **Napoli Ristorante e Pizzeria.** On busy Ferry Street, Napoli is just a five-minute drive from Clifton Hill but it's a local joint that manages to be both casual and refined. Sit in the back room if possible, where exposed-brick columns and black-and-white photos of Naples on the walls set the scene for the southern Italian pasta dishes and thin-crust pizzas. The extensive menu includes 10 pizzas with crisp, wafer-thin crusts and generous dollops of tomato sauce, and plenty of pasta dishes and hearty meat dishes to choose from. Start with a garlicky bruschetta before an entrée like homemade roasted sausage with baked polenta and rapini or fettuccine in a red-pepper-spiced oil-and-garlic sauce with anchovies, bread crumbs, and Pecorino. Wines are mostly Italian or Niagara. You can order pizzas for pick-up. *Average main: C$16 ✉ 5485 Ferry St. ☎ 905/356–3345 🌐 www.napoliristorante.ca ⏲ No lunch.*

$$$$ AMERICAN ✕ **Skylon Tower.** The big draw here is the view from the **Revolving Dining Room:** perched 520 feet above the Horseshoe Falls, it's simply breathtaking. And the atmosphere puts this restaurant above those serving similar cuisine in the area, drawing an eclectic crowd of couples in cocktail attire and families in casual clothes. The menu revolves as well: prime rib with horseradish sauce and chicken cordon bleu have made appearances. **The Summit Suite Buffet Dining Room,** an all-you-can-eat buffet restaurant one level up, doesn't revolve, but has comparable

views for slightly less and serves a popular Sunday brunch. A reservation at either restaurant includes free admission to the observation deck, which makes the prices (upward of C$50 per person at the Revolving Dining Room; C$40 prix-fixe dinner at the Summit Suite) a little easier to digest, considering the food is secondary to the view. *Average main: C$55* ✉ *5200 Robinson St.* ☎ *905/356–2651, 800/814–9577* 🌐 *www.skylon.com* *Reservations essential* *Summit Suite closed Nov.–Apr. but open for Sun. brunch year-round.*

WHERE TO STAY

For expanded hotel reviews, visit Fodors.com.

A room with a view of the falls means staying in a high-rise hotel, usually a chain. Hotels with falls views are clustered near the two streets leading down to the falls, Clifton Hill (and adjacent Victoria Avenue), and Murray Street (and adjacent Fallsview Boulevard), also called Murray Hill. Families gravitate toward Clifton Hill, with its video arcades, chain restaurants, and *Maid of the Mist* docking at the end of the street. Murray Hill, where the Fallsview Casino is, is less ostentatious and closer to the falls.

Niagara Falls has plenty of B&Bs, but they're mediocre compared to those in Niagara-on-the-Lake, 20 km (12 miles) north. All the hotels we recommend here are within walking distance of the falls.

$ HOTEL **Country Inn & Suites.** If you're on a budget but not willing to stay at a dingy motor lodge, this seven-story hotel is probably your best choice. **Pros:** low-cost parking (C$8 a day); breakfast and high-speed Internet included; within walking distance of Clifton Hill. **Cons:** no views to speak of; 15-minute walk down to the falls. *Rooms from: C$110* ✉ *5525 Victoria Ave.* ☎ *905/374–6040, 800/263–2571* 🌐 *www.countryinns.com* *49 rooms, 59 suites* *Breakfast.*

$$$$ HOTEL Fodor's Choice ★ **Fallsview Casino Resort.** With the most coveted rooms and the best restaurants, shopping, gaming facilities, and views—all 35 stories overlook the Horseshoe, American, and Bridal Veil falls thanks to its lofty locale—Fallsview Casino Resort is *the* place to be in Niagara Falls. ⇨ *Where to Eat***Pros:** the most glamorous address in Niagara Falls; first-class accommodation; great entertainment; biggest casino in town; excellent fitness, spa, and pool facilities, amenities, and service. **Cons:** pricey; rooms fill up fast. *Rooms from: C$349* ✉ *6380 Fallsview Blvd.* ☎ *905/358–3255, 888/946–3255* 🌐 *www.fallsviewcasinoresort.com* *289 rooms, 85 suites* *No meals.*

$$$$ RESORT FAMILY **Great Wolf Lodge.** Instead of the usual casino-and-slot-machine ambience in other area hotels, you'll find a spectacular water park of 12 slides, seven pools, water fort, outdoor hot tubs, and other fun water facilities for the kids. **Pros:** great variety of water slides and facilities. **Cons:** rooms are mostly open concept, so there is less privacy for the parents. *Rooms from: C$320* ✉ *3950 Victoria Ave.* ☎ *905/354–4888, 888/878–1818* 🌐 *www.greatwolf.com* *406 suites* *No meals.*

$$$ HOTEL **Sheraton on the Falls.** Just steps from the Niagara Parkway and *Maid of the Mist* ticket booth is this 22-story tower at the corner of Clifton Hill, and it's the most polished option in that area. **Pros:** at the bottom of Clifton Hill and very close to the falls; updated rooms; breakfast

overlooking all three falls is a great start to the day. **Cons:** no views from rooms below sixth floor; expensive Wi-Fi and parking. *Rooms from: C$239* ✉ *5875 Falls Ave.* ☎ *905/374–4445, 888/229–9961* 🌐 *www.sheratononthefalls.com* *660 rooms, 10 suites* *No meals.*

$$$ B&B/INN **Sterling Inn & Spa.** Unique among the chain options in Niagara Falls is this boutique hotel in a converted 1930s milk factory—hence the bottle-shaped building face. **Pros:** big rooms; modern design; AG restaurant serves good locally sourced cuisine; romantic setting; noteworthy spa. **Cons:** no views; subterranean restaurant; north of Victoria Avenue opposite the top of Clifton Hill, about a 20-minute walk to the base of Clifton Hill. *Rooms from: C$250* ✉ *5195 Magdalen St.* ☎ *289/292–0000, 877/783–7772* 🌐 *www.sterlingniagara.com* *41 rooms* *Breakfast.*

SPORTS AND THE OUTDOORS

Niagara Glen. The 82.5-acre Niagara Glen nature reserve has 4 km (2.5 miles) of hiking trails through forested paths that pass giant boulders left behind as the falls eroded the land away thousands of years ago. Some trails are steep and rough, and the Glen has an elevation change of more than 200 feet. 🌐 *www.niagaraparks.com/nature-trails.*

Niagara Parks Commission. The Niagara Parks Commission has information on hiking and biking trails, local parks, restaurants, and the Niagara Gorge. ☎ *905/371–0254, 877/642–7275* 🌐 *www.niagaraparks.com.*

Niagara River Recreation Trail. From Fort Erie to Niagara-on-the-Lake, this recreation trail is 56 km (35 miles) of bicycle trails along the Niagara River. The 29-km (18-mile) route between Niagara Falls and Niagara-on-the-Lake is paved. The trail is divided into four sections, each with site-specific history: Niagara-on-the-Lake to Queenston; Queenston to the Whirlpool Aero Car; Chippawa to Black Creek; and Black Creek to Fort Erie. 🌐 *www.niagaraparks.com/nature-trails.*

Ontario Trails Council. Ontario Trails Council has information and maps about hikes in the province. ☎ *877/668–7245, 613/389–7678* 🌐 *www.ontariotrails.on.ca.*

NIAGARA WINE REGION

Ontarians have been growing Concord grapes for (sweet) wine in the Niagara region since the 1800s, but experiments with European *Vitis vinifera* species between the 1950s and 1970s led to more serious wine production. Today, the Niagara Peninsula is Canada's largest viticulture area, accounting for nearly 80% of the country's growing volume. More than 60 wineries reside here, either north of St. Catharines spread out across the largely rural Niagara Escarpment, or south of St. Catharines, in close proximity to pretty, Victorian-tinged Niagara-on-the-Lake.

But wine tasting isn't the only game in the Peninsula. Niagara-on-the-Lake draws theatergoers to its annual Shaw Festival and food lovers to its unparalleled restaurants. The Niagara Escarpment is a prime Sunday-drive destination, with winding country roads, the charming town of Jordan, and a couple of diamond-in-the-rough restaurants.

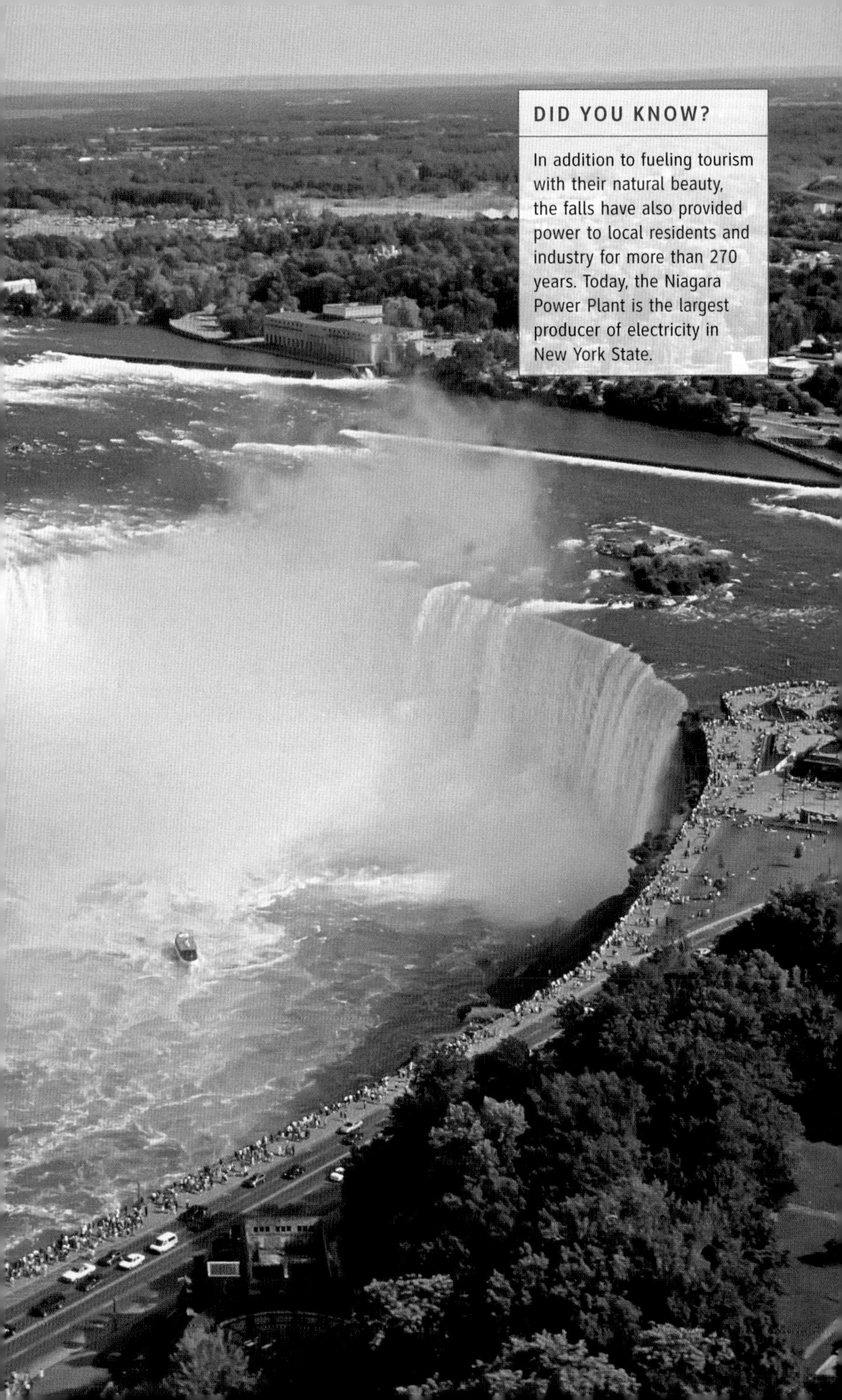

DID YOU KNOW?

In addition to fueling tourism with their natural beauty, the falls have also provided power to local residents and industry for more than 270 years. Today, the Niagara Power Plant is the largest producer of electricity in New York State.

NIAGARA-ON-THE-LAKE

15 km (9 miles) north of Niagara Falls and 130 km (80 miles) south of Toronto.

The hub of the Niagara wine region is the town of Niagara-on-the-Lake (sometimes abbreviated NOTL). Since 1962 this town of 14,000 residents has been considered the southern outpost of fine summer theater in Ontario because of its acclaimed Shaw Festival. As one of the country's prettiest and best-preserved Victorian towns, Niagara-on-the-Lake has architectural sights, shops, flower-lined streets and plentiful ornamental gardens in summer, quality theater nearly year-round, and some of the best chefs and hoteliers in the country.

WHEN TO GO

The town is worth a visit at any time of the year for its inns, restaurants, and proximity to the wineries (open year-round), but the most compelling time to visit is from April through November, during the Shaw Festival, and when the weather allows alfresco dining. Wine-harvesting tours and events take place in the fall and, for ice wine, in December and January. Be warned that the tiny town can get packed over Canadian and American holiday weekends in summer: parking will be scarce, driving slow, and you might have to wait for tastings at wineries.

GETTING HERE AND AROUND

From Buffalo or Toronto, Niagara-on-the-Lake is easily reached by car via the QEW. NOTL is about a two-hour drive from Toronto, a bit far for just a day trip. From Niagara Falls or Lewiston, take the Niagara Parkway. There's no public transport in Niagara-on-the-Lake or to Niagara Falls, 15 km (9 miles) south.

Niagara-on-the-Lake is a very small town that can easily be explored on foot. Parking downtown can be nightmarish in peak season. Parking along the main streets is metered, at C$2 per hour. On most residential streets parking is free but still limited.

TOURS

Sentineal Carriages conducts year-round tours in and around Niagara-on-the-Lake. Catch a carriage at the Prince of Wales hotel or make a reservation for a pick-up. The private, narrated tours are C$80 for 30 minutes, C$115 for 45 minutes, and C$145 for 1 hour (prices are per carriage).

ESSENTIALS

Tour Contacts Sentineal Carriages ☎ *905/468–4943* 🌐 *www.sentinealcarriages.ca.*

Visitor Information Niagara-on-the-Lake Chamber of Commerce and Visitor & Convention Bureau ✉ *26 Queen St.* ☎ *905/468–1950* 🌐 *www.niagaraonthelake.com.*

TOP EXPERIENCE: WINERIES

Château des Charmes. Founded in 1978, this is one of Niagara's first wineries, and one of the two largest family-owned wineries in Niagara (Peller is the other). Originally from France, the Bosc family were pioneers in cultivating European varieties of grapes in Niagara. Wines here consistently win awards, and the winery is particularly known for its Chardonnay and Gamay Noir Droit, made from a grape variety that was accidentally created through a mutation. The wine is proprietary, and this is the only winery allowed to make it. Château des Charmes is pioneering again and in the process of developing brand-new wholly Canadian grape varieties. ✉ *1025 York Rd.* ☎ *905/262–4219* 🌐 *www.chateaudescharmes.com* 🎫 *Tasting flights C$10; tours C$10–15* ⏲ *Daily 10–6; tours at 1, 3, and 4 pm.*

Frogpond Farm. Ontario's only certified-organic winery is a small, family-owned affair with exclusively organic wines. The setting is truly farm-like: sheep and guinea hens mill about outside while you taste. With only ten varieties, all VQA and including a nice ice wine, you can become an expert in this label in one sitting. The wines are available on-site, online, at selected restaurants in Ontario; many of the labels are available at the LCBO. ✉ *1385 Larkin Rd. (Line 6)* ☎ *905/468–1079, 877/989–0165* 🌐 *www.frogpondfarm.ca* 🎫 *Tastings free* ⏲ *Retail and tastings May–Oct., daily 11–6; Nov.–Apr., daily 11–5.*

Jackson-Triggs Niagara Estate Winery. An ultramodern facility, this famous winery blends state-of-the-art winemaking technology with age-old, handcrafted enological savvy, as evidenced by the stainless steel trough by the entrance. A multitude of tours, workshops, and events are offered. The hourly public tour is a great introduction to winemaking and includes three tastings and a mini-lesson in wine tasting. Its premium award-winning VQA wines can be sipped in the tasting gallery and purchased in the retail boutique. ✉ *2145 Niagara Stone Rd.* ☎ *905/468–4637, 866/589–4637* 🌐 *www.jacksontriggswinery.com* 🎫 *Tastings C$1 (C$5–C$7 ice wine). Tours C$5* ⏲ *June–Sept., daily 10:30–6:30; Oct.–May, Sun.–Fri. 10:30–5:30, Sat. 10:30–6:30. Tours June–Sept., daily every hr on the hr; Oct.–May, daily at 10:30, 12:30, and 2:30.*

8

Konzelmann Estate Winery. An easygoing winery with a friendly staff and sociable tasting bar, Konzelmann has garnered praise (and awards) from various authoritative sources like the *Wall Street Journal*, for its fruitier wines in particular, and it's known for high-quality ice wines, one of which made *Wine Spectator*'s top 100 wines list in 2008, the first Canadian wine ever to make the list. Konzelmann's vineyards border Lake Ontario, and the winery has a viewing platform with vistas of the vines and water. The retail shop is well stocked with wine-related gifts. ✉ *1096 Lakeshore Rd.* ☎ *905/935–2866* 🌐 *www.konzelmann.ca* 🎫 *Tours C$8–22* ⏲ *May–Oct., daily 10–6; Nov.–Apr., Mon.–Sat. 10–5, Sun. 11–5. Tours May–mid-Sept., daily at 11, 1, and 3; specialty tours by appointment.*

Stratus. Standing out from a vast landscape of single varietal wines, Stratus specializes in assemblage: combining multiple varieties of grapes to create unique blends. Established in 2000, and emerging on the Niagara wine scene in 2005, they continue to perfect what has traditionally been a recipe for disaster for winemakers. A fine example is the Stratus White, a mix of six grape varieties, that's complex and unlike anything you've ever tasted (in a good way). Sip all three assemblage

Fort George National Historic Site **3**
Niagara Apothecary **1**
Niagara Historical Society & Museum **2**
St. Mark's Church **4**
Whirlpool Jet Boat Tours **5**

wines (white, red, and ice wine) and a handful of single varietals in the modern glass-walled tasting room, installed in the world's first LEED-certified winery. **TIP→ Tours must be reserved in advance and can include cheese and charcuterie, or a beer-and-wine pairing with the craft brewery next door, Oast House.** ✉ *2059 Niagara Stone Rd.* ☎ *905/468–1806* 🌐 *www.stratuswines.com* 🎟 *Tastings C$10 (4 wines)* 🕓 *May–Dec., daily 11–5; Jan.–Apr., Wed.–Sun., noon–5.*

Trius Winery at Hillebrand. With more than 300 wine awards, this winery—one of Niagara's first and largest—produces many excellent varieties. Its reds (especially Trius Red and Trius Cabernet Franc) are some of the best in Niagara, consistently taking top prizes at competitions; the Trius Brut is another gold medalist. After the half-hour cellar and vineyard tour are three complimentary tastings. Another dozen themed tours and regular events include a seminar where you can blend your own Trius Red and an evening of chef-hosted meals at their terrific restaurant. **TIP→ Book in advance for tours.** ✉ *1249 Niagara Stone Rd.* ☎ *905/468–7123, 800/582–8412* 🌐 *www.triuswines.com* 🎟 *Tastings C$2, C$5 (ice wine). Tours C$10–C$15* 🕓 *Daily 10–9; tours every hour on the hour 11–5.*

EXPLORING

FAMILY
Fodor's Choice ★

Fort George National Historic Site. On a wide stretch of parkland south of town sits this fort that was built in the 1790s but lost to the Yankees during the War of 1812. It was recaptured after the burning of the town in 1813 and largely survived the war, only to fall into ruins by the 1830s. Thankfully, it was reconstructed a century later, and you can explore the officers' quarters, the barracks rooms of the common soldiers, the kitchen, and more. Staff in period uniform conduct tours and reenact 19th-century infantry and artillery drills. ✉ *Queens Parade, Niagara Pkwy.* ☎ *905/468–4257* 🌐 *www.pc.gc.ca/lhn-nhs/on/fortgeorge/index.aspx* 🎟 *C$11.70 (C$5.90 parking)* ⏲ *Mar., Sat.–Sun. noon–4; Apr. and Nov. Sat.–Sun. 10–5; May.–Oct. daily 10–5.*

Niagara Apothecary. Restored to look like a 19th-century pharmacy that opened here in 1869, the apothecary has glass-fronted walnut cabinets that display vintage remedies such as Merrill's System Tonic, which "Purifies the Blood and Builds up the System." Among the boxes and bottles is a rare collection of apothecary flasks. ✉ *5 Queen St.* ☎ *905/468–3845, 800/220–1921 off season and for group tours* 🌐 *www.niagaraapothecary.ca* 🎟 *Free* ⏲ *Early May–early Sept., daily noon–6; early Sept.–2nd Mon. in Oct., weekends noon–6; closed Oct.–May.*

Niagara Historical Society & Museum. In connected side-by-side buildings—one the 1875 former Niagara High School building and the other the first building in Ontario to have been erected as a museum, in 1906—this extensive collection relates to the often colorful history of the Niagara Peninsula from earliest times through the 19th century. **■ TIP→ During June, July, and August, the museum offers guided walking tours of the town (C$5) at 11 am on Thursday, Friday, and Saturday; and Sunday at 2 pm.** ✉ *43 Castlereagh St.* ☎ *905/468–3912* 🌐 *www.niagarahistorical.museum* 🎟 *C$5* ⏲ *May–Oct., daily 10–5; Nov.–Apr., daily 1–5.*

Queen Street. You can get a glimpse of the town's rich architectural history walking along this single street, with Lake Ontario to your north, and it is the core of NOTL's commercial portion. At the corner of Queen and King Streets is Niagara Apothecary. This high-style, mid-Victorian building was an apothecary from 1866 to 1964. The Court House is situated across the street. It became the Town Hall in 1862. Presently, it houses a small 327-seat theatre during Shaw Festival. At No. 209 is the handsome Charles Inn, formerly known as Richardson-Kiely House, built in 1832 for Charles Richardson, who was a barrister and Member of Parliament. **■ TIP→ The ten or so blocks of shopping includes an olive tasting room, upscale restaurants and cafés, designer-label boutiques, old-fashioned ice-cream parlors, and a spa. You could easily spend an entire day in this area.**

St. Mark's Church. One of Ontario's oldest Anglican churches, this was built in 1804, and St. Mark's parish is even older, formed in 1792. The stone church still houses the founding minister's original library of 1,500 books, brought from England. During the War of 1812, American soldiers used the church as a barracks, and still-visible rifle pits were dug in the cemetery. The church is open for concerts, lectures, and Sunday services only. ✉ *41 Byron St.* ☎ *905/468–3123* 🌐 *stmarks1792.com.*

Niagara-on-the-Lake, in the heart of the Niagara wine region, has gained fame for its fine wines and food, beautiful setting, and the annual summer Shaw Festival.

FAMILY **Whirlpool Jet Boat Tours.** A one-hour thrill ride, these tours veer around and hurdle white-water rapids that follow Niagara canyons up to the wall of rolling waters, just below Niagara Falls. Children must be at least six years old for the open-boat Wet Jet Tour and four years old for the covered-boat (dry!) Jet Dome Tour; minimum height requirements also apply. Tours depart from Niagara-on-the-Lake or Niagara Falls, Ontario (June–August only) and Lewiston, NY. ✉ *61 Melville St.* ☎ *905/468–4800, 888/438–4444* 🌐 *www.whirlpooljet.com* 🎟 *C$61* 🕑 *Mid-Apr.–mid-Oct., weather permitting.*

WHERE TO EAT

George Bernard Shaw once said, "No greater love hath man than the love of food," and Niagara-on-the-Lake, which hosts a festival devoted to the playwright, is a perfect place to indulge your epicurean desires. Many eateries serve fine produce and wines from the verdant Niagara Peninsula, and the glut of high-end options fosters fierce competition. A number of inns and wineries here have restaurants. Especially in summer, make reservations whenever possible. Many restaurants serve dinner only until 9.

$$$$ INTERNATIONAL Fodor's Choice ★ ✕ **Hillebrand Winery Restaurant.** Niagara-on-the-Lake's first winery restaurant is still one of its best. After a complimentary winery tour and tasting, you can continue to indulge in the spacious, light-filled dining room with big double doors framing vineyards almost as far as the eye can see. The menu of locally inspired cuisine changes every six weeks. Tasting menus (C$85) are available to try such culinary masterpieces as wild sockeye salmon with asparagus and fennel slaw, and Perth lamb potpie with tomato-and-rhubarb terrine. Niagara strawberry shortcake is just one delicious dessert from the pastry chef that

goes nicely with one of the in-house ice wines. **TIP→ Lunch is more affordable and just as luxurious as dinner; Sunday brunch with starter, main, and dessert is a steal at C$48.** *Average main: C$38* ✉ *1249 Niagara Stone Rd., at Hwy. 55* ☎ *905/468–7123, 800/582–8412* 🌐 *www.triuswines.com* *Reservations essential.*

DID YOU KNOW?

The moderate climate of the Niagara region doesn't benefit only grapes: about 40% of Canada's apples and 70% of its peaches as well as berries, cherries, and pears are grown in this area smaller than Rhode Island.

$$ BRITISH
Olde Angel Inn. You can request a Yorkshire pudding to accompany any meal at this tavern just off Queen Street, which should tip you off to its British leanings, played out further in the decor: a warren of rooms with creaky floors and worn (or well-loved, depending on how you see it) wooden tables and chairs, low ceilings and exposed beams, and convivial chatter throughout. In Ontario's oldest operating inn (it's believed to have opened in 1789) the Olde Angel sets out pub fare such as shepherd's pie, bangers and mash, and steak-and-kidney pie. Entrées change periodically but always include the house specialty, prime rib of beef au jus. Twenty-four domestic and imported (European) brews are on tap. **TIP→ The pub has live music, ranging from Celtic to 1970s covers, on most nights of the week, beginning at 9:30.** *Average main: C$15* ✉ *224 Regent St.* ☎ *905/468–3411* 🌐 *www.angel-inn.com.*

$$$$ EUROPEAN Fodor's Choice ★
Peller Estates Winery Restaurant. Frequently cited as the best restaurant in Niagara-on-the-Lake—an impressive feat in a town with so many excellent restaurants—Peller manages refinement without arrogance and has a superior view to its main competitor, Hillebrand. The stately Colonial revival dining room is anchored by a huge fireplace at one end and has windows running the length of the room overlooking a large patio and the estate vineyards. A menu of ever-changing expertly prepared entrées often weaves the Peller Estates wine into modern Canadian cuisine, such as the ice-wine lobster with basil cannelloni and double-smoked bacon, or Ontario elk with Cabernet-juniper sausage. Tasting menus are available at lunch (C$58) and dinner (C$89). Inventive desserts have included a honey-lemon soufflé with cardamom crème anglaise. *Average main: C$35* ✉ *290 John St. E* ☎ *905/468–4678* 🌐 *www.peller.com* *Reservations essential.*

$$$ ITALIAN
Ristorante Giardino. The real treat at this modern Italian restaurant is to sit on the large patio out front, set back from Queen Street across the lawn under the shade of tall trees. Nibble on antipasti such as Atlantic salmon carpaccio and classic caprese salad (with tomatoes and mozzarella), and then dig into the seasonal menu, always full of fresh (made daily) pasta, pizza, grilled fish, chicken, veal, and lamb dishes. A light fish course like the oven-roasted Chilean sea bass with black olives and cherry tomatoes is perfect for spring and summer. Find the perfect bottle from the extensive wine list to go with the meal and leave space to indulge in the kitchen's classic Italian desserts. *Average main: C$30* ✉ *Gate House Hotel, 142 Queen St.* ☎ *905/468–3263* 🌐 *www.gatehouse-niagara.com* *Closed Jan.–mid-Mar.*

8

Peller Estates Winery, known for its award-winning Rieslings and ice wines, provides visitors an elegant experience, from winery tours to tastings to fine dining.

$$$ CANADIAN ✕ **Tiara Restaurant at Queen's Landing.** Niagara-on-the-Lake's only waterfront restaurant, the regal Tiara sits beside a marina with a view of the Niagara River beyond the sailboat masts. The elegant, amber-hued Georgian-meets-contemporary dining room is buttoned up but accented by a pretty stained-glass ceiling and near-panoramic windows that give nearly every table a water view. The outdoor tables next to the marina, however, are the ones to request to go with the exquisite French-influenced menu which might include Ontario lamb duo—edamame-crusted chop and rosemary-rubbed broil with spearmint foam—and free-range roast chicken with spiced Niagara rhubarb. Round out the meal with homemade ice cream topped with seasonal berries. *Average main: C$25* ✉ *155 Byron St.* ☎ *905/468–2195, 888/669–5566* 🌐 *www.vintage-hotels.com* ✍ *Reservations essential.*

$$$$ MODERN CANADIAN ✕ **Treadwell.** New on the Niagara-on-the-Lake scene, Treadwell recently relocated from its former space in Port Dalhousie and brought with it a long-established clientele and sterling reputation. This brainchild of chef-owner Stephen Treadwell, his chef de cuisine, Matthew Payne, and his son, wine sommelier James Treadwell embodies the philosophy of farm-to-table. Sit down for dinner on the sidewalk patio or in the sleek dining room and indulge in seared Lake Huron whitefish with creamy leeks and lobster fritters, or Cumbrae Farms pork tenderloin wrapped in prosciutto and sage. A Sunday brunch favorite is lemony East Coast lobster on duck fat–fried bread with crumbled goat's cheese and bacon. *Average main: C$33* ✉ *114 Queen St.* ☎ *905/934–9797* 🌐 *www.treadwellcuisine.com* ✍ *Reservations essential.*

$$$ ECLECTIC **Zee's Grill.** For alfresco dining, it's hard to beat Zee's huge wraparound patio with heat lamps across from the Shaw Festival Theatre. More informal than most similarly priced restaurants in town, Zee's has a seasonal menu that brings panache to homegrown comfort foods, such as seared rainbow trout with Jerusalem artichoke ravioli and crispy leeks or grilled beef tenderloin with double-smoked bacon hash and cabernet *jus*. Appetizers follow the same philosophy—elegant, yet whimsical—as represented by a lobster poutine of butter poached lobster in a classic herbed Hollandaise sauce, and the duck confit pâté en croûte of confit duck leg, baked in a pastry shell served with chutney. Breakfast is served daily. *Average main: C$30 92 Picton St. 905/468–5715 www.niagarasfinest.com/properties/zeesgrill Reservations essential No lunch Dec.–mid-Apr.*

WHERE TO STAY

For expanded hotel reviews, visit Fodors.com.

In terms of superior lodging, you're spoiled for choice in Niagara-on-the-Lake and it's hard to go wrong with any of the properties within the town's historic center. Prices are high, but hotels sometimes offer significant deals online.

Niagara-on-the-Lake may be Canada's B&B capital, with more than 100 to its name. Their service and quality can rival some of the priciest hotels.

Niagara-on-the-Lake Bed & Breakfast Association. For B&B listings, contact the Niagara-on-the-Lake Bed & Breakfast Association. *905/468–0123, 866/855–0123 www.niagarabedandbreakfasts.com.*

Niagara-on-the-Lake Historic Bed & Breakfasts. The Niagara-on-the-Lake Historic Bed & Breakfasts website maintains a list of historic B&Bs, all built before 1850 and all within two blocks from Queen/Picton Street, the center-of-town shopping and dining strip. *www.historicbb.com.*

$$$ B&B/INN **The Charles Inn.** An air of old-fashioned civility permeates this 1832 Georgian gem. **Pros:** historic details with modern touches; highly lauded restaurant; impeccably decorated. **Cons:** some historic "quirks" like variable water temperature; some verandas are connected (shared with neighbors). *Rooms from: C$239 209 Queen St. 905/468–4588, 866/556–8883 www.niagarasfinest.com 12 rooms Breakfast.*

$$$$ HOTEL Fodor's Choice ★ **Harbour House.** The closest hotel to the waterfront in town is this luxurious and romantic boutique hotel with a contemporary-cottage theme just a block from the river. **Pros:** staff cater to every need; approachable luxury; full breakfast included. **Cons:** virtually no public spaces; no restaurant, gym, or spa on-site; a few rooms without water views. *Rooms from: C$399 85 Melville St. 905/468–4683, 866/277–6677 www.harbourhousehotel.ca 28 rooms, 3 suites Breakfast.*

$$ HOTEL **Moffat Inn.** A central location on Picton Street next to the Prince of Wales hotel, reasonable prices, and expert management make this 1835 stucco inn a real find. **Pros:** great location at reasonable price; impeccably clean; bathrooms have been recently updated; upscale linens; free

Wi-Fi and parking. **Cons:** rooms small and not as posh as other area hotels; dated decor and worn carpets. *Rooms from: C$174 ✉ 60 Picton St. ☎ 905/468–4116, 888/669–5566 ⊕ www.vintage-hotels.com ⇆ 23 rooms, 1 2-bedroom apartment 🍴 No meals.*

BREAKFAST BASICS

At local inns and B&Bs, breakfasts are often lavish multicourse affairs. But be wary of lodging that does not include it, as it's tough to find breakfast outside hotel restaurants that tend to charge an arm for eggs and a leg for toast.

$$ B&B/INN **Olde Angel Inn.** Though established in the late 1700s, this coach-house inn burned down during the War of 1812 and was rebuilt in 1816. **Pros:** excellent price at the heart of town; on-site English-style tavern *(⇨ Where to Eat)*. **Cons:** historic inn means poor soundproofing, which is a problem for rooms over the pub; dedicated parking for cottages only. *Rooms from: C$169 ✉ 224 Regent St. ☎ 905/468–3411 ⊕ www.angel-inn.com ⇆ 3 rooms, 2 2-bedroom suites, 2 2-bedroom cottages 🍴 No meals.*

$$$ HOTEL Fodor's Choice ★ **Pillar and Post.** A two-story hotel six (long) blocks from the heart of town, this building has been a cannery, barracks, and basket factory in its 100-plus-year history. **Pros:** exceptional staff; unaffected mix of historic and modern; cool spa and pool; free parking and high-speed Internet. **Cons:** not as central as some other hotels (a brisk 20-minute walk to Queen/Picton Street); no elevator to second-floor rooms. *Rooms from: C$250 ✉ 48 John St. ☎ 905/468–2123, 888/669–5566 ⊕ www.vintage-hotels.com ⇆ 122 rooms 🍴 No meals.*

$$$$ HOTEL **Prince of Wales.** A visit from the Prince of Wales in 1901 inspired the name of this venerable hostelry that still welcomes the occasional royal guest or film star (AKA Hollywood royalty). **Pros:** nice spa; over-the-top-elegant public spaces; highly trained staff; high-quality toiletries, Bose stereos, and Keurig coffeemakers in each room. **Cons:** some views of the parking lot; rabbit warren of corridors can be confusing; breakfast not included. *Rooms from: C$369 ✉ 6 Picton St. ☎ 905/468–3246, 888/669–5566 ⊕ www.vintage-hotels.com ⇆ 110 rooms 🍴 No meals.*

$$$ HOTEL **Queen's Landing.** About half the rooms at this Georgian-style brick mansion have knockout views of the fields of historic Fort George or the marina—ask for one when making a reservation. ⇨ **Pros:** elegant, historic look; excellent service. **Cons:** breakfast not included; not historic. *Rooms from: C$250 ✉ 155 Byron St. ☎ 905/468–2195, 888/669–5566 ⊕ www.vintage-hotels.com ⇆ 138 rooms, 4 suites 🍴 No meals.*

$$$$ B&B/INN **Riverbend Inn & Vineyard.** Surrounded by its own private vineyard, this beautifully restored, green-shuttered historic 1820 mansion is formal in style: it's fronted by a grand portico, and an enormous original 19th-century crystal chandelier greets you in the lobby. **Pros:** charming atmosphere, especially out on the patio if the weather permits; next to Peller Estates Winery. **Cons:** no elevators; far from central shopping district. *Rooms from: C$295 ✉ 16104 Niagara Pkwy. ☎ 905/468–8866, 888/955–5553 ⊕ www.riverbendinn.ca ⇆ 19 rooms, 2 suites 🍴 No meals.*

$$$ HOTEL **Shaw Club Hotel & Spa.** Clean lines, neutral colors, and modern elements like steel and glass give Shaw Club an edgy and hip vibe over its competitors, in a town that's largely Georgian or Victorian in style. ⇨ **Pros:** hip cosmopolitan style unique in NOTL; ideal location just across the street from Shaw Festival Theatre; easygoing staff. **Cons:** small rooms; Standard and Annex rooms lack the wow factor of the rest of the hotel. *Rooms from: C$250 92 Picton St. 905/468–5711, 800/511–7070 www.shawclub.com 29 rooms, 1 suite Breakfast.*

DID YOU KNOW?

The Shaw Festival is the only theater festival in the world that specializes in the plays of George Bernard Shaw and plays written during and about the period of Shaw's life.

$$$$ RENTAL **Victorian Villas.** A breath of fresh air in Niagara-on-the-Lake, this brand-new lodging option offers ultramodern, beautifully appointed, self-contained condo-like properties right in the heart of the Queen Street shopping district. **Pros:** centrally located; perfect for longer stays, big groups, and families; in the heart of the action; renowned spa (Sanctuary) and restaurant (Treadwell), plus a Starbucks in the same complex. **Cons:** pricey; only 28 units, so they fill up fast. *Rooms from: C$400 118 Queen St. 905/468–4552, 855/988–4552 www.thevictorianvillas.com 28 units No meals.*

NIGHTLIFE AND THE ARTS

Fodor's Choice ★ **Shaw Festival.** Niagara-on-the-Lake remained a sleepy town until 1962, when local lawyer Brian Doherty organized eight weekend performances of two George Bernard Shaw plays, *Don Juan in Hell* and *Candida*. The next year he helped found the festival, whose mission is to perform the works of Shaw and his contemporaries, including Noël Coward, Bertolt Brecht, J. M. Barrie, J. M. Synge, and Anton Chekhov. Now, the festival has expanded to close to a dozen plays, running from April to October, including some contemporary plays by Canadian playwrights, and one or two musicals (which are performed unmiked). All are staged in one of four theaters within a few blocks of one another. The handsome **Festival Theatre,** the largest of the three, stands on Queen's Parade near Wellington Street and houses the box office. The **Court House Theatre,** on Queen Street between King and Regent streets, served as the town's municipal offices from the 1840s until 1969, and is a national historic site. At the corner of Queen and Victoria streets, the **Royal George Theatre** was originally built as a vaudeville house in 1915. The **Studio Theatre,** the smallest of the four, hosts mostly contemporary performances. The festival is one of the biggest events in the summer. **TIP→ Regular-price tickets cost C$45 to C$110, but discounts abound; see "Ways to Save"**on the website. *905/468–2172, 800/511–7429 www.shawfest.com.*

8

SHOPPING

Niagara-on-the-Lake's historic Queen Street is lined with Victorian storefronts housing art galleries; women's clothing stores; gourmet food stores selling olives, marinades, and vinaigrettes; and tea and sweets shops.

Greaves Jams & Marmalades. Greaves Jams & Marmalades has been making jams, jellies, and marmalades from mostly local produce using family recipes, since the company began in 1927. The spreads have no preservatives, pectin, or additives. The brand has expanded into an operation with an online store, and its jams are often served for afternoon tea in upscale hotel restaurants. ✉ *55 Queen St.* ☎ *905/468–7831* 🌐 *www.greavesjams.com.*

EN ROUTE

From midsummer to late fall, the Niagara Peninsula's roadside fruit and vegetable stands and farmers' markets are in full bloom, with an abundance of berries, peaches, and cherries, as well as late-summer vegetables like corn and field tomatoes. Some of the best stands are on Highway 55, between Niagara-on-the-Lake and the QEW, and along Lakeshore Road, between Niagara-on-the-Lake and St. Catharines, some with pick-your-own options.

Harvest Barn Country Markets. There are many fruit stands and produce markets along the streets of Niagara-on-the-Lake, but just outside the area is the mother lode that dwarfs the others. Harvest Barn Country Markets, in a barn with a red-and-white-striped awning, sells regional fruits and vegetables and tempts with its fresh-baked goods: sausage rolls, bread, and fruit pies. After shopping for fresh and local ingredients, satisfy your hunger with lunch at the deli, or soup and salad bar, and join locals at the picnic tables. It's open year-round. ✉ *1822 Niagara Stone Rd./Hwy. 55* ☎ *905/468–3224* 🌐 *www.harvestbarn.ca.*

THE NIAGARA ESCARPMENT

Vineland is 102 km (63 miles) southeast of Toronto and 41 km (25 miles) west of Niagara-on-the-Lake.

The Niagara Peninsula north of St. Catharines is known as Niagara Escarpment or the Twenty Valley, for the huge valley where the region's main towns of Jordan, Vineland, and Beamsville are. This area is much less visited than Niagara-on-the-Lake, and the wineries more spread out. Peach and pear trees, hiking trails, and long stretches of country road are the lay of the land. Aside from wine tasting, you can also visit the cute-as-a-button town of Jordan.

WHEN TO GO

Unlike Niagara-on-the-Lake, this area doesn't get overcrowded in summer, the ideal season for puttering along the country roads. Many restaurants, cafés, and shops have abbreviated hours between mid-September and late May. Most wineries do open for tastings in winter, but call ahead to be sure and to check on driving conditions, as some of these spots are on steep or remote rural roads.

GETTING HERE AND AROUND

Aside from booking a structured winery tour, getting behind the wheel yourself is the only way to visit the attractions in this region. This area is about 75 minutes from Toronto and 45 minutes from Niagara-on-the-Lake and is a feasible day trip.

ESSENTIALS

Twenty Valley Tourism Association ✉ *3720 19th St., Jordan* ☎ *905/562–3636* 🌐 *www.twentyvalley.ca.*

TOP EXPERIENCE: WINERIES

Fodor'sChoice ★ **Cave Spring Cellars.** On Jordan's Main Street, Cave Spring is one of the leading wine producers in Canada, with Ontario's oldest wine cellars, in operation since 1871. Go for the Riesling, Chardonnay, and ice wine. It shares ownership with Inn on the Twenty and On the Twenty restaurant (next door) and produces custom blends for the latter. **TIP→ There are public tours every day at 1:30 pm between June and September (only Friday, Saturday, and Sunday the rest of the year).** ✉ *3836 Main St., Jordan* ☎ *905/562–3581* 🌐 *www.cavespring.ca* 🎟 *Tastings C$1–C$4* ⏲ *June and Sept. daily 10–6; July and Aug. daily 10–7; Oct.–May Sun.–Thur. 10–5, Fri. and Sat. 10–6.*

Fielding Estate. Two Adirondack chairs by the cedar framed entrance set the tone for the warm and charming winery within. Inside the modern West Coast–style cedar building with corrugated tin roof and massive stone chimney, Fielding has envious views of vineyards and Lake Ontario from huge picture windows and a big stone fireplace for chilly days. A young team—husband-and-wife owners and two winemakers—has been making quick strides here. The vineyard produces a low yield that enables flavors to be concentrated. **TIP→ Try the 2010 Syrah or 2010 Cabernet Franc, both prizewinners.** ✉ *4020 Locust Ln., Beamsville* ☎ *888/778–7758, 905/563–0668* 🌐 *www.fieldingwines.com* 🎟 *Tastings C$5 (3 wines); tours C$10* ⏲ *May–Oct., daily 10:30–6; Nov.–Apr., daily 10:30–5:30.*

Tawse. Eco-friendly and partially geothermally powered, Tawse is so committed to producing top-notch Pinot Noir that it installed a six-level gravity-flow system to avoid overhandling the delicate grape. The investment seems to be paying off, especially considering they were voted "Winery of the Year" three years in a row (2010–12) at the Canada Wine Awards. The rural hillside winery is modern, its big stainless steel vats visible from the tasting room. **TIP→ Don't leave empty handed because tasting fees are waived if you buy two or more bottles.** ✉ *3955 Cherry Ave., Vineland* ☎ *905/562–9500* 🌐 *www.tawsewinery.ca* 🎟 *Tastings C$5 (3 wines)* ⏲ *May–Oct. daily 10–6; Nov.–Apr. weekdays 10–5, weekends 10–6.*

Vineland Estates Winery. One of Ontario's most beautiful wineries occupies 75 acres that were once a Mennonite homestead established in 1845. The original buildings have been transformed into the visitor center and production complex. Several tour and tasting options are available on Saturdays, including a wine and cheese tour and tasting for $20 at 1 pm, and ice-wine tour and tasting for $25 at 3:30 pm. The excellent Restaurant@Vineland Estates Winery (⇨ *Where to Eat*) serves

8

DID YOU KNOW?

Numerous waterfalls trickle along the Niagara Escarpment's beloved Bruce Trail. At more than 800 km (500 miles) long, it is the longest footpath in Canada.

lunch and dinner, and you can find a guesthouse and a B&B cottage on the property. ✉ *3620 Moyer Rd., 40 km (25 miles) west of Niagara-on-the-Lake, Vineland* ☎ *905/562–7088, 888/846–3526* 🌐 *www.vineland.com* 🎫 *Tastings C$5 (3 wines)* 🕙 *May–Oct. 10–6; Nov.–Apr. Sun.–Thurs. 11–5:30, Fri. and Sat. 10–6.*

EXPLORING

Jordan Village. Charming Main Street Jordan, aka Jordan Village, is a small enclave of cafés and shops selling antiques, garden supplies, and artisanal foods. The Inn on the Twenty, the On the Twenty Restaurant, and Cave Spring Cellars are also here. Just a few blocks long, Jordan Village can be fully explored in a morning or afternoon. Home store **CHIC** (✉ *3836 Main St., Unit 9*) is worth a wander to gawk at items like Siberian fox throws and a bronze bear the size of an actual bear cub, even if you can't afford a $4,000 cedar canoe. **Irongate Garden Elements** (✉ *3845 Main St.*) is a favorite with gardeners. ✉ *Off QEW Exit 55 (Jordan Rd.); follow Jordan Rd. south 3 km (1.9 miles), take right onto Fourth Ave.; follow signs to Cave Spring Cellars from here, Jordan* 🌐 *www.jordanvillage.com.*

WHERE TO EAT

$$$$ EUROPEAN Fodor's Choice ★

✕ **Inn on the Twenty Restaurant.** The huge windows framing the Twenty Valley conservation area are reason enough to dine at this restaurant on Jordan's boutiques-lined Main Street. Many come from far away to enjoy a meal at what is known as one of the best restaurants around Toronto. Regional specialties and local and organic produce are emphasized on a seasonal menu that has included Wellington County boneless rib-eye steak served with mushroom-and-onion fricassée and blue-cheese butter; and wild Huron trout with potato "mille-feuille" in spring leek cream. The dining room reminiscent of the French and Italian countryside is lovely, with a soaring ceiling, whitewashed exposed beams, and a view of the gardens. Cave Spring Cellars, which has a shop next door, provides many of the wines. They have a mid-afternoon menu (3–4:30 pm), which includes light dishes such as an heirloom beet salad with feta and pistachio brittle, and an artisanal cheese and charcuterie platter. 💲 *Average main: C$32* ✉ *3836 Main St., off QEW Exit 55 or 57 (follow Cave Spring Cellars signs), Jordan* ☎ *905/562–7313* 🌐 *www.innonthetwenty.com* ✍ *Reservations essential.*

$$$$ CANADIAN Fodor's Choice ★

✕ **Restaurant@Vineland Estates Winery.** Exquisite, progressive Canadian food and venerable wines are served by an enthusiastic staff on this bucolic property with three 19th-century Mennonite stone buildings. Sit on the large outdoor patio overlooking vineyards and Lake Ontario beyond or in the glassed-in restaurant, where many of the tables have a similar panoramic view. The menu is locally sourced and seasonal; salmon from Canada is seared and rests upon sautéed greens and fingerling potatoes blanketed under olive and caper rémoulade. Carnivorous cravings are answered with rare-seared venison haunch with wild rice and juniper *jus*. Desserts, like spiced pumpkin cheesecake served with mascarpone gelato, is the perfect demonstration of simplicity and innovation. 💲 *Average main: C$35* ✉ *3620 Moyer Rd., Vineland* ☎ *905/562–7088, 888/846–3526* 🌐 *www.vineland.com* ✍ *Reservations essential* 🕙 *Closed Mon. and Tues., Jan.–Apr.*

8

WHERE TO STAY

For expanded hotel reviews, visit Fodors.com.

$$$$ B&B/INN **Inn on the Twenty.** Seven of the 24 suites in the main building of this Main Street Jordan inn are 600-square-foot, two-story affairs, but the rooms to book—in nice weather at least—are the five ground-level suites with very private garden patios. ⇨ **Pros:** large rooms; impeccably decorated; central location for the Twenty Valley. **Cons:** not as much to do in Jordan as in surrounding areas. *Rooms from: C$289* ✉ *3845 Main St., off QEW Exit 55 or 57 (follow Cave Spring Cellars signs), Jordan* ☎ *905/562–5336, 800/701–8074* 🌐 *www.innonthetwenty.com* *28 suites* *Breakfast.*

SPORTS AND THE OUTDOORS

Bruce Trail. Canada's oldest and longest footpath, the Bruce Trail stretches 885 km (550 miles) along the Niagara Escarpment, with an additional 400 km (250 miles) of side trails. It takes in scenery from the orchards and vineyards of the Niagara Escarpment—one of Canada's 15 UNESCO World Biosphere Reserves—to the craggy cliffs and bluffs at Tobermory, 370 km (230 miles) north of Niagara-on-the-Lake. You can access the hiking trail at just about any point along the route; the main trail is marked with white blazes, the side trails with blue blazes. Northern parts of the trail are remote. ✉ *Niagara Falls* ☎ *905/529–6821, 800/665–4453* 🌐 *brucetrail.org.*

STRATFORD

145 km (90 miles) west of Toronto.

In July 1953 Alec Guinness, one of the world's greatest actors, joined with Tyrone Guthrie, probably the world's greatest Shakespearean director, beneath a hot, stuffy tent in a quiet town about a 90-minute drive from Toronto. This was the birth of the Stratford Shakespeare Festival, which now runs from April to late October or early November and is one of the most successful and admired festivals of its kind.

Today Stratford is a city of 32,000 that welcomes more than 500,000 visitors annually for the Stratford Shakespeare Festival alone. But Shakespeare is far from the only attraction. The Stratford Summer Music Festival (July and August) is another highlight, shopping in the enchanting city core is a favorite pastime, and with more amazing restaurants than you could hope to try in one visit, dining out in Stratford could be a reason to return.

WHEN TO GO

The festival runs from mid-April through late October or early November. Most visitors choose their travel dates based on the play(s) they want to see. About half of the city's restaurants and B&Bs close off-season; the city is quiet in the colder months, but shops and art galleries stay open, hotels have reduced rates, and you'll rub elbows with locals rather than visitors.

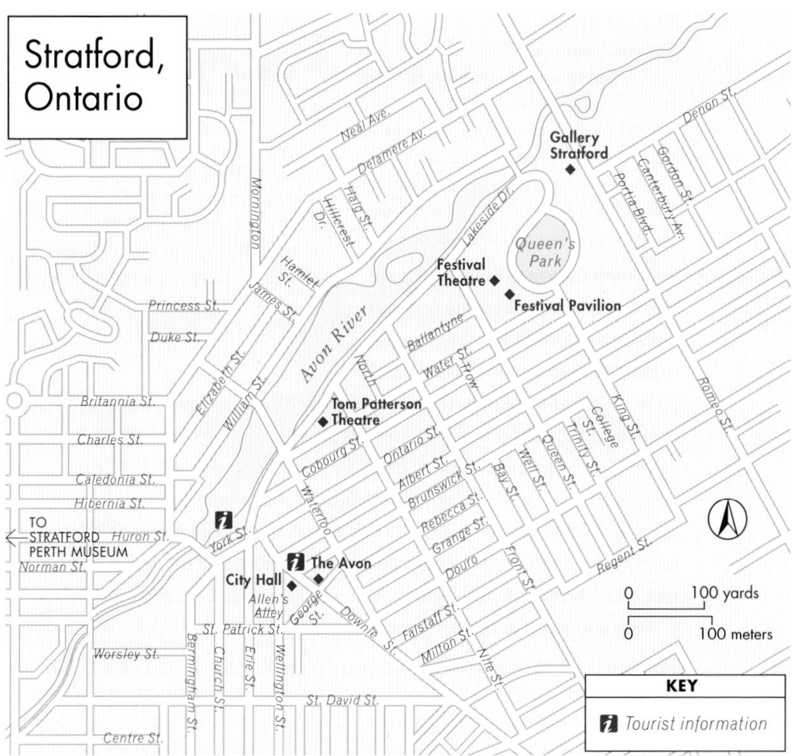

GETTING HERE AND AROUND

Ontario's main east–west highway, the 401, which traverses the province all the way from Michigan to Québec, is the main route from Toronto to Kitchener-Waterloo; from there, Highway 7/8 heads to Stratford. Traffic-free driving time is about two hours. VIA Rail has daily service to downtown Stratford from Toronto's Union Station; the trip is about two hours.

Stratford is an ideal town for cruising via bicycle. Totally Spoke'd rents cruisers, mountain bikes, and tandem bikes (C$35–C$47/day; C$20–C$35/half day).

ESSENTIALS

Bicycle Rental Totally Spoke'd ✉ *29 Ontario St.* ☎ *519/273–2001* 🌐 *www.totallyspoked.ca* ⏲ *Oct.–Apr. closed Mon..*

Train Information Stratford Train Station ✉ *101 Shakespeare St.* ☎ *888/842–7245.* **VIA Rail** ☎ *888/842–7245* 🌐 *www.viarail.ca.*

Visitor Information Stratford Shakespeare Festival ✉ *55 Queen St.* ☎ *519/273–1600, 800/567–1600* 🌐 *www.stratfordfestival.ca.*
Stratford Tourism Alliance ✉ *47 Downie St.* ☎ *519/271–5140, 800/561–7926* 🌐 *www.visitstratford.ca.*

EXPLORING

Gallery Stratford. Regular exhibits of Canadian visual art and, in summer, of local artists' work are displayed here. Great for groups of all ages. ✉ *54 Romeo St.* ☎ *519/271–5271* 🌐 *www.gallerystratford.on.ca* 🎟 *C$5* ⏲ *Jun.–Sept., Tues.–Sun. 10–5; Oct.–May., Tues.–Sun. 11–3.*

STRATFORD WALKING TOURS

The Stratford Tourism Alliance produces several themed, self-guided walking tours, such as Historic Downtown; Landmarks; and Shakespearean Gardens. Pick one up from the tourism office at ✉ *47 Downie St.*, or for a more modern spin, download the tour podcasts from 🌐 *www.visitstratford.ca.*

QUICK BITES

Boomer's Gourmet Fries. The humble potato rises to become a star at Boomer's Gourmet Fries, equipped with a take-out window and a handful of stools at a counter. Toppings of every ilk can be found here, like veg chili, hickory sticks, and salsa. The imaginative pairings apply to burgers as well, with options like bruschetta and goat cheese and the "Parisienne" with Brie, grilled onions, and Dijon mustard on the menu. Fish-and-chips is done simply with cod. Try one of the many unique and delicious takes on a Canadian "delicacy," *poutine:* the traditional version is fries topped with cheese curds and gravy. ✉ *26 Erie St.* ☎ *519/275–3147* 🌐 *www.boomersgourmetfries.com.*

Stratford Perth Museum. You can brush up on Stratford and Perth County history with permanent displays and changing exhibits that cover such topics as hockey in Stratford, the city's railroad, and the settlement of the area in the early 1800s. There are hiking trails and picnic areas on the property. ✉ *4275 Huron Rd.* ☎ *519/393–5311* 🌐 *www.stratfordperthmuseum.ca* 🎟 *C$5* ⏲ *May–Aug., Tues.–Sat. 10–4, Sun. and Mon. noon–4; Sept.–Apr., Tues.–Sat. 10–4, closed Sun. and Mon.*

WHERE TO EAT

For a tiny town, Stratford is endowed with an unusual array of excellent restaurants. Perth County is a locavore's dream of farmers' markets, dairies, and organic farms. The proximity of the Stratford Chefs School supplies a steady stream of new talent, and the Shakespeare festival ensures an appreciative audience.

$$$ EUROPEAN ✕ **Bijou.** A husband-and-wife team, both Stratford Chefs School grads, operates this small, self-professed "culinary gem." The chalkboard menu changes daily, and nearly everything on it is locally sourced. Two- or three-course prix-fixe dinners have French, Italian, and Asian influences: duck confit steamed in cabbage leaves with French lentils and bok choy may be an option for your main course. For dessert, there might be an Ontario peach tarte with black-pepper ice cream and basil syrup. **TIP→ The small entrance, next to the Stratford Hotel, is easy to miss: to get here, cross the parking lot on Erie Street, or pass through Allen's Alley, off Wellington Street.** 💲 *Average main: C$27* ✉ *105 Erie St.* ☎ *519/273–5000* 🌐 *www.bijourestaurant.com* ✍ *Reservations essential* ⏲ *Closed Mon. and Sun.; May–Oct. no lunch Tues.–Thurs.; Nov.–Apr. no lunch Sat.*

CLOSE UP

Bringing the Bard to Ontario

The origins of Stratford are modest. After the War of 1812, the British government granted a million acres of land along Lake Huron to the Canada Company, headed by a Scottish businessman. Surveyors came to a marshy creek surrounded by a thick forest and named it "Little Thames," noting that it might make "a good mill-site." It was Thomas Mercer Jones, a director of the Canada Company, who renamed the river the Avon and the town Stratford. The year was 1832, 121 years before the concept of a theater festival would take flight and change Canadian culture.

For years Stratford was considered a backwoods hamlet. Then came the first of two saviors of the city, both of them also (undoubting) Thomases. In 1904 an insurance broker named Tom Orr transformed Stratford's riverfront into a park. He also built a formal English garden, where flowers mentioned in the plays of Shakespeare—monkshood to sneezewort, bee balm to bachelor's button—bloom grandly to this day.

Next, Tom Patterson, a fourth-generation Stratfordian born in 1920, looked around; saw that the town wards and schools had names like Hamlet, Falstaff, and Romeo; and felt that some kind of drama festival might save his community from becoming a ghost town. The astonishing story of how he began in 1952 with C$125 (a "generous" grant from the Stratford City Council), tracked down Tyrone Guthrie and Alec Guinness, and somehow, in little more than a year, pasted together a long-standing theater festival is recounted in his memoirs, *First Stage: The Making of the Stratford Festival.*

Soon after it opened, the festival wowed critics worldwide with its professionalism, costumes, and daring thrust stage. The early years brought giants of world theater to the tiny town of some 20,000: James Mason, Alan Bates, Christopher Plummer, Jason Robards Jr., and Maggie Smith. Stratford's offerings are still among the best of their kind in the world—the next-best thing to seeing the Royal Shakespeare Company in mother city Stratford-upon-Avon, in England—with at least a handful of productions every year that put most other Canadian summer arts festivals to shame. *For planning information see The Arts, below.*

8

$$$$ FRENCH **Church Restaurant and Belfry.** Constructed in 1873 as a Congregational church, the building has most of the original architecture in place, but today white tablecloths gleam in the afternoon light that pours through the stained-glass windows. The artfully plated modern French meals—grilled rib-eye steak with red-wine braising *jus,* celeriac *pomme* purée, and wilted spinach—are complex production numbers. The menu usually includes lamb, at least one fish entrée, and an interesting three-course tasting menu (C$55). The bistro-style and slightly less expensive Belfry ($$$), upstairs, has more down-to-earth but still-stylish food, such as ice wine–glazed quail with double-smoked bacon, *boudin noir* (blood sausage), and baby vegetables. *Average main: C$35 70 Brunswick St. 519/273–3424 www.churchrestaurant.com Reservations essential Church closed Mon. and Jan.–Mar. Belfry closed Sun. and Mon. and Jan.–Mar.*

$$$ ECLECTIC ✕ **Down the Street Bar and Restaurant.** Funky and eclectic, this bistro-bar is the hottest place in town and a go-to spot for Festival actors. Chatter and jazz tunes are the soundtrack in the whimsical bordello-meets-Macbeth space, decorated with low-hung chandeliers and red rococo-style wallpaper and drapes—even the ceilings are red. The seasonal menu of only seven entrées is as playful as the decor, ranging from rib eye with herb shallot butter to panko-crusted black cod to sweet chili-fried tofu with coconut curry rice noodles. A late-night menu of dressed-up sandwiches, burgers, and antipasti is served till midnight. On tap is a comprehensive selection of imported beers and microbrews. *Average main: C$23 ✉ 30 Ontario St. ☎ 519/273–5886 ⊕ www.downthestreet.ca ⚠ Reservations essential ⊙ Closed Mon. No lunch Tues.–Thurs. Closed Sun. mid-Oct.–mid-June.*

$$$ ITALIAN ✕ **Pazzo Pizzeria and Taverna.** A corner of Stratford's main crossroads is home to one of the city's best and most convivial Italian restaurants. Have a drink and people-watch at the bar or on the patio. Led by new chef Yva Santini, the kitchen creates hearty regional Italian mains—like porchetta with crispy pork belly and balsamic cipollini onions—and house-made pastas—such as lobster cannelloni with confit fennel and salmon caviar—that make good use of locally sourced produce and meat and sustainable fish. Downstairs, at the Pizzeria, go for the straightforward pasta dishes or the thin-crust pizzas—two favorites are the Soprano, with Calabrese sausage, portobello mushrooms, and asiago; and the Italian Stallion with prosciutto, Italian sausage and bacon, spicy Calabrese sausage, and *bocconcinci* (bite-sized Mozzarella balls). It's a popular meeting place after a play, the decor is soothing and modern, and the service is quick and friendly. *Average main: C$22 ✉ 70 Ontario St. ☎ 519/273–6666 ⊕ www.pazzo.ca ⚠ Reservations essential ⊙ Closed Mon.*

$$$$ CANADIAN ✕ **The Prune.** A converted 1905 house holds a number of charming gray-purple dining rooms with white table linens surrounded by a tidy courtyard. Chef Bryan Steele, who is also senior cookery instructor at Stratford Chefs School, coaxes fresh local ingredients into innovative dishes with the best of what's available globally. Dishes change with the harvest but have included Lake Huron whitefish meunière with asparagus, cinnamon cap mushrooms; and spring risotto with Parmesan, crispy egg, wild-leek pesto. The owners proudly source their lamb from small family-owned Church Hill Farm, just 30 km (18 miles) away. The restaurant has a knowledgeable sommelier on staff, a solid vegetarian selection, and a strong wine list, with many Ontario options. Desserts are made fresh for each meal by an in-house pastry chef. *Average main: C$40 ✉ 151 Albert St. ☎ 519/271–5052 ⊕ theprune.com ⚠ Reservations essential ⊙ Closed Nov.–mid-May and Mon. No lunch.*

$$$$ EUROPEAN Fodor's Choice ★ ✕ **Rundles Restaurant.** At Stratford's top choice for sophisticated haute cuisine the look is summery and modern: brick is exposed, windows are unadorned and panoramic, and, with a theatrical flourish, flowing white silk scarves hang from primitive stone masks. Diners have five to seven choices for each course (appetizer, entrée, and dessert) on the prix-fixe menu (C$92.50). Offerings change frequently, but regulars

would protest the removal of the grilled duck breast with carrot-and-parsnip purée and pickled dates. The more relaxed **Sophisto-Bistro,** at the same location, has two- and three-course dinners (C$50–62) that might include hot-smoked trout salad with fingerling potatoes in a hot bell pepper cream or, for dessert, poached apples and candied apple ice cream. Considerable artistry is lavished on preparation and presentation. *Average main: C$94 9 Cobourg St. 519/271–6442 www.rundlesrestaurant.com Reservations essential Closed Oct.–May and Mon. No lunch weekdays.*

$$$ ECLECTIC **Sun Room.** Stir-fries and noodle dishes were joined by Continental choices when new owners took over this Stratford institution in 2010. Additional options draw from the bounty of nearby wine and food producers and may include such dishes as Perth County pork tenderloin stuffed with caramelized apple and chèvre from C'est Bon Cheese (in St. Mary's) or pan-seared elk with a red-wine *jus* and blue-potato hash. The casual dining room is modernized with painted black tables, globe lights, high-back leather chairs, and artwork by Stratford Festival set designer John Pennoyer on the walls. Service is welcoming. *Average main: C$30 55 George St. 519/273–0331 www.sunroomstratford.com Reservations essential Closed Sun. No lunch Mon.*

$$ CAFÉ **York Street Kitchen.** Locals come to this casual spot across from the waterfront for the signature generously portioned and juicy sandwiches and, for dinner, homemade comfort dishes, such as meat loaf with Yukon Gold mashed potatoes or lamb potpie, but especially for the breakfast served daily: favorites are the French toast with homemade apple compote and the Canadiana sandwich with peameal bacon, mustard, tomato, and egg on a toasted kaiser roll. A build-your-own sandwich menu is available for lunch and at the take-out window in summer. The bright dining room is decorated with vibrant-patterned vinyl tablecloths. During festival season the lines form early. *Average main: C$15 24 Erie St. 519/273–7041 www.yorkstreetkitchen.com.*

WHERE TO STAY

For expanded hotel reviews, visit Fodors.com.

Stratford has a wide range of atmospheric B&Bs, motels on the outskirts of downtown, and inns around the center. Room rates are discounted substantially in winter, sometimes by more than 50%.

Stratford Area Bed & Breakfast Association. The Stratford Area Bed & Breakfast Association conducts regular inspections of area B&Bs and maintains a list of those that pass muster. *519/272–2961 www.sabba.ca.*

$$$ B&B/INN **Avery House.** This 1874 Gothic Revival brick home transformed into an impeccably decorated B&B has an eclectic interior. **Pros:** continually updated; affable host; big breakfasts. **Cons:** communal dining and set breakfast time (9 am) not everyone's cup of tea; on a busy road; ground-floor unit's bathroom isn't directly en suite. *Rooms from: C$189 330 Ontario St. 519/273–1220, 800/510–8813 www.averyhouse.com 5 rooms, 1 suite Closed Nov.–May Breakfast.*

8

$$ HOTEL **Festival Inn.** Stratford's largest hotel—east of town and about 10 minutes by car from the theaters—offers a mixture of lodging types: motel rooms, suites with Jacuzzis, and a modern inn. **Pros:** fair prices; modern rooms; exceptional staff; outdoor pool; pet-friendly. **Cons:** slightly out of town on a commercial strip. *Rooms from: C$145 1144 Ontario St. 519/273–1150, 800/463–3581 www.festivalinnstratford.com 169 rooms Breakfast.*

$$$ B&B/INN **Foster's Inn.** Two doors away from the Avon and Studio theaters, this brick building dates to 1906 and has a bit of history—it once housed the International Order of Odd Fellows, a fraternal organization that started in the United Kingdom. **Pros:** great deals in winter; excellent locale; full breakfast menu at restaurant; free Wi-Fi. **Cons:** fills up fast in summer; sometimes a two-night minimum stay required. *Rooms from: C$179 111 Downie St. 519/271–1119, 888/728–5555 www.fostersinn.com 9 rooms No meals.*

$$ B&B/INN **Queen and Albert B&B Inn.** A 1901 storefront, now bright blue with a striped awning, is the unique facade of this residential-neighborhood B&B, a 10-minute walk to Stratford's main shopping and eating strip. **Pros:** friendly host; large rooms; two rooms with a shared balcony. **Cons:** no elevator and only one ground-floor room, which has twin beds and is not as impressively decorated as upper-floor rooms. *Rooms from: C$175 174 Queen St. 519/272–0589 www.queenandalbert.com 4 suites Closed Nov.–Apr. Breakfast.*

$$$$ B&B/INN **Stewart House Inn.** The interior of this elegant 1870s home draws on the Victorian period but with modern conveniences. **Pros:** exceptional service; in-house massage; private breakfast tables; on-site outdoor pool; complimentary espresso available around the clock. **Cons:** not as central as some other inns; ground-floor Garden Room available only in summer. *Rooms from: C$289 62 John St. N 519/271–4576, 866/826–7772 www.stewarthouseinn.com 6 rooms Breakfast.*

$ HOTEL **Swan Motel.** The original 1960s motel sign still marks this single-story tawny-brick motel 3 km (2 miles) south of downtown, behind which you'll find clean-as-a-whistle, albeit utilitarian, rooms at good prices. **Pros:** one of the best deals in town; warm hosts; on a private lot backed by farmland; outdoor pool. **Cons:** basic rooms with parking-lot views; not walkable to downtown; motor-lodge layout around a parking lot. *Rooms from: C$110 960 Downie St. 519/271–6376 www.swanmotel.ca 24 rooms Closed Nov.–May No meals.*

$$$ B&B/INN **The Three Houses.** On a quiet residential street, this elegant and tastefully decorated trio of two Edwardian houses and one Victorian has been frequented by the likes of Kevin Spacey, Julie Andrews, and Christopher Plummer. **Pros:** star appeal; exquisite decorative taste; heated saltwater pool. **Cons:** irregular hours in winter; sometimes entire house is rented out to film crews. *Rooms from: C$225 100 Brunswick St. 519/272–0722 www.thethreehouses.com 6 suites Breakfast.*

The award-winning Festival Theatre, the largest of the Stratford Shakespeare Festival's four venues, has been staging great drama for theater lovers since 1957.

THE ARTS

Fodor's Choice ★ **Stratford Shakespeare Festival.** One of the two largest classical repertory companies in the world—England's Royal Shakespeare Company is the other—the Festival presents not only Shakespeare plays, but also works by other dramatists (including new plays) and popular musicals and musical revues in its four theaters.

8

The 1,800-seat **Festival Theatre** (✉ *55 Queen St.*), with its hexagonal wooden thrust stage and permanent wooden stage set, is the largest and the oldest of the Festival's theaters—in its first incarnation in 1953 it was just a stage under a tent. The 1,100-seat **Avon Theatre** (✉ *99 Downie St.*) has a traditional proscenium stage. The **Tom Patterson Theatre** (✉ *111 Lakeside Dr.*) has a long, runway-style thrust stage and 480 steeply stacked seats. The petite **Studio Theatre** (✉ *34 George St. E*), with only 260 seats, is the go-to space for experimental and new works; built in 2002, it has a modern appearance and a hexagonal thrust stage.

Throughout the season, 12 to 16 productions are mounted, and at the height of the festival in July and August you may be able to choose from among eight performances. The Festival also offers numerous concerts, workshops, tours, lectures, and talks, such as Meet the Festival, where the public can ask questions of actors and artists. The Festival has both matinees and evening performances (and many visitors do see two plays per day). Theaters are closed most Mondays. For tickets, information, and accommodations, contact the Festival office directly. ✉ *55 Queen St.* ☎ *519/273–1600, 800/567–1600* 🌐 *www.stratfordfestival.ca.*

Fodor's Choice ★ **Stratford Summer Music.** For five weeks in July and August, Stratford Summer Music brings musicians—from string quartets to Mexican mariachi bands—to indoor and outdoor venues around town. Outdoor performances, like those sounding from a barge on the Avon River, are free. Series may include Saturday-night cabaret at the Church restaurant and classical-music lunches at Rundles. Some performances do sell out, so get tickets in advance. ☎ *519/271–2101* 🌐 *www.stratfordsummermusic.ca.*

DISCOUNT TICKETS

Regular Stratford Festival tickets are around C$55 to C$110, but there are many ways to pay less. Spring previews and some fall performances are discounted 30%. Savings of 30% to 50% can be had for students and seniors, and theatergoers aged 16 to 29 can buy seats online for C$25 for select performances two weeks prior. Also available are early-ordering discounts, rush seats, half-price Tuesdays, and family and group discounts.

SHOPPING

Downtown Stratford is a great place for daytime distractions and is utterly devoid of chain stores. Ontario Street alone is lined with quaint bookstores stocking great local reads, chocolatiers, myriad colorful housewares and women's clothing shops, and catch-all gift stores.

The Theatre Store. In two locations (at the Avon and Festival theaters), this is the place for Shakespeare finger puppets, every Shakespeare play ever written, original costume sketches, soundtracks to the musicals, and Bard-themed children's books. Visit their online store if you missed the chance to go in person. ✉ *Avon Theatre, 100 Downie St.* ☎ *519/271–0055* 🌐 *store.stratfordfestival.ca* ✉ *Festival Theatre, 55 Queen St.* ☎ *519/271–0055* 🌐 *store.stratfordfestival.ca.*

Watson's Chelsea Bazaar. At this brimming curio shop you might find a cat curled up among the reasonably priced china, glassware, French soaps, kitchen gadgets, and other bric-a-brac. The Bradshaw family has owned a store at this location in various forms (it used to be a high-end china hall) since the 1800s. ✉ *84 Ontario St.* ☎ *519/273–1790* 🌐 *www.watsonsofstratford.com.*

EN ROUTE

The tiny village of St. Jacobs, in Mennonite country 50 km (30 miles) northeast of Stratford, has a main street lined with quilt shops, fresh-from-the-farm food stores, and restaurants whose menus feature locally raised and grown meat and produce.

St. Jacobs Farmers' Market. Just outside Waterloo, this biweekly farmers' market (Thursday and Saturday) features 100 vendors selling local produce, cheeses, baked goods, and meat. There are also hundreds of permanent indoor and outdoor booths (open every day) with homemade foods straight from the farm—preserves, pies, smoked meats, and cheeses—and flea-market fare like crafts and handmade furniture. **TIP→ Don't miss the fresh hot apple fritters, a made-to-order treat worth queuing up for.** ✉ *878 Weber St. N, Waterloo* ☎ *519/747–1830* 🌐 *www.stjacobs.com* ⏲ *Market: year-round Thurs. and Sat. 7–3:30; mid-June–early Sept. Thurs. and Sat. 7–3:30 and Tues. 8–3. Stores: Jan.–Mar. Mon.–Fri. 10–5, Sat. 10–6, Sun. noon–5:30; Apr.–Dec. Mon.–Sat. 10–6, Sun. noon–5:30.*

SOUTHERN GEORGIAN BAY

Collingwood is 150 km (90 miles) north of Toronto on Hwys. 400 and 26. Midland is 145 km (90 miles) north of Toronto on Hwys. 400 and 93.

The southern shores of Lake Huron's Georgian Bay are home to waterfront towns and beaches that are popular getaways for Torontonians in summer. Ski resorts—Blue Mountain is the most popular—draw city folk as well once the snow falls and become biking and adventure resorts in summer. The region's largest city is Barrie (population 130,000), on the shore of Lake Simcoe, originally a landing place for the area's aboriginal inhabitants and, later, for fur traders. Today it's a big-box-store-filled suburb and one of Toronto's farther-flung bedroom communities. More interesting are the quiet towns of Midland and Penetanguishene (also called Penetang by locals), occupying a small corner of northern Simcoe County known as Huronia, on a snug harbor at the foot of Georgian Bay's Severn Sound. These are docking grounds for trips to the Georgian Bay Islands National Park. To the west, the attractive harbor town of Collingwood, on Nottawasaga Bay, is at the foot of Blue Mountain, the largest ski hill in the province.

WHEN TO GO

After Labour Day and before Victoria Day weekend (late May), few tourist attractions apart from ski resorts are open.

GETTING HERE AND AROUND

Georgian Bay towns and attractions are west of Highway 400, either via Highway 26 toward Collingwood or well-marked off Highway 400 north of Barrie. These towns and regions are 2½ to 4 hours from Toronto and are generally long weekend or even weeklong trips from the city.

TIP→ If you are heading north of Barrie in winter, go with a four-wheel-drive vehicle. Resorts, especially, are usually well off the highway and may require navigating twisting backcountry routes.

ESSENTIALS

Tourism Information Visit Southern Georgian Bay ☎ *705/445–7722, 888/227–8667* ⊕ *www.visitsouthgeorgianbay.ca.* **Georgian Bay Coastal Route** ⊕ *www.visitgeorgianbay.com.*

EXPLORING

Georgian Bay Islands National Park. A series of 63 islands in Lake Huron's Georgian Bay, the park can be visited only via boat. Organized boat tours with the park or private companies operate from the weekend closest to May 24 through mid-October, weather permitting. The park's campground, on Beausoleil Island, was refurbished in 2010. The only way to explore one of the islands on foot is to book a trip on the park's *Daytripper* boat, bring your own boat, or take a water taxi in Honey Harbour (contact the park for details).

The park's own boat, the ***Daytripper*** (☎ *705/526–8907* ⊕ *www.pc.gc.ca/georgianbay* *C$15.70* ⊙ *June–early Oct.; call for schedules*), makes the 15-minute trip to Beausoleil Island, which has hiking trails and beaches, from Honey Harbour, 15 km (9 miles) north of Port Severn at Highway 400 Exit 156.

8

PLANNING YOUR OUTDOOR ADVENTURE

The Ontario Tourism Marketing Partnership's website (www.ontariotravel.net) is a one-stop-shop for information on outdoor adventures from cycling to snowmobiling. It also publishes a free outdoor-adventure guide. The nonprofit Ontario Trails Council (*877/668-7245* *www.ontariotrails.on.ca*) has information on every trail and trail sport in the province; click the Central tab for the Muskokas and Georgian Bay. *For Georgian Bay cruises, see Georgian Bay Islands National Park, in the Southern Georgian Bay section. For Algonquin Park tours, see the "Dogsledding and Moose-spotting" feature in the Algonquin Provincial Park section.*

CAMPING

Peak season in Ontario parks is June through August. Reserve a campsite if possible, though all provincial parks with organized camping have some sites available on a first-come, first-served basis.

Ontario Parks. For detailed information on parks and campgrounds provincewide, to make campground reservations, or to get the *Ontario Parks Guide*, contact Ontario Parks. *www.ontarioparks.com.*

FISHING

Ministry of Natural Resources. Fishing licenses are required for Ontario and may be purchased from Ministry of Natural Resources offices and from most sporting-goods stores, outfitters, and resorts. A C$9.68 Outdoors Card, good for three years, is also required for fishing beyond a day (Canadian residents always need the Outdoors Card). For non-Canadians, the most restrictive (i.e., cheapest) one-day fishing license is C$21.88 (C$12.95 for Canadians); eight-day and one-year licenses are also available. All prices include taxes. *800/667-1940* *www.mnr.gov.on.ca.*

Go Fish Ontario (*www.gofishinontario.com*), operated by Ontario Tourism, is an excellent planning tool for fishing trips.

SKIING

Ski resorts with downhill runs are concentrated north and west of Barrie. *See recommended resorts in the Sports and the Outdoors section, below.* The central Ontario region also has more than 1,600 km of cross-country ski trails.

Ontario Snow Resorts Association. Ski Ontario has information on the condition of slopes across the province. *705/443-5450* *www.skiontario.ca.*

Two companies do cruises through the Georgian Bay but don't allow you to disembark on any of the islands.

The 300-passenger *Miss Midland*, operated by **Midland Tours** (*705/549-3388 or 888/833-2628* *www.midlandtours.com* *C$27*), leaves from the Midland town dock and offers 2½-hour sightseeing cruises daily at 2 pm mid-May to mid-October. The company can arrange departures from Toronto, which includes time to explore the town of Midland. From the Penetanguishene town dock, **Penetanguishene 30,000 Island Cruises** (*705/549-7795 or 800/363-7447* *www.georgianbaycruises.com* *C$20-C$27*) takes passengers on

Penetanguishene Harbour and the Georgian Bay islands tours, including 1½- and 2½-hour cruises of Penetanguishene Harbour and 3½-hour cruises of the 30,000 islands of Georgian Bay, on the 200-passenger MS *Georgian Queen*. Lunch and dinner cruises are available. Captain Steve, the owner and your tour guide, has operated these tours—a family business—since 1985. Cruises depart one to three times daily in July and August; less frequently (but usually Saturday, Sunday, and Wednesday) in May, June, September, and October. ✉ *Town and park welcome center: off Hwy. 400 Exit 153 or 156, Port Severn* ☎ *705/526–9804* 🌐 *www.pc.gc.ca/georgianbay* 🎫 *C$5.80* ⏲ *Late May (Victoria Day weekend)–early Oct.*

Huronia Museum. Nearly one million artifacts on native and maritime history are on display at the museum building, and there's also a replica Huron/Ouendat village. Visitors can expect contemporary art and extensive photography pieces, in addition to native art and archaeological collections. ✉ *549 Little Lake Park* ☎ *705/526–2844, 800/263–7745* 🌐 *huroniamuseum.com* 🎫 *C$10* ⏲ *May–Oct., daily 9–5; Nov.–Apr., weekdays 9–5.*

Martyrs' Shrine. On a hill overlooking Sainte-Marie among the Hurons, a twin-spired stone cathedral was built in 1926 to honor the eight missionaries stationed in Huronia who were martyred between 1642 and 1649. In 1930 all eight were canonized by the Roman Catholic Church. ✉ *16163 Hwy. 12 W, Midland* ☎ *705/526–3788* 🌐 *www.martyrs-shrine.com* 🎫 *C$4* ⏲ *Mid-May–mid-Oct., daily 8 am–9 pm.*

FAMILY **Sainte-Marie among the Hurons.** A Jesuit mission was originally built on this spot in 1639. The reconstructed village, which was once home to a fifth of the European population of New France, was the site of the first European community in Ontario; it had a hospital, farm, workshops, and a church. Workers also constructed a canal from the Wye River. A combination of disease and Iroquois attacks led to the mission's demise. Twenty-two structures, including two native longhouses and two wigwams, have been faithfully reproduced from a scientific excavation. Staff members in period costume demonstrate 17th-century trades, share native stories and legends, and grow vegetables—keeping the working village alive. ✉ *16164 Hwy. 12 W, 5 km (3 mi) east of Hwy. 93, Midland* ☎ *705/526–7838* 🌐 *www.saintemarieamongthehurons.on.ca* 🎫 *Apr.–mid-May and mid–late Oct., C$10; mid-May–early-Sept., C$12* ⏲ *Apr.–mid-May and mid–late Oct., weekdays 10–5; mid-May–early-Sept., daily 10–5; last entry at 4:45.*

FAMILY **Scenic Caves Nature Adventures.** Explore ancient caves, hike along craggy hilltop trails, get a thrill on zipline rides, or brave the suspension footbridge, 25 meters (82 feet) above the ground with amazing views of the bay, 300 meters (985 feet) below. Hiking boots or sneakers are required. ✉ *260 Scenic Caves Rd., Collingwood* ☎ *705/446–0256* 🌐 *www.sceniccaves.com* 🎫 *C$22.57* ⏲ *Late Apr.–Jun., Sept., and Oct. weekdays 9–5, weekends 9–6; July and Aug. 9–8. Last admission 2 hrs before close.*

8

WHERE TO STAY

For expanded hotel reviews, visit Fodors.com.

$$$$ RESORT Fodor's Choice ★ **Blue Mountain Resort.** The largest ski resort in Ontario, and only getting bigger, this huge property near Collingwood revolves around its brightly painted Scandinavian-style alpine "village" with several blocks of shops, restaurants, bars, a grocery, and a plaza with live music. **Pros:** just a skip and a hop from the pedestrian village where all shops and restaurants are located; wide range of accommodations; excellent skiing. **Cons:** Blue Mountain Inn needs renovation; other accommodations pricey in season. *Rooms from: C$400 ⊠ 108 Jozo Weider Blvd., Blue Mountains ☎ 705/445–0231, 877/445–0231 ⊕ www.bluemountain.ca Blue Mountain Inn: 93 rooms, 2 suites; Westin Trillium House: 222 suites; Mosaïc: 85 suites; Village Suites: 447 suites; Historic Snowbridge Mountain Homes: 150 units No meals.*

$$ RESORT **Horseshoe Resort.** Recently renovated, modern accommodations at this lodge on a 1,600-acre property come in a variety of shapes and sizes: choose from two-level lofts, spacious hotel rooms, or condos. **Pros:** free Wi-Fi; fun programs for kids; fresh, modern rooms; never-ending list of on-site facilities. **Cons:** scenic but isolated location. *Rooms from: C$169 ⊠ 1101 Horseshoe Valley Rd., Barrie ☎ 705/835–2790, 800/461–5627 ⊕ www.horseshoeresort.com 56 rooms, 45 suites No meals.*

SPORTS AND THE OUTDOORS

Most ski resorts have a multitude of summer activities, such as mountain biking, golf, and adventure camps.

Fodor's Choice ★ **Blue Mountain Resort.** The province's highest vertical drop, 720 feet, is at Blue Mountain Resort. Ontario's most extensively developed and frequented ski area has 42 trails, 22 of which are available after dark for night skiing, served by high-speed six-person lifts; quad, triple, and double lifts; and magic carpets. Summer activities include a roller coaster, golfing, tennis, beaches, mountain biking, open-air gondola rides, and ziplines. *⊠ 108 Jozo Weider Blvd., Blue Mountains ☎ 705/445–0231, 416/869–3799 from Toronto ⊕ www.bluemountain.ca.*

Horseshoe Resort. One of the few resorts to offer snowboarding, tubing, snowmobiling, snowshoeing, and cross-country and downhill skiing trails and facilities is Horseshoe Resort, about an hour's drive north of Toronto, off Highway 400. The resort has a terrain park, competition-level half-pipe and 26 alpine runs, 15 of which are lit at night, served by six lifts and a magic carpet. The vertical drop is only 304 feet, but several of the runs are rated for advanced skiers. Winter sports are only half the fun. Treetop trekking, horseback riding, and other summer adventures are available as well. *⊠ 1101 Horseshoe Valley Rd., Barrie ☎ 705/835–2790, 800/461–5627 ⊕ www.horseshoeresort.com.*

FAMILY **Mount St. Louis Moonstone.** Skiers and snowboarders can take advantage of 40 runs at Mount St. Louis Moonstone, 26 km (16 miles) north of Barrie. The majority of slopes are for beginner and intermediate skiers, though there's a sprinkling of advanced runs. The resort's Kids

Camp, a day-care and ski-school combination, attracts families. Inexpensive cafeterias within the two chalets serve decent meals. ⚠ **No overnight lodging is available.** ✉ *24 Mount St. Louis Rd., Off Hwy. 400 Exit 131, Coldwater* ☎ *705/835–2112, 877/835–2112* 🌐 *www.mountstlouis.com.*

THE MUSKOKAS

Outcroppings of pink and gray granite, drumlins of conifer and deciduous forest, and thousands of freshwater lakes formed from glaciers during the Ice Age characterize the rustic Muskoka region north of Toronto. Called Muskoka for Lake Muskoka, the largest of some 1,600 lakes in the area, this region is a favorite playground of those who live in and around Toronto. Place names such as Orillia, Gravenhurst, Haliburton, Algonquin, and Muskoka reveal the history of the land's inhabitants, from Algonquin tribes to European explorers to fur traders. This huge 4,761-square-km (1,838-square-mile) swath of land and lakes is also referred to colloquially as cottage country. (In Ontario, "cottage" is broadly used to describe any vacation home, from a fishing shack to a near-mansion.) The area became a haven for the summering rich and famous during the mid–19th century, when lumber barons who were harvesting near port towns set up steamship and rail lines, making travel to the area possible. Since then, cottage country has attracted urbanites who make the pilgrimage to hear the call of the loon or swat incessant mosquitoes and black flies. A few modern-day celebrities are reported to have cottages here as well, such as Bill Murray and Steven Spielberg. For the cottageless, overnight seasonal camping in a provincial park is an option, as is a stay in a rustic lodge or posh resort. 8

Tourism Information Haliburton County Tourism ☎ *705/286–1333, 800/461–7677* 🌐 *www.haliburtoncounty.ca.* **Muskoka Tourism** ☎ *705/689–0660, 800/267–9700* 🌐 *www.discovermuskoka.ca.*

GRAVENHURST

74 km (46 miles) north of Barrie on Hwy. 11.

Gravenhurst is a town of approximately 10,000 and the birthplace of Norman Bethune, a surgeon, inventor, and political activist who is a Canadian hero. The heart of town is the colorful Muskoka Wharf, with its boardwalk along the water, restaurants, steamship docks, vacation condos, and plaza that hosts festivals and a Wednesday farmers' market from mid-May to early October. Still, Gravenhurst is a tiny town and can be seen in a day or even an afternoon.

WHEN TO GO

As with everywhere in the Muskokas, Gravenhurst comes alive in the summer months, with many attractions opening only after Victoria Day and closing between Labour Day and mid-October, as the weather dictates. Nevertheless, area resorts do plan winter activities—snowshoeing, sleigh rides, and the like—and restaurants are open (with shorter off-season hours) year-round.

GETTING HERE AND AROUND

From Toronto, take Highway 400 north, which intersects with the highly traveled and often congested Highway 11. Gravenhurst is about 70 km (40 miles) north of the junction on Highway 11. Driving time in good traffic is a bit over two hours. Ontario Northland buses and trains operate six days a week between Toronto's Union Station and downtown Gravenhurst; travel time is 2 hours 10 minutes.

ESSENTIALS

Transportation Information Ontario Northland ☎ *800/461–8558* 🌐 *www.ontarionorthland.ca.* **Gravenhurst Bus and Railway Station** ✉ *150 Second St. S.* ☎ *705/687–2301.*

Visitor Information Gravenhurst Chamber of Commerce ✉ *685-2 Muskoka Rd. N* ☎ *705/687–4432* 🌐 *www.gravenhurstchamber.com.*

EXPLORING

Bethune Memorial House. An 1880-vintage frame structure, this National Historic Site honors the heroic efforts of field surgeon and medical educator Henry Norman Bethune (1830–1939), who worked in China during the Sino-Japanese War in the 1930s and trained thousands to become medics and doctors. There are period rooms and an exhibit tracing the highlights of his life. The house has become a shrine of sorts for Chinese diplomats visiting North America. ✉ *235 John St. N* ☎ *705/687–4261* 🌐 *www.pc.gc.ca/lhn-nhs/on/bethune/index.aspx* 🎫 *C$3.90* ⏲ *June Wed.–Sun., 10–4; July–Oct., daily 10–4.*

Muskoka Boat & Heritage Centre. Learn about steamboat history and technology in this museum with a rotating collection of historic boats that have included a 1924 propeller boat, a 30-foot 1894 steamboat, and gleaming wooden speedboats. ✉ *275 Steamship Bay Rd., Muskoka Wharf* ☎ *705/687–2115, 866/687–6667* 🌐 *realmuskoka.com* 🎫 *C$7.50* ⏲ *Mid-June–late Oct., Tues.–Fri. 10–6, Sat.–Mon. 10–4; late Oct.–mid-June, Tues.–Sat. 10–4.*

FAMILY **Muskoka Steamships Cruises.** In warm weather, cruises tour the Muskoka lakes on historic and reproduction vessels. Excursions range from one to eight hours and include lunch and dinner cruises, sightseeing cruises, and themed trips, like the murder-mystery cruise and, for kids, a cruise with a magic show, a visit to a wildlife park, or pirate dress-up. The restored 128-foot-long, 99-passenger *RMS Segwun* (the initials stand for Royal Mail Ship) is North America's oldest operating steamship, built in 1887, and is the sole survivor of a fleet that provided transportation through the Muskoka Lakes. The 200-passenger *Wenonah II* is a 1907-inspired vessel with modern technology. Reservations are required. Learn about steamboat history and technology in the **Muskoka Boat and Heritage Centre** with a rotating collection of historic boats that have included a 1924 propeller boat, a 30-foot 1894 steamboat, and gleaming wooden speedboats. ✉ *185 Cherokee Ln., Muskoka Wharf* ☎ *705/687–6667, 866/687–6667* 🌐 *realmuskoka.com* 🎫 *Sightseeing cruises C$20–C$50; lunch and dinner cruises C$52–C$87* ⏲ *June–Oct. 8:30–4:30; Nov.–May weekdays 8:30–4:30.*

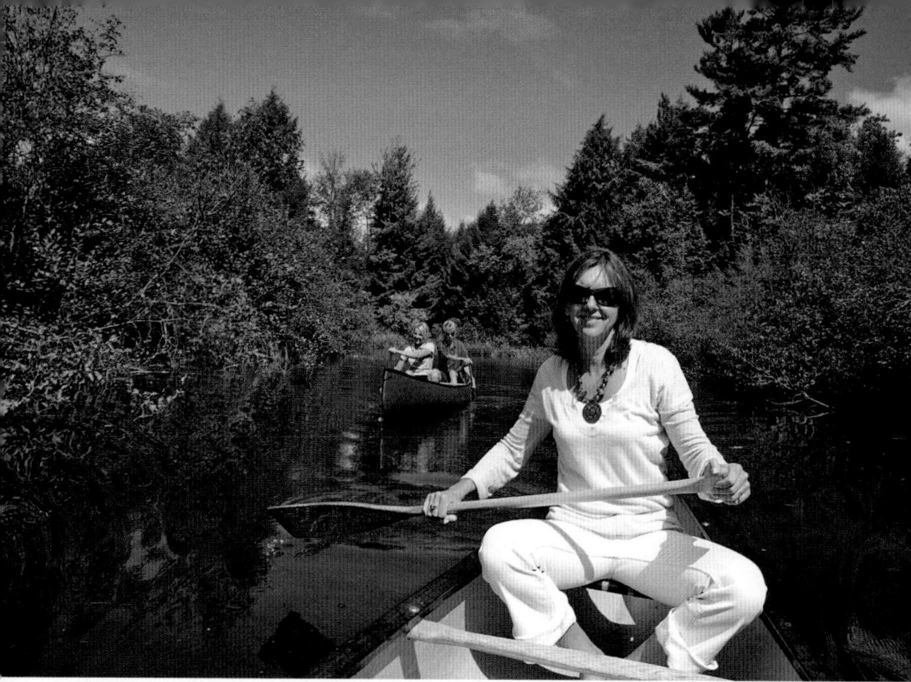

The Muskoka region north of Toronto is a popular destination for people wanting to escape the faster pace of city life.

WHERE TO EAT

$$ CAFÉ ✕ **Blue Willow Tea Shop.** The dozen or so petite tables are set with Blue Willow–pattern china in this quaint restaurant serving traditional English fare on the Muskoka Wharf overlooking the bay. Afternoon tea—a three-tier platter of shortbread, scones with Devonshire cream, and savory finger sandwiches, plus a pot of tea per person—is served every day from 2 to 5 pm, for C$23. Other than tea, sandwiches, such as grilled bacon and Brie, quiches, and specials like homemade stews are offered for lunch. Popular items on the short dinner menu include baked fish-and-chips, prime rib with Yorkshire pudding, and classic bangers and mash. The attached shop sells loose-leaf teas and other food items for your own tea party at home. It often opens for special meals on holidays. *Average main: C$15 ✉ 900 Bay St., Muskoka Wharf ☎ 705/687–2597 ⊕ www.bluewillowteashop.ca ⊙ Sun., Tues.–Thurs. 11–3, Fri.–Sat. 11–8 ⊙ Closed Mon. and Sept.–June.*

$$$ CANADIAN ✕ **Elements.** Consistent with the aesthetics of Taboo Resort, Elements offers luxurious and contemporary international cuisine in a structured, modern, and subdued dining room, with sleek black wood veneers, hardwood floors, and a wall of lakefront windows. The Mediterrean, French, and Canadian-inspired menu changes seasonally but is well represented by dishes like steelhead trout with Ontario asparagus and couscous, and grilled rib eye with shallot bordelaise and king oyster mushrooms. The wine list features more than 350 consignment wines, not available in the LCBO, and includes their own private label. For the highly acclaimed **Culinary Theatre** experience (C$100 per person; C$160 with wine), bar stools surround the chef's station, giving you an up-close view of the preparation of your meal. Wine

classes are offered on Saturdays. *Average main: C$30 ⊠ Taboo Resort, 1209 Muskoka Beach Rd. ☎ 705/687–2233, 800/461–0236 ⊕ www.tabooresort.com ✍ Reservations essential.*

$ CAFÉ **✕ Marty's World Famous Café.** Duck into this cozy café in the afternoon for what is possibly the best butter tart you've ever tasted. The chalkboard on the wall lists other home-cooked dishes like pies, quiche, and daily soups and sandwiches. Food and decor is simple, natural, and homey, just like the neighborhood. It's located outside of Gravenhurst in Bracebridge. *Average main: C$10 ⊠ 5 Manitoba St., Bracebridge ☎ 705/645–4794 ⊕ www.martysworldfamous.com.*

$$$$ CANADIAN **✕ North.** Since opening in 2007 in the center of Gravenhurst, North has been praised as one of the best restaurants in Muskoka, serving hearty Canadian fare that makes good use of local meats and produce. The small dining room, with walls lined with paintings by local artists, high-backed dark leather chairs and white tablecloths paired with rustic-looking stained pine floors, has a clean and rustic farm-to-table chic. Chef Alain Irvine's menu changes seasonally but patrons can expect staples such as grilled strip steak in in red wine with horseradish sour cream potatoes and baby carrots; wild boar with roasted fingerlings and green peppercorn *jus*; and fish-and-chips with house-made tartar sauce. Popular dessert includes brownies made with local Muskoka Brewery brown ale. Despite its being one of the classiest establishments in town, the atmosphere is relaxed and the service friendly and attentive. *Average main: C$32 ⊠ 530 Muskoka Rd. N ☎ 705/687–8618 ⊕ northinmuskoka.com ✍ Reservations essential ⏲ Closed Sun. and Mon. No lunch.*

WHERE TO STAY

For expanded hotel reviews, visit Fodors.com.

$$$ RESORT ALL-INCLUSIVE FAMILY **Bayview-Wildwood Resort.** Seemingly remote but truly only a 20-minute drive south of Gravenhurst, this all-inclusive lakeside resort dates to 1898 and is particularly geared to outdoor types and families. **Pros:** great for families; casual atmosphere; free activities for kids. **Cons:** strict meal times; noisy cargo trains pass by day and night. *Rooms from: C$250 ⊠ 1500 Port Stanton Pkwy., R.R. 1, Severn Bridge ☎ 705/689–2338, 800/461–0243 ⊕ www.bayviewwildwood.com 28 rooms, 26 suites, 16 cottages, 3 houses All-inclusive.*

$$$$ RESORT Fodor's Choice ★ **Taboo Resort, Golf and Spa.** A magnificent 1,000-acre landscape of rocky outcrops and evergreen trees typical of the Muskoka region surrounds this Alpine lodge–style, deluxe resort. **Pros:** fantastic golf course; forest and lake views; excellent spa and restaurant. **Cons:** expensive; too easy to never leave the resort grounds. *Rooms from: C$289 ⊠ 1209 Muskoka Beach Rd. ☎ 705/687–2233, 800/461–0236 ⊕ www.tabooresort.com 79 rooms, 22 suites, 15 Cottage Chalets.*

SHOPPING

Muskoka Cottage Brewery. It's a real treat to visit this brewery, tasting room, and retail store for one of the most popular beers in Ontario, especially if you come for the free tour. While you're here, taste a few popular beers like the cream ale and Mad Tom IPA, or seasonal ales like summer weiss or double chocolate cranberry stout. It's halfway between Gravenhurst and Bracebridge, off Highway 11. ⊠ *1964 Muskoka*

Beach Rd., Bracebridge ☎ 705/646–1266 🌐 www.muskokabrewery.com ⏲ Mon., Tues., and Sat. 11–5, Wed. and Thurs. 11–6, Fri. 11–8. Tours: June–Aug. Thurs.–Sat. 12:30, 1:30, 2:30, and 3:30.

HUNTSVILLE

51 km (32 miles) north of Gravenhurst on Hwy. 11.

Muskoka's Huntsville region is filled with lakes and streams, stands of virgin birch and pine, and deer—and no shortage of year-round resorts. It is usually the cross-country skier's best bet for an abundance of natural snow in Southern Ontario. All resorts have trails.

WHEN TO GO

Summer is high season for vacationers in Huntsville, but the town is also ideal for cross-country skiing, ice fishing, and other backcountry winter adventures.

GETTING HERE AND AROUND

From Toronto, take Highway 400 north just past Barrie and then take Highway 11 north about 120 km (75 miles). Without traffic, the trip is about three hours. At least four Ontario Northland buses operate between Toronto's Union Station and Huntsville daily; travel time is four hours, and the station is in the north of the city, a short walk to Main Street.

From Gravenhurst, Huntsville is about 55 km (35 miles) north on Highway 11, a 45-minute drive.

ESSENTIALS

Transportation Information Huntsville Bus Station ✉ *77 Centre St. N* ☎ *705/789–6431.* **Ontario Northland** ☎ *705/789–6431, 800/461–8558* 🌐 *www.ontarionorthland.ca.*

Visitor Information Huntsville/Lake of Bays Chamber of Commerce ✉ *8 West St. N* ☎ *705/789–4771* 🌐 *huntsvillelakeofbays.on.ca.*

WHERE TO EAT

$$$ CANADIAN **✕ The Norsemen Restaurant.** Generations of devotees have returned to this lakeside restaurant in the wooded hills near Huntsville for the warm hospitality and modern Canadian cuisine with French flair, some of whom may even come by canoe or kayak. Built in the 1920s, the lodge became a restaurant in 1970 and is unabashedly rustic and homey: double-sided stone fireplace, locally harvested beams overhead, and oxbows over the doorways. Even the coffee is roasted in-house on a daily basis. Ask to be seated by the screened-in porch for a view of the lake to soak in the leisurely evening. Popular and enduring dishes include Ontario rack of lamb and prime rib with Yorkshire pudding. Menu of seven or so entrées include at least one vegetarian option. Round out the meal with fun and modern desserts like s'mores mousse and green-tea poached pear. The extensive wine list is a point of pride. Seatings are between 5:30 and 9:30. *$ Average main: C$27 ✉ 1040 Walker Lake Dr., 2 km (1 mile) north of Hwy. 60 ☎ 705/635–2473, 800/565–3856 🌐 www.norsemen-walkerlake.com ⏲ Dec.–Mar. closed Sun.–Thurs.; Apr.–June, Sept. and Oct. closed Mon. and Tues.; June–Aug. closed Mon. Closed Nov.*

8

WHERE TO STAY

For expanded hotel reviews, visit Fodors.com.

$$$ RESORT **Deerhurst Resort.** This deluxe resort along Peninsula Lake is a 780-acre, self-contained community with restaurants and lodgings to fit every budget and style, from weddings to corporate events. **Pros:** wide-range of amenities; something for everyone; recently renovated. **Cons:** size can be overwhelming for some; busy check-in and check-out mean occasional waits. *Rooms from: C$219 ✉ 1235 Deerhurst Dr., just south of Rte. 60 ☎ 705/789–6411, 800/461–4393 ⊕ www.deerhurstresort.com 400 rooms No meals.*

$$ RESORT FAMILY **Walker Lake Resort.** Rustic two- and three-bedroom cottages overlook Walker Lake at this resort, and many come with Jacuzzi tubs and fireplaces. **Pros:** very peaceful setting; lively and cheery restaurant. **Cons:** no TVs; cottages are by weekly rental only. *Rooms from: C$175 ✉ 1040 Walker Lake Dr., R.R. 4 ☎ 705/635–2473, 800/565–3856 in Canada ⊕ www.norsemen-walkerlake.com 7 cottages No meals.*

SPORTS AND THE OUTDOORS

Hidden Valley Highlands Ski Area. The ski area has 35 skiable acres with 13 hills and three quad lifts. It's great for beginner and intermediate skiers, with a couple of black-diamond runs for daredevils. ✉ *1655 Hidden Valley Rd., off Hwy. 60, 8 km east of town* ☎ *705/789–1773, 800/398–9555* ⊕ *www.skihiddenvalley.on.ca.*

ALGONQUIN PROVINCIAL PARK

35 km (23 miles) east of Huntsville on Hwy. 60.

WHEN TO GO

Most people go to Algonquin in the summer, but the many winter attractions—ice fishing, cross-country skiing, dogsled tours—make it a popular destination in cold months as well. The only time to avoid is the notorious blackfly season, usually sometime in May. The mosquito population is healthy all summer, so pack repellent, pants, and long-sleeved shirts. Algonquin Provincial Park can be done in a weekend, but four days is the average stay; the park is huge and there's a lot of ground to cover.

GETTING HERE AND AROUND

A good four-hour drive from Toronto, Algonquin is most readily reached via Highway 400 north to Highway 60 east. The huge park has 29 different access points, so call to devise the best plan of attack for your visit based on your interests. The most popular entry points are along the Highway 60 corridor, where you'll find all the conventional campgrounds. If you're heading into the park's interior, spring for the detailed Algonquin Canoe Routes Map (C$4.95), available from the park's website. The visitor centers, at the park gates, or on the Highway 60 corridor, 43 km (27 miles) east of the west gate, have information on park programs, a bookstore, a restaurant, and a panoramic-viewing deck. **TIP→ In winter, go with a four-wheel-drive vehicle.**

ADVENTURE TOURS NEAR ALGONQUIN

If planning an Algonquin Park adventure seems daunting, leave it to the pros. Transport from Toronto, meals, and accommodations are included. You might, for example, do a multiday paddle-and-portage trip, catered with organic meals. Most companies have cabins, some quite luxurious, in Algonquin Park for tour participants; other tours may require backcountry tent camping.

Call of the Wild. Call of the Wild offers guided trips of different lengths—dogsledding and snowmobiling in winter, canoeing and hiking in summer—deep in the park away from the more touristy areas. The tour company's in-park Algonquin Eco Lodge is powered only by waterfall. A popular package is a four-day canoe trip and three days relaxing at the lodge. ☎ *905/471–9453, 800/776–9453* 🌐 *www.callofthewild.ca.*

Northern Edge Algonquin. Northern Edge Algonquin eco-adventure company provides adventurous learning vacations and retreats with themes such as moose-tracking (via canoe), sea kayaking, yoga, shamanism, and women-only weekends. Home-cooked comfort food is local and organic; lodging ranges from new cabins to tents. ☎ *888/383–8320* 🌐 *www.northernedgealgonquin.com.*

Voyageur Quest. Voyageur Quest has a variety of adventure wilderness trips year-round in Algonquin Park and throughout northern Ontario, including a number of family-geared vacations. ☎ *416/486–3605, 800/794–9660* 🌐 *www.voyageurquest.com.*

Winterdance Dogsled Tours. Winterdance Dogsled Tours takes you on half-day, full-day, multiday, and moonlight dogsledding adventures in and near Algonquin Provincial Park. Canoe tours are available in summer, as are kennel visits with the sled dogs. ✉ *6577 Haliburton Lake Rd., Haliburton* ☎ *705/457–5281* 🌐 *www.winterdance.com.*

8

EXPLORING

This park stretches across 7,650 square km (2,954 square miles), containing nearly 2,500 lakes, 272 bird species, 45 species of mammals, and 50 species of fish and encompassing forests, rivers, and cliffs. The typical visitor is a hiker, canoeist, camper, or all three. But don't be put off if you're not the athletic or outdoorsy sort. About a third of Algonquin's visitors come for the day to walk one of the 17 well-groomed and well-signed interpretive trails or to enjoy a swim or a picnic. Swimming is especially good at the Lake of Two Rivers, halfway between the west and east gates along Highway 60. Spring, when the moose head north, is the best time to catch a glimpse of North America's largest land mammal. Getting up at the crack of dawn gives you the best chance of seeing the park's wildlife. Park naturalists give talks on area wildflowers, animals, and birds, and you can book a guided hike or canoe trip. Expeditions to hear wolf howling take place in late summer and early autumn. The park's **Algonquin Logging Museum** (🕑 *late-June–mid Oct., daily 9–5*) depicts life at an early Canadian logging camp. ✉ *Hwy. 60, main and east gate is west of town of Whitney; west gate is east of town of Dwight*

Highway 60 takes drivers on a scenic route through Ontario's famed Algonquin Provincial Park.

705/633–5572 www.algonquinpark.on.ca C$16 per vehicle Apr.–mid-Oct., daily 8 am–10 pm; mid-Oct.–Mar., daily 9–5. Park attractions may have their own operating hrs; call ahead.

WHERE TO EAT

If you'd like wine with dinner, bring your own: park restrictions prohibit the sale of alcohol here.

$$$$ CANADIAN **Arowhon Pines Restaurant.** A meal at this breathtaking, circular log-cabin restaurant in the heart of Algonquin Park is the highlight of many visits. A view of the lake is a great accompaniment to the food, but a towering stone fireplace in the center of the room is an attraction, too. Menu changes daily, but guests can expect hearty Canadian dishes with local and seasonal ingredients like Northern Ontario trout with sautéed potatoes and squash, rack of lamb scented with garlic and rosemary, or roasted loin of pork stuffed with apples and prunes. The menu always includes plenty of vegetarian options, and other diets are readily accommodated. Bring your own wine for no corkage fee. If you have kids in tow, take advantage of the early kids' dinner (5:30 pm) followed by a group babysitting service until 8 pm. Dinners are C$75 prix-fixe for the public; lunch (C$35) and breakfast (C$25) are also served. *Average main: C$75 Algonquin Provincial Park, near west entrance, 8 km north of Hwy. 60 705/633–5661, 866/633–5661 arowhonpines.ca Reservations essential Closed mid-Oct.–late-May.*

$$$$ CANADIAN **Bartlett Lodge Restaurant.** In the original 1917 lodge building, this small lakeside pine dining room offers an ever-changing prix-fixe menu of comtemporary Canadian cuisine, which might kick off with fennel and mustard rubbed pork belly and move on to pistachio and

CLOSE UP

Camping in Algonquin Provincial Park

Algonquin Provincial Park. Campgrounds, backcountry camping, and cabins are all available inside the park. Along the parkway corridor, a 56-km (35-mile) stretch of Highway 60, are eight organized campgrounds. Prices range from C$37 to C$48 depending on the location and whether you require electricity. Within the vast park interior you won't find any organized campsites (and the purists love it that way). Interior camping permits are C$12 per person, available from Ontario Parks. Contact Algonquin Park's main number (☎ *705/633–5572*) to learn about the guidelines for of interior camping before calling Ontario Parks to reserve. In between the extremes of the corridor campgrounds and interior camping are the lesser-known peripheral campgrounds—Kiosk, Brent, and Achray—in the northern and eastern reaches of the park, which you access by long dirt roads. These sites do not have showers, and Brent has only pit toilets. The Highway 60 corridor campsites have showers, picnic tables, and, in some cases, RV hookups.

A bit less extreme than pitching a tent in Algonquin's interior but just as remote is a stay in one of the park-run ranger cabins (C$58–C$134 per person, C$11 each additional adult), which have woodstove or propane heat and, in some cases, mattresses and electricity. Four of the 13 cabins are accessible by car; the rest are reached by canoe, which can take from one hour to two days.

Reservations are required for all campsites, cabins, and for interior camping; call the **Ontario Parks reservations line** (☎ 888/668–7275 🌐 www.ontarioparks.com). ☎ *705/633–5572* 🌐 *www.algonquinpark.on.ca.*

8

cherry crusted Australian rack of lamb or the house specialty, beef tenderloin. Fish and vegetarian options, such as sweet-potato gnocchi with shaved Gruyère, are always available. Desserts, included with the meal, all made on-site, feature cheesecakes, some variation of crème brûlée (perhaps a chocolate-chili version), and homemade pie. Breakfast is served from 8 am to 9:30 am, and dinner seatings are at 6 pm and 8 pm only. **TIP→ You must bring your own wine.** $ *Average main: C$64 ✉ Algonquin Park, by boat from Cache Lake Landing, just south of Hwy. 60, Huntsville ☎ 705/633–5543, 866/614–5355 🌐 www.bartlettlodge.com ✍ Reservations essential ⏲ Closed late-Oct.–mid-May. No lunch.*

WHERE TO STAY

For expanded hotel reviews, visit Fodors.com.

$$$$ RESORT ALL-INCLUSIVE **Arowhon Pines.** The stuff of local legend, Arowhon is a family-run wilderness retreat deep in Algonquin Provincial Park known for unpretentious rustic "luxury" and superb dining. **Pros:** all-inclusive swimming, sailing, canoeing, kayaking, hiking, and birding on a private lake in a gorgeous setting; excellent restaurant. **Cons:** limited cell phone service; pricey considering rusticity of cabins; only half the rooms have water views. $ *Rooms from: C$251 ✉ Algonquin Park, near west entrance, 8 km north of Hwy. 60 ☎ 705/633–5661,*

866/633–5661 toll-free year-round ⊕ www.arowhonpines.ca ⇨ 50 rooms in 13 cabins ⊙ Closed mid-Oct.–late May ¶ All-inclusive.

$$$ RESORT **Bartlett Lodge.** Smack in the center of Algonquin Provincial Park, this impressive 1917 resort is reached by a short boat ride on Cache Lake (just make your reservation and use the phone at the landing to call the lodge when you arrive), and one of only two that is inside the provincial park. **Pros:** completely quiet; each cabin has its own canoe and porch. **Cons:** restaurant is expensive and only offers dinner (or picnic lunches). *[$] Rooms from: C$200 ⊠ Algonquin Park, by boat from Cache Lake Landing, just south of Hwy. 60 ☎ 705/633–5543, 905/338–8908 in winter ⊕ www.bartlettlodge.com ⇨ 12 cabins, 2 artist suites, 2 platform tents ⊙ Closed late Oct.–early May ¶ Some meals.*

SPORTS AND THE OUTDOORS

OUTFITTERS **Algonquin Outfitters.** Algonquin Outfitters is the most well-known outfitter and has multiple locations in and around the park, specializing in canoe trip packages and rentals, outfitting and camping services, sea kayaking, and a water-taxi service to the park's central areas. Stores are at Oxtongue Lake (the main store—near the west Highway 60 park entrance), Huntsville, Opeongo Lake, Bracebridge, Haliburton, and Brent Base on Cedar Lake. Call to confirm equipment rentals. Visit their website and blog for updates on park conditions and other happenings. *⊠ Oxtongue Lake store, 1035 Algonquin Outfitters Rd., R.R. 1, just north of Hwy. 60, Dwight ☎ 705/635–2243, 800/469–4948 ⊕ algonquinoutfitters.com.*

Portage Store. If you plan to camp in the park, you may want to contact the Portage Store, which provides extensive outfitting services and guided canoe trips. It rents canoes and sells self-guided canoe "packages" that include all the equipment you need for a canoeing-and-camping trip in the park. Also available are bike rentals, maps, detailed information about routes and wildlife, and an on-site general store and casual restaurant. When you arrive, employees can help you brush up on your paddling and portaging skills. *⊠ Hwy. 60, Canoe Lake ☎ 705/633–5622 in summer, 705/789–3645 in winter ⊕ www.portagestore.com.*

TRAVEL SMART TORONTO

GETTING HERE AND AROUND

Most of the action in Toronto happens between just north of Bloor and south to the waterfront and from High Park in the west to the Beach in the east. It's easy to get around this area via subway, streetcar, and bus. Service is frequent.

Yonge Street (pronounced "young") is the official dividing line between east and west streets. It's a north–south street that stretches from the waterfront up through the city. Street numbers increase heading away from Yonge in either direction. North–south street numbers increase heading north from the lake.

AIR TRAVEL

Flying time to Toronto is 1½ hours from New York and Chicago and 5 hours from Los Angeles. Nonstop to Toronto from London is about 7 hours.

Most airlines serving Toronto have numerous daily trips. Allow extra time for passing through customs and immigration, which are required for all passengers, including Canadians. The 2½-hour advance boarding time recommended for international flights applies to Canada. The Toronto airport has check-in kiosks for Air Canada flights, which cut back on time spent in line.

Brace yourself for the possibility of weather delays in winter.

All travelers must have a passport to enter or reenter the United States. U.S. Customs and Immigration maintains offices at Pearson International Airport in Toronto; U.S.-bound passengers should arrive early to clear customs before their flight.

Security measures at Canadian airports are similar to those in the United States.

Airline Security Issues Canadian Transportation Agency ☎ *888/222-2592* 🌐 *www.cta-otc.gc.ca.* **Transportation Security Administration** 🌐 *www.tsa.gov.*

NAVIGATING TORONTO

- The CN Tower can be seen from most anywhere in the city except on very cloudy days. Remember its location (Front and John streets) to get your bearings.
- Lake Ontario is the ultimate landmark. It's always south, no matter where you are.
- The subway is the fastest way to get around. Stay at a hotel near a subway line to make navigating the city easier.
- The streetcar and bus signs can be easy to miss. Look for the red, white, and blue signs with a black streetcar picture on electrical poles near street corners every five blocks or so along the route.

AIRPORTS

Most flights into Toronto land at Terminals 1 and 3 of Lester B. Pearson International Airport (YYZ), 32 km (20 miles) northwest of downtown. There are two main terminals, so check in advance which one your flight leaves from to save hassles. The automated LINK cable-line shuttle system moves passengers almost noiselessly between Terminals 1 and 3 and the GTAA Reduced Rate Parking Lot.

Wi-Fi Internet access is free in both terminals. There are several chain hotels at the airport.

Porter Airlines—which flies to Boston, Chicago, Halifax, Montréal, Newark, Ottawa, Québec City, and Washington, D.C.—is the only airline operating from Billy Bishop Toronto City Airport (YTZ), often called Toronto Island Airport. There are few amenities at this smaller airport, but it is very convenient to downtown.

Airport Information Lester B. Pearson International Airport ✉ *Toronto* ☎ *416/776-9892* 🌐 *www.torontopearson.com.* **Billy Bishop Toronto City Airport** ✉ *Toronto* ☎ *416/203-6942* 🌐 *www.torontoport.com/airport.aspx.*

GROUND TRANSPORTATION

Although Pearson International Airport isn't far from downtown, the drive can take well over an hour during weekday rush hours from 6:30 to 9:30 am and 3:30 to 6:30 pm. Taxis to a hotel or attraction near the lake cost C$53 and have fixed rates to different parts of the city. (Check fixed-rate maps at *www.torontopearson.com*.) You must pay the full fare from the airport, but it's often possible to negotiate a lower fare going to the airport from downtown with regular city cabs. It's illegal for city cabs to pick up passengers at the airport, unless they're called—a time-consuming process sometimes worth the wait for the lower fare. Likewise, airport taxis can't pick up passengers going to the airport; only regular taxis can be hailed or called to go to the airport.

A 24-hour Airport Express coach service runs daily to several major downtown hotels and the Toronto Coach Terminal (Bay and Dundas streets). It costs C$26.95 one-way, C$40 round-trip. Pickups are from the arrivals levels of the terminals at Pearson. Look for the curbside bus shelter, where tickets are sold.

GO Transit interregional buses transport passengers to the Yorkdale and York Mills subway stations from the arrivals levels. Service can be irregular (once per hour) and luggage space limited, but at C$5.35 it's one of the least expensive ways to get to the city's northern sections (or onto the subway line).

Two Toronto Transit Commission (TTC) buses also run from any of the airport terminals to the subway system. Bus 192 (Airport Rocket bus) connects to the Kipling subway station; Bus 58 Malton links to the Lawrence West station. Luggage space is limited and no assistance is given, but the price is only C$3 in exact change (⇨ *See Bus Travel*).

If you rent a car at the airport, ask for a street map of the city. Highway 427 runs south some 6 km (4 miles) to the lakeshore. Here you pick up the Queen Elizabeth Way (QEW) east to the Gardiner Expressway, which runs east into the heart of downtown. If you take the QEW west, you'll find yourself swinging around Lake Ontario, toward Hamilton, Niagara-on-the-Lake, and Niagara Falls.

From Toronto Island Airport a free ferry operates to the terminal at the base of Bathurst Street; the trip takes less than 10 minutes. At the time of writing, a pedestrian tunnel was under construction. It's expected to be operational by early 2014. Porter Airlines also runs a free shuttle from Union Station to the ferry terminal/tunnel entrance.

Contacts GO Transit ☎ *416/869–3200, 888/438–6646* ⊕ *www.gotransit.com.* **Airport Express** ☎ *905/564–3232, 800/387–6787* ⊕ *www.torontoairportexpress.com.* **Toronto Transit Commission or TTC** ☎ *416/393–4636* ⊕ *www.ttc.ca.*

TRAVEL TO DOWNTOWN TORONTO FROM PEARSON AIRPORT

Mode of Transport	Duration	Price
Taxi	45–90 min	C$53
Airport Express bus	45–90 min	C$26.95
GO train	40 min	C$5.35
Car	45–90 min	NA
TTC	40 min	C$3

FLIGHTS

Toronto is served by Air Canada, American, Delta, United, and US Airways as well as more than a dozen European and Asian carriers with easy connections to many U.S. cities. Toronto is also served within Canada by WestJet, Porter, and Air Transat, a charter airline.

Airline Contacts Air Canada ☎ *888/247–2262, 514/393–3333* ⊕ *www.aircanada.com.* **Air Transat** ☎ *877/872–6728, 514/906–5196* ⊕ *www.airtransat.ca.* **American Airlines** ☎ *800/433–7300* ⊕ *www.aa.com.* **Delta Airlines** ☎ *800/221–1212 for U.S. reservations, 800/241–4141 for international reservations* ⊕ *www.delta.com.*

Porter Airlines ☎ *888/619–8622, 416/619–8622* 🌐 *www.flyporter.com.* **United Airlines** ☎ *800/864–8331* 🌐 *www.united.com.* **US Airways** ☎ *800/428–4322 for U.S. and Canada reservations, 800/622–1015 for international reservations* 🌐 *www.usairways.com.* **WestJet** ☎ *888/937–8538* 🌐 *www.westjet.com.*

BOAT TRAVEL

Frequent ferries connect downtown Toronto with the Toronto Islands. In summer, ferries leave every 15 to 30 minutes for Ward's Island, every hour for Centre Island, and every 30 to 45 minutes for Hanlan's Point. Ferries begin operation between 6:30 and 7:30 am and end between 11 and 11:45 pm. Fares are C$7 round-trip.

Boat Information

Toronto Islands Ferry ☎ *416/392–8193* 🌐 *www.toronto.ca/parks/island.*

BUS TRAVEL

ARRIVING AND DEPARTING

Most buses arrive at the Toronto Coach Terminal, which serves a number of lines, including Greyhound (which has regular service to Toronto from all over the United States), Coach Canada, Ontario Northland, and Can-AR. The trip takes 6 hours from Detroit, 3 hours from Buffalo, and 11 hours from Chicago and New York City. During busy times, such as around holidays, border crossings can add an hour or more to your trip as every passenger must disembark and be questioned.

Information on fares and departure times is available online or by phone. Tickets are purchased at the Toronto Coach Terminal before boarding the buses.

Some Canadian bus lines don't accept reservations, but Coach Canada and Greyhound Canada allow online ticket purchases, which can then be printed out ahead of time or picked up at the station. On most lines, there are discounts for senior citizens (over 60), children (under 12), and students (with ISIC cards). Purchase your tickets as far ahead as possible, especially for holiday travel. Seating is first-come, first-served; arriving 45 minutes before your bus's scheduled departure time usually gets you near the front of the line.

A low-cost bus company, Megabus, runs from Buffalo, New York, to Toronto through Niagara Falls. The further in advance tickets are purchased, the less expensive they are.

WITHIN TORONTO

Toronto Transit Commission (TTC) buses and streetcars link with every subway station to cover all points of the city. ⇨ *See Public Transportation Travel.*

Bus Information Can-AR ☎ *905/738–2290, 800/387–7097* 🌐 *www.can-arcoach.com.* **Coach Canada** ☎ *800/461–7661* 🌐 *www.coachcanada.com.* **Greyhound Lines of Canada Ltd.** ☎ *416/594–1010, 800/661–8747* 🌐 *www.greyhound.ca.* **Megabus** ☎ *866/488–4452* 🌐 *www.megabus.com.* **Ontario Northland** ☎ *705/472–4500, 800/363–7512* 🌐 *www.ontc.on.ca.* **Toronto Coach Terminal** ✉ *610 Bay St., just north of Dundas St. W, Dundas Square Area* ☎ *416/393–7911.*

CAR TRAVEL

Given the relatively high price of gas, Toronto's notoriously terrible traffic, and the ease of its public transportation system, car travel is recommended only for those who wish to drive to sites and attractions outside the city, such as the Niagara Wine Region, Niagara Falls, and live theater at Stratford or Niagara-on-the-Lake. The city of Toronto has an excellent transit system that's inexpensive, clean, and safe, and cabs are plentiful.

In Canada your own driver's license is acceptable for a stay of up to three months. In Ontario, you must be 21 to drive a rental car. There may be a surcharge of C$10–C$30 per day if you are between 21 and 25. Agreements may require that the car not be taken out of Canada, including the U.S. side of Niagara Falls; check when booking.

CAR RENTAL

Rates in Toronto begin at C$30 a day and C$150 a week for an economy car with unlimited mileage. This does not include tax, which is 13%. If you prefer a manual-transmission car, check whether the rental agency of your choice offers it; some companies don't in Canada. All the major chains listed *below* have branches both downtown and at Pearson International Airport.

Contacts Alamo ☎ *888/233-8749* 🌐 *www.alamo.com.* **Avis** ☎ *800/331-1084* 🌐 *www.avis.com.* **Budget** ☎ *800/472-3325* 🌐 *www.budget.com.* **Discount Car and Truck Rental** ☎ *800/263-2355 outside Ontario or in U.S., 416/249-5800 in Toronto, 888/820-7378 in Ontario* 🌐 *www.discountcar.com.* **Enterprise** ☎ *416/798-1465, 800/261-7331* 🌐 *www.enterprise.com.* **Hertz** ☎ *800/654-3001* 🌐 *www.hertz.com.* **National Car Rental** ☎ *800/227-7368* 🌐 *www.nationalcar.com.*

GASOLINE

Distances are always shown in kilometers, and gasoline is always sold in liters. (A gallon has 3.8 liters.)

Gas prices in Canada are higher than in the United States and have been on the rise. At this writing, the per-liter price is between C$1.25 and C$1.35 (US$4.73–$5.10 per gallon). Gas stations are plentiful; many are self-service and part of small convenience stores. Large stations are open 24 hours; smaller ones close after the dinner rush. For up-to-date prices and where to find the cheapest gas in the city (updated daily), go to 🌐 *www.torontogasprices.com.*

PARKING

Toronto has green parking-meter boxes everywhere. Parking tickets net the city C$50 million annually, so they are frequently given out. Boxes are computerized; regular rates between C$1 and C$2.50 per half hour are payable with coins—the dollar coin, the two-dollar coin, and nickels, dimes, and quarters are accepted—or a credit card (AE, MC, or V). Parking lots are found under office buildings or on side streets near main thoroughfares.

ROAD CONDITIONS

Rush hours in Toronto (6:30 to 9:30 am and 3:30 to 6:30 pm) are bumper-to-bumper, especially on the 401 and Gardiner Expressway. Avoid them like the plague, particularly when coming into or leaving the city.

ROADSIDE EMERGENCIES

The American Automobile Association (AAA) has 24-hour road service in Canada, provided via a partnership with the Canadian Automobile Association (CAA).

Emergency Services Canadian Automobile Association ☎ *416/221-4300, 800/268-3750* 🌐 *www.caa.ca.*

RULES OF THE ROAD

By law, you're required to wear seat belts and to use infant seats in Ontario. Fines can be steep. Drivers are prohibited from using handheld cellular phones. Right turns are permitted on red signals unless otherwise posted. You must come to a complete stop before making a right turn on red. Pedestrian crosswalks are sprinkled throughout the city, marked clearly by overhead signs and very large painted yellow Xs. Pedestrians have the right of way in these crosswalks; however, Toronto pedestrians rarely heed crosswalk signals, so use caution in driving along downtown streets. The speed limit in most areas of the city is 50 kph (30 mph) and usually within the 90–110 kph (50–68 mph) range outside the city.

Watch out for streetcars stopped at intersections. Look to your right for a streetcar stop sign (red, white, and blue signs on electrical poles). ⚠ **It's illegal to pass or pull up alongside a streetcar stopped at an intersection—even if its doors aren't open—as it might be about to pick up or drop off passengers.** Stop behind the streetcar and wait for it to proceed.

Ontario is a no-fault province, and minimum liability insurance is C$200,000. If you're driving across the Ontario border, bring the policy or the vehicle-registration forms and a free Canadian Non-Resident Insurance Card from your insurance agent.

If you're driving a borrowed car, also bring a letter of permission signed by the owner.

Driving motorized vehicles while impaired by alcohol is taken seriously in Ontario and results in heavy fines, imprisonment, or both. It's illegal to refuse to take a Breathalyzer test. The possession of radar-detection devices in a car, even if they are not in operation, is illegal in Ontario. Studded tires and window coatings that do not allow a clear view of the vehicle interior are forbidden.

FROM THE UNITED STATES

Expect a wait at major border crossings. The wait at peak visiting times can be 60 minutes. If you can, avoid crossing on weekends and holidays at Detroit–Windsor, Buffalo–Fort Erie, and Niagara Falls, New York–Niagara Falls, Ontario, when the wait can be even longer.

Highway 401, which can stretch to 16 lanes in metropolitan Toronto, is the major link between Windsor, Ontario (and Detroit), and Montréal, Québec. There are no tolls anywhere along it, but you should be warned: between 6:30 and 9:30 each weekday morning and from 3:30 to 6:30 each afternoon, the 401 can become very crowded, even stop-and-go; plan your trip to avoid rush hours. A toll highway, the 407, offers quicker travel; there are no tollbooths, but cameras photograph license plates and the system bills you, if it has your address. It has access to plates registered in Georgia, Maryland, Maine, Michigan, New York, Ohio, Ontario, Québec, and Wisconsin. If you aren't identified then you don't have to pay. The 407 runs roughly parallel to the 401 for a 65-km (40-mile) stretch immediately north of Toronto.

If you're driving from Niagara Falls (U.S. or Canada) or Buffalo, New York, take the Queen Elizabeth Way (QEW), which curves along the western shore of Lake Ontario and eventually turns into the Gardiner Expressway, which flows right into downtown.

Insurance Information **Insurance Bureau of Canada** ☎ *416/362–2031* 🌐 *www.ibc.ca.*

PUBLIC TRANSPORTATION

The Toronto Transit Commission (TTC), which operates the buses, streetcars, and subways, is safe, clean, and reliable. There are three subway lines, with 65 stations along the way: the Bloor–Danforth line, which crosses Toronto about 5 km (3 miles) north of the lakefront, from east to west; the Yonge–University line, which loops north and south like a giant "U," with the bottom of the "U" at Union Station; and the Sheppard line, which covers the northeastern section of the city. A light rapid transit (LRT) line extends service to Harbourfront along Queen's Quay.

Buses and streetcars link with every subway station to cover all points of the city. Service is generally excellent, with buses and streetcars covering major city thoroughfares about every 10 minutes; suburban service is less frequent.

TICKETS

The single fare for subways, buses, and streetcars is C$3. An all-day unlimited-use pass (valid from the start of service until 5:30 am the next day) is C$10:75; three tickets or tokens are available for C$7.95; and seven tickets or tokens cost $18.55. **TIP→ On weekends and holidays, up to two adults and four children can use the C$10.75 day pass—an excellent savings.**

Tokens and tickets are sold in each subway station and many convenience stores. All vehicles accept tickets, tokens, or exact change, but you must buy tickets and tokens before you board. With tickets or exact change on the subway, you must use the turnstile closest to the station agent window and drop the ticket or money into the clear receptacle, whereas a token or swipecard can be used at any turnstile. Paper transfers are free; pick one up from the driver when you pay your fare on the bus or streetcar or get one from the transfer machines just past the turnstiles in the subway, then give the driver or station agent the transfer on the next leg of your journey. Note that transfers are time-sensitive from your start point, and TTC staff knows how long it takes to get to your transfer point to prevent misuse.

If you plan to stay in Toronto for a month or longer, consider the Metropass, a prepaid card (C$128.50) that allows unlimited rides during one calendar month.

TTC TICKET/PASS	PRICE
Single Fare	C$3
Day Pass	C$10.75
3-Ticket or -Token Pack	C$7.95
7-Ticket or -Token Pack	C$18.55
Monthly Unlimited Pass	C$128.50

HOURS AND FREQUENCY

Subway trains run from approximately 6 am to 1:30 am Monday through Saturday and from 9 am to 1:30 am Sunday; holiday schedules vary. Subway service is frequent, with trains arriving every two to five minutes. Most buses and streetcars operate on the same hours as the subway. On weekdays, subway trains get very crowded (especially on the Yonge–University line northbound and the Bloor–Danforth line eastbound) from 8 to 10 am and 4 to 7 pm.

Late-night buses along Bloor and Yonge streets, and as far north on Yonge as Steeles Avenue, run from 1 am to 5:30 am. Streetcars that run 24 hours include those on King Street, Queen Street, and College Street. Late-night service is slower, with buses or streetcars arriving every 30 minutes or so. All-night transit-stop signs are marked with reflective blue bands.

Streetcar lines, especially the King line, are interesting rides with frequent service. Riding the streetcars is a great way to capture the flavor of the city as you pass through many neighborhoods.

STOPS AND INFORMATION

Streetcar stops have a red pole with a picture of a streetcar on it. Bus stops usually have shelters and gray poles with bus numbers and route maps posted. Both buses and streetcars have their final destination and their number on both the front and back and side windows. The drivers are friendly and will be able to help you with your questions.

The free *Ride Guide,* published annually by the TTC, is available in most subways. It shows nearly every major place of interest in the city and how to reach it by public transit. The TTC's telephone information line provides directions in 20 languages.

Smoking is prohibited on all subway trains, buses, and streetcars, a rule that is strictly enforced.

Subway and Streetcar Information
Toronto Transit Commission or TTC
☎ *416/393–4636 recorded message, 416/393–4100 for lost and found, 416/393–4000 switchboard* 🌐 *www.ttc.ca.*

TAXI TRAVEL

Taxis can be hailed on the street, but if you need to make an appointment (e.g., for an early-morning airport run) or if you're in a residential neighborhood, it's necessary to call ahead. Taxi stands are rare and usually only at hotels and at the airport.

Taxi fares are C$4.25 for the first 0.143 km and C25¢ for each 31 seconds not in motion and for each additional 0.143 kilometers. A C$0.25 surcharge is added for each passenger in excess of four. The average fare to take a cab across downtown is C$8–C$9, plus a roughly 15% tip (⇨ *see Tipping*), when the traffic is flowing normally. The largest companies are Beck, Co-op, Diamond, Metro, and Royal.

TIP→ Call ☎ 416/829-4222 to be connected to one of many taxi companies for free via an automated system.

Taxi Companies **Beck** ☎ *416/751–5555, 877/883–2325* 🌐 *www.becktaxi.com.* **Co-op** ☎ *416/504–2667, 877/471–4023* 🌐 *www.co-opcabs.com.* **Diamond** ☎ *416/366–6868* 🌐 *www.diamondtaxi.ca.* **Metro** ☎ *416/504–8294.* **Royal** ☎ *416/777–9222* 🌐 *www.royaltaxi.ca.*

TRAIN TRAVEL

Amtrak has service from New York and Chicago to Toronto (both 12 hours), providing connections between its own United States–wide network and VIA Rail's Canadian routes. VIA Rail runs trains to most major Canadian cities; travel along the Windsor–Québec City corridor is particularly well served. Amtrak and VIA Rail operate from Union Station on Front Street between Bay and York streets. You can walk underground to a number of hotels from the station, and there's a cab stand outside its main entrance.

Trains to Toronto may have two tiers of service: business class and reserved coach class. Business class is usually limited to one car, and benefits may include more legroom, meals, free Internet access, and complimentary alcoholic beverages.

To save money, look into rail passes, but be aware that if you don't plan to cover many miles, you may come out ahead by buying individual tickets.

VIA Rail's Canrail pass allows seven one-way trips in coach-class within a 21-day period, between two pre-determined points, with one stopover per trip permitted. Sleeping cars are available, but they sell out very early and must be reserved at least a month in advance during high season (June through mid-October). The Economy Pass (high season: C$1,008; low season: C$630) must be purchased three days prior to the first trip; the more expensive Plus Pass (high season: C$1,159; low season: C$725) can be booked up to the day before. There are discounts for youths and senior citizens aged 60 and over.

Children under two travel for free in a parent's seat, and children up to 11 can get their own seat for roughly half the price of an adult ticket.

Major credit cards, debit cards, and cash are accepted.

Reservations are strongly urged for inter-city and interprovincial travel and for journeys to and from the United States. If your ticket is lost, it is like losing cash, so guard it closely. If you lose your reservation number, your seat can still be accessed in their reservation system by using your name or the train you have been booked on.

GO Transit is the Greater Toronto Area's commuter rail. (It also runs buses.) The double-decker trains are comfortable and have restrooms.

Train Contacts **Amtrak** ☎ *800/872–7245* 🌐 *www.amtrak.com.* **GO Transit** ☎ *416/869–3200, 888/438–6646* 🌐 *www.gotransit.com.* **Union Station** ✉ *65–75 Front St., between Bay and York Sts.* ☎ *416/366–7788* 🌐 *www.toronto.ca/union_station.* **VIA Rail Canada** ☎ *888/842–7245* 🌐 *www.viarail.ca.*

ESSENTIALS

BUSINESS SERVICES AND FACILITIES

FedEx Office—where you can fax, copy, print, and rent computers—has several locations in Toronto.

Contacts FedEx Kinko's ✉ *357 Bay St., at Temperance St., Financial District* ☎ *416/363-2705* 🌐 *www.fedexkinkos.ca* ✉ *505 University Ave., at Dundas St. W, Chinatown* ☎ *416/979-8447* ✉ *459 Bloor St. W, at Major St., The Annex* ☎ *416/928-0110.*

COMMUNICATIONS

INTERNET

Most hotels in Toronto have some Internet access, and more and more are offering Wi-Fi. Chain hotels usually charge around C$15 per day for Wi-Fi. In boutique hotels and bed-and-breakfasts, Wi-Fi charges are rare. There are many designated Internet cafés around town, or cafés that provide Wi-Fi for customers.

Note that cybercafés frequently change hands and names but often stay in the same location. Rates are usually C$2–C$3 per hour. Two areas are hubs for 24-hour cybercafés: Bloor and Bathurst (heading east) and Church-Wellesley on Yonge. Cybercafes lists more than 4,000 Internet cafés worldwide.

Contacts Cybercafes 🌐 *www.cybercafes.com.*

PHONES

The good news is that you can now make a direct-dial telephone call from virtually any point on earth. The bad news? You can't always do so cheaply. Calling from a hotel is almost always the most expensive option; hotels usually add huge surcharges to all calls, particularly international ones. Calling cards usually keep costs to a minimum but only if you purchase them locally. And then there are mobile phones, which are sometimes more prevalent than landlines; as expensive as mobile phone calls can be, they are still usually a much cheaper option than calling from your hotel.

When you are calling Canada, the country code is 1. The country code is 1 for the United States as well so dialing a Canadian number is like dialing a number long distance in the U.S.—dial 1, followed by the 10-digit number.

CALLING WITHIN CANADA

Local calls in Canada are exactly the same as local calls in the United States. Despite the ubiquity of cell phones, pay phones still appear every few blocks and take quarters (C50¢ for the first three minutes). Ask at your hotel whether local calls are free—there may be hefty charges for phone use. Buying a prepaid calling card or renting a cell phone may be worthwhile if you plan to make many local calls.

CALLING OUTSIDE CANADA

Calling to the United States from Canada is billed as an international call, even though you don't have to dial anything but 1 and the 10-digit number. Charges can be $1 per minute or more on cell phones. Prepaid calling cards are the best option.

CALLING CARDS

Prepaid phone cards, which can be purchased at convenience stores, are generally the cheapest way to call the United States. You can find cards for as little as C$5 for eight hours of talk time. With these cards, you call a toll-free number, then enter the code from the back of the card. You can buy the cards online before you leave home.

MOBILE PHONES

If you have a multiband phone and your service provider uses the world-standard GSM network (as do T-Mobile, AT&T, and Verizon), you can probably use your phone in Canada. Roaming fees can be steep, however: 99¢ a minute is considered reasonable. And internationally you normally pay the toll charges for incoming calls. It's almost always cheaper to send a text message than to make a call as text messages have a very low set fee (often less than C5¢).

If you just want to make local calls, consider buying a new SIM card (note that your provider may have to unlock your phone for this) and a prepaid service plan in the destination. You'll then have a local number and can make local calls at local rates. If your trip is extensive, you could also simply buy a new cell phone in your destination, as the initial cost will be offset over time. Fido, a Canadian cell-phone company, sells prepaid SIM cards with a rate of C40¢-per-minute for the first five minutes of the day (C20¢-per-minute after that) to the U.S. and long-distance in Canada, but you have to go to a Fido store to buy and install the card.

TIP→ If you travel internationally frequently, save one of your old mobile phones or buy a cheap one on the Internet; ask your cell phone company to unlock it for you and take it with you as a travel phone, buying a new SIM card with pay-as-you-go service in each destination.

There are plenty of mobile-phone stores in downtown Toronto for renting phones. You can rent cell phones for as little as US$29 per week with Cellular Abroad, but international rates to the U.S. are 66¢ per minute.

Cellular Abroad rents and sells GSM phones and sells SIM cards that work in many countries. Mobal rents mobiles and sells GSM phones with SIM cards (starting at US$29) that will operate in 140 countries. Per-call rates vary throughout the world. Planet Fone rents cell phones, but the per-minute rates are expensive.

Contacts Cellular Abroad ☎ *800/287–5072* 🌐 *www.cellularabroad.com.* **Fido** ✉ *218 Yonge St., between Queen and Dundas, Dundas Square Area* ☎ *416/597–1436* 🌐 *fido.ca.* **Mobal** ☎ *888/888–9162* 🌐 *www.mobalrental.com.* **Planet Fone** ☎ *888/988–4777* 🌐 *www.planetfone.com.*

CUSTOMS AND DUTIES

You're always allowed to bring goods of a certain value back home without having to pay any duty or import tax. But there's a limit on the amount of tobacco and liquor you can bring back duty-free, and some countries have separate limits for perfumes; for exact figures, check with your customs department. The values of so-called duty-free goods are included in these amounts. When you shop abroad, save all your receipts, as customs inspectors may ask to see them as well as the items you purchased. If the total value of your goods is more than the duty-free limit, you'll have to pay a tax (most often a flat percentage) on the value of everything beyond that limit.

Clearing customs is fastest if you're driving over the border. Unless you're pulled aside or traffic is backed up, you'll be through in a matter of minutes. When arriving by air, wait times can be lengthy—plan on at least 45 minutes. If you're traveling by bus, customs is a slow process, as all passengers must disembark, remove their luggage from the bus, and be questioned. Make sure all prescription drugs are clearly labeled or bring a copy of the prescription with you.

American and British visitors may bring in the following items duty-free: 200 cigarettes, 50 cigars, and 7 ounces of tobacco; 1 bottle (1.5 liters or 53 imperial ounces) of wine, 1.14 liters (40 ounces) of liquor, or 24 355-milliliter (12-ounce) bottles or cans of beer for personal consumption. Any alcohol and tobacco products in excess of these amounts are subject to duty fees, provincial fees, and taxes. You can also bring in gifts of no more than C$60 in value per gift.

A deposit is sometimes required for trailers, which is refunded upon return. Cats and dogs must have a certificate issued by a licensed veterinarian that clearly identifies the animal and certifies that it has been vaccinated against rabies during the preceding 36 months. Certified assistance dogs are allowed into Canada without restriction. Plant material must be declared and inspected. There may be restrictions on some live plants, bulbs, and seeds. With certain restrictions or prohibitions on some fruits and vegetables—including oranges, apples, and bananas—visitors may bring food with them for their own use, provided the quantity is consistent with the duration of the visit.

Canada's firearms laws are significantly stricter than those in the United States. All handguns and semiautomatic and fully automatic weapons are prohibited and cannot be brought into the country. Sporting rifles and shotguns may be imported provided they are to be used for sporting, hunting, or competing while in Canada. All firearms must be declared to Canada Customs at the first point of entry. Failure to declare firearms will result in their seizure, and criminal charges may be made. Regulations require visitors to have a confirmed "Firearms Declaration" to bring any guns for sporting, hunting, or competition into Canada; a fee of C$25 applies, good for 60 days. For more information, contact the Canadian Firearms Centre.

Information in Canada **Canada Revenue Agency** ☎ *800/284–5942 for international and non-resident inquiries* 🌐 *www.cra.gc.ca.* **Canadian Firearms Centre** ☎ *800/731–4000* 🌐 *www.rcmp-grc.gc.ca.*

U.S. Information **U.S. Customs and Border Protection** 🌐 *www.cbp.gov.*

ELECTRICITY

Canada's electrical capabilities and outlet types are no different from those in the United States. Residents of the United Kingdom, Australia, and New Zealand will need adapters to type A (not grounded) or type B (grounded) plugs. Voltage in Canada is 110, which differs from the United Kingdom, Australia, and New Zealand. Newer appliances should be fine, but check with the manufacturer and buy a voltage converter if necessary.

DID YOU KNOW?

Though Canada is a bilingual country—it has two official languages, French and English—Toronto is the Anglophone center of Canada, and 99% of the people living here will speak to you in English. By law, product labels must also be in French, but you won't find French road signs or hear much French here.

EMERGENCIES

For a complete listing of emergency services, you can always check the Yellow Pages or ask for assistance at your hotel desk. The Dental Emergency Clinic operates from 8 am to midnight. Many Pharma Plus Drugmarts are open until midnight; some branches of Shoppers Drug Mart are open 24 hours.

All international embassies are in Ottawa; there are some consulates in Toronto, including a U.S. consulate. The consulate is open weekdays 8:30–3, but most services are offered only before noon.

Doctors and Dentists **Dental Emergency Clinic** ✉ *1650 Yonge St., Greater Toronto* ☎ *416/485–7121.*

Foreign Consulates **Consulate General of the United States** ✉ *360 University Ave., Queen West* ☎ *416/595–1700, 416/595–6506 emergency line for U.S. citizens, 416/201–4056 emergency line for U.S. citizens (after hours)* 🌐 *toronto.usconsulate.gov.*

General Emergency Contacts **Ambulance, fire, and police** ☎ *911.*

Hospitals and Clinics **St. Michael's Hospital** ✉ *30 Bond St., fronting Queen St. East, Dundas Square Area* ☎ *416/360–4000* 🌐 *www.stmichaelshospital.com.* **Toronto General Hospital** ✉ *200 Elizabeth St., Queen's Park* ☎ *416/340–3111* 🌐 *www.uhn.ca.*

24-Hour and Late-Night Pharmacies **Rexall Pharma Plus** ✉ *777 Bay St., at College St., Dundas Square Area* ☎ *416/977–5824* 🌐 *www.rexall.ca* ⏲ *Daily 8 am–midnight* ✉ *63 Wellesley St. E, at Church St., Church-Wellesley*

416/924–7760 Daily 8 am–midnight. **Shoppers Drug Mart** *465 Yonge St., at College St., Dundas Square Area 416/408–4000 www.shoppersdrugmart.ca 24 hrs 388 King St. W, at Spadina Ave., Entertainment District 416/597–6550 Daily 8 am–midnight 390 Queen's Quay W, at Spadina Ave., Harbourfront 416/260–2766 Daily 8 am–midnight.*

HEALTH

Toronto does not have any unique health concerns. It's safe to drink tap water. Pollution in the city is generally rated Good to Moderate on the international Air Quality Index. Smog advisories are listed by the Ontario Ministry of the Environment at *www.airqualityontario.com.*

HEALTH CARE

Consider buying trip insurance with medical-only coverage. Neither Medicare nor some private insurers cover medical expenses anywhere outside the United States. Medical-only policies typically reimburse you for medical care (excluding that related to preexisting conditions) and hospitalization abroad, and provide for evacuation. You still have to pay the bills and await reimbursement from the insurer, though.

Another option is to sign up with a medical-evacuation assistance company. A membership in one of these companies gets you doctor referrals, emergency evacuation or repatriation, 24-hour hotlines for medical consultation, and other assistance. International SOS Assistance Emergency and AirMed International provide evacuation services and medical referrals. MedjetAssist offers medical evacuation.

Medical Assistance Companies
AirMed International *www.airmed.com.* **International SOS Assistance Emergency** *www.internationalsos.com.* **MedjetAssist** *www.medjetassist.com.*

Medical-Only Insurers International Medical Group *www.imglobal.com.* **International SOS** *www.internationalsos.com.* **Wallach & Company** *www.wallach.com.*

OVER-THE-COUNTER REMEDIES

OTC medications available in Canada are nearly identical to those available in the United States. In some cases, brand names are different, but you'll recognize common brands like Tylenol, Midol, and Advil. Nonprescription medications can be found at drugstores and in some grocery and convenience stores.

HOURS OF OPERATION

Post offices are closed weekends, but post-office service counters in drugstores are usually open on Sunday. When open, hours are generally 8 to 6 or 9 to 7. There is no mail delivery on weekends. The Beer Store, which sells beer only, and the LCBO (Liquor Control Board of Ontario), which sells wine, beer, and liquor, close on holidays.

Most banks are open Monday through Thursday 10 to 5 and Friday 10 to 6. Some are open longer hours and on Saturday. All banks are closed on national holidays. Most have ATMs accessible around the clock.

As in most large North American urban areas, many highway and city gas stations in and around Toronto are open 24 hours, although there's rarely a mechanic on duty Sunday. Smaller stations close at 7 pm.

Toronto museums have an array of opening and closing times; it's best to phone ahead or check websites. *Opening hours of sites and attractions are denoted in this book by a clock icon.*

Most retail stores are open Monday through Saturday 10 to 6, and many now open on Sunday (generally noon to 5) as well. Downtown stores are usually open until 9 pm seven days a week. Some shops are open Thursday and Friday evenings, too. Shopping malls tend to be open weekdays from 9 or 10 am to 9 pm, Saturday from 9 am to 6 pm, and Sunday from noon to 5 pm, although many extend their hours pre-Christmas. Corner convenience stores are often open until midnight, seven days a week.

HOLIDAYS

Standard Canadian national holidays are New Year's Day, Good Friday, Easter Monday, Victoria Day (Monday preceding May 25), Canada Day (July 1), Civic Day (aka Simcoe Day in Toronto; first Monday in August), Labour Day (first Monday in September), Thanksgiving (second Monday in October), Remembrance Day (November 11), Christmas, and Boxing Day (December 26).

MAIL

Canada's national postal system is called Canada Post. There are few actual post-office buildings in Toronto. Instead, many drugstores have post-office counters that offer full mail services. Check the Canada Post website for locations; a red, blue, and white Canada Post sign will also be affixed to the storefront. Post offices are closed weekends, and there is no mail delivery on weekends. During the week most post offices are open from 8 to 6 or from 9 to 7.

You can buy stamps at the post office, railway stations, airports, bus terminals, many retail outlets, and some newsstands. Letters can be dropped into red Canada Post boxes on the street or mailed from Canada Post counters in drugstores or post offices. If you're sending mail to or within Canada, be sure to include the postal code—six digits and letters. Note that the suite number may appear before the street number in an address, followed by a hyphen. The postal abbreviation for Ontario is ON.

Main postal outlets for products and services in the downtown area are the Adelaide Street Post Office; the Atrium on Bay Post Office near the Marriott, the Eaton Chelsea Hotel, and the Eaton Centre; and Postal Station "F," one block southeast of the major Bloor-Yonge intersection.

The Canadian postal system is almost identical to the U.S. system. To send regular letters within Canada, just ask for a letter stamp, which is C63¢. Stamps for letters to the United States are C$1.10. Stamps for letters to countries other than the United States are C$1.85. Envelopes that exceed 30 grams (1 ounce) or are oversized cost incrementally more. Letter stamps are also sold in books of 10 or rolls of 100 for domestic and in books of six or rolls of 50 for international.

When sending mail other than a letter weighing less than 30 grams, take your envelope or package to a postal counter in a drugstore or to the post office to have it weighed and priced accordingly.

Mail may be sent to you care of ✉ *General Delivery, Toronto Adelaide Street Post Office, 36 Adelaide Street East, Toronto, ON M5C 1J0.*

Info Canada Post ☎ *416/979–8822, 866/607–6301 in Canada* 🌐 *www.canadapost.ca.*

Main Branches Adelaide Street Post Office ✉ *31 Adelaide St. E, Financial District* ☎ *866/607–6301.* **Atrium on Bay Post Office** ✉ *595 Bay St., Dundas Square Area* ☎ *416/506–0911.* **Postal Station "F"** ✉ *50 Charles St. E, Yorkville* ☎ *416/413–4815.*

SHIPPING PACKAGES

Customs forms are required with international parcels. Parcels sent regular post typically take up to two weeks. The fastest service is FedEx, which has 24-hour locations at University and Dundas and at Bloor and Spadina. "Overnight" service with Canada Post usually takes two days.

Express Services FedEx ✉ *505 University Ave., at Dundas St. W, Chinatown* ☎ *416/979–8447* 🌐 *www.fedex.ca* ✉ *459 Bloor St. W, at Major St., The Annex* ☎ *416/928–0110* ✉ *357 Bay St., at Temperance St., Entertainment District* ☎ *416/363–2705.*

MONEY

Unless otherwise stated, all prices, including dining and lodging, are given in Canadian dollars. Toronto is the country's most expensive city.

Prices throughout this guide are given for adults. Substantially reduced fees are almost always available for children, students, and senior citizens.

ATMS AND BANKS

Your own bank will probably charge a fee for using ATMs abroad; the foreign bank you use may also charge a fee. Nevertheless, you'll usually get a better rate of exchange at an ATM than at a currency-exchange office or even when changing money in a bank. And extracting funds as you need them is a safer option than carrying around a large amount of cash.

TIP→ PINs with more than four digits are not recognized at ATMs in many countries. If yours has five or more, remember to change it before you leave.

ATMs are available in most bank, trust company, and credit union branches across the country, as well as in many convenience stores, malls, and gas stations. The major banks in Toronto are Scotiabank, CIBC, HSBC, Royal Bank of Canada, the Bank of Montréal, and TD Canada Trust.

ITEM	AVERAGE COST
Cup of Coffee	C$1.50
Glass of Wine	C$6–C$9
Glass of Beer	C$3–C$6
Sandwich	C$6–C$8
One-Mile Taxi Ride	C$2.50 (plus initial C$4.25)
Museum Admission	C$8–C$20

CREDIT CARDS

It's a good idea to inform your credit card company before you travel, especially if you're going abroad and don't travel internationally very often. Otherwise, the credit-card company might put a hold on your card owing to unusual activity—not a good thing halfway through your trip. Record all your credit-card numbers—as well as the phone numbers to call if your cards are lost or stolen—in a safe place, so you're prepared should something go wrong. Both MasterCard and Visa have general numbers you can call (collect if you're abroad) if your card is lost, but you're better off calling the number of your issuing bank as MasterCard and Visa usually just transfer you to your bank; your bank's number is usually printed on your card.

If you plan to use your credit card for cash advances, you'll need to apply for a PIN at least two weeks before your trip. Although it's usually cheaper and safer to use a credit card abroad for large purchases (so you can cancel payments or be reimbursed if there's a problem), note that some credit-card companies *and* the banks that issue them add substantial percentages to all foreign transactions, whether they're in a foreign currency or not. Check on these fees before leaving home so there won't be any surprises when you get the bill.

TIP→ Before you charge something, ask the merchant whether or not he or she plans to do a dynamic currency conversion (DCC). In such a transaction the credit-card processor (shop, restaurant, or hotel, not Visa or MasterCard) converts the currency and charges you in dollars. In most cases you'll pay the merchant a 3% fee for this service in addition to any credit-card company and issuing-bank foreign-transaction surcharges.

Dynamic currency conversion programs are becoming increasingly widespread. Merchants who participate in them are supposed to ask whether you want to be charged in dollars or the local currency, but they don't always do so. And even if they do offer you a choice, they may well avoid mentioning the additional surcharges. The good news is that you *do* have a choice. And if this practice really gets your goat, you can avoid it entirely thanks to American Express; with its cards, DCC simply isn't an option.

Reporting Lost Cards American Express ☎ *800/297-8500 in the U.S., 336/393-1111 collect from abroad* 🌐 *www.americanexpress.com.* **Diners Club** ☎ *800/234-6377 in the U.S., 514/877-1577 collect from abroad* 🌐 *www.dinersclub.com.* **Discover** ☎ *800/347-2683 in the U.S., 801/902-3100 collect from abroad* 🌐 *www.discover.com.* **MasterCard** ☎ *800/627-7309 in the U.S., 636/722-7111 collect from abroad* 🌐 *www.mastercard.com.* **Visa** ☎ *800/847-2911 in the U.S., 303/967-1096 collect from abroad* 🌐 *www.visa.com.*

CURRENCY AND EXCHANGE

U.S. dollars are sometimes accepted—more commonly in the Niagara region close to the border than in Toronto. Some hotels, restaurants, and stores are skittish about accepting Canadian currency over $20 due to counterfeiting, so be sure to get small bills when you exchange money or visit an ATM. Major U.S. credit cards and debit or check cards with a credit-card logo are accepted in most areas. Your credit-card-logo debit card will be charged as a credit card.

The units of currency in Canada are the Canadian dollar (C$) and the cent, in almost the same denominations as U.S. currency ($5, $10, $20, 1¢, 5¢, 10¢, 25¢, etc.). The $1 and $2 bill are no longer used; they have been replaced by $1 and $2 coins (known as a "loonie," because of the loon that appears on the coin, and a "toonie," respectively). At this writing the exchange rate is US96¢ to C$1.

Even if a currency-exchange booth has a sign promising no commission, rest assured that there's some kind of huge, hidden fee. (Oh . . . that's right. The sign didn't say no *fee*.) And as for rates, you're almost always better off getting foreign currency at an ATM or exchanging money at a bank.

Google does currency conversion. Just type in the amount you want to convert and an explanation of how you want it converted (e.g., "14 Swiss francs in dollars"), and voilà. Oanda.com also allows you to print out a handy table with the current day's conversion rates. XE.com is a good currency conversion website.

Conversion sites Google 🌐 *www.google.com.* **Oanda.com** 🌐 *www.oanda.com.* **XE.com** 🌐 *www.xe.com.*

PACKING

You may want to pack light because airline luggage restrictions are tight. For winter, you need your warmest clothes, in many layers, and waterproof boots. A scarf that covers your face is a good idea—winds can be brutal. In summer, loose-fitting, casual clothing will see you through both day and evening events. It's a good idea to pack a sweater or shawl for cool evenings or restaurants that run their air conditioners full blast. Men will need a jacket and tie for the better restaurants and many of the nightspots. Jeans are as popular in Toronto as they are elsewhere and are perfectly acceptable for sightseeing and informal dining. Be sure to bring comfortable walking shoes. Consider packing a bathing suit for your hotel pool and a small umbrella.

PASSPORTS AND VISAS

Anyone who is not a Canadian citizen or Canadian permanent resident must have a passport to enter Canada. Passport requirements apply to minors as well. Anyone under 18 traveling alone or with only one parent should carry a signed and notarized letter from both parents or from all legal guardians authorizing the trip. It's also a good idea to include a copy of the child's birth certificate, custody documents if applicable, and death certificates of one or both parents, if applicable. (Most airlines do not allow children under age five to travel alone, and on Air Canada, for example, children under age 12 are allowed to travel unaccompanied only on nonstop flights. Consult the airline, bus line, or train service for specific regulations if using public transport.) Citizens of the United States, United Kingdom,

Australia, and New Zealand do not need visas to enter Canada for a period of six months or less.

PASSPORTS

U.S. passports are valid for 10 years. You must apply in person if you're getting a passport for the first time; if your previous passport was lost, stolen, or damaged; or if your previous passport has expired and was issued more than 15 years ago or when you were under 16. All children under 18 must appear in person to apply for or renew a passport. Both parents must accompany any child under 16 (or send a notarized statement with their permission) and provide proof of their relationship to the child.

TIP→ Before your trip, make two copies of your passport's data page (one for someone at home and another for you to carry separately). Or scan the page and email it to someone at home and yourself.

If you're renewing a passport, you can do so by mail. Forms are available at passport acceptance facilities and online. The cost to apply for a new passport card and book (or a renewal) is $165 for adults, $120 for children under 16; renewals are $140. Allow six weeks for processing, both for first-time passports and renewals. For an expediting fee of $60 you can reduce this time to about two weeks. If your trip is less than two weeks away, you can get a passport even more rapidly by going to a passport office with the necessary documentation. Private expediters can get things done in as little as 48 hours.

U.S. Passport Information U.S. Department of State ☎ *877/487–2778* 🌐 *travel.state.gov/passport.*

U.S. Passport and Visa Expediters A. Briggs Passport & Visa Expeditors ☎ *800/806–0581 toll-free, 202/338–0111* 🌐 *www.abriggs.com.* **American Passport Express** ☎ *800/455–5166, 603/559–9888* 🌐 *www.americanpassport.com.* **Passport Express** ☎ *800/362–8196* 🌐 *www.passportexpress.com.* **Travel Document Systems** ☎ *800/874–5100, 202/638–3800* 🌐 *www.traveldocs.com.*

RESTROOMS

Toronto is often noted for its cleanliness, which extends to its public restrooms. In the downtown shopping areas, large chain bookstores and department stores are good places to stop. If you dart into a coffee shop, you may be expected to make a purchase. Gas stations downtown don't typically have restrooms. Only a few subway stations have public restrooms; their locations are noted on the subway map posted above the doors in each car on the train.

SAFETY

Toronto is renowned as a safe city, but you should still be careful with your valuables—keep them in a hotel safe when you're not wearing them. Downtown areas are generally safe at night, even for women alone. Most of the seedier parts of the city are on its fringes. Nevertheless, areas east of Dufferin on Queen Street, College, or Bloor can feel desolate after dark as can most of Dundas Street, though a few pioneer hipster bars are popping up in these areas.

Panhandling happens in Toronto, especially in Queen West and Kensington Market. Jaywalking isn't illegal in Toronto and it happens frequently. Be alert when driving or walking—streetcars, jaywalkers, and plentiful bicyclists make downtown navigation somewhat hazardous.

TIP→ Distribute your cash, credit cards, IDs, and other valuables between a deep front pocket, an inside jacket or vest pocket, and a hidden money pouch. Don't reach for the money pouch once you're in public.

Advisories U.S. Department of State 🌐 *travel.state.gov.*

TAXES

Toronto has a Harmonized Sales Tax (HST) of 13% (the combination of the former 5% national GST and the 8% provincial PST) on most items purchased in shops and on restaurant meals. (Be aware that taxes and tip add at least 30% to your food and beverage total when dining out.) The HST also applies to lodging and alcohol purchased at the Liquor Control Board of Ontario (LCBO). Prices displayed in LCBO stores include tax, so you won't see the extra taxes levied at the register. Other stores that sell wine charge only GST, but as they have to pay the LCBO a 10% tax, it's fair to assume they've marked up their prices accordingly.

TIME

Toronto is on Eastern Standard Time (EST), the same as New York. The city is three hours ahead of Pacific Standard Time (PST), which includes Vancouver and Los Angeles, and is one hour behind Atlantic Standard Time, which is found in the Maritime Provinces. The Province of Newfoundland and Labrador is 1½ hours ahead of Toronto.

Timeanddate.com can help you figure out the correct time anywhere.

Timeanddate.com 🌐 *www.timeanddate.com/worldclock.*

TIPPING

Tips and service charges aren't usually added to a bill in Toronto. In general, tip 15–20% of the total bill. This goes for food servers, barbers and hairdressers, and taxi drivers. Porters and doormen should get about C$2 a bag. For maid service, leave C$2–C$5 per person a day.

VISITOR INFORMATION

The website of the City of Toronto has helpful material about everything from local politics to public transit. The monthly magazine *Toronto Life* and the weekly alternative papers *Now* and *The Grid* list the latest art and nightlife events and carry information about dining, shopping, and more. Another site, 🌐 *toronto.com*, is one-stop shopping for nuts-and-bolts info like traffic or transportation, as well as for cultural events and links to a lot of other Toronto websites and blogs.

Written by locals, for locals, Blog TO includes commentary on Toronto life and upcoming cultural events.

Official websites

Canadian Tourism Commission ☎ *604/638–8300* 🌐 *www.canadatourism.com.*

City of Toronto 🌐 *www.toronto.ca.*

Ontario Travel ☎ *800/668–2746* 🌐 *www.ontariotravel.net.*

Tourism Toronto ☎ *416/203–2500, 800/499–2514* 🌐 *www.seetorontonow.com.*

Other Helpful websites

The Grid 🌐 *www.thegridto.com.*

Toronto Life 🌐 *www.torontolife.com.*

Toronto.com 🌐 *www.toronto.com.*

NOW 🌐 *www.nowtoronto.com.*

Blog TO 🌐 *www.blogto.com.*

INDEX

A

B

C

PHOTO CREDITS

Front cover: dbimages/Alamy [Description: Royal Ontario Museum (ROM)]. Back cover (from left to right): Lissandra Melo / shutterstock.com; Tourism Toronto; Tourism Toronto. Spine: jiawangkun / shutterstock.com. 1, RENAULT Philippe / age fotostock. Chapter 1: Experience Toronto. 2, Barrett & MacKay/age footstock. 8-9, Peter Mintz / age fotostock. 10, Tourism Toronto. 11 (left), Joshua Jensen/ Flickr. 11 (right), Nikki Leigh McKean. 12, OTMP. 13 (left), nicblockley/Flickr. 13 (right), Tourism Toronto. 16 (left), Tourism Toronto. 16 (top center), Garyisajoke/Flickr. 16 (bottom right), Tourism Toronto. 16 (top right), OTMP. 17 (top left), Emily Sheff. 17 (bottom left), lmnop88a/Flickr. 17 (right), Sam Javanrouh/ wvs.topleftpixel.com . 18, torontowide.com. 19 (left), Tourism Toronto. 19 (right), Jeff Denberg/Flickr. 20, gorillaimages/Shutterstock. 21, Tourism Toronto. 23 (left), David Cooper. 23 (right), Jeff Karpala/Flickr. 25 (left), Garyisajoke/Flickr. 25 (right), Laslovarga/wikipedia.org. 28, Jim Lopes/Shutterstock. 29 (left), Tourism Toronto. 29 (right), Ontario Science Centre. Chapter 2: Exploring Toronto. 33, P. Narayan / age fotostock. 34, Ontario Science Centre. 38, Chris Cheadle / age fotostock. 39 (left), Robert Lesser/Flickr. 39 (right), Loozrboy/Flickr. 40, Aude/wikipedia.org. 42, Roy Rainford / age fotostock. 48, Charles Leonio/iStockphoto. 50, Brian Summers / age fotostock. 54, © Fpro | Dreamstime.com. 55, Peter Mintz / age fotostock. 57, Toronto Star / age fotostock. 58, Rolf Hicker /age fotostock. 60, Oleksiy Maksymenko / age fotostock. 63, Josephers/wikipedia.org. 67, Angelo Cavalli / age fotostock. 69, Ron Erwin / age fotostock. 70, Alan Marsh / age fotostock. 71, Emily Sheff. 73, OTMP. 76, Aron Brand/Shutterstock. 82, Tourism Toronto. 84, Vast Photography / age fotostock. 86, Oleksiy Maksymenko / age fotostock. 87, Ingorrr/Flickr. 91, Ontario Science Centre. Chapter 3: Where to Eat. 95, Jean Heguy / age footstock. 96, Nikki Leigh McKean. Chapter 4: Where to Stay. 131, George Whiteside Photography. 132, The Hazelton Hotel. Chapter 5: Nightlife. 149, Toronto Star / age fotostock. 150, Tourism Toronto. Chapter 6: The Performing Arts. 167, ckchiu/Shutterstock. 168, Peter Albrektsen/Shutterstock. 170, George Pimentel/Tourism Toronto. 171, Joshua Jensen/Flickr. 173, 416style/Flickr. 176, David Hou. 181, Alan Marsh / age fotostock. Chapter 6: Shopping. 183, Tourism Toronto. 184, Tourism Toronto. 195, Toronto Eaton Centre. Chapter 7: Side Trips from Toronto. 215, Kevin Tavares/iStockphoto. 216, OTMP. 217 (top left), Marco Maccarini/iStockphoto. 217 (top right), Richard Bain/Stratford Shakespeare Festival. 217 (bottom), Niagara Falls Tourism. 218, Nitin Sanil/ iStockphoto. 219 (left), Niagara Falls Tourism. 219 (right), Willem Dijkstra/iStockphoto. 220, Henry Georgi / age fotostock. 221, Tasting Room by Craig Hatfi eld http://www.flickr.com/photos/craighatfi eld/376120113/ Attribution License. 222, Elena Elisseeva/Shutterstock. 226, JTB Photo / age fotostock. 233, Adam Booth/iStockphoto. 238-39, Dennis MacDonald / age fotostock. 244, JTB Photo / age fotostock. 246, Tourism Toronto. 252, Klaus Lang / age fotostock. 261, Kerry Hayes/Stratford Shakespeare Festival. 269, Design Pics / age fotostock. 274, Glenn Davy / age fotostock.

NOTES

NOTES